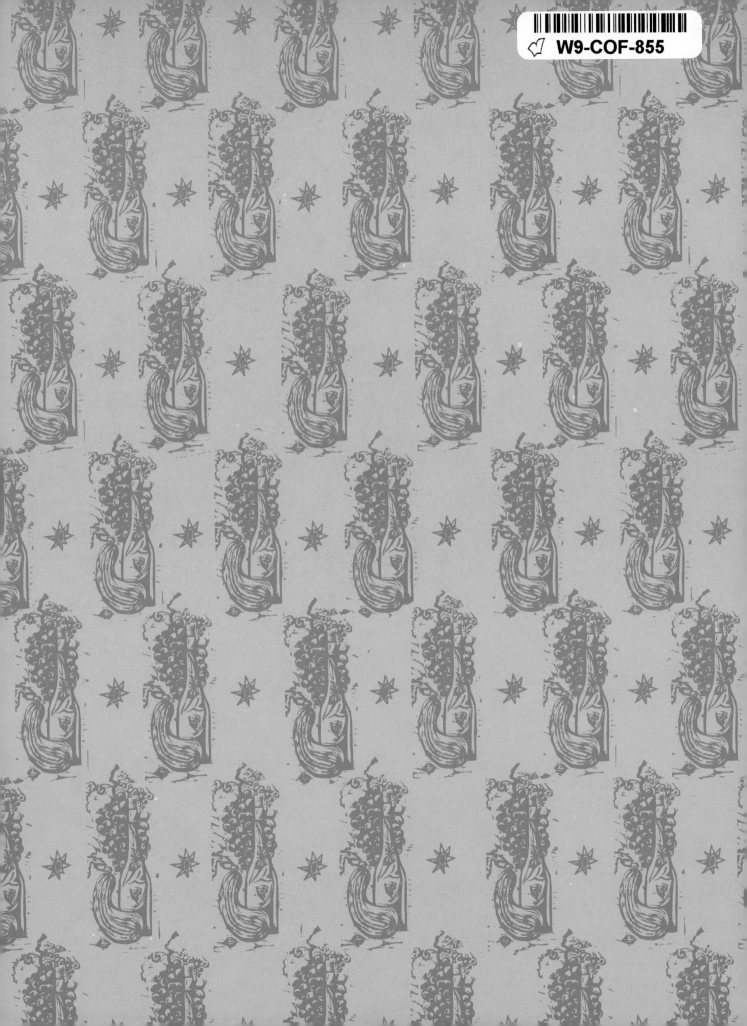

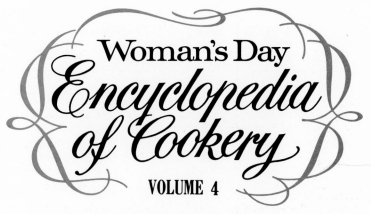

Woman's Day
Encyclopedia of Cookery

VOLUME 4

in 12 volumes—over 2,000 pages—
with more than 1,500 illustrations in color,
1,000 entries and 8,500 recipes
1,200 menus, 50 specialty cook books
and a host of delightful features by distinguished food writers.

Prepared and edited by the Editors of Woman's Day
Editor: EILEEN TIGHE
Managing Editor: EVELYN GRANT   *Food Editor:* GLENNA MCGINNIS
Art Consultant: HAROLD SITTERLE   *Photographic Editor:* BEN CALVO
Associates: OLIVIA RISBERG, CHARLOTTE SCRIPTURE,
CAROLYN STORM, JOHANNA BAFARO

SPECIAL PROJECT STAFF
Editor: NIKA STANDEN HAZELTON   *Art Director:* LEONARD A. ROMAGNA
Associates: L. GERALDINE MARSTELLER, HELEN FEINGOLD,
SUSAN J. KNOX, INEZ M. KRECH

FAWCETT PUBLICATIONS, INC.   NEW YORK

PRINTED AND BOUND BY
FAWCETT-HAYNES PRINTING CORPORATION
ROCKVILLE, MARYLAND

Table of Contents

VOLUME 4

CREOLE COOKERY TO FINNAN HADDIE

Definitions and 666 Recipes
How to buy, store, prepare, cook, and serve •
Nutritive Food Values • Caloric Values

To help you plan more varied meals
with the recipes in this volume

Foreword

To the best of our knowledge, no work of this magnitude ever has been undertaken by any author, editor, or publisher in America. The editors of Woman's Day, with a special staff of experts, present to you this Encyclopedia of Cookery, a comprehensive and colorful library on all culinary matters. The twelve-volume encyclopedia contains in its 2,000 pages over 8,500 recipes from all over the world, 1,500 food illustrations in color, 1,200 menus, 50 special cook books and over 1,000 food definitions. In addition, there are full details about all foods, their nutritive and caloric values, how to buy, serve, prepare, and cook them. There is a history of food and cooking, articles on nutrition, diet, entertaining, menu planning, herbs and spices. Every topic of culinary interest is covered. Five years of intensive work have gone into its preparation, backed by twenty-five years of food and cookery experience in the publication of Woman's Day.

We think you will find this Encyclopedia of Cookery the most complete and authoritative work ever published on the subject. It is a library for everyone who cares about good food and the fine art of preparing it.

The Editors

VOLUME 4

CREOLE COOKERY—There are those who say that Creole cooking is America's most original contribution to good food, and that it ranks with Europe's finest cuisines. Be this as it may, there is no doubt that Creole cooking has made its hometown, New Orleans, a mecca to which gourmets from every part of the world come joyfully and as often as they can afford.

Creole cooking is a combination of classic French, Spanish, and Anglo-Saxon cuisine, prepared with the skilled assistance of Negro cooks, and spiced and seasoned with ingredients used by the local Choctaw Indians. It is a product of abundant native foods such as game, saltwater and fresh-water fish, oysters, crayfish, and shrimps, and of historic and geographical circumstances.

Creole cooking is native to Louisiana and the Gulf States, where the original Spanish and French settlers, anxious to maintain their language and culture, were called "Creole." Being a "Creole" implied a cultural background and a taste for elegant living. The records of the early Creoles tell of their luxurious homes, their lavish entertaining, and the subtlety and grand scale of their cooking on the plantation or in the town house.

The dishes most closely associated with Creole cookery are the bouillabaisse, the gumbos, and the jambalayas which are made with the wealth of succulent seafood that is one of the bounties of the region. It is the seasoning—leaning heavily on pepper, onions, garlic, green peppers, and spices—that makes many Creole dishes so individual. The most typical of these seasonings is filé, made from powdered sassafras leaves, which both flavors

and textures food. It disintegrates in the long, slow cooking of most Creole dishes, and should be added at the last moment. Another typical ingredient is okra. The African word for okra has been modified to "gumbo," and thus, Creole gumbos are dishes which use okra for flavoring and thickening. Another interesting feature of Creole cooking is the combining of meats and/or poultry and seafood in one dish that is neither solid nor liquid, but a stew. Some of these dishes are called jambalayas, and are characterized by the addition of rice. Also distinctly Creole is the cooking of fish and chicken in paper bags to retain the delicate flavor.

In essence, Creole cooking reflects the Spanish love for highly flavored foods and for rice; the French gift for delicacy in the kitchen as shown in their ways of cooking chicken and game birds; of making custards and fritters, and of using wines and liqueurs in cooking. Added to this are the skill and infinite patience of the Negro cooks who introduced some of their own foods, such as okra and other vegetables, into their masters' kitchens, and the herbs traditional with the Indians. The result of it all is a piquant, inventive, and extremely varied cuisine, whose tools were the heavy iron pot or skillet, whose fire was slow, and whose fat was pure lard. To crown the cuisine is Creole coffee, always strong, and served in many ways, from the breakfast *café au lait* to the after-dinner brews sparked with brandy and liqueurs.

Dining out in style has always been a custom in New Orleans, and no other American city can boast of so many fine restaurants known to so many people throughout the country. To bring nostal-

gia into the hearts of those readers who have dined in New Orleans, we have included a number of dishes from such famous restaurants as Corinne Dunbar's, Brennan's, Commander's Palace, and Arnaud's in our medley of Creole cookery.

CREOLE BOUILLABAISSE
2 tablespoons butter
2 tablespoons all-purpose flour
2 onions, chopped
2 garlic cloves, minced
2 teaspoons curry powder
Dash of hot pepper sauce
8 whole cloves
2 bay leaves
½ teaspoon crumbled dried thyme
1 teaspoon salt
3½ cups (one 1-pound, 13-ounce can) tomatoes
1 cup water
2 pounds red snapper
2 pounds redfish
½ cup sherry
1 can (4 ounces) whole mushroom caps, undrained

Melt butter in large skillet. Add flour and cook over low heat until golden brown, stirring constantly. Add onion and garlic; continue cooking for 2 to 3 minutes. Then add curry, hot pepper sauce, half of cloves, 1 bay leaf, the thyme, and salt. After a minute or two add tomatoes and water. Simmer slowly, covered, for 30 minutes. Put fish, cut into small pieces, in another skillet. Cover with boiling water; add remaining cloves and bay leaves and half of sherry. Gently simmer fish for 8 minutes; drain. Put fish and mushrooms into sauce; heat for 5 minutes. Add remaining sherry and serve. Makes 12 servings.
Note: Cooking the seasonings in brown flour and butter *roux* gives this famous dish a very special flavor.

ARNAUD'S OYSTERS BIENVILLE

3 tablespoons butter
2 onions, minced
3 tablespoons all-purpose flour
1½ cups chicken consommé
⅔ cup white wine
1 cup minced raw mushrooms
1½ cups chopped cooked shrimps
3 dozen oysters
  Rock salt
2 egg yolks
2 tablespoons heavy cream
  Dry bread crumbs
  Grated Parmesan cheese

Melt butter and sauté onions until golden brown. Stir in flour and cook, stirring, until the mixture is lightly browned. Gradually stir in consommé, wine, mushrooms, and shrimps. Cook slowly over low heat, stirring constantly, for 10 minutes. Open oysters and put them in their deep shells on individual ovenproof baking dishes. A bed of rock salt will help the shells stand firmly upright. Bake the oysters in their own juices in preheated moderate oven (350°F.) for about 6 minutes. Beat egg yolks with cream and beat hot sauce into the mixture. Reheat the sauce but do not boil. Cover each oyster with some of the sauce and sprinkle lightly with equal parts of dry bread crumbs and Parmesan cheese. Return the oysters to the oven for about 10 minutes, until the topping is browned. Makes 6 to 8 servings.

BRENNAN'S SHRIMP CLEMENCEAU

8 cups water
2 bay leaves
1 thyme sprig
7 dried pepper pods
2 tablespoons salt
½ teaspoon cayenne
2 pounds shrimps
2 large potatoes, peeled and diced
  Deep fat or oil
2 tablespoons butter
8 mushrooms
2 parsley sprigs, chopped
4 garlic cloves, minced
1 cup cooked green peas

Boil water with bay leaves, thyme, pepper pods, salt, and cayenne for 25 minutes. Add shrimps and simmer for 5 minutes longer, or until shrimps turn pink. Peel and devein shrimps. Fry potatoes in deep fat or oil until they are golden brown. Drain on absorbent paper towel. Melt butter. Sauté mushrooms, parsley, and garlic until lightly browned. Combine mushroom mixture with the potatoes, the cooked shrimps, and the cooked peas. Toss lightly over medium heat and serve piping hot. Makes 4 to 6 servings.

OYSTER AND SHRIMP JAMBALAYA

2 tablespoons olive oil
1 pint oysters
2 onions, chopped
1 garlic clove, pressed
1 small green pepper, minced
1 pound raw shrimps, shelled and deveined
1 cup uncooked rice
2 cups (one 1-pound can) tomatoes
2 cups chicken bouillon or water
1 bay leaf
  Pinch of ground thyme
1 teaspoon salt
⅛ teaspoon pepper
1 teaspoon sugar
  Minced parsley

Heat olive oil in large skillet. Add oysters and cook over low heat until edges begin to curl. Remove from pan; refrigerate. Cook onions, garlic, and green pepper in skillet for 2 to 3 minutes. Add shrimps. Cook until shrimps turn pink. Remove from pan. Put rice in skillet; heat, stirring constantly, until rice browns. Add tomatoes, bouillon, and seasonings. Cover and simmer over low heat until rice is tender and liquid has been absorbed. Add oysters and shrimps. Heat through, stirring gently. Serve garnished with minced parsley. Makes 6 servings.

DUNBAR'S JAMBALAYA

3 tablespoons butter
1 small onion, minced
1 garlic clove
1½ pounds raw shrimps
3 small pork sausages
¼ pound cooked ham
1 tablespoon all-purpose flour
1 can (6 ounces) tomato paste
4 parsley sprigs, minced
2 thyme sprigs, minced
2 cups hot water
  Salt and pepper
⅓ cup uncooked rice

Melt 1 tablespoon butter and brown onion and garlic. Peel and devein shrimps. If shrimps are very large, cut them into halves lengthwise. Add shrimps and cook, stirring, for about 5 minutes, until shrimps are bright pink. Cut sausages into small pieces and brown pieces in a separate pan. Cut ham into cubes the same size as the sausages and sauté with the sausages for a few minutes. Blend in flour. Combine meat with shrimps and add tomato paste, parsley, and thyme. Add hot water and bring to a boil. Add salt and pepper to taste. Cover. Simmer for 1 hour. Cook rice according to directions on package until it is barely tender. Stir rice into the meat mixture and add remaining butter. Set the pan into a pan of hot water and continue to cook for about 30 minutes longer, or until the rice has absorbed all the liquid and the mixture is quite dry. Makes 6 servings.

COMMANDER'S PALACE STUFFED FLOUNDER

  Butter or margarine (about ⅔ cup)
½ cup minced white onions
¾ cup chopped celery
¼ cup minced shallots
1 large garlic clove, chopped
1 tablespoon all-purpose flour
½ cup each of dry white wine and milk
¼ cup each of chopped cooked shrimps and crabmeat
1 cup soft bread crumbs
  Salt and pepper
6 small flounder, split
  Lemon wedges
  Parsley

Melt ½ cup butter and sauté onions, celery, shallots, and garlic until tender but not brown. Sprinkle with flour. Cook, stirring constantly, for 2 minutes, until mixture browns. Gradually stir in white wine and milk. Cook, stirring, over low heat until mixture is smooth and thickened. Fold in shrimps and crabmeat and soft bread crumbs. Season with salt and pepper to taste. Have flounder split without separating the halves. Remove the backbone. Spread half of each fish with stuffing, reshape fish, and spread it liberally with butter. Season with salt and pepper to taste. Lay the fish side by side in a buttered heatproof serving dish and brown the bottom over direct heat. Put the dish under broiler heat to brown the top. Serve hot, garnished with lemon wedges and parsley. Makes 6 servings.

HOTEL PONTCHARTRAIN SHRIMP REMOULADE

¼ cup tarragon vinegar
1 tablespoon ketchup
2 tablespoons horseradish mustard
1½ teaspoons paprika
½ teaspoon salt
¼ teaspoon cayenne
½ cup salad oil
¼ cup minced green onions and tops
2 pounds cleaned, cooked large shrimps
  Shredded lettuce

In small bowl beat together first 6 ingredients. Gradually add oil and beat until well blended. Stir in onions and celery. (If electric blender is available, whirl first 6 ingredients with onions and celery in blender for 15 seconds. With cover ajar, gradually blend in oil.) Pour sauce over shrimps and marinate in refrigerator for 4 to 5 hours. For each serving, arrange 6 shrimps on shredded lettuce in cocktail or sherbet glass. Makes 8 servings.

HOTEL PONTCHARTRAIN RED-SNAPPER COURT BOUILLON

3½ to 4 pounds red snapper
  Salt and pepper to taste
  Water
1 large onion, chopped
6 stalks celery, chopped
1 green pepper, chopped
½ cup bacon fat
1 can (6 ounces) tomato paste
1 cup dry red or white wine
  Cayenne
¼ cup Worcestershire
½ teaspoon dried basil
6 bay leaves

Oyster and Shrimp Jambalaya

Louisiana Pecan Cake

Chicken and Okra Gumbo

¼ teaspoon oregano
Small bunch green onions, chopped
Small bunch parsley, chopped
Hot cooked rice

Cut the thick, meaty part of the fish in 2-inch squares, and set aside. Put the remainder of the fish (head, bones, and small bits of fish) in saucepan. Add salt and pepper and 1 cup water. Simmer for 15 to 20 minutes. Remove head and bones, and reserve stock with bits of fish. In kettle sauté onion, celery, and green pepper in bacon fat very slowly until vegetables are almost congealed but not browned. Add tomato paste, 1 can water, and fish stock. Add wine, and remaining ingredients, except fish and rice. Simmer, covered, for half hour. Add fish, and cook for 10 minutes longer. Serve on hot rice. Makes 6 servings.
Note: This is a thick mixture, not a soup.

GRILLADES
1½ pounds round steak, cut ½ inch thick
Salt and pepper to taste
1 tablespoon lard
1 onion, sliced
1 garlic clove, minced
1 tomato, chopped
Parsley

Cut meat in 4 squares or serving pieces. Season meat with salt and pepper, rubbing seasonings in thoroughly. Heat lard in heavy skillet, and cook onion and garlic in the fat until golden. Add tomato and grillades. Cover and cook slowly, turning occasionally until brown and tender. Serve with a garnish of parsley. Makes 4 servings.
Note: Round steak is always used for this. The steak is cut in squares and each piece is called a "grillade."

VENISON IN CHAFING DISH
8 to 10 slices venison, ⅛ inch thick
Salt and pepper to taste
2 tablespoons butter or margarine, melted
1 tablespoon currant jelly
1 tablespoon water

Season venison with salt and pepper. Heat 1 tablespoon butter in top pan of chafing dish over heat. Add venison, and cook for 1 minute. Turn slices and cook for 1 minute longer. Mix 1 tablespoon butter, the jelly, and water. Spread on venison, and continue cooking and turning, not more than 5 minutes in all. Serve at once. Makes 4 servings.

CHICKEN AND OKRA GUMBO
1 frying chicken (about 3 pounds), cut up
2 tablespoons lard or butter
1 pound smoked ham, cut in ½-inch dice
1 onion, chopped
6 large fresh tomatoes, peeled and chopped

2 pints okra, sliced ½ inch thick
Salt and cayenne to taste
Few sprigs parsley, chopped
1 bay leaf
1 pod dried red pepper, without seeds
6 cups water
12 shelled oysters
Hot cooked rice

Cut chicken into 12 pieces. Heat lard in heavy kettle. Add chicken and ham. Cover, and cook slowly for 10 minutes. Add onion, tomatoes, and okra. Cook over high heat, stirring, for 4 or 5 minutes. Season with salt and cayenne. Add parsley, bay leaf, dried pepper, and water. Bring to boil, cover, and simmer for 1½ to 2 hours. Add oysters, and cook a few minutes longer. Add additional salt and cayenne, if necessary. Serve with rice. Makes about 3½ quarts, or 6 servings.

ARNAUD'S BREAST OF CHICKEN EN PAPILLOTE
3 cups water
1 teaspoon salt
1 onion
1 carrot
Celery stalk with leaves
½ bay leaf
Few parsley sprigs
3 whole chicken breasts, cut into halves
¼ cup butter
6 large mushroom caps
¼ cup coarsely diced smoked ham
2 tablespoons all-purpose flour
1 egg yolk
2 tablespoons sherry

Simmer water with salt, onion, carrot, celery, bay leaf, and parsley for 20 minutes. Add chicken breasts to hot broth and simmer gently until tender. Strain broth and reserve. Cut out 6 heart-shape pieces of aluminum foil or parchment paper and place 1 skinned and boned chicken breast on half of each piece. Melt butter and lightly brown mushroom caps. When brown, remove caps and reserve. Add ham and sauté for a few minutes. Sprinkle mixture with flour and cook, stirring for 2 minutes. Gradually stir in 1½ cups reserved chicken broth. Cook over low heat, stirring constantly, until smooth and thickened. Beat egg yolk with sherry and stir hot sauce into the mixture. Replace over heat and reheat but do not boil. Spoon sauce over chicken breasts and top with mushroom caps. Fold other half of hearts over and crimp edges to seal, making into an airtight package. Lay packages side by side on a baking sheet. Bake in preheated moderate oven (350°F.) for about 10 minutes. Each guest splits open his own papillote at the table. Makes 6 servings.

BRENNAN'S EGGS HUSSARDE
On individual serving plates put a piece of Holland rusk. Cover the rusk with a slice of broiled ham cut to fit, and pour over the ham a spoonful of Brennan's Marchand de Vin Sauce. Cover the slice with a slice of tomato, peeled and lightly broiled if desired, and on the tomato arrange a poached egg. Top with a dollop of Brennan's Hollandaise Sauce.

Brennan's Marchand de Vin Sauce
½ pound mushrooms
¼ pound cooked ham
4 shallots
1 onion
¼ cup butter
½ cup beef bouillon
½ cup red wine
½ tablespoon all-purpose flour
Salt and pepper

Chop finely first 4 ingredients. Cook in the butter until onion is golden. Stir in bouillon and wine. Mix flour with a little water and stir into the hot mixture. Cook, stirring constantly, until mixture is smooth and thickened. Simmer for 20 minutes longer, stirring occasionally to prevent scorching. Add salt and pepper to taste. Makes enough for 6 to 8 servings.

Brennan's Hollandaise Sauce
4 eggs
Juice of 1 lemon
½ cup butter, melted
Salt and white pepper

Beat eggs in the top part of double boiler. Add lemon juice and beat again. Put the pan over, but not touching, hot water in the bottom of the boiler. Stir in melted butter gradually. Cook, stirring with a wooden spoon, until the sauce is thick and fluffy. Keep the heat low so that the water in the bottom pan does not boil. Season the sauce with salt and white pepper to taste. Makes enough for 6 to 8 servings.

CREOLE BLACKEYE PEAS
1 pound dried blackeye peas
6 cups cold water
2 dried hot red peppers
½ cup each chopped red and green pepper
Butter or margarine
Salt and pepper
1 small onion, cut in rings

Cover peas with the cold water. Bring to boil, and boil for 2 minutes. Let stand for 1 hour. Add dried peppers, bring to boil, and simmer, covered, for 30 minutes, or until peas are tender, adding more water, if necessary. Stir in red and green pepper, and cook a few minutes longer. Season to taste with butter, salt, and pepper. Serve hot with a garnish of onion rings. Makes 8 servings.

CANDIED YAMS, AMANDINE
6 yams
1 cup brown sugar, packed
¼ cup butter or margarine
¼ cup water
½ teaspoon salt

2 whole cloves
¼ cup toasted slivered blanched almonds
Parsley

Cook, and drain yams. Peel, and put in shallow baking dish. Mix sugar, butter, water, salt, and cloves. Bring to boil, and boil for 5 minutes. Pour over yams. Bake in preheated moderate oven (375°F.) for about 30 minutes, basting occasionally. Sprinkle with almonds, and garnish with parsley. Makes 6 servings.

DUNBAR'S STUFFED SQUASH

6 summer squash
¼ pound cooked lean ham
½ pound cooked and shelled shrimps
2 onion slices
⅔ cup butter
    Stale French-bread crumbs
2 thyme sprigs
2 tablespoons chopped parsley
1 garlic clove, chopped
    Salt and pepper
    Pimiento
    Parsley sprigs

Wash squash and cook them in boiling salted water to cover until they are tender enough to be pierced with a skewer. Cut squash into halves and scoop out the pulp, being careful not to break the shells. Reserve the shells. Mash the pulp and put it through a food chopper with the ham, shrimps, and onion. Melt ½ cup butter in a heavy skillet and add the chopped ingredients. Simmer over low heat, stirring occasionally, for 20 minutes. Soak 1 cup stale bread crumbs in water and press them dry. Add bread to skillet along with thyme, parsley, and garlic. Season mixture to taste with salt and pepper and toss it well to blend. Simmer over low heat for 10 minutes, stirring constantly. Pile this stuffing into reserved squash shells, mounding it high. Sprinkle with bread crumbs and dot with remaining butter. Bake in preheated moderate oven (350°F.) for about 25 minutes, or until the topping is browned. Garnish each with a strip of pimiento and a parsley sprig. Makes 12 servings as a side dish.

CALAS TOUT CHAUDS
(Hot Rice Fritters)

2 cups cooked rice
3 eggs, well beaten
½ teaspoon vanilla extract
1 teaspoon granulated sugar
¼ teaspoon salt
6 tablespoons all-purpose flour
3 teaspoons baking powder
    Fat for deep frying
    Sifted confectioners' sugar

Combine rice, eggs, and vanilla and mix thoroughly. Stir sugar, salt, flour, and baking powder into rice mixture. Drop by spoonfuls into hot deep fat (360°F.) and fry until brown. Drain on absorbent paper. Sprinkle with confectioners' sugar. Serve very hot. Makes about 18 fritters.

PECAN TARTS

4 eggs, beaten
1¼ cups dark corn syrup
1½ tablespoons melted butter
1½ teaspoons vanilla extract
¼ teaspoon salt
1¼ cups chopped pecans
    Pastry for 14 to 18 tart shells, unbaked

Beat eggs with next 4 ingredients. Add nuts and mix lightly. Pour into pastry-lined tart pans. Bake in preheated hot oven (400°F.) for 10 minutes. Reduce heat to slow (300°F.) and continue baking for 20 to 30 minutes, or until filling is set. Makes 14 to 18 tarts.

PRALINES

1 pound (2¼ cups, firmly packed) brown sugar
¼ cup water
2 tablespoons butter or margarine
2 cups pecans (some halves, some chopped coarsely)

Put sugar and water in heavy saucepan. Bring to boil and cook rapidly, stirring constantly, until a small amount of mixture dropped in very cold water forms a soft ball (236°F. on a candy thermometer). This will take only 2 or 3 minutes. Remove from heat and stir in butter and pecans. Beat about 30 seconds, or just until mixture begins to sugar. Drop from spoon onto wax paper, and let stand until firm. Makes about 1½ pounds, or 1 dozen 12-inch pralines.

Note: True Creole pralines should be thin, sugary, and rather hard.

BRENNAN'S BANANAS FOSTER

2 tablespoons butter
4 small bananas, cut into halves lengthwise
2 tablespoons brown sugar
    Dash of ground cinnamon
1 tablespoon banana liqueur
½ cup rum
    Ice cream

Melt butter and sauté bananas until golden. Sprinkle with brown sugar and cinnamon. Remove bananas to a serving dish and pour pan juices over them. Heat banana liqueur and rum, pour over the fruit, and set aflame. Serve blazing, with ice cream. Makes 4 servings.

ARNAUD'S ANANAS FLAMBÉS

1 ripe fresh pineapple
    All-purpose flour
    Milk
¼ cup butter
    Sugar
    Maraschino cherries
¼ cup brandy

Peel pineapple and cut it into slices ½ inch thick. Remove the hard center core. Dip the rings of pineapple into flour, then into milk, then into flour again. Lay slices on a paper towel to dry. Melt butter and pour off the clear liquid which

rises to the top of the milky sediment in the pan. Heat this clarified butter in a skillet and brown the floured pineapple rings on both sides. Remove the rings to a heatproof serving dish and sprinkle them generously with sugar. Put a maraschino cherry into the center of each ring. Bake the pineapple rings in a preheated hot oven (400°F.) for about 5 minutes, watching them carefully so that they may be removed from the oven as soon as the sugar begins to brown. Warm brandy in a silver ladle, blaze it by touching it with a match, and pour the flaming spirits over the fruit. Serve flaming. Makes 4 to 6 servings.

CRÊME BRÛLÉE

4 egg yolks
    Light brown sugar
¼ teaspoon salt
2 cups heavy cream
1 tablespoon dark rum or 1 teaspoon vanilla extract
    Sliced peaches, raspberries, or whole strawberries

Beat egg yolks with ¼ cup light brown sugar, and the salt until light and creamy. Slowly stir scalded cream into egg-yolk mixture. Cook, stirring constantly, over simmering water until the consistency of thin mayonnaise. Add rum, and pour into a shallow broilerproof serving dish. Refrigerate several hours or overnight. Sift light brown sugar over custard to the depth of about ¼ inch. Place under broiler, watching every minute, until sugar caramelizes and begins to brown. Refrigerate immediately. Serve with fruit. Makes 4 servings.

LOUISIANA PECAN CAKE

1½ packages seeded raisins, cut into halves
1 cup whiskey
1 cup softened butter or margarine
2¼ cups granulated sugar
1 nutmeg, grated
6 eggs, well beaten
4½ cups sifted all-purpose flour
3½ cups coarsely chopped pecans
2 teaspoons baking powder
1 teaspoon salt
    Confectioners' sugar

Soak raisins in whiskey overnight. Cream butter and granulated sugar. Add nutmeg and eggs. Beat thoroughly. Mix 1 cup of the flour with the nuts. Sift together remaining flour, baking powder, and salt. Add dry ingredients to creamed mixture. Fold in nuts, then raisins. Mix lightly and pour into well-greased and floured 10-inch tube pan. Bake in slow oven (325°F.) for 1¼ hours, or until top seems firm and sides of cake begin to shrink away from pan. Do not overbake. Let cool in pan for 5 minutes. Turn out and cool on a cake rack. Sprinkle with confectioners' sugar.

Crêpes Suzette in a blaze of glory are a fitting finale to a fine dinner. The lacy crêpes, bathed in a suave orange-butter sauce,

CRÊPE—The French word for a type of pancake. It is a very thin, delicate pancake made of flour and eggs: with or without flavoring, sweetened or unsweetened. Sweetened crêpes are served for dessert, with fruit or a sauce or just with sugar. The most famous member of the dessert crêpe family is Crêpes Suzette, which are folded into quarters and served with a flaming liqueur sauce. Unsweetened crêpes are stuffed with meat, vegetables, fish, or cheese, rolled or folded, and sauced to be served as a main dish.

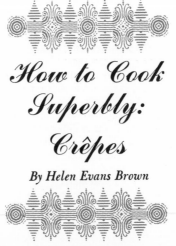

How to Cook Superbly: Crêpes

By Helen Evans Brown

Making a perfect crêpe is not as hard as it looks and once you've learned, you will also be able to produce many magnificent main dishes and delectable desserts, for these tissue-thin delicate pancakes are tremendously versatile. Best known of the desserts is the famous Crêpes Suzette, a flaming glory with as many versions as stories of its origin. The famous Jewish blintzes, the Russian *blinchiki,* and crêpes filled with fruit, preserves, or jellies, and served with whipped, sour, or ice cream, or with various syrups, also make fitting finales for any meal. You can make Chinese egg

are flamed at the table in a chafing dish with a mixture of orange-flavored liqueur and brandy.

rolls with crêpes, and a delicious variety of the popular Italian *cannelloni*. Crêpes filled with cheese, meat, seafood, or poultry, then sauced and glazed, are considered the most elegant of main courses, and these same savory crêpes, cut into pieces, rolled in crumbs, and fried, are fine appetizers. Even leftover crêpes, cut into strips, are highly esteemed as a garnish for clear soups. Crêpes freeze beautifully, too, so you can make extra fine ones and keep them for future treats. (Be careful to wrap them well, but have them completely thawed and slightly warm before trying to separate them. Although

sugar is added to the batter for dessert crêpes, the unsweetened kind can also be used if served with a fruit sauce or sprinkled with powdered sugar.

Recipes for crêpe batter vary greatly, yet the pancakes made from them are quite similar. This is because the secret is in the cooking. However, after experimenting with a dozen different formulas, I have decided that the one given below is the tenderest and most flavorsome of them all.

EQUIPMENT

The pan: As for an omelet, you will need a small frying pan or skillet, with a bot-

tom measurement of 6 to 8 inches, depending upon the size of crêpes you desire. The pan should be of heavy cast aluminum, iron, or enameled iron, and should be treated exactly like an omelet pan. There are special crêpe pans made of heavy cast iron that are imported from France and are very fine.

Other utensils: You will also need an electric blender or a bowl and beater, measuring spoons and cups, a small brush, a small spatula or table knife, and a warm plate slightly larger than the crêpes are to be.

INGREDIENTS

For 24 to 32 crêpes, depending on size:

- 3 eggs
- 2 egg yolks (or 1 additional egg)
- ½ cup milk
- ½ cup water*
- 2 tablespoons clarified butter (see below)
- 2 tablespoons brandy (optional)
- 1 cup all-purpose flour
- ¾ teaspoon salt
- 1 to 2 tablespoons sugar (for dessert crepes)
- 1 teaspoon vanilla extract or 1 teaspoon grated lemon or orange rind (for dessert crepes, optional)

*You may use all milk, but the water gives extra lightness, as does the brandy. **To make clarified butter**—Put ½ cup butter in a heavy pan and heat until it is foaming. Skim off top and allow to stand for a few minutes, then carefully pour off the clear amber liquid, leaving the milky residue in the bottom. Discard the residue. Use this clarified butter in the recipe and for cooking the crêpes. It will not burn or stick as easily as untreated butter. Any surplus will be useful for other cooking.

HERE'S HOW

1. Measure all the ingredients into a blender and whirl until smooth. Or, if you are using the bowl method, beat eggs and yolks, add remaining ingredients, and beat until smooth. In either case, let the batter stand at room temperature for at least 1 hour.

2. Have batter, remaining clarified butter, and utensils near the stove. Put pan on to become very hot. It is ready when a couple of drops of water will skitter across the pan and disappear in a second.

3. Brush bottom of pan quickly and thoroughly with clarified butter and pour about 2 tablespoons batter into the pan. (A ¼-cup measure, half full, makes a good ladle for pouring batter. You will find that the 8-inch pan takes about that amount, the smaller ones slightly less. After practice, you may be able to pour the correct amount from a pitcher, gauging with your eye.) Turn and tip pan immediately so that the batter will form a thin film over the bottom. It should be so hot that it will sizzle and set almost immediately into a thin lacy pancake. If you've used too much batter, quickly pour off the excess. The crêpe can be trimmed later. If you have any holes where the batter has missed the pan, just add a drop or two of batter for a patch. Work quickly, for the crêpe will be ready to turn in 15 to 20 seconds.

4. Using the spatula or knife, loosen the edge all the way around, then lift to make sure it has browned on the bottom. If it has, turn up the edge at the far side of the pan and, using both hands, quickly lift it up and toward you, flipping so that it lies flat and upside down in the pan. You may find it easier to pick up the crêpe at the near side and flip it away from you. This will not burn you if you work quickly and is almost the only way to turn a crêpe without wrinkling it (the other way is by flipping it high in the air, but it takes a Boy Scout or expert chef to do that!).

5. Let the crêpe cook for another few seconds, about 15, on that side, then slide it onto the warmed plate.

6. Repeat procedure, buttering the pan before each crêpe. If the crêpes are to be filled, it is not necessary to turn them, as the unbrowned side can be kept inside. These crêpes will have a lacy look with a slightly crisp edge, and will be very thin. Keep them covered and warm until ready to use. One good way is to put the plate over a pan of hot water and cover the crêpes with transparent plastic wrapping.

DESSERT CRÊPES

The very simplest way to serve crêpes is to spread them with jelly or preserves, roll or fold them, arrange on a fireproof dish, sprinkle with sugar, and slip under the broiler or into a hot oven until hot and glazed. They may also be filled with sugared fruit, rolled, and served with whipped cream or dairy sour cream.

CRÊPES SUZETTE

For 12 crêpes (enough for 4 servings) cream together ¼ cup sweet butter and ¼ cup confectioners' sugar. Grate the zest of an orange (only the orange outside part of the peel) and add to the mixture, then stir in the juice of the orange and 3 tablespoons of Cointreau, Curaçao, or Grand Marnier liqueur. Make dessert crêpes, following the basic recipe. When ready to serve, put the flavored butter into a hot chafing dish or electric skillet and heat until it bubbles and reduces slightly. Using a fork and spoon, dip each crêpe into this hot mixture, then fold in quarters and put to one side of the pan. When all are dipped, sprinkle with a little more sugar, then add 3 tablespoons of whichever liqueur you used in the butter and ¼ cup brandy to the pan. Stand as far away as possible and light the liquid with a match. Spoon the flaming liquid over the crêpes and serve as soon as the flames die down.

BLINTZES

Make a filling by mixing a cup of farmer-style cottage cheese, 1 egg yolk, 1 tablespoon sugar, few grains of salt, and 1 teaspoon grated lemon rind or vanilla extract, or dash of ground cinnamon. This makes enough filling for 8 to 10 crêpes. Make dessert crêpes, following the basic recipe. Put a spoonful of filling on each crêpe and roll, tucking in the sides, or fold like an envelope. Place on a buttered pan, seam side down, brush with butter, and brown in the oven or broiler. Serve with dairy sour cream and preserves, if desired.

CRÊPES AS A MAIN DISH

Cut cooked poultry, shellfish, or meat into small pieces and mix with an equal amount of cream, béchamel, or cheese sauce. Make crêpes, following the basic recipe. Put a spoonful of filling on each crêpe, roll, and arrange on a buttered fireproof dish. Mix whichever sauce you have used in the filling with an equal amount of hollandaise sauce and/or whipped cream. Pour over rolled crêpes and put under the broiler to heat and become golden brown.

CRÊPES GÂTEAU

Spread a crêpe with any hot savory filling of cheese, meat, seafood, or game that has been minced fine and mixed with gravy, dairy sour cream, or sauce. Top with another crêpe and continue until the stack is 4 or 5 inches high. Brush with butter, sprinkle with cheese or crumbs, and reheat in preheated moderate oven (350°F.) until hot and brown. Cut into wedges to serve with or without dairy sour cream or sauce. A stack of 16 crêpes prepared in this way will make 4 to 6 good servings.

CRÊPE CASSEROLE

Line a casserole with crêpes, having those at the sides hang over the edge. Fill with any creamed mixture and fold overhanging crêpes over the top. Put another crêpe on top and heat well. This is a good way to use both leftover crêpes and cooked meat, seafood, or vegetables.

CRIMP—This culinary term refers to two widely different methods of food preparation.

In pastry-making: Crimping means pressing down a fork or a similar tool on the outer edges of uncooked pastry. This is an easy way to achieve a decorative pattern and, in the case of two-crust pies, it seals the upper and lower crusts together so that the filling won't escape. When crimping a pie, it is well to moisten the edges of the pastry with cold water first, thus holding them together.

In preparing fresh fish: Crimping means gashing a freshly caught fish on both sides of the body, at 1- or 2-inch intervals. The fish is then plunged into icy water for about 30 minutes to 1 hour, depending on size. This firms the flesh of the fish.

CRISP—When used as a verb, "to crisp" means to revive freshness by placing in chilled liquid or moist air, as celery is crisped, or by placing in a warm oven, as crackers are crisped. "To crisp" also means to make firm by frying as fritters.

As an adjective crisp implies that the texture of a food is brittle and crackly: a crisp crust on bread, a crisp dry cereal, or crisp bacon.

CROAKER—The name is given to a number of different fish that make croaking or grunting noises. They include the Atlantic croaker, the fresh-water drum, and the queenfish. The noise is produced by the air bladder. Croakers are usually small fish, and are eaten either fried or broiled.

BROILED CROAKER FILLETS WITH HERBS

1½ pounds fresh, or thawed frozen, croaker fillets
1 onion, grated
Juice of 1 lemon
3 tablespoons melted butter or margarine
½ teaspoon salt
⅛ teaspoon pepper
¼ teaspoon ground marjoram
2 teaspoons minced watercress or chives
1 tablespoon minced parsley

Wipe fish with damp cloth or paper towel; arrange on greased broiler rack. Mix remaining ingredients and pour over fish. Broil for about 6 minutes under medium heat, or until fish flakes easily with a fork. Remove to hot platter; pour drippings from pan over top and garnish with additional parsley or watercress. Makes 4 servings.

DEEP-FRIED CROAKERS WITH TARTARE SAUCE

4 croakers, cleaned
Seasoned all-purpose flour
1 egg, beaten
2 tablespoons cold water
Fine dry bread crumbs or cracker meal
Fat for deep frying
Tartare Sauce

Wipe fish with a damp cloth or paper towel. Roll in seasoned flour and dip into mixture of egg and water. Roll in crumbs and arrange fish in frying basket just to cover the bottom. Do not overlap. Fry in hot deep fat (370°F. on a frying thermometer) until golden brown. Drain and serve with Tartare Sauce. Makes 4 servings.

Tartare Sauce

Mix ¼ cup mayonnaise and 1 tablespoon each of chopped sweet pickle, cream, and chopped stuffed olives.

CROISSANT—This French word means "crescent" and it describes a buttery, flaky roll baked in the shape of a crescent.

The French, Swiss, Austrians, and other central Europeans eat freshly baked *croissants* for breakfast, a habit enthusiastically embraced by foreigners visiting these countries. *Croissants* are also excellent for tea or at any time of the day, provided they are fresh. *Croissants* can be bought in many American bakeries, and they are one of the most popular foreign pastries.

Croissants were created in Budapest, Hungary, in 1686, to commemorate the withdrawal of the invading Turks. Bakers, working at night, heard the Turks tunneling into the city and spread the alarm which led to the defeat of the Turkish troops. As a reward for their vigilance, the bakers were commissioned to produce a commemorative pastry, shaped like a crescent, the emblem of Turkey.

CROISSANTS

1½ cups butter or margarine
3⅓ cups sifted all-purpose flour (about)
2 packages active dry yeast or 2 cakes compressed yeast
½ cup warm water*
¾ cup plus 1 tablespoon milk
¼ cup sugar
1 teaspoon salt
1 egg, beaten
1 egg yolk

Cream butter with ⅓ cup flour. Chill and roll out between 2 sheets of wax paper into an oblong 12 x 6 inches. Chill until ready to use. *Use very warm water (105°F. to 115°F.) for dry yeast; use lukewarm water (80°F. to 90°F.) for compressed yeast. Sprinkle or crumble cake into water. Let stand for a few minutes, then stir to dissolve. Scald ¾ cup milk, then add sugar and salt, and cool to lukewarm. Add dissolved yeast. Stir in egg. Beat in enough flour to make a soft

dough. Knead on a floured board until smooth and elastic. Roll into a 14-inch square. Remove wax paper from chilled butter; turn upside down on half of the dough. Remove remaining wax paper. Fold dough over butter and seal edges. Roll dough carefully into an oblong 20 x 12 inches. Working quickly, fold dough in thirds and roll again to an oblong 20 x 12 inches. Fold and roll 2 more times. If you cannot work quickly, chill dough between rollings for about 30 minutes. After last rolling chill for 45 minutes. When ready to shape *croissants,* cut dough into 4 equal pieces. Roll each piece into a circle 12 inches in diameter. Cut each circle into 10 wedges. Roll up each wedge beginning at the long end. Curve into crescent shape after placing point side down, about 3 inches apart. on an ungreased cookie sheet. Cover and let rise until doubled in bulk. Beat egg yolk with 1 tablespoon milk and brush rolls lightly with the mixture. Bake in preheated moderate oven (375°F.) for 12 to 15 minutes. Makes 40 rolls.

CROQUETTE—The word is a derivative of the French word *croquer* which means "to crunch" or "to crackle under the teeth." The culinary term covers a little savory morsel, which should be crisp on the outside and creamy on the inside. Croquettes are made in the shape of a cone or a sausage, and consist of such cooked foods as minced fish, eggs, meats, vegetables, and fruits, held together by a thick sauce and deep-fried.

Croquettes have come to be associated in this country with the use of assorted leftovers. This is unfortunate because they can be absolutely delicious when properly made. In fact, croquettes are considered one of the specialties of fine French cooking. Here are some hints for their success:

Basic Croquette Mixture—Use ¾ cup thick sauce for 2 cups ground or minced solid foods. The solid foods should be drained.

Shaping Croquettes—The quickest method is to spread the mixture in a greased flat pan, in the thickness desired. Chill, then cut into squares, oblongs, or any wanted shapes. (Chilling makes shaping soft mixtures easier.) Or form croquettes into cones or sausages with hands. After shaping chill again for several hours or overnight, so that crumbs will stick even better. Shaped uncooked croquettes may be frozen on flat sheets until solid, and then wrapped individually for freezer storage.

Coating or Crumbing Croquettes—This process protects the inside filling by sealing the croquette so that cooking fat cannot penetrate and cause sogginess. Beaten eggs or egg yolk may be varied with the addition of water, milk, or oil. Croquettes, depending on the crispness of the crust wanted, may be first rolled in flour, then in egg and fine, dry bread crumbs, or, more simply, in eggs and crumbs only. For an extra-thick coating, the process may be repeated; this may be desirable in the case of an especially creamy filling. Croquettes can also be coated with cracker crumbs, or pasta crumbs. *Croquettes must be coated evenly so that the filling doesn't ooze out during the cooking.*

Frying Croquettes—Croquettes are usually fried in deep fat or oil ranging in temperature from 375°F. to 385°F. for 1 to 5 minutes, or until evenly browned on all sides, depending on ingredients and size. For skillet frying, flat-shape croquettes are browned, turning as needed in shallow fat. When done, croquettes are drained on absorbent paper; kept warm in slow oven (300°F.) or reheated in a hot oven (400°F.).

Serving—Sauces are selected for accent or contrasting flavors, texture, and color for either the savory or sweet-type croquette.

TUNA CROQUETTES

2 tablespoons butter
¼ cup all-purpose flour
¾ teaspoon salt
⅛ teaspoon pepper
1 cup milk
2 cans (7 ounces each) tuna, drained
2 tablespoons chopped parsley
½ teaspoon fresh lemon juice
    Fine dry bread crumbs
1 egg
2 tablespoons water
    Fat for deep frying

Melt butter; add flour, salt, and pepper and mix well. Gradually add milk and cook until thick, stirring constantly. Combine tuna, parsley, and lemon juice with the white sauce; mix well. Chill. Shape into 8 croquettes; roll in crumbs, dip into slightly beaten egg mixed with water, and roll again in crumbs. Fry in deep fat (375°F. on a frying thermometer) for about 5 minutes, or until golden. Makes 4 servings.

CHICKEN CROQUETTES

2 tablespoons butter
¼ cup all-purpose flour
¾ teaspoon salt
⅛ teaspoon pepper
1 cup milk
1 teaspoon each of minced parsley and onion
2 cups ground cooked chicken
½ teaspoon fresh lemon juice
    Salt and pepper to taste
    Pinch of ground sage
    Fine dry bread crumbs
1 egg
1 tablespoon water
    Fat for deep frying

Melt butter; add flour, salt, and pepper

and mix well. Gradually add milk and cook until thick, stirring constantly. Combine next 7 ingredients with white sauce. Chill. Shape into 8 croquettes; roll in crumbs, dip into slightly beaten egg mixed with water, and then roll again in crumbs. Fry in deep fat (375°F. on a frying thermometer) for about 5 minutes, or until golden. Makes 4 servings.

EGG CROQUETTES

1 tablespoon butter
3 tablespoons all-purpose flour
1 cup milk
4 hard-cooked eggs
1 teaspoon grated onion
2 tablespoons minced parsley
3 tablespoons minced celery
¼ cup grated process American cheese
    Salt and pepper to taste
    Fine dry bread crumbs
1 egg
2 tablespoons water
    Fat for deep frying

Melt butter; stir in flour; gradually add milk, and cook until thick, stirring constantly. Press hard-cooked eggs through a coarse sieve; add to sauce with onion, parsley, celery, cheese, and seasonings. Chill mixture. Shape into 8 croquettes. Dip into crumbs, then into egg beaten with water, and then again into crumbs. Fry in deep fat (375°F. on a frying thermometer) until croquettes are golden. Makes 4 servings.

SWEET-POTATO CROQUETTES

4 medium sweet potatoes, cooked, peeled, and mashed (2 cups)
2 tablespoons butter or margarine
1 teaspoon salt
¼ teaspoon pepper
2 tablespoons brown sugar
    Fine dry bread crumbs
1 egg
1 tablespoon water
    Fat for deep frying

Beat potatoes with next 4 ingredients until smooth and blended. Chill. Shape mixture into 8 croquettes; roll in crumbs, dip into slightly beaten egg mixed with water, then roll again in crumbs. Fry in hot deep fat (375°F. on a frying thermometer) until golden. Drain. Makes 4 servings.

LEMON-RICE CROQUETTES

½ cup boiling water
½ cup uncooked rice
1 teaspoon salt
1 cup milk
1 egg
1 tablespoon sugar
    Grated rind of 1 lemon
1 tablespoon butter
1 egg
2 tablespoons water
    Fine dry bread crumbs
    Fat for deep frying
    Custard Sauce

In a saucepan mix first 3 ingredients; cover and cook slowly until water is absorbed, about 10 minutes. Add milk and stir lightly with a fork; cover and cook

until rice is tender. Stir in egg, sugar, lemon rind, and butter. Refrigerate until cool. Shape into 8 croquettes, dip into egg mixed with water, then into crumbs. Fry in deep fat (375°F. on frying thermometer) until golden, about 5 minutes. Serve warm topped with Custard Sauce. Makes 4 servings.

Custard Sauce

In top part of small double boiler, beat together 1 cup milk, dash salt, 1 egg (or 2 egg yolks), and 2 tablespoons sugar. Put over simmering water and cook, stirring, until mixture thickens slightly and coats a metal spoon. Remove from hot water and pour into small bowl. Add ¼ teaspoon vanilla extract or a little grated lemon rind. Cool, and chill. Makes 1 cup.

ALMOND CROQUETTES

2¼ cups milk
3 tablespoons all-purpose flour
3 tablespoons cornstarch
½ cup sugar
⅛ teaspoon salt
2 egg yolks, beaten
½ cup slivered blanched almonds
¼ teaspoon almond extract
1 egg, slightly beaten
    Cracker crumbs
    Fat for deep frying

Scald 2 cups of the milk. Sift together flour, cornstarch, sugar, and salt in top part of double boiler; add half to egg yolks. Stir in ¼ cup cold milk; add rest of dry mixture. Mix in remaining scalded milk and cook mixture over boiling water until smooth and thick. Add almonds and almond extract. Pour into 8-inch square pan and chill until firm. Cut into 9 squares. Dip each square into slightly beaten egg and then into cracker crumbs. Fry in hot fat (375°F. on a frying thermometer) until golden, about 5 minutes. Makes 9 croquettes.

Note: These dessert croquettes should be served immediately.

CROUSTADE—A term used in French cooking for a browned case or shell made of bread, rice, potato, hominy, or pastry and used to hold a creamed meat, seafood, vegetable, or hors-d'oeuvre mixture.

TO MAKE CROUSTADES

Remove the crust from unsliced, day-old bread. Cut into large 3-inch cubes. Hollow out, leaving a ½-inch shell. Brush inside and out with melted butter. Seasoned butter may be used. Toast on a greased cookie sheet in a moderate oven (350°F.) for 10 to 12 minutes, or until brown.

■ **To Prepare Shells from Bread Slices**—Remove crusts; butter bread on both sides. Mold the bread slices into muffin-pan cups and bake in moderate oven

(350°F.) for 8 to 10 minutes, or until crisp and brown.

■ **Variations**—Prepare croustades from hard rolls, frankfurter rolls, or 3-inch lengths of French bread. Hollow out, brush with butter and bake as directed above. Croustades may also be prepared from flaky or puff pastry. Cut into rounds or squares or oblongs. Cut 1 layer of pastry for bottom and top with rings of the same size until a side about 1 inch deep is formed. Bake as usual.

CROUTON

CROUTON—The word refers to a small piece of bread, any kind of bread, such as white, whole-wheat, rye, or even pumpernickel, usually cut into the shape of cubes and fried in oil or butter, or browned in the oven. Croutons are served principally as a garnish for soup or scrambled eggs, in salads, stuffings, or bread puddings, or as casserole toppings. The word "crouton" is derived from the French word for the crusty end of a long loaf of bread.

Croutons, either plain or seasoned, are available in food stores. To crisp them for serving, heat in a moderate oven.

CROUTONS

Trim the crusts from day-old bread. Cut them into ¼-inch cubes. Sauté in butter and drain. Or, butter sliced bread on both sides, cube, and brown in preheated moderate oven (350°F.). The length of time needed for this depends on the type of bread used and its moisture content. Stale bread will brown more quickly than fresh bread.

Note: To make croutons in decorative shapes, use small heart and diamond cookie cutters.

Cheese Croutons
Sprinkle grated Parmesan on croutons before browning.

French-Bread Croutons
Cut slices from small loaf of French bread. Prepare as above.

Savory Croutons
Sprinkle sautéed croutons with curry powder, marjoram, thyme, chili seasoning, onion, or garlic salt, or any favorite herb or spice.

CRULLER—A fried cake, sister to the doughnut, which takes its name from the Dutch word *krulle,* meaning "twisted cake." Crullers are made by rolling out dough, cutting it into strips, doubling the strips, twisting them, and pinching the ends together. They are then fried in deep fat and brushed with sugar. French crullers are made in a round shape with a cream-puff batter, and fried in deep fat.

They have a thin icing.

CRULLERS
¼ cup butter
1 cup sugar
2 eggs, well beaten
4 cups sifted all-purpose flour
1 tablespoon baking powder
¼ teaspoon ground nutmeg
½ teaspoon salt
1 cup milk
   Fat for deep frying
   Confectioners' sugar

Cream butter and sugar; add well-beaten eggs. Sift flour with baking powder, nutmeg, and salt and add, alternating with milk. Chill dough and roll out to ¼-inch thickness. Cut dough into strips 1 x 8 inches. Fold each strip in half lengthwise; twist several times and pinch ends together. Fry in hot deep fat (380°F. on a frying thermometer) until brown. Drain on absorbent paper, and cool. Sprinkle with confectioners' sugar. Makes 6 dozen.

FRENCH CRULLERS
¼ cup sugar
½ teaspoon salt
¼ cup shortening
1 cup boiling water
1 cup sifted all-purpose flour
3 eggs
1 teaspoon vanilla extract
   Fat for deep frying
   Confectioners' Sugar Frosting (p. 543)

Combine sugar, salt, shortening, and boiling water in a saucepan. Mix and bring to a rapid boil. Add flour all at once and mix and cook until thickened, stirring constantly. Remove from heat. Add eggs one at a time, beating thoroughly after each addition. Add vanilla. Force mixture through pastry tube onto greased paper, forming circles. Heat deep fat to 375°F. on frying thermometer. Carefully turn paper upside down so crullers will drop into fat. Fry until golden brown. Spread with thin Confectioners' Sugar Frosting. Makes about 1 dozen.

CRUMB, TO—This phrase has two related meanings in culinary practice. "To crumb" can mean to coat food with bread, cereal, or cracker crumbs: the food may simply be topped with plain, buttered, or sweet crumbs; or it may be dipped into a liquid such as milk or beaten eggs first, and then coated with crumbs. The first method is used for casseroles or cakes; the second for seafood, meat, and vegetables, which are then sautéed, fried, or baked. Crumbed foods are also called "breaded" foods.

"To crumb" is also used to describe breaking, crushing, rolling, or grinding food into small pieces. Bread is torn into crumbs with the fingers, cookies are crushed, and crackers, dry bread, or

cereals are placed between sheets of wax paper or in a paper bag and rolled with a rolling pin or other heavy object.

There are various kinds of crumbs:
Dry Crumbs—Made from dried breads, zwieback, melba toast, dry cereals, or dried cake. If not dry enough, the crumbs can be dried further by spreading on a cookie sheet and crisping in a slow oven (250°F.). Light-colored dry crumbs are used for breading fried foods, thickening sauces, and topping casseroles. Browned dry crumbs are used as a topping for vegetables or creamed dishes, and for any dish that requires little or no cooking after the crumbs have been used. To make browned dry crumbs, heat in a skillet one-third cup butter or margarine for each cup of crumbs and brown crumbs slowly in it. They should be used immediately.

Soft Bread Crumbs—Made by crumbling two- to four-day-old bread lightly with the fingers, or by gently pulling it apart with a fork. Soft bread crumbs are used for meat loaves and stuffings, and for any dish that needs body and thickening.

Sweet Crumbs—Dry cookies or cake can be crumbled for dessert use.

The following types of prepared crumbs are available in food stores: Bread crumbs, flavored or plain; cracker crumbs; matzo meal; corn flake crumbs; and graham-cracker crumbs.

CRUMPET—A small, patty-cake-shape, unsweetened, leavened bread made of flour, milk, butter, salt, yeast, and egg. The word comes from the Middle English word for "wafer." Crumpet dough is stiff but can be spoon-beaten and spoon-dropped for shaping. Crumpets are cooked twice, first on a griddle until well risen and browned on both sides; then they are split and toasted to complete the cooking. They are served hot with butter and jam.

The British dote on them for tea and, when away from home, they wax soulful at the thought of fresh, hot buttered crumpets eaten before an open fire.

Although they are similar to their English-muffin cousins, crumpets are softer in texture with surface holes appearing during the pan cooking; these holes enable them to absorb great quantities of butter.

CRUMPETS
1 package active dry yeast or
  1 cake compressed yeast
¼ cup water*
2 tablespoons sugar
1 teaspoon salt
3 tablespoons butter or margarine
1 cup milk, scalded
1 egg
3 cups all-purpose flour

*Use very warm water (105°F. to 115°F.) for dry yeast; use lukewarm (80°F. to 90°F.) for compressed. Sprinkle dry yeast or crumble cake into water. Let stand for a few minutes; then stir until dissolved. Add sugar, salt, and butter to warm milk, stirring to dissolve; cool to lukewarm. Add egg, yeast mixture, and flour and beat thoroughly. Let batter rise in warm place for 30 minutes; with spoon, beat for 3 minutes. Repeat rising and beating and then rising again. Pour batter into greased 4-inch muffin rings on medium hot greased griddle (325°F. on electric griddle), filling one third full. Bake until well risen and browned on one side. Turn over, rings and all, and brown on other side (should take about 18 to 20 minutes). Remove, cool, split, and toast. Serve with butter and orange marmalade or jam. Makes 8 to 10.
Note: If rings are not available, roll dough to ½-inch thickness on lightly floured board. Cut with floured 4-inch cutter. Bake 5 minutes on each side.

CRUST—The word has several meanings in cookery. It is used to describe a firm, hardened covering formed as a result of cooking: in meats, poultry, or breads, for example. It also describes a thin layer of pastry, as used in pies, or to top a casserole, or to encase a pâté, a ham, or other meat in order to seal in the juices.

Crusts are made from flour, liquid, and shortening. They can be savory or sweet and they may be flavored with herbs, spices, cheese, citrus rind, or nuts. They can be of any variety, such as biscuit, short, or puff paste. Crusts can also be made from cracker or cake crumbs. All these crusts should be crisp.

Another type of crust, made from a flour and water paste, is used as a sort of outer coating to hold in the juices during the baking of such foods as ham. After baking, the crust is cracked off and discarded.

The outer rinds of some cheeses, Camembert, for instance, are called crusts.

Sometimes the word crust is used to describe a hard, dried-out coating which forms on a food. With foods such as custards and puddings, a crust is not desirable. To prevent one from forming on top of a pudding or a thick custard, either sprinkle with sugar, place wax paper directly on pudding, or cover tightly with a lid or foil while still warm.

CUBE, TO—When used as a culinary term, "to cube" means to cut food into small, uniform, and sometimes decorative chunks: cheese, bread, potatoes, or carrots, for example. When the size of a cube is important (½-inch or 1-inch cubes), it will generally be specified in a recipe.

"To dice" is the term used for cutting food into cubes less than ½ inch in size.

CUCUMBER—The succulent fruit of a rough-stemmed trailing vine belonging to the gourd family. The word comes from the fruit's Latin name, *cucumis*. A native of southern Asia, the cucumber has been cultivated since early historic times.

Cucumbers come in a number of varieties, from thick, stubby little fruit three to four inches long to greenhouse giants which are grown in England by competing gardeners and may reach two feet in length. The most popular cucumbers have a smooth dark-green rind. Others, popular in Russia, a great cucumber-eating country, are short and thick with a tough netted brown skin. There are also large white cucumbers grown chiefly in France for cosmetic purposes, because it is believed that cucumbers whiten and soften the skin.

Pickles, called gherkins, are made from small cucumbers. They are soaked in brine, treated with boiling vinegar, and flavored with dill or with spices.

Cucumbers have always been a staple vegetable, both fresh or pickled. Indians, Hebrews, Greeks, and Romans referred to them as long as 4,000 years ago. The Romans forced them to grow out of season for the Emperor Tiberius, who is said to have eaten them daily. Charlemagne, the emperor who was also an experimental farmer, grew them in France in the 8th century. The English began to grow them in the 13th century. Columbus planted cucumbers in Haiti in 1494, and the Spaniards brought them to the mainland of North America. They were grown in Virginia in 1609 and in Massachusetts in 1629. They have been grown in enormous quantities ever since, to the delight of weight watchers, since cucumbers are 96 per cent water.

Availability—Cucumbers are available all year. Peak crop from May to August.

Purchasing Guide—Look for cucumbers that are well shaped, crisp, firm, fresh, and bright-green in color with a whitish tip. Overmature cucumbers are dull in color, yellowish, or puffy. Avoid shriveled cucumbers. They are tough and have a bitter flavor.
☐ 1 medium cucumber = 1½ cups diced

Storage—Wash to remove dirt, wipe dry and store in refrigerator. Do not peel or slice until you are ready to use them.
☐ Refrigerator shelf, raw: 1 to 2 weeks
☐ Refrigerator shelf, cooked: 1 to 2 days
Do not freeze cucumbers.

Caloric Value
☐ One, 7½ x 2 inches, raw = 25 calories

Basic Preparation—Peel, if desired. Cut a slice from each end and discard.
☐ **To Serve Raw**—Cut into thin slices, flute and slice, cut into strips, or dice. To flute: score skin with a fork before slicing. *For canapés:* place fluted, thin slices on buttered rounds of bread or crackers and top with strips of pimiento or a slice of hard-cooked egg. *For shells:* cut into halves lengthwise and scoop out the seeds. Fill with chicken, egg, or fish.
☐ **To Marinate**—Peel and slice very thin

and chill for several hours in a mixture of vinegar, sugar, salt, and pepper. Sprinkle with parsley or dill before serving.

☐ **To Boil**—Peel and quarter lengthwise or cut into thick slices and cook in small amount of boiling salted water; or steam until tender, about 10 to 15 minutes. Drain; season to taste.

☐ **To Sauté**—Cut into ¼-inch slices. Dip into seasoned flour or egg and bread crumbs; sauté in butter until golden brown.

☐ **To Bake and Stuff**—Do not peel. Boil in a small amount of salted water for 5 to 7 minutes. Cut lengthwise and remove seeds. Stuff with a mixture of chopped ham, cheese, and bread crumbs. Moisten with cream. Place in a baking dish and add stock or bouillon. Bake in a preheated moderate oven (350°F.) for 30 minutes.

CUCUMBER AND TOMATO SOUP

½ cucumber, peeled and grated
1 can (10½ ounces) condensed tomato soup
1 soup-can water
¼ cup chopped green onion
1 teaspoon Worcestershire
1 teaspoon salt
⅛ teaspoon pepper
½ cup heavy cream
Chopped parsley

Mix all ingredients except last 2. Chill for several hours. Strain and add heavy cream. Chill again. Serve garnished with parsley. Makes 4 servings.

BRAISED CUCUMBERS

3 medium cucumbers
2 tablespoons butter or margarine
1 bouillon cube, beef or chicken
1 tablespoon boiling water
Salt and pepper

Peel cucumbers; cut once lengthwise and crosswise. Brown lightly in butter. Add bouillon cube dissolved in water. Cook, covered, over low heat for about 5 minutes. Season to taste. Makes 4 servings.

CUCUMBER-ONION SALAD

2 mild onions
2 large cucumbers
Salt
Water
½ cup tarragon vinegar
1 teaspoon sugar
Pepper

Peel onions and cucumbers and cut into wafer-thin slices. Cover with salted ice water and let stand in refrigerator for several hours. Drain, and add ¼ cup cold water, vinegar, sugar, and salt and pepper to taste. Makes 4 to 6 servings.

Cucumber-Onion Salad with Sour-Cream Dressing

After draining vegetables in recipe above, add ½ cup dairy sour cream and ½ cup tarragon vinegar and garnish with chopped chives.

Tomatoes Stuffed with Dilled Cucumbers
Cucumber and Tomato Soup
Cucumber Sandwiches

CUCUMBER-ALMOND SALAD

2 cucumbers
Salt
1 cup dairy sour cream
¼ cup chopped blanched almonds
2 tablespoons minced chives or green onion
1 teaspoon fresh lemon juice
Coarsely ground pepper to taste
½ teaspoon salt

Peel cucumbers and slice paper-thin. Sprinkle with salt and let stand while assembling remaining ingredients. Drain cucumbers and add remaining ingredients. Blend well. Chill. Makes 4 to 6 servings.

CUCUMBERS IN CHEESE SAUCE

2 large cucumbers
2 tablespoons butter or margarine
1 cup medium white sauce
½ cup shredded sharp Cheddar cheese

Peel cucumbers and cut into ¼-inch slices. Cook in butter until lightly browned and tender. Add white sauce made with 2 tablespoons butter, 2 tablespoons flour, and 1 cup milk, seasoned to taste. Sprinkle with cheese. Heat. Makes 4 servings.

CUCUMBER SAUCES FOR FISH

Cucumber Sauce

Peel cucumbers, grate or chop, and drain thoroughly. Season to taste with salt, pepper, and fresh lemon juice.

Cucumber-Cream Sauce

Peel and chop 1 cucumber. Drain thoroughly. Add ¼ teaspoon salt and dash of pepper. Whip ½ cup dairy sour cream or heavy sweet cream until stiff. Fold in 2 tablespoons vinegar, then cucumber mixture.

CUCUMBER SANDWICH FILLINGS

Use these fillings with rye or white bread spread lightly with mayonnaise.
■ Chopped cucumber, green pepper, and pimiento.
■ Slices of cucumber and watercress sprigs.
■ Chopped cucumber with chives.
■ Sliced cucumber, sliced tomato, and grated onion.
■ Sliced cucumber, Boston-style baked beans, and grated onion.

PICKLED CUCUMBERS

2 to 3 cucumbers
1 tablespoon salt
¾ cup cider or white vinegar
1 tablespoon sugar, or more, according to taste
¼ teaspoon white pepper
1 tablespoon chopped parsley or dill

Scrub cucumbers free of waxy coating. Dry. Score with the tines of a fork. Slice as thinly as possible, preferably with a vegetable slicer. The slices should be transparent. Place in deep bowl and sprinkle with salt. Cover with a plate and weight with something heavy, such as a can of coffee or fruit. Let stand at room temperature for 1 to 2 hours. Drain thoroughly and press out remaining juice. Combine vinegar, sugar, and pepper. Pour over cucumbers. Correct seasoning, if necessary. Chill cucumbers thoroughly. At serving time, drain and sprinkle with parsley or dill. Makes 4 to 6 servings.

DILLED CUCUMBERS

Peel and dice 1 large cucumber. Season with chopped fresh dill. Moisten with French dressing. Makes 4 servings.

Tomatoes Stuffed with Dilled Cucumbers

Cut tops from 4 ripe medium tomatoes. Scoop out pulp and sprinkle inside with salt; turn upside down and drain. Prepare Dilled Cucumbers as above. Fill the tomatoes with cucumbers.

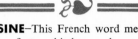

CUISINE—This French word means two things: first, a kitchen and, second, the style of cooking of a family, a restaurant, or a nation.

CULINARY—This adjective means "of, or pertaining to, the kitchen or cookery." It comes straight from the Latin word of the same meaning, *culinarius,* which was itself formed from *culina,* "kitchen." Culinary is used in such expressions as "culinary arts" or "culinary standards."

CUMIN (**Cuminum cyminum**)—The cumin plant, source of the aromatic cuminseed, is a delicate member of the parsley family, an annual, which rarely grows more than five to six inches high. The seed is tiny and oval, with a strong, warm, and slightly bitter taste. The plant is native to the Mediterranean countries, North Africa, and western Asia, where it has been used since antiquity as a stimulant to the appetite and as a flavoring for fish and meats, especially stews, as well as breads. To this day cuminseed flavors most oriental meat cooking and it is used also in the preparation of curries. It has become one of the national spices of Mexican cooking, as in chili con carne and hot tamales. Cuminseed also flavors cheeses, and it is used for liqueurs such as kümmel.

Cuminseed was one of the herb seeds used by the ancient Persians, Greeks, and Romans. In Biblical times the ancient scribes and Pharisees were charged with punctiliously tithing mint, dill, and cumin. The Romans spread the use of cuminseed throughout their empire and north to the Saxons, who roasted peacocks flavored with cuminseeds on festive occasions. Many superstitions and legends have been built around this spicy seed. Pliny said eating great quantities of cuminseed would produce a scholarly pallor in those wishing to look as though they had been spending long hours studying. In the Middle Ages it was believed that cuminseed had the power to bind a person to a place or another person. For this reason in Germany the bride and groom carried cuminseed in their pockets during the marriage ceremony.

Since cuminseed resembles caraway seed in flavor as well as looks, its uses are much the same. Cuminseed is stronger, however, and should be used sparingly at first. It is used in the preparation of pickling spices, curry powders, chili powders, and chutney. Both the whole and the ground seeds are used to season appetizers, breads, cookies, cheeses, eggs, fish, poultry, game, meats, and vegetables.

Cuminseed is available in whole and ground seeds.

LAMB STEW WITH OKRA AND CUMINSEED

1½ pounds fresh okra or 2 packages (10 ounces each) frozen okra, thawed
¼ cup white vinegar
3 tablespoons olive oil
2 pounds lean boneless lamb, cut into 1½-inch cubes
½ cup onions, minced
1½ teaspoons salt
½ teaspoon pepper
½ to ⅔ teaspoon ground cuminseed
2 cups tomato sauce or juice
2 tablespoons fresh lemon juice

Trim stems off okra. Pour vinegar over it. Let stand for 30 minutes. Drain and rinse under cold water. Heat oil in Dutch oven or large casserole. Brown lamb and onions in it. Add salt, pepper, cuminseed, tomato sauce, lemon juice, and okra. Bring to a boil. Simmer, covered, over low heat, stirring occasionally, for about 1 hour, or until meat is tender. Serve with boiled rice or pilaf. Makes 4 to 6 servings.

NEPALESE POTATO SALAD

2 large potatoes, peeled and boiled
2 teaspoons sesame seeds, toasted and ground

Juice of ½ lemon
Salt to taste
¼ teaspoon ground cuminseed
Dash of red pepper
1 small green pepper, chopped
Few chopped coriander seeds

Chop potatoes finely. Combine all ingredients and mix well. Makes 4 to 6 servings.

MEXICAN EGG SALAD

6 hard-cooked eggs, coarsely chopped
⅓ cup minced celery
¼ cup minced pickle
1 teaspoon seasoned salt
¼ teaspoon dry mustard
¼ teaspoon crushed cuminseed or ground cuminseed
⅛ teaspoon white pepper
1 teaspoon vinegar
Mayonnaise
Salad greens

Mix all ingredients except last 2. Add mayonnaise to moisten. Serve on greens. Makes 4 servings.

CANDIED APPLES WITH CUMINSEED

1 cup sugar
2 cups boiling water
1 teaspoon ground cuminseed
¼ teaspoon salt
6 firm baking apples
Sweetened whipped cream

Combine sugar, boiling water, cuminseed, and salt in 1½-quart saucepan. Bring to a boil. Simmer for 5 minutes. Meanwhile, peel, quarter, and core apples. Place a few at a time into syrup. Simmer, covered, for 10 minutes, or until apples are tender but still firm. Do not overcook. Lift out cooked apples with slotted spoon and place in serving dish. Repeat process until all apples are used. Cool. Cook syrup until it is thick as molasses. Pour over apples. Chill, and serve with whipped cream. Makes 6 to 8 servings.

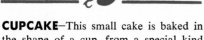

CUPCAKE—This small cake is baked in the shape of a cup, from a special kind of cake batter. The cup may be a muffin pan, a custard cup, a small cup mold, or a cupcake paper. If pans are used, they must be greased and floured for easy removal of cakes; cupcake paper will peel off.

COFFEE-MOLASSES CUPCAKES

¼ cup butter or margarine
½ cup sugar
1 egg
½ cup dark molasses
1¾ cups sifted all-purpose flour
½ teaspoon each of salt and baking soda
¼ teaspoon each of ground ginger and cinnamon
½ cup coffee

Cream butter; add sugar gradually, beating until light and fluffy. Add egg and molasses and beat well. Sift dry ingredients and add to first mixture alternately with coffee. Fill greased muffin tins ⅔ full and bake in preheated moderate oven (350°F.) for 25 minutes. Cool for 5 minutes; turn out on racks and cool. Makes about 1 dozen.

PRUNE POUND CUPCAKES

½ cup butter or margarine
1 cup sugar
1 teaspoon vanilla extract
2 eggs
1 cup pitted cooked prunes
1¾ cups sifted all-purpose flour
1½ teaspoons baking powder
½ teaspoon salt
1 teaspoon ground cinnamon
¼ teaspoon ground cloves
½ cup milk
½ cup chopped nuts

Cream butter; add sugar gradually, beating until light and fluffy. Add vanilla, then eggs, one at a time, beating well after each. Fold in prunes. Sift together dry ingredients and add to first mixture alternately with milk, beating until smooth. Add nuts. Half fill greased 2½-inch muffin pans; bake in preheated moderate oven (375°F.) for 20 minutes. Let stand for 5 minutes; turn out on a rack to cool. Makes 21.

CURRANT-ORANGE CUPCAKES

1¼ cups sugar
⅓ cup water
1 tablespoon grated orange rind
1 cup dried currants
½ cup soft butter or margarine
2 eggs
1 teaspoon vanilla extract
2 cups sifted all-purpose flour
3 teaspoons baking powder
½ teaspoon salt
¾ cup milk

In small saucepan combine ½ cup sugar, the water, and orange rind. Bring to boil and remove from heat. Stir in currants and let stand for 30 minutes. Drain thoroughly, reserving syrup. Cream butter; gradually add ¾ cup sugar and beat until light and fluffy. Add eggs, one at a time, beating thoroughly after each addition. Add vanilla. Add sifted dry ingredients alternately with milk, beating after each addition until smooth. Add drained currants. Half fill muffin cups lined with paper baking cups. Bake in preheated moderate oven (350°F.) for 20 to 25 minutes. Prick tops. Heat reserved syrup and spoon ½ teaspoon over each hot cupcake. Cool. Makes about 2 dozen.

VANILLA CUPCAKES

½ cup butter or margarine, softened
1 cup sugar
½ teaspoon vanilla extract
2 eggs
1½ cups sifted cake flour
1¼ teaspoons baking powder
¼ teaspoon salt
⅓ cup milk
Favorite frosting
Candied fruit
Colored sugar

Cream butter. Gradually beat in sugar, a little at a time. Beat in vanilla extract and eggs, one at a time, beating well after each addition. Sift together cake flour, baking powder, and salt. Add to first mixture alternately with milk, beating until smooth. Grease twelve 2¾-inch cupcake pans. Line cupcake pans with wax paper. Half fill them with batter. Bake in preheated moderate oven (375° F.) for about 20 minutes. Cool. Frost with any favorite frosting and decorate with candied fruit and colored sugar. Makes 12.

CURE—The word, when used as a verb relating to food, refers to an age-old method of preserving meat, poultry, and vegetables using salt as a preservative. Sugar is sometimes added for flavor and counteracts the tendency the saltpeter has to harden the meat. Saltpeter is added to preserve and intensify the red color. Commercially mixed curing preparations are sold containing ingredients to improve color and retard rancidity.

Pork is the most frequently cured meat. Vegetables particularly well adapted to preservation by curing are snap beans, corn, spinach, chard, beet tops, turnip tops, and dandelion greens. Fresh vegetables in prime condition should be chosen. They should be of the same maturity throughout, and not overripe.

CURED BACON

Put sides of bacon from fresh-killed hogs on a board and rub with salt, using 8 pounds fine salt per 100 pounds of meat. Let stand for 48 hours. For each 100 pounds meat, mix 3 pounds brown sugar, 3 ounces saltpeter, and 4 gallons water. Bring to boil and simmer for 15 minutes. Skim, and cool. Put bacon in clean oak barrel and cover with the liquid. Put heavy weight on meat to keep it immersed. Remove meat after 5 weeks and hang up to dry. When thoroughly dried, smoke at smokehouse as needed.

CURED HAMS

Allow 5 pints fine salt, 3 ounces saltpeter, ½ pound brown sugar, and 2 ounces black pepper per 100 pounds of meat. Mix 1 pint salt, the saltpeter, and sugar and rub over hams. Let stand for 24 hours. Then rub with the pepper and 2 pints salt. Let stand for 5 days, then rub again with remaining salt. Let stand for 30 days, then hang meat and brush off salt. Have hams smoked 10 days with hickory or apple wood. Rub lightly with cayenne, wrap in brown paper, then in muslin bags, and hang up, hock down. Coat cloth with shellac or suspend hams in a loose bag surrounded by finely chopped straw to the thickness of two or three inches.

OLD-FASHIONED SALTED GREEN BEANS
    16 pounds green beans
    4 pounds (6 cups) salt

Remove tips and wash beans thoroughly. Cut beans in long thin slivers. Line a clean 2-gallon stone jar with a muslin bag. Sprinkle a layer of salt ¼ inch thick across the bottom. Add a 2-inch layer of beans and press down very firmly; repeat, being careful to press firmly around edges. Continue until all ingredients are used, making the last layer salt. Fold top of bag over beans or tie shut. Put a plate on top and weight down with a clean, heavy stone or a quart jar filled with water or sand and closely sealed. If brine does not form within 24 hours, make a strong brine, using 1 pound of salt to 2 quarts of water. Pour just enough over beans to cover them.

■ **To Cook Beans**—If salted for only a short time, rinse in cold water and cook as usual, omitting salt. If salted for several months, soak beans in cold water for 1 to 2 hours before cooking, changing the water several times. Cook as usual, omitting salt.

CURRANT—This name is applied to two totally different fruits. One, a fresh currant, is a berry of the genus *Ribes*, a member of the gooseberry family; the other, a dry currant, is a dried grape of the genus *Vitis*. Since the fresh currant is first mentioned as a garden fruit plant in the 15th century, it probably took its name from the dry currant, which had been cultivated for centuries before that time and which it resembles.

FRESH CURRANTS
These tiny, sweet-tart berries are native to the colder regions of both Europe and America and come in red, white. or black varieties. Red currants are by far the best known and most frequently used.

Popular in northern Europe, currants crossed the Channel and then the Atlantic. Currants were on the listing of fruit and vegetable plants sent to the Massachusetts Bay Colony in 1627. The colonists cultivated currants in their gardens before strawberries, raspberries, and blackberries were domesticated. Today cultivation is carefully controlled, for the bushes harbor a fungus that kills the valuable white, or five-needle, pine.

Red currants are eaten fresh as a fruit, as well as cooked in jams and jellies. White currants are used in salads and fruit cups, and black currants are used primarily in jams, jellies, and beverages.

Availability—Available June through August, with peak in July.

Purchasing Guide—Select bright, clean, and plump currants with good color and stem attached. Slightly underripe currants are best for jelly.

☐ 1 quart = 3¾ cups

Storage—Sort, cover, and refrigerate. Use within 1 to 2 days.

Nutritive Food Values—Small amounts of vitamins A and C.

☐ 3½ ounces, raw = 54 calories

Basic Preparation—Wash and stem before using.

DRY CURRANTS
These tiny, dried, seedless grapes are used chiefly in cakes and cookies, either singly or in conjunction with raisins and other fruit. Currants are tarter and more highly flavored than raisins. The name "currant" is a corruption of Corinth, the Greek city from which they originally came. The fruit is also known as Zante currants, after one of the Greek islands where they are grown, and Zante currants are still Corinth's main export.

Availability—Boxed, in either black or white Zante varieties.

☐ 5 ounces = 1 cup

Storage—Refrigerate, tightly covered, once box is opened.

☐ Kitchen shelf: 6 months
☐ Refrigerator shelf, opened and covered: 6 months

Nutritive Food Values—High in carbohydrates, good amounts of calcium, phosphorus, and iron.

☐ 1 tablespoon = 26 calories

FRESH CURRANT JELLY
    4 pounds (3 quarts) ripe fresh currants
    1 cup water
    7 cups sugar
    ½ bottle fruit pectin

Crush currants. Add water, bring to boil and simmer, covered, for 10 minutes. Put in jelly cloth or bag and squeeze out juice. Measure 5 cups into a very large saucepan. Add sugar and mix well. Put over high heat and bring to boil, stirring constantly. Stir in pectin at once. Then bring to a *full rolling boil and boil hard for 1 minute,* stirring constantly. Remove from heat, skim off foam with metal spoon, and pour quickly into glasses. Cover at once with ⅛ inch hot paraffin. Makes about 11 medium glasses.

GLAZED FRESH CURRANT TARTS
    1 quart fresh currants
    6 4-inch tart shells, baked (1½ cups flour recipe)
    Water
    ¾ cup sugar
    Dash of salt
    2 tablespoons cornstarch
    1 package (3 ounces) cream cheese, cut into 6 cubes

Wash currants; remove stems from 3 cups of them and fill 6 tart shells. Cook remaining currants in 3 tablespoons water for about 5 minutes and force through sieve. Add enough water to make 1¼ cups. Mix sugar, salt, and cornstarch. Gradually stir in sieved berries and cook, stirring constantly, over low heat for 5 minutes, or until thickened. Cool. Pour cornstarch mixture over currants in tarts, and chill. Garnish each with a cube of cream cheese. Makes 6 servings.

FRESH CURRANT ICE
    1 quart fresh currants
    2¼ cups water
    1 teaspoon unflavored gelatin
    1 cup sugar
    Juice of ½ lemon
    ⅛ teaspoon salt

Turn refrigerator control to coldest setting. Wash currants, remove stems, and put in saucepan with 2 cups water. Bring to boil and simmer for 5 minutes, or until currants are soft. Force through fine sieve and bring to boil. Sprinkle gelatin on remaining ¼ cup water to soften; add hot currant pulp and stir until dissolved. Stir in remaining ingredients. Pour into refrigerator tray and partially freeze. Transfer to chilled bowl. Beat with a rotary beater until fluffy and light in color. Return to tray and freeze until firm. Makes 6 servings.

FRESH CURRANT PIE
    1 quart fresh currants
    Sugar
    3 tablespoons quick-cooking tapioca
    ¼ cup water
    ⅛ teaspoon salt
    8-inch pie shell, baked
    3 egg whites
    ¼ teaspoon salt

Wash currants. Combine currants, 1 cup sugar, tapioca, water, and salt. Cook for 15 minutes, or until tapioca is transparent. Cool. Pour into 8-inch pie shell. Beat egg whites and salt until foamy. Add 6 tablespoons sugar gradually, 1 tablespoon at a time, continuing to beat until stiff and glossy. Spread over pie, making sure meringue is spread out to the crust. Bake in preheated slow oven (300°F.) for 25 minutes, or until meringue is firm. Makes 6 servings.

FAT RASCALS
(Dry Currant Tea Cakes)

    4 cups sifted all-purpose flour
    1 teaspoon baking powder
    1 cup butter
       Sugar
    ¼ teaspoon salt
    1⅓ cups dry currants, washed and
       dried
    ½ cup of water
       Milk

Sift together flour and baking powder. Cut in butter until mixture resembles coarse meal. Add 2 tablespoons sugar, salt, and currants. Stir in the water and ½ cup of milk to make a firm dough. Roll out dough to ½-inch thickness. Cut into rounds with 2-inch cookie cutter. Brush with milk and sprinkle with sugar. Bake in preheated hot oven (400°F.) for 20 minutes. Makes about 2½ dozen.

CURRY—The word is used to describe a blend of ground spices, also called "curry powder," and the spiced sauce and stew dishes made using these blended spices.

Curries are native to India, where they are mentioned as early as 477 A.D. The word, from the Tamil *kari,* is recorded in the English language in the 16th century and from then on, throughout the world, curry has been the name for this native Indian dish.

Thanks to certain spices, all curry powders have a characteristic flavor. Turmeric, fenugreek, cuminseed, coriander, and red or cayenne pepper are basic. Beyond that, a curry powder may include allspice, cinnamon, cardamom, cloves, fennel, ginger, mace, yellow mustard, and black or white pepper. The various combinations and amounts determine the flavor of the curry.

Traditionally, and to this day, housewives in India daily grind or bruise their curry spices into a paste with a little water on their "curry stone." The ingredients and proportions are entirely dependent on the taste and judgment of the cook and on the kind of curry dish she is going to make, for there are hundreds of them in the various regions of India, made with fish, meat, fowl, eggs, vegetables, and legumes. Each has its own name. In general, southern Indian curries are more pungent, northern Indian ones milder.

Before the early 16th century, curries and curry powders were made without red peppers. When Columbus discovered

America he also discovered many members of the great capsicum family: the pod peppers from which red pepper is made. Word of this spice spread as fast as ships could sail and within a decade capsicums were brought to India by the Portuguese. It was at this time that curries became hot.

Curry powder is probably the world's earliest spice blend. Rare cook books, two hundred years old, call for curry powder in Indian-style dishes. The well-known Williamsburg cook book has a recipe for Gumbo dating from 1837. This delicious-sounding concoction uses curry powder to season a chicken, twenty to thirty oysters, and a handful of okra. Seafaring men brought curry powder home from the Far East a century ago as an exotic treasure for wife or mother.

Curries are usually served on rice, since they need a base that will absorb the sauce. A variety of accompaniments can be served with them. They include chutneys, pickles, fried chopped bananas, fried raisins, coconut, salted nuts, chopped green pepper, chopped onions, crumbled bacon, chopped eggs, etc.

Popadams, a flat, crisp, fried bread, are a curry accompaniment in India. Another traditional accompaniment is Bombay Duck, a fish the size of a herring which is dried and salted. This fish is available, canned, in food stores and should be prepared according to the directions on the can.

Apart from its use in Indian curries, curry powder adds an intriguing flavor to innumerable old-time American favorites, from soups to salted nuts, where a pinch added to the salt will improve their interest. And a little curry powder will bring new interest to white sauces and creamed dishes, as well as to plain buttered vegetables and potatoes, and mayonnaise and salad dressings. One word of caution: Use curry powder with a light hand, tasting as you go on adding it.

BASIC RULES FOR PREPARING CURRIES

■ All spices should be *cooked* first. They must be cooked at the temperature of a hot fat for 3 to 4 minutes over a slow fire. In India this step is known as *bhoon.*

Any kind of fat can be used, such as butter, lard, margarine, or oil.

■ Onions and garlic should be chopped as fine as possible.

■ Onions should never be allowed to brown, but cooked only until soft and white. Browned onions spoil the flavor and looks of a curry.

■ Curries need an acid. In India, tamarind juice is used, but lemon or lime juice will prove satisfactory substitutes.

■ Fresh coconut is better for curry than canned or packaged coconut.

■ Coconut milk is often used for curries. Cow's milk, sweet or sour, can be substituted; experiment with the taste.

■ Never thicken a curry with flour. If too thin, add a little milk, coconut milk, or dried coconut, or cook without a lid to allow evaporation to the proper consistency.

■ Curries can be cooked in any kind of utensil and over any kind of heat.

BEEF CURRY

    1½ pounds boneless beef chuck
       Salt and pepper
       Flour
    2 tablespoons butter or margarine
    2 large onions, sliced
    1 cup boiling water
    ¾ teaspoon ground coriander
    ½ teaspoon turmeric
    ½ teaspoon ground cuminseed
       Dash cayenne
    ½ cup tomato juice
       Hot cooked rice
       Condiments

Cut meat in 1-inch cubes, and roll in seasoned flour. Brown on all sides in butter in kettle. Remove meat and cook onions in the drippings remaining in kettle until golden. Add meat, water, and spices. Bring to boil, cover, and simmer for about 2 hours, or until meat is tender. Stir in tomato juice. Serve on hot cooked rice, accompanied by condiments such as chutney, raisins, coconut, peanuts, etc. Makes 4 to 6 servings.
Note: If preferred, 2 teaspoons curry powder may be substituted for the coriander, turmeric, cuminseed, and cayenne.

CHICKEN KORMA CURRY

    1 fryer (2½ pounds), cut up
    2 onions
    1 garlic clove
    1 teaspoon salt
    ⅛ teaspoon powdered ginger
    1 pint yogurt
    ¼ cup butter or margarine
    ½ teaspoon turmeric
    ½ teaspoon ground cuminseed
    ¼ teaspoon mustard seed, crushed
    4 peppercorns, crushed
       Seed from 2 cardamom pods, crushed
    ½ cup water

Cut chicken in 12 pieces and prick with fork. Dice 1 onion and crush in a mortar with garlic and the salt. Add with ginger to yogurt. Mix with chicken pieces and marinate for 30 minutes to 1 hour. Slice remaining onion and brown lightly in the butter. Add turmeric, cuminseed, and mustard seed and cook over low heat for 1 minute. Add chicken mixture and cook uncovered, over high heat, stirring occasionally, until sauce cooks down, about 25 minutes. Add peppercorns, cardamom, and water. Cover, and simmer for 15 to 20 minutes, or until chicken is tender, adding more water if necessary to prevent sticking. (Gravy should be thick and adhere to chicken.) Makes 4 servings.

LAMB KOFTA CURRY

2 onions
1 garlic clove
Few sprigs fresh mint
½ teaspoon powdered cloves
½ teaspoon powdered ginger
2½ teaspoons salt
1½ pounds ground lamb
1 egg white
3 hard-cooked eggs, cut into quarters
½ teaspoon turmeric
⅛ teaspoon cayenne
1 teaspoon ground coriander
¼ cup butter or margarine
1 tablespoon tomato purée or ketchup
1 pint yogurt

Mince 1 onion, the garlic, and mint. Put in bowl and add cloves, ginger, 2 teaspoons salt, and meat. Add egg white and mix lightly but thoroughly. Shape meat mixture around egg quarters to form balls. Slice remaining onion, add spices and cook lightly in the butter. Add ½ teaspoon salt, tomato purée, and yogurt. Add meatballs and bring to boil. Cover and simmer for about 20 minutes. Makes 6 servings.

CABBAGE CURRY

1 medium head of green cabbage
1 small onion, sliced
Pinch each of ground ginger, garlic salt, ground turmeric, and salt
¼ cup cooking oil
¼ cup water

Trim outer leaves of cabbage. Cut cabbage into halves and remove cores. Cut cabbage into very small thin slices. Add remaining ingredients. Cover and steam over medium heat, stirring occasionally, for 25 to 30 minutes, or until cabbage has the consistency of thick stew. Makes 4 servings.

Curries
from Ceylon
by Lilian O. Feinberg

Curries red, curries white, curries hot or curries cool, but curries *three* times a day! That's the menu in Ceylon, the miniature Eden in the Indian Ocean, formed like a teardrop near the tip of India. Twenty-four million curries are served daily and that's a conservative estimate. What's special about curries? Well, as with chop suey and pizza, the blend of flavors may delight you. Nutritionally, curry meals are well balanced, but even if they are not you'd like the flavor of meat cooked in milk (preferably coconut milk) and the use of exotic spices. New ways to serve old foods are always fun to discover, and you can experiment your way to a perfect curry for your family.

Any flesh, fish, vegetable, leaf, or flower can be cooked with spices and coconut milk to form a curry. In Ceylon, how the curry is prepared depends upon where it is prepared. The island's food has been influenced by the Portuguese (1517-1658) and the Dutch (1658-1796) who invaded the island, the British who evicted the Dutch and ruled until 1948 when the island gained Dominion status, and the Tamils, natives of south India, who settled in the northern provinces. There are three authentic curry variations then: Tamil curry, up-country curry (the area of the Kandyan highlands), and low-country curry (influenced by Europeans). The first uses dried tamarind, Indian curry powder, coconut oil, and is red hot; the second uses fresh limes, less seasoning, more gravy; the third is tempered to European tastes. Our recipes are a combination of all three, with suggested substitutes.

All curries are either red or white, hot or cool. The Ceylonese divide all foods into two classes: the "heating" and the "cooling," but these terms have come to refer not to temperature but seasoning, and an uninitiated visitor finds it hard to tell the difference. Both of them blow off the top of her head! Traditionally, red curries are made with fish, beef, pork, lamb, mutton, or poultry. Popular white curries are spinach and potatoes with lentils, cabbage with potatoes, cauliflower with carrots or peas, peas and potatoes, sweet potatoes, eggplant, okra, beets, fresh tomatoes, eggplant, pineapple and bananas, either alone or combined with nuts, usually cashews. You can make up additional combinations.

 **BASIC INGREDIENTS**

COCONUT MILK

Ceylonese friends of mine who have lived in Europe and were unable to get coconut milk substituted cow's milk and cream, but coconut milk is really part of the habit-forming flavor of a good curry. (Coconut milk as used in Ceylonese curries is *not* the liquid inside a fresh coconut; it is the heavy-bodied "milk" squeezed from the grated meat of the coconut, and every home in Ceylon, from the poorest mud and wattle hut to the Colombo mansions, has a coconut grater in its kitchen.) Fortunately for us, packages of dried, finely grated coconut are available in most of the United States. Coconut milk extracted from this dried coconut is almost like coconut milk from a fresh coconut. To extract the milk from a 1-pound package of dried coconut (4 cups), soak the dried coconut in 1 cup boiling water for 5 minutes. Then, using a food mill or colander, squeeze out and strain the liquid. (Ceylonese do this squeezing with their hands.) Add another cup of boiling water to the coconut and repeat the squeezing, but keep the liquids separate. The first extract has the consistency of cream, the second that of milk. If you are making a large quantity of curry, you can add more water and squeeze the coconut a third time. For a rich gravy, use 2 cups water to 4 cups dried coconut. But a less fattening and more economical product can be obtained from 2 cups water to 2 cups dried coconut; thus 1 pound dried coconut can yield 4 cups or more coconut milk: 2 cups first extract, 2 cups second extract.

In red (meat, fish, and poultry) curries, both extracts are used together. In white (vegetable) curries, you use first the second extract; then just before the curry has finished cooking, you add the first extract; simmer the curry for 2 or 3 minutes, until the gravy begins to boil, stirring constantly; remove from heat and serve. The constant stirring prevents curdling and is one of the secrets of making a good curry. The vegetables should be simmered until tender before the first extract is added. White curries are not as thick as red curries, for about ¾ of the coconut milk remains in the gravy. The coconut milk in red curries must cook down to half or less (until thickened) before the curry is ready.

CONDIMENTS

*Chili Powder, for vegetable curry
*Roasted Chili Powder, preferred for meat curries (1 tablespoon chili powder, roasted in hot oven, 400°F., until it begins to darken; remove from oven; pound into powder. A mortar and pestle is standard Ceylonese kitchen equipment.)
*Curry Powder, for vegetable curry
*Roasted Curry Powder, preferred for meat curries (1 tablespoon curry powder, 1 tablespoon ground coriander; roast as above.)
*Indian Curry Powder, preferred by Tamils (1 tablespoon chili powder, 2 tablespoons ground coriander, 1 teaspoon white cuminseed, 1 bay leaf, 2 peppercorns. Roast in hot oven, 400°F., until it begins to darken. Remove from oven; add 1 teaspoon ground saffron; pound into powder. This is *hot*.)
Saffron
Dillseed
White Cuminseed

Sweet Cumin (aniseed)
Coriander
Cardamom (use ground or whole)
Cloves (usually used whole, but ground cloves can be substituted)
Peppercorns
Cinnamon (whole and ground)
Salt
Gingerroot (either dried or ground)
Garlic; Onions (red or white)
Dried Salted Fish (Maldive fish is used in Ceylon, but dried herring or cod may be substituted.)
Red or Green Chilies (we call these dry red or green peppers. Fresh peppers may be substituted.)
Curry Leaf (substitute bay leaf)
Lemongrass (substitute drop of lemon extract, *not* lemon peel or juice.)
Powdered Mustard

Any one of the three powders may be used in any recipe. In practice, most cooks do not discriminate between the chili and curry powders for meat and vegetables. They use whichever they like best for both. Ceylonese cooks, however, use at least 2 tablespoons curry powder and 1 tablespoon chili powder in red curries, far too hot for Western palates.

BASIC RED CURRIES

CHICKEN CURRY

1 medium-size chicken (2 to 3 pounds)
1 teaspoon ground coriander
  or 1 teaspoon curry powder
½ teaspoon chili powder
¼ teaspoon ground saffron
2 tablespoons minced onion
1 teaspoon minced garlic
  Pinch of ground ginger
1 bay leaf
2 drops of lemon extract
½-inch piece of cinnamon stick
1 teaspoon salt
1 tablespoon melted shortening
  Coconut milk to cover, about 2 cups
  (1 cup FIRST extract, 1 cup SECOND extract; if more is needed, add SECOND extract.)
1 teaspoon lemon or lime juice
  or vinegar
1 teaspoon ground mixed spices:
  cardamom, cinnamon, cloves

Disjoint chicken. Mix all ingredients together except coconut milk, lemon juice, and 1 teaspoon mixed spices, and toss over chicken. Put chicken in saucepan and heat for 10 minutes, or until chicken and onions are golden brown and partly fried. Add coconut milk, cover, and simmer for about 1 hour, or until gravy is thick and chicken is tender. (Coconut milk will have cooked down to about half of original quantity.) Stir occasionally to prevent sticking. Remove from heat, add lemon juice, and immediately sprinkle surface of curry with 1 teaspoon mixed spices. Serve with rice and other accompaniments. Makes 4 servings.

Beef Curry

Have 1 pound round steak or other boneless beef cut into 1-inch cubes. Brown beef in fat before adding spices and coconut milk. Proceed as in Chicken Curry. Makes 4 servings.

Lamb Curry

Have 1 pound of boneless lamb cut into 1-inch cubes. Fry the onions and garlic in the melted shortening; then proceed as in Chicken Curry. Makes 4 servings.

Pork Curry

Have 1 pound of lean boneless pork cut into 1-inch cubes. Omit milk and use water instead. Proceed as in Chicken Curry. Makes 4 servings.

FISH CURRY

Seer, mullet, and shark are much used in the Far East, but halibut, whitefish, mackerel, trout, or any fish in plentiful supply will be good. Wash 1 pound of fish (whole rather than sliced, if you can get it) and soak it for 15 minutes in a brine made of 1 tablespoon vinegar and 1 teaspoon salt. Rinse; sprinkle with ½ teaspoon lemon juice and season, omitting the coriander or curry powder. Add coconut milk and simmer for about 45 minutes or until a red oil forms on top of the gravy and the fish is soft. Shake the pan during cooking; do not stir or the fish will fall apart. Add ½ teaspoon lemon juice and serve, either flaked or in chunks. Makes 2 or 3 servings.

BASIC WHITE CURRIES

VEGETABLE CURRY

⅛ teaspoon ground saffron
1 teaspoon salt, or more to taste
1 tablespoon minced onion
  Pinch of dillseeds
1 bay leaf
½-inch piece of green or red chili, if desired, either dried or fresh
  Pinch of dried fish (optional)
1 pound vegetables, any kind (if potatoes, quarter or halve each potato, depending on size. A 2-inch chunk or slice of a vegetable is average.)
2 cups coconut milk (1 cup FIRST extract, 1 cup SECOND extract)

Blend all seasonings together with the vegetables. Add 1 cup SECOND extract of coconut milk. Cover. Simmer until gravy has cooked down to half of original quantity, or vegetables are tender. Add FIRST extract; simmer for another 5 minutes, stirring constantly, until gravy boils. Remove from heat; serve. Makes 4 servings.

Plantain or Banana Curry

Soak sliced or chunked bananas in salted water to prevent discoloration before cooking. Select green bananas rather than white ones. (These also make delicious "chips" or deep-fried bananas, without batter.) Proceed as in Vegetable Curry.

ACCOMPANIMENTS

MALLUNG

½ pound outer cabbage leaves (or carrot tops, leek tops, kohlrabi leaves, or any other vegetable leaves)
1 teaspoon salt
1 tablespoon minced onion
½ small green chili (about 1-inch piece)
1 bay leaf
¾ cup dry ground coconut
1 teaspoon lime or lemon juice or vinegar
1 teaspoon minced garlic
¼ teaspoon ground saffron
⅛ teaspoon powdered mustard
⅛ cup water

Wash vegetable leaves in cold salted water. Drain and shred very fine. Add salt, minced onions, chili, and bay leaf. Cook (almost steam) over very low heat without adding water. Stir constantly to prevent sticking. When leaves are very tender, add dried coconut to which has been added the lime juice, garlic, saffron, and mustard. Then add water to moisten; stir, remove from heat, and serve. Makes 4 servings.

BADUN

Follow the directions for Red Curries but cook down the coconut milk until the gravy dries up, or leave out all of the coconut milk and, instead, add just enough water to prevent burning. Green or wax beans, or vegetable leaves finely minced, are a new experience served this way. Beet tops, spinach, and grape leaves are unusual. All meat, fish, and poultry can be made into a *Badun*. A word of caution: this dry-fry curry is not for the amateur. It is hot, and you'll have to work up to it.

SAMBALS

Sambals can be RED or WHITE. Traditionally, they are a hot dish made by grinding together chilies, onions, salt, Maldive fish, and grated coconut. When the chili is omitted or cut down, the *sambal* is "cooling" or WHITE.

COCONUT SAMBAL

2 cups dried coconut
¼ cup milk (cow's milk)
1 tablespoon minced onion
¼ teaspoon chili powder
¼ teaspoon salt
¼ teaspoon lime or lemon juice or vinegar

Soak coconut in milk for 10 minutes. Add onion, chili powder, salt, and lime juice. Mix well. This is fluffy, not a paste. Makes 4 to 6 servings.

STRING HOPPERS

Use fine egg noodles and follow the directions on the package. Serve with curries and *sambals* in place of rice.

OTHER ACCOMPANIMENTS

Chutneys, pickles, jams, preserves, nuts, sliced bananas, vegetable and fruit salads form a delightful accompaniment to rice and curry. This is a "smörgåsbord" with a relish!

Chicken Curry,
one of the red,
hot curries of Ceylon,
served with rice
and all the
proper Ceylonese
complements

CUSK—This large, salt-water fish has a continuous black fin running from the back of the head to the tail. It is related to the cod and is found in the North Atlantic. Cusk has firm, lean white meat and can be prepared like cod or haddock.

Availability—Available fresh as fillets in the northeastern United States.

Storage—Refrigerate immediately.
- Refrigerator shelf, raw: 24 hours
- Refrigerator shelf, cooked and covered: 1 to 2 days
- Refrigerator frozen-food compartment, prepared for freezing: 2 to 3 weeks
- Freezer, prepared for freezing: 1 year

Caloric Value
- 3½ ounces, steamed = 106 calories

BAKED CUSK WITH VEGETABLES
¼ cup olive oil
1 cup each of sliced raw cabbage and carrots
1 cup each of coarsely diced raw potatoes, eggplant, and tomatoes
1 cup snap beans, cut into 1-inch pieces
½ cup fresh or frozen green peas
¼ cup instant minced onion
½ teaspoon ground thyme
Salt and pepper
1½ pounds cusk fillets or steaks
1 tablespoon fresh lemon juice
Paprika

Put 3 tablespoons oil in shallow baking dish. Mix vegetables, thyme, 2 teaspoons salt, and ½ teaspoon pepper. Put in dish with oil. Cover with foil and bake in preheated hot oven (400°F.) for about 1 hour. Sprinkle fish with salt and pepper. Mix remaining 1 tablespoon oil with the lemon juice and brush on fish. Uncover vegetables and put fish on top. Bake, uncovered, for about 20 minutes longer. Sprinkle with paprika. Makes 6 servings.

CUSK AND POTATO CASSEROLE
2 pounds cusk fillets
4 potatoes, sliced
3 onions, sliced
Few celery tops
1 bay leaf
4 whole cloves
1 garlic clove, minced
¼ teaspoon dried dillseed
¼ teaspoon white pepper
2½ teaspoons salt
¼ pound butter or margarine
½ cup dry white wine
2 cups boiling water
2 cups light cream
Chopped parsley

Put all ingredients, except last 2, in 3-quart casserole. Cover, and bake in preheated moderate oven (375°F.) for 1 hour. Add scalded cream. Garnish with parsley. Makes 6 servings.

CUSTARD—A mixture of eggs and milk, sweetened and flavored and cooked over hot water on top of the stove or set in a pan of hot water and baked in the oven.

SOFT CUSTARDS
3 eggs or 6 egg yolks
¼ cup sugar
Dash salt
2 cups milk
½ teaspoon vanilla extract

Beat all ingredients, except vanilla, until blended in top part of double boiler. Put over simmering water and cook, stirring, for about 7 minutes, or until mixture thickens slightly and coats a metal spoon. Remove from over hot water and pour into bowl. Add vanilla. Cool and chill. Makes 2 cups.

BAKED CUSTARDS
1 cup undiluted evaporated milk
1 cup water
4 egg yolks
⅓ cup sugar
¼ teaspoon salt
½ teaspoon vanilla extract
Nutmeg

Combine milk and water and heat to scalding. Beat egg yolks slightly; add sugar, salt, and vanilla. Gradually add milk, stirring constantly. Divide into 4 custard cups, and set in pan of hot water. Bake in preheated slow oven (325°F.) for 50 minutes, or until tip of inserted knife comes out clean. Serve warm or cold, with nutmeg. Makes 4 servings.

Caramel Custards
Follow recipe above for the custard mixture. Before pouring into cups, melt ½ cup sugar over low heat, stirring constantly, until caramelized and syrupy. Divide into 4 custard cups, turning the cups to coat sides with syrup. Pour custard mixture in cups, and bake as directed.

COCONUT CUSTARD PIE
2¼ cups milk
½ cup sugar
½ teaspoon salt
Grating of nutmeg
½ teaspoon vanilla extract
3 eggs, slightly beaten
½ cup flaked coconut
Pastry for 1-crust 9-inch pie, unbaked

Scald milk; add sugar, salt, nutmeg, and vanilla. Mix well. Gradually pour milk mixture over beaten eggs, stirring constantly. Grease a deep 9-inch pie pan with cooking oil; pour in custard mixture. Sprinkle with the coconut. Put pie pan in larger shallow pan and pour in hot water to depth of about 1 inch. Bake in preheated slow oven (300°F.) for 55 minutes, or until set. Remove pan of custard from water; let stand until cold, then chill. Fit pastry into a pie pan exactly like the one containing custard; bake and cool. Just before serving, carefully loosen custard from sides of pan, using a small spatula. Shake gently to loosen custard from bottom; carefully but quickly slide custard from pan into the baked shell. Allow custard filling to settle down into the crust for a few minutes before serving. Makes 6 to 8 servings.

CUSTARD APPLE—Aside from the common custard apple (*Annona reticulata*), the name covers several fruits of tropical and subtropical America, such as the cherimoya and the sweetsop, or sugar apple, all of which have a sweet soft pulp. They don't taste in the least like other apples. The outside of the true custard apple looks scaly, rather like an artichoke. The fruit is four to six inches in length, heart-shape, and the pulp is cream-colored.

All custard apples have a bland taste, refreshing in a hot climate. The cherimoya is the best tasting, and the most fragrant. The pulp of custard apples is eaten as is, either directly from the fruit or spooned into a serving dish. The pulp should be chilled before serving and it is improved by a squeeze of lemon or lime juice.

Availability—From January to May, in southern California, where it is grown.

Storage—Refrigerate.
- Refrigerator shelf: 2 to 3 days

Caloric Value
- 3½ ounces, raw = 101 calories

CUT—As a noun used in connection with food, the word refers to a natural or customary segment of meat. Porterhouse steak and brisket are cuts of meat, for example.

As a verb, "to cut" means anything done with a knife or other sharp instrument. Cutting includes chopping, slicing, dicing, mincing, and slashing.

When using a knife the proper method of holding it is important. The thumb and the index finger grip the top of the blade nearest the handle, with the other fingers resting around the handle.

CUT IN—In culinary terms, this phrase means to break fat into small particles and combine them with dry ingredients. Cutting in is done with two knives or with a pastry blender.

CZECHOSLOVAKIAN COOKERY—

Czechoslovakian cookery reflects the fact that the Czech lands lay in the heart of Europe and were traveled as crossroads from north to south, west to east. From the Slavic east comes the custom of souring foods with sour cream, lemon, vinegar, or even the juice of green grapes. From Vienna come the schnitzels, from Hungary the goulash, from Germany the duck, goose, sauerkraut, and the dumplings, big and small, sweet or savory, that are the cornerstones of Czech cooking. Czech food isn't light food, but it is mighty good food, cooked in butter or lard, in a robust well-seasoned way, and washed down with Pilsener beer, the famous native drink.

Czechoslovakia is a country of deep mountain forests rich in venison and wild boar; streams and lakes filled with trout, pike, and carp, the latter the traditional Christmas dish. Her towns and villages are architectural gems. Historic Prague, the capital, is one of the world's most beautiful cities, with triumphs of baroque architecture in old castles and palaces.

From her picturesque farms come the famous Czech geese, ducks, and chickens which the farm wives fatten to make succulent and juicy. From the farms come also the noble Czech pigs, whose meat, fresh or smoked, is the mainstay of the country's meat cookery. Czechoslovakian hams, known as Prague hams, are a delicacy prized by connoisseurs everywhere.

Scores of different kinds of delicious edible mushrooms are found in Czechoslovakian woods and meadows. They're put in soups and cooked with eggs, used in sauces and stuffings, and eaten pickled.

Most Czechoslovakian meals begin with soup and many meals consist of a main-dish soup, especially in the countryside. The people like their soups substantial, thickened with flour, potatoes, cream, or egg yolks; handsomely garnished with dill, marjoram, parsley, and chives.

Dumplings are varied and light beyond belief. Praise of the fine Czechoslo-vakian hand with dumplings, sweet and savory, has been sung by native poets. Dumplings range from plain bread or potato dumplings to those made with eggs and flour, resembling soufflés. Some Czech dumplings are made light with yeast or baking powder; others with beaten egg whites. Dumplings can contain any number of delicious additions, from crisp bits of bacon to meats, cheese, and fruits. They vary in shape too; some dumplings are small and round; others are made into long rolls to be cut across into slices. Dumplings are cooked in soup, boiled in water or in fruit juices, or steamed, rolled in a napkin. Dessert dumplings, wrapped around juicy plums or apricots, are served with butter and sugar or with a sauce.

The Czechs, an earthy people, are also fond of cereal products such as noodles and groats. And they make the most delicious light and dark rye breads to serve with their cold meats and cheeses.

Volumes could be written on the Czechoslovakian cooks' ways with cakes and pastries of all kinds. Czech yeast cakes and sweet breads, in particular, are outstanding even among the finest of their kind in Europe.

POLÉVKA S JATERNIMI KNEDLÍKY
(Soup with Liver Dumplings)
- ½ pound beef liver, ground
- 2 tablespoons butter or beef marrow
- ½ garlic clove, mashed
- ½ teaspoon grated lemon rind
  Dash each of ground marjoram and mace
- 2 eggs
- 1 cup fine dry bread crumbs
- 2 tablespoons all-purpose flour
- 1 teaspoon salt
- ¼ teaspoon pepper
- 2 quarts consomme

Cream ground beef liver with butter, garlic, lemon rind, marjoram, and mace. Beat in eggs. Beat in bread crumbs, flour, salt, and pepper. Let stand at room temperature for about 1 hour. Shape into balls the size of golf balls. Bring consomme to a boil. Drop in liver dumplings. Cover and lower heat. Simmer for 10 minutes. Makes 6 servings.

KAPR PECENY S KYSELOU OMACKOU
(Carp with Sour-Cream Sauce)
- ¼ cup butter
- 2 bay leaves
  One 3- to 4-pound carp, cleaned and ready for cooking
  Salt and pepper to taste
- ⅓ cup dairy sour cream
  Juice of 1 lemon

Grease a shallow baking dish with the butter. Place bay leaves on butter. Season carp inside and out with salt and pepper. Lay in baking dish. Cover with sour cream and add lemon juice. Bake in preheated moderate oven (350°F.) for 35 to 40 minutes, or until golden brown and flaky. Baste frequently during baking time. Serve with buttered noodles sprinkled with poppy seeds. Makes 4 servings.

BEEFSTEAK NA KYSELO
(Steak with Sour-Cream Gravy)
- 1½ pounds round steak, thinly sliced
- 1 tablespoon lard
- 1 teaspoon salt
- 1 large onion, sliced
- 1 cup boiling water
- 1 cup dairy sour cream
- 2 tablespoons all-purpose flour
  Salt and pepper
- 1 tablespoon tomato ketchup (optional)

Trim meat slices. Cut into 1½-inch pieces. Heat lard in heavy skillet. When smoking hot, sauté meat in it until browned on both sides. Lower heat. Sprinkle salt over meat and top with onion slices. Pour water over meat. Simmer, covered, for 50 to 60 minutes, or until tender. Check liquid; at the end of cooking time, there should be about 1 cup of it. Remove meat to hot dish. Blend sour cream with flour. Stir into skillet and mix thoroughly with pan juices. Season with salt and pepper to taste and add ketchup. Heat through and pour sauce over meat. Serve very hot with boiled noodles or boiled potatoes. Makes 4 servings.

TELECÍ MASO S VINNOU OMACKOU
(Veal Roast with Wine Sauce)
  One 5- to 6-pound leg of veal, boned
- ¼ pound lean bacon, cut into thin strips
- 2 teaspoons salt
- 1 teaspoon pepper
- 2 large onions, sliced
- 1 carrot, sliced
- 1 celery stalk with leaves, sliced
- 1 parsley root, peeled and sliced, or 1 cup parsley, chopped
  Butter (about ½ cup)
- 2 cups boiling water
- 1 cup dry white wine
- 1 teaspoon all-purpose flour
- ½ cup dairy sour cream

Sauce
- ½ cup dry white wine
  Grated rind of 1 lemon
- 2 teaspoons all-purpose flour
- ½ cup heavy cream
  Salt and pepper

Trim meat free of fat and gristle. With larding needle or with knitting needle, push bacon strips through the meat. Rub with salt and pepper. Place onions, carrot, celery, parsley, and 3 tablespoons butter on bottom of roasting pan. Top with meat. Rub about 2 tablespoons butter into meat. Add boiling water. Roast in preheated moderate oven (350°F.) for 25 to 30 minutes per pound, or until 170°F. registers on meat thermometer and veal is tender. When half done, add wine. Melt 2 teaspoons butter and stir in flour and sour cream. When meat is ¾ done, turn around in baking pan. Spread ⅓ of sour-cream mixture on top and sides. Cook until this has been absorbed, and repeat process twice. Dot with 2 tablespoons butter and cook until meat is browned. Remove roast to hot serving platter and keep hot.

Strain pan juices. To make sauce, add wine and lemon peel to pan juices. Simmer for 5 minutes. Stir flour into cream. Add to liquid, stirring constantly until sauce is smooth and thick. Season with salt and pepper to taste. Serve with noodles or potatoes and a green vegetable. Makes 6 to 8 servings.

VEPŘOVÉ S KRENEM
(Piquant Pork with Horseradish)

2 pounds lean pork, cut into 1½-inch cubes
2 tablespoons butter or margarine
2 cups water
1 cup vinegar
1 medium onion, stuck with 3 cloves
1 medium carrot
1 small celery root (knob celery), peeled, or 1 celery stalk
1 tablespoon salt
1 teaspoon caraway seeds
½ teaspoon pepper
¼ cup prepared horseradish

Brown pork in hot butter on all sides in deep kettle. Add water and all other ingredients except horseradish. Simmer, covered, for 1½ hours, or until tender. Transfer meat to hot platter; keep hot. Force stock through sieve or purée in electric blender. Pour stock over meat. Top with horseradish. Serve with boiled potatoes. Makes 4 to 6 servings.

HOUBY S VEJCI
(Mushrooms with Eggs)

1 pound fresh mushrooms, sliced
⅓ cup butter
1 teaspoon salt
¼ teaspoon pepper
½ teaspoon crushed caraway seeds
2 tablespoons chopped parsley
6 eggs, beaten

Sauté mushrooms in hot butter with salt, pepper, caraway seeds, and parsley. When mushroom liquid has evaporated, add beaten eggs and scramble mixture. Makes 4 servings.

SVESTKOVE KNEDLÍKY
(Plum Dumplings)

Butter
2 eggs
¼ teaspoon salt
2 cups sifted all-purpose flour
2 cups boiled potatoes, riced
12 to 15 plums, pitted
12 to 15 blanched almonds
¼ cup cinnamon sugar
1 cup fine bread crumbs

Cream 2 tablespoons butter until soft. Beat in eggs and salt. Gradually beat in flour and riced potatoes, beating well after each addition. Dough should be stiff enough to knead thoroughly. On floured board roll out dough to ¼-inch thickness. Cut into 3-inch squares. Stuff each plum with 1 almond. Lay 1 plum on each square of dough. Sprinkle with a little cinnamon sugar. Fold dough edges over plum, encasing it completely. Shape with hands into a ball. Drop dumplings into gently boiling salted water. Simmer, covered, for about 10 minutes. Test for doneness by removing 1 dumpling and tearing it apart. Remove dumplings. Brown bread crumbs in ⅓ cup hot butter. Roll dumplings in buttered bread crumbs. Sprinkle with cinnamon sugar. Makes 6 servings.

KNEDLÍKY S VISNOVÉ
(Cherry Dumplings)

2¼ cups about (one 1-pound, 4-ounce can) pitted red sour cherries
¾ cup sugar
Dumpling Batter

Put undrained cherries and sugar in large deep skillet and bring to boil. Drop Dumpling Batter into boiling fruit from a tablespoon to make 4 to 6 dumplings. Cover and cook gently for 20 minutes. Serve at once.

Dumpling Batter

1 cup sifted cake flour
¼ cup sugar
1 teaspoon baking powder
¼ teaspoon salt
Grated rind of 1 orange
⅓ cup milk
2 teaspoons melted margarine

Sift dry ingredients into bowl. Add remaining ingredients, mixing quickly and lightly until blended; do not mix smooth.

BOZI MILOSTI
(Celestial Crusts)

3 tablespoons butter
¼ cup sugar
1 egg
2 egg yolks
1 tablespoon light cream
3 tablespoons grape or any sweet fruit juice
Grated rind of 1 lemon
2½ cups sifted all-purpose flour
Fat for deep frying
Granulated sugar

Cream butter and sugar. Beat in egg and egg yolks, one at a time, beating well after each addition. Beat in cream, grape juice, and lemon rind. Gradually stir in flour. Wrap dough in wax paper and chill for 30 minutes. Divide dough into 4 parts. Roll out each part on floured board as thinly as possible, the thinner the better. Cut into 1½-inch squares. Drop into deep hot fat (375°F. on frying thermometer) and fry until golden brown. Drain on absorbent paper. Sprinkle with granulated sugar while hot.

Serve hot or cold. Makes about 7 dozen.

KOLÁCKY (Bohemian Tarts)

1 package active dry yeast
2 tablespoons warm water*
4 cups sifted all-purpose flour
¼ cup sugar
1 teaspoon salt
1 teaspoon grated lemon rind
¾ cup butter
3 egg yolks
1 cup heavy cream
Prune Filling
Apricot Filling
Frosting

Soften yeast in the water.* Use very warm water (105°F. to 115°F.) for dry yeast. Sift flour, sugar, and salt. Add lemon rind and yeast and blend in butter. Beat egg yolks and add the cream. Add to first mixture and blend well. Cover and refrigerate overnight. Next day, toss on lightly floured board and roll to ¼-inch thickness. Cut with 2-inch cutter and put on ungreased cookie sheets. Cover and let rise until double in bulk, about 1 hour. Make a depression in the center of each and put in one of the fruit Fillings. Bake in preheated moderate oven (375°F.) for about 10 minutes. Spread with Frosting while warm. Makes about 4 dozen.

Prune Filling

Cook and drain 1½ cups dried prunes. Pit and mash with fork. Add ¼ cup sugar and ½ teaspoon ground cinnamon. Makes enough to fill 4 dozen Kolácky.

Apricot Filling

Cook and drain 1½ cups dried apricot halves. Force through sieve and add ½ cup sugar. Makes enough to fill 4 dozen Kolácky.

Frosting

Mix well 1½ cups confectioners' sugar, 1 teaspoon fresh lemon juice, and 2 tablespoons boiling water.

MAKOVÝ KOLÁC
(Poppy-Seed Layer Torte)

¼ cup sweet butter
1 cup sugar
6 eggs, separated
½ cup raisins, plumped
1 cup ground poppy seeds
Grated rind of 1 large lemon
½ teaspoon ground cinnamon
¼ teaspoon each of ground cloves and mace
½ cup apricot, strawberry, or raspberry jam
1 cup heavy cream, whipped

Cream butter until soft. Gradually add sugar, beating well after each addition. Beat in egg yolks, one at a time, beating thoroughly. Stir in remaining ingredients except jam and cream. Beat egg whites until stiff. Fold in batter. Grease and flour two 9-inch layer cake pans. Spoon half of batter into each. Bake in preheated moderate oven (350°F.) for about 30 minutes, or until layers test done. Cool. Fill cold layers with jam. Top with whipped cream. Makes 8 to 10 servings.

DAMSON—A variety of plum tree and its fruit, which, like all plums, belongs to the great rose family. It originated in Asia Minor. The word "damson" itself is derived from Damascus, capital of Syria, where these plums were cultivated before the time of Christ.

Damson plums are small, firm, oval purple plums. They grow wild and are also cultivated in orchards. There is a variety with yellow flesh. These are spicier and more acid than ordinary plums.

Damson plums are not eaten raw, but they are a superlative fruit for cooking and are made into delicious pies, compotes, jams, and preserves. They should be pitted before cooking. To pit: Halve with paring knife, circle pit with knife, and remove.

Availability—Available in specialty fruit stores from May through September.

Damson jam is also available.

Purchasing Guide—Select damsons at peak ripeness, shown by fresh appearance, full color, and firm plumpness yielding slightly when gently pressed. Plums are best in flavor, sweetness, and nutritional value when picked at maturity. Avoid underripe, hard, or shriveled plums with poor color; they will not ripen satisfactorily. Overripe fruit, generally soft and sometimes leaky, will have poor flavor and will spoil quickly, as will those with growth cracks.

Storage—Buy in amounts that can be used within the week. Wash, pick over plums, drain, and refrigerate in a covered container.

☐ Refrigerator shelf, fresh: 4 to 5 days
☐ Refrigerator shelf, stewed: 4 to 5 days
☐ Jam, kitchen shelf: 6 months
☐ Jam, refrigerator shelf, opened and covered: 4 to 5 weeks

Caloric Values

☐ 1 plum = 10 to 15 calories
☐ Jam, 1 tablespoon = 55 calories

STEWED DAMSON PLUMS

¾ to 1 cup sugar, depending on tartness of fruit
½ cup water
1 cinnamon stick
2 pounds damson plums, pitted

Combine sugar, water, and cinnamon stick. Boil for 3 minutes, or until thick. Add damson plums. Bring to a gentle boil. Simmer, covered, for about 10 minutes, or until plums are tender. Chill before serving. Makes 6 servings.

DAMSON-PLUM PIE

2 cups pitted damson plums
1½ cups sugar
2 eggs, beaten
1 cup milk
¼ cup cream
Pastry for 2-crust 9-inch pie, unbaked
1 tablespoon butter or margarine

Cook plums in small amount of water

until tender. Drain and force through a sieve or colander. Stir in sugar, eggs, milk, and cream. Roll out half the pastry and line a 9-inch pie pan. Pour in filling and dot with butter. Roll out rest of pastry; cover pie and crimp edge. Bake in preheated hot oven (425°F.) for 15 minutes. Reduce heat to moderate (375° F.) and bake for about 30 minutes longer. Makes 8 servings.

DAMSON-PLUM JAM

4½ cups prepared fruit (about 3 pounds ripe damson plums)
7½ cups (3¼ pounds) sugar
½ bottle liquid fruit pectin

Pit (do not peel) about 3 pounds fully ripe damson plums. Cut into small pieces and chop. Add ½ cup water; bring to boil and simmer, covered, for 5 minutes. Measure 4½ cups into a very large saucepan. Add sugar and mix well. Put over high heat, bring to a full rolling boil, and boil hard for 1 minute, stirring constantly. Remove from heat; stir in pectin at once. Skim off foam with metal spoon. Then stir and skim for 5 minutes to cool slightly and prevent floating fruit. Ladle at once into hot sterilized glasses. Seal with paraffin. Makes eleven 8-ounce glasses.

DAMSON-PLUM CONSERVE

6 pounds damson plums
3 pounds seedless raisins
5 oranges
9 to 11¼ cups (4 to 5 pounds) sugar
2 cups chopped walnuts

Pit plums, cover with water, and cook until soft. Add raisins, pulp from oranges, and sugar. Cook until smooth and thick. Add nuts and cook for 12 to 15 minutes longer. Pour into hot sterilized jars and seal. Makes about 6 pints.

DANDELION—A familiar weed of the chicory family which grows wild throughout Asia, Europe, and North America. The name comes from the French *dent de lion* or "lion's tooth," which the sharply indented leaves of the plant are said to resemble. Generations of children and lovers have blown the fuzzy winged seeds from the hoary seed balls to know when they would get married, how many children they would have, and whether or not their love was requited.

Wild or cultivated, dandelion leaves are eaten as a vegetable, raw or cooked. They have a somewhat bitter flavor. They should be harvested in the spring, before the plant flowers, when the leaves are still young, tender, and delicate.

In Europe, dandelion greens have long been an accepted spring vegetable. To our colonial forefathers, a mess of dandelion greens on the table meant a spring

tonic, a blood purifier, and a cure for heart trouble and rheumatism.

There's more to dandelion eating than the leaves. The roots can be eaten as vegetables, or roasted and ground and made into a root coffee. To prepare as a vegetable: dig up the dandelion plant, root and all. Peel the roots with a potato peeler. Slice them thinly crosswise. Cover with water, bring to a boil, and drain. Repeat the process and serve with salt, pepper, and butter.

To make dandelion-root coffee: roast the roots in a slow oven for about 4 hours. They should snap easily and show a very dark brown interior. Grind and use as you do coffee.

Availability—Cultivated and wild dandelion greens are usually found in the market in early spring. During the winter months some greens may be available in southern areas.

Purchasing Guide—Look for very young, fresh green plants with tender leaves. Cultivated dandelion greens are more blanched, tender, and not as bitter as the wild variety. Avoid plants with wilted, tough, or yellow leaves.

Storage—Wash dandelion greens well and drain thoroughly. Discard damaged leaves and roots. Wrap greens in plastic film and keep in the vegetable compartment of the refrigerator.

☐ Refrigerator shelf or vegetable compartment, raw: 3 to 8 days
☐ Refrigerator shelf, cooked: 4 to 5 days
☐ Refrigerator frozen-food compartment, prepared for freezing: 2 to 3 months
☐ Freezer, prepared for freezing: 1 year

Nutritive Food Values—Dandelion greens are an excellent source of vitamin A, very good for iron, and good for calcium.
☐ 3½ ounces, raw = 45 calories
☐ 3½ ounces, cooked = 33 calories

Basic Preparation—Tear greens into bite-size pieces for use in salads. Chop or cut into 2-inch pieces for cooking.

☐ **To Cook**—Have about ½ inch of water boiling in a saucepan. Add greens and salt. Cover and cook for 10 to 20 minutes, or until tender. Drain and season to taste.

For very young and tender greens, use no water. Place washed greens in a covered saucepan. The greens will cook in the water that clings to the leaves after washing.

☐ **To Freeze**—Remove tough stems and blemished leaves. Wash in cold running water. Scald greens for 2 minutes in boiling water. Chill in ice water. Drain and pack tightly, allowing ½-inch headspace.

DANDELION GREENS WITH LENTILS

½ cup lentils
2 cups water
¼ pound bacon or salt pork, diced
1 onion, diced
1 pound dandelion greens, cooked
   Salt and pepper

Soak lentils in water overnight; do not drain. Cook with bacon and onion until lentils are tender and liquid almost evaporated. Drain greens; mix with lentils. Season to taste and heat for 5 minutes. Makes 4 servings.

DANDELION GREENS, ITALIAN STYLE

1 pound dandelion greens
1 onion, diced
1 garlic clove, minced
1 small dried whole red pepper, crushed
¼ cup cooking oil
   Salt and pepper
   Parmesan cheese

Discard roots and wash greens thoroughly in salted water: cut leaves into 2-inch pieces. Cook uncovered in about ½-inch of boiling salted water until tender, about 10 minutes. Sauté onion, garlic, and red pepper in oil. Drain greens; add to onion mixture and season to taste. Heat slowly. Serve with grated cheese. Makes 4 servings.

RAW DANDELION SALAD

½ pound dandelion greens
½ cup thinly sliced red or Spanish onions
2 tomatoes, quartered
   Pinch of basil
   Salt and pepper
   French dressing

Use young tender leaves of dandelion; wash thoroughly; cut into 2-inch pieces and pat dry with towel. Add other ingredients; toss and mix well. Makes 4 servings.

DANDELION WINE

Dandelion wine is a time-honored drink and ranks among the better homemade wines. Here is an old recipe for it: Place 1 gallon dry dandelion flowers in a 2-gallon crock. Pour 1 gallon boiling water over flowers. Cover and let stand for 3 days. Strain through a cloth and squeeze all the liquid from flowers. In a deep kettle combine liquid, 3 pounds of sugar, and the juice of 3 oranges and 1 lemon. Simmer for 20 minutes. Return liquid to crock. Cool until barely lukewarm. Toast a slice of rye bread. Sprinkle top with ½ package dry yeast or ½ cake compressed yeast. Place bread on top of liquid in crock. Cover with a cloth and keep at room temperature (70° to 75°F.) for 6 days. Strain wine into a gallon jug. Plug jug loosely with a wad of cotton. Keep in dark place for 3 weeks. Decant into a bottle. Cap or cork bottle tightly. Keep for at least 5 months before serving.

Danish Cookery

by Helen Evans Brown

Danes are proud of their food and with good reason. Their coffeecake—known in this country as Danish pastry, and in Denmark as *Wienerbrød,* or Vienna bread—is world famous. Their open-faced sandwiches, or *smørrebrød,* are conversation pieces wherever they are served, and other Danish specialties such as cucumber salad *(agurkesalat),* meatballs *(frikadeller),* and doughnuts *(aebleskiver)* are becoming very popular. The Danes' fish cookery is probably the best in the world, and that is because they buy their fish live, so there's no chance of it not being fresh. Danish hams, bacons, and cheeses are now found in many American food stores and so is Danish beer. Restaurants in Copenhagen and other Danish cities, and many Danish homes as well, serve Continental cuisine along with the native specialties. This is because the royal family, many years ago, imported cooks from France, and the fame of their food (as well as the recipes) soon spread to the populace. But whether the food is Danish or Continental, it is excellent, for the Danes not only love cooking, they love to eat.

SMØRREBRØD

These open-faced Danish sandwiches are to be found almost anywhere in Denmark. They are sold from little kiosks on the street corners, on boats going to the islands, on trains, and in restaurants. One restaurant, Oskar Davidsen's, has a yard-long menu listing 177 different smørrebrød.

They are made on white, rye, sour-rye, or crisp bread, always buttered. Rye is the favorite. On top goes the main ingredient, always tastefully arranged, and the garnishes. Usually a small leaf of lettuce is tucked under the filling at one or two corners. They are always eaten with knife and fork. Some smørrebrød that are particularly popular have names, such as "Rush Hour," "Hans Andersen's," "Mussels in Bed," and "Vet's Breakfast."

REJER I TRAENGSEL
(Rush Hour Shrimp)
This is one of the most famous of the smørrebrød and one of the simplest. Butter white bread and arrange on it 2 layers of tiny shrimps, symmetrically placed. On top put another double row of shrimps. These Danish shrimps are the best in the world. They're caught at night, cooked alive next morning, and shelled and used at once. As many as 60 to 100 shrimps go on each "Rush Hour."

MUSLINGER I SENG
(Mussels in Bed)
Spread rye bread with butter, then with cream cheese. Cover with smoked mussels (smoked oysters would make it "oysters in bed") and garnish with chopped chives and sliced radishes.

ROGET AAL
(Smoked Eel)
This can be bought canned in specialty food stores. It is best on buttered rye bread, garnished with Aeggestand (page 538). It needs nothing else.

ROGET LAKS
(Smoked Salmon)
Butter rye bread and use thinly sliced lox, or smoked salmon, laid on in waves. Garnish with rings of raw onion and with Asier (page 538) if desired.

KRYDDERSILD
(Pickled Herring)
This can be bought in most food stores. Arrange it on buttered rye bread and garnish with raw onion rings and pimiento strips.

HANS ANDERSEN'S
Cover buttered rye bread with crisp bacon; on this put sliced tomato and garnish with slices of Leverpostej (see below), Sky (page 538), and shavings of fresh horseradish, if available.

VET'S BREAKFAST
The rye bread is spread with Skysovs (page 538). On this goes a slice of Leverpostej (see below), and the whole is garnished with Sky (page 538). Paper-thin slices of salami are laid on top in waves. The "Vet's Midnight Snack" is the same, with sliced veal instead of salami.

LEVERPOSTEJ
(Liver Pâté)
1 pound fresh pork fat
½ pound chicken livers or calf's liver
¼ pound lean pork
1 medium onion
2 anchovies
1½ teaspoons salt
¼ teaspoon pepper
1 egg
½ cup all-purpose flour
1 cup cream
¼ teaspoon each of ground allspice and thyme

Slice the pork fat thin and line the sides and bottom of a 1½-quart glass bread pan with it, reserving remainder. (If fresh pork fat is unavailable, use salt pork and soak overnight after slicing.) Pour boiling water over the livers and drain. This firms them. Grind remaining pork fat, livers, lean pork, onion, and anchovies. Repeat grinding at least twice more, or purée them in blender. Add remaining ingredients and mix thoroughly. Put into fat-lined pan and cover with a piece of foil. Place in a pan containing 2 inches of hot water. Bake in preheated moderate oven (350°F.) for 1 hour. Put a light weight on top (another bread pan is fine) and allow to cool. Slice. Makes about sixteen 1-inch slices.
Note: Place slices on buttered rye bread. Garnish with Agurkesalat (page 542), or with Asier (page 538).

BØF
(Roast Beef)
The beef should be rare and sliced paper-thin. Arrange it in billows on buttered rye bread and garnish with Frisk Stegt Løg and Sky (page 538).

CLIPPER SANDWICH
This can be made on white or rye bread, buttered, of course. It is spread with raw scraped beef. This is easy and much better than ground, although you can use the latter. To scrape, use fresh sirloin, round, or rump steak and scrape, using a heavy not-too-sharp knife. Use the connective tissue that remains to add rich-

ness to stock. On the beef put a diagonal strip of Danish lump caviar, and put strips of smoked salmon on either side.

TUNGE
(Tongue)
Place thinly sliced beef tongue on buttered bread. Garnish with Sky (page 538) and sliced hard-cooked egg.

RULLEPØLSE
(Meat Rolls)
2 large breasts of lamb (about 4 pounds each)
¼ cup minced parsley
1 tablespoon salt
¼ cup minced onion
¼ teaspoon each of ground ginger, cloves, allspice, and pepper
1 cup salt
½ teaspoon saltpeter
¼ cup sugar
8 cups boiling water

Have bones removed from breasts of lamb. Skewer and lace pieces together. Mix parsley, 1 tablespoon salt, onion, and spices together and spread over meat. Roll very firmly and tie securely. Make brine by combining 1 cup salt, the saltpeter, sugar, and boiling water. Cool brine and then pour over meat. Cover. Let stand in a cool place for 4 days. Drain and cook in simmering water for 2½ hours, or until fork-tender. Remove from stock and pull out skewers. Remove lacing. Save stock for soup. Put the roll between 2 bread boards or baking sheets. Weight with something heavy; large filled cans do nicely. When cold, slice thin.
Note: Place slices on bread and garnish with lettuce and Asier (page 538).

STEGT AND
(Roast Duck)
Slice duck thin and arrange on buttered bread of your choice. Garnish with cold Rødkaal (page 542), and with a salad made by mixing diced apple and diced celery with mayonnaise.

SAMSØ OR GRUYÈRE CHEESE
Samsø is a Danish cheese rather like Gruyère. Slice it paper-thin and put it on buttered rye bread; garnish with sliced stuffed olives and raw onion.

CAMEMBERT
Spread rye bread with butter and then with Danish Camembert (available in cans). Top with crisp bacon and sliced tomatoes.

ROQUEFORT OST
(Danish Blue Cheese)
Spread rye bread with butter and Danish blue cheese, garnished with Frisk Stegt Løg (page 538) and sliced tomatoes.

Of course, there are as many more pos-

Røget Laks
Vet's Breakfast
Kryddersild
Camembert
Rejer i Trængsel

sibilities as there are meats, fish, poultry, and garnishes. You will find that you can compose your own, using bits of leftovers for both sandwich and its garnish. This is the thrifty Danes' way of using up tidbits.

SNITTER

This is an endearing term for miniature open-faced sandwiches, ideal to serve as appetizers or with afternoon tea or morning coffee. Cut slices of bread into quarters, making squares or triangles, or cut into rounds about 1½ inches in diameter. Butter and spread and garnish like *smørrebrød,* above, or use any cheese, meat, or fish spread, tastefully garnished.

GARNISHES

Frisk Stegt Løg (fried onions) are a favorite garnish, as are *Aeggestand* (cold scrambled eggs—really an unsweetened custard), *Asier* (pickled cucumbers), *Sky* (chopped aspic), thinly sliced dill pickles, radishes, hard-cooked eggs, cucumbers, and lemons. The last two are sliced thin, slit from one side to the center, then given a half twist so that they look like a figure S humped up in the middle.

FRISK STEGT LØG
(Fried Onions)

There's nothing better than the crisply fried onions that so often garnish the *smørrebrød* in Denmark. Unlike our French-fried onions, they are not dipped into batter or crumbs. Cut large onions into halves from pole to pole. Remove skins, and slice about ⅛ inch thick. Fry about 1 onion at a time in deep fat heated to 370°F. on a frying thermometer. They will take about 5 minutes to become brown, crisp, and sweet. Drain on paper toweling and sprinkle with salt. These are good cold, but can easily be reheated by a sojourn in a preheated moderate oven (350°F.) for about 5 minutes.

AEGGESTAND
(Cold Scrambled Eggs)

Beat 1 egg slightly and mix with ¼ cup milk and a few grains of salt. Pour into a shallow buttered dish, an 8-inch pie pan is fine, and set in a pan of water. Bake in preheated slow oven (300°F.) for 20 minutes, or until set. Cool and cut into slices. This is used on smoked salmon.

SKY
(Chopped Aspic)

Soften ½ envelope unflavored gelatin in ¼ cup cold water and add to 1 can (10½ ounces) consommé. Heat, stirring, until the gelatin is dissolved. Pour into a loaf pan (a glass bread pan is ideal) and allow to set. Turn out on a cold board and chop into crystals with a cold knife. Keep chilled until time to use as a garnish.

ASIER
(Pickled Cucumbers)

18 long cucumbers
⅓ cup salt
6 cups vinegar
1½ cups sugar
3 tablespoons salt
1 tablespoon mustard seeds
1 teaspoon whole peppercorns
1 teaspoon celery seeds
½ teaspoon each of ground turmeric and ginger
12 small dried red peppers
12 sprigs of fresh dill

Peel the cucumbers and cut into halves crosswise and lengthwise. Split each piece into quarters, to give 16 pieces for each cucumber. Sprinkle with salt and let stand overnight. Drain and rinse. Combine vinegar, sugar, and seasonings except peppers and dill. Bring to a boil and simmer for 5 minutes. In the meantime, sterilize 12 pint jars and pack the cucumbers into them, asparagus style. Put a pepper and a sprig of dill (or ½ teaspoon dillweed) in each jar and fill with the boiling syrup. Seal at once. Makes 12 pints.

Note: These are very different from our American cucumber pickles, both in appearance and taste.

SKYSOVS
(Spiced Drippings)

Heat drippings from roast pork or bacon. In it fry some chopped onion and a little dried thyme or rosemary. Strain and use in place of butter.

SOUPS

GULE AERTER
(Yellow Pea Soup)

1 pound dried yellow peas
1 pound lean bacon or salt pork
   Bouquet garni made from 1 bay leaf, 2 parsley sprigs, and ½ teaspoon dried thyme
   Water
3 celery stalks, sliced
3 carrots, diced
1 large potato, diced
2 large onions, diced
½ cup (one 4-ounce can) Danish cocktail sausages, sliced
   Salt and pepper

Soak peas in water according to package directions. Or place first 3 ingredients in deep kettle. Add 6 cups water. Cook, covered, for about 2 hours, or until very soft. Remove bacon and *bouquet garni.* Dice bacon. Force soup through a sieve or whirl in a blender. Cool, and skim off fat. Cook celery, carrots, potato, and onions in 2 cups water until tender. Combine soup, vegetables, diced bacon, and sliced cocktail sausages. Season with salt and pepper to taste. Simmer, covered, for 20 minutes to blend flavors and heat through. If too thick, thin with a little water. Serve with Danish rye bread. Makes 3 quarts or 6 servings.

AGURKESUPPE
(Cucumber Soup)

¼ cup butter or margarine
1 large onion
4 large or 5 medium cucumbers
2 bay leaves
6 peppercorns
¼ cup all-purpose flour
5 cups chicken bouillon
   Salt
   Hot pepper sauce
1 cup heavy cream
1 tablespoon fresh lemon juice
   Dairy sour cream
   Chopped dill

Melt the butter, chop the onion, and peel and slice all but half of 1 cucumber very thinly. Combine the sliced cucumber with the butter and onion and add bay leaves and peppercorns. Cook, covered, until the vegetables are transparent. Add flour and stir until smooth. Gradually stir in the bouillon. Simmer, covered, for 30 minutes; then force through a sieve or whirl in electric blender. Add salt to taste and a dash of hot pepper sauce. Chill thoroughly. Before serving, add cream, lemon juice, and more salt if needed. Peel the remaining ½ cucumber and split it. Scrape out the seeds. Slice very thinly and add to the soup. Serve each cupful garnished with a spoonful of dairy sour cream and a generous sprinkling of chopped dill. Makes 6 to 8 servings.

ASPARGESSUPPE
(Asparagus Soup)

1 pound asparagus
   Beef bouillon
2 tablespoons butter
1 tablespoon all-purpose flour
3 egg yolks
2 tablespoons light cream
   Salt, pepper, sugar

Wash asparagus and break off tips. Cook tips for about 10 minutes, or until just tender, in 1 cup bouillon. Cut the remaining stalks into pieces (discard very tough ends) and cook in 3 cups bouillon until very tender; then force through a sieve. Cream butter with flour. Add paste to asparagus-stalk mixture and bring to a boil. Beat egg yolks with cream and pour in a little of the boiling soup. Combine

this with remaining soup, add asparagus tips and bouillon, and season to taste with salt, pepper, and a pinch of sugar. Serve with croutons. Makes 6 servings.

KAERNEMAELKSKOLDSKAAL
(Cold Buttermilk Soup)

Beat 2 eggs until light. Then add ¼ cup sugar and 1 quart buttermilk. Beat some more. Add 1 teaspoon vanilla extract and the juice and grated rind of 1 lemon. Mix well and serve very cold, topped with whipped cream. Makes 4 to 6 servings.

ØLLEBRØD
(Beer and Bread Soup)

½ pound pumpernickel bread
2½ cups water
2¼ cups beer, preferably Danish
1 tablespoon sugar
1-inch piece of cinnamon stick
Grated rind of ½ lemon
½ teaspoon salt, or to taste
Fresh lemon juice to taste
Whipped cream or dairy sour cream

Break bread into pieces and soak in water until soft. Cook, stirring, until it becomes a thick smooth mush. Add beer and seasoning and simmer for 20 minutes. If too thick, add a little water. Discard cinnamon stick and taste for seasoning. Serve with whipped cream on each portion. Makes enough for 6 ordinary mortals or 3 Danes.

KIRSEBAERSUPPE
(Cherry Soup)

Cook 2 cups sour cherries in 6 cups water until tender. Strain off liquid, discarding cherries. Then add 1 cinnamon stick, ½ lemon, sliced, and sugar to taste. Simmer for 5 minutes, then add another cup of cherries, these pitted. Thicken with 1 tablespoon cornstarch mixed with ¼ cup water, cook until clear, and serve with sweet croutons (cube bread, sauté in butter, and sprinkle with sugar while still hot) or with *Brødboller* (see page 542). Makes 6 to 8 servings.

FISH

KLIPFISK
(Salted Dried Cod)

Soak salt cod in water or milk to cover for 4 to 5 hours; drain, cover with cold water, and bring to a boil. Simmer for 20 minutes, or until tender. Put on a heated platter, surround with boiled potatoes, garnish with parsley and sliced hard-cooked eggs, and pour a generous quantity of melted butter over all. Serve with mustard sauce. Allow 1 pound of fish for 4 servings.

FISKEFRIKADELLER
(Fish Balls)

Drop *Fiskefars* (see recipe below) from a spoon into hot butter or oil and brown on both sides. Serve with Sennepssovs (page 542), dairy sour cream, caper, or lemon sauce, if desired. Makes 4 servings.
Note: Serve hot to the family or cold at a buffet party.

Fiskefars
(Fish Forcemeat)

1 pound lean white fish
3 tablespoons melted butter
2 tablespoons each of all-purpose flour and cornstarch
1 teaspoon salt
Pepper
1 egg, well beaten
⅓ cup milk

Grind fish, using the fine blade on your food grinder, or whirl in a blender, a little at a time, until all is smooth. You should have 2 cups of fish. Add butter, flour, and cornstarch. Add seasonings to taste, and beaten egg. Mix very well, using an electric mixer if available. Gradually add milk, beating constantly, until absorbed.

FISKEBUDDING
(Fish Pudding)

Butter a 1-quart mold and sprinkle with crumbs. Add *Fiskefars* (recipe above). Set mold in a pan of hot water and bake in preheated slow oven (325°F.) for 1 hour. Makes 4 servings.
Note: This may be served hot, or chilled and sliced. If served cold, garnish with sliced hard-cooked eggs, mayonnaise, and sliced tomatoes or cucumber and dill.

STEGT AAL I KARRY
(Fried Eel with Curry Sauce)

Prepare eel; cut the skin around the head. With a sharp knife, cut under skin slowly to loosen a small flap. Hold the head in one hand and grasp the skin with the other hand. Or use a pair of pliers. Strip the skin off as you would a glove, in one motion. Cut off head. Cut eel into desired lengths and sprinkle cut pieces with salt. Let stand for 30 minutes; rinse and dry on towels. Dip into seasoned flour (½ teaspoon salt and some freshly ground pepper to each ½ cup flour), then dip into slightly beaten egg, and roll in bread crumbs. Fry in plenty of butter until golden. Serve with *Karry*. Two average-size eels make 4 to 8 servings, depending on size of eel.

Karry
(Curry Sauce)

Chop 1 apple and 1 onion and cook until soft in 2 tablespoons butter. Add 1 tablespoon curry powder and simmer for 3 to 4 minutes; then stir in 2 tablespoons

flour and 1 cup stock made from the trimmings of the eel. Simmer for 15 minutes, adding salt to taste, a little lemon juice, and more curry powder if needed.

AAL I GELÉ
(Jellied Eel)

1 eel, skinned and cut into 2-inch pieces
Water
1 onion, sliced
1 carrot, sliced
Bouquet garni of 1 bay leaf, parsley sprig, thyme sprig, and 3 to 4 peppercorns
Cider vinegar
Salt
Unflavored gelatin

Select a gelatin mold that has a hole in the middle, like an angel-food pan. Fill the mold with water and pour the water into a large saucepan. Bring to a boil and place eel in water with onion, carrot, and *bouquet garni*. Simmer until eel is just tender. Strain, reserving liquid and herbs. Season the liquid with vinegar and salt to taste and add 1 envelope unflavored gelatin for each 2 cups liquid, soaking the gelatin in ¼ cup water for each package of gelatin. Let gelatin soak for 5 minutes. Add to hot liquid and heat until gelatin is dissolved. Pour liquid into mold to the depth of 1 inch. Chill until firm. Add eel and sprinkle with reserved herbs, minced. Add enough gelatin to hold pieces in place. Chill until firm. Add remaining gelatin and chill until firm. Unmold by standing mold in lukewarm water for a few seconds. Garnish with lemon and parsley. If mold is a large one, you will need 2 average-size eels. Makes 4 to 8 servings, depending on size of eel.
Note: Usually served with hot creamed potatoes.

MEAT

SKINKE MED MADEIRA
(Ham with Madeira)

Ham half (about 5 pounds)
2 bay leaves
1 cinnamon stick
4 whole cloves
4 peppercorns
3 cups Madeira wine
¼ cup butter
¼ cup all-purpose flour
2 cans (10½ ounces each) consomme

Bake ham as usual. Tie spices in a small cheesecloth bag and place in the pan. While roasting, baste ham with Madeira. Remove skin, score fat, and return to oven, continuing to baste with the wine until the ham is brown and shiny. Cream butter with flour and cook over low heat for 3 to 4 minutes. Skim fat from ham pan.

Gradually stir 1 cup of liquid from the ham, and the consommé into butter-flour mixture. Cook over low heat, stirring constantly, until thickened and smooth. Serve with ham. Makes 8 to 10 servings.

FLAESKESTEG
(Roast Pork)

Select a fresh ham or shoulder or loin of pork with the skin on. In this country, it may be difficult to find a loin with the skin, but fresh shoulders and hams are usually available. Score the skin with a sharp knife, cutting through to the fat beneath. Do this either in parallel cuts about ⅛ inch apart, or in ¼-inch squares. Put the pork in a cold oven and set at slow (325°F.). Roast until the meat thermometer reads 185°F. internal temperature, and the skin is crisp and blistered. This will take 5 hours or more for a leg weighing about 8 to 10 pounds. Makes 16 to 18 servings.

Note: Roasting pork with the skin on gives it a wonderful crispness.

FYLDT SVINEMORBRAD
(Stuffed Pork Tenderloin)

2 pork tenderloins (about 1 pound each)
2 large apples, peeled and chopped
   Salt and pepper to taste
12 cooked prunes, pitted
2 tablespoons butter
½ cup beef bouillon
1 cup heavy cream

Split tenderloins the long way, cutting two thirds of the way through. Open flat and pound to an even thickness. Place apples on meat and sprinkle with salt and pepper. Lay 6 prunes across the short end of each tenderloin and roll like a jelly roll. Tie securely, then brown on all sides in butter. Add bouillon and heavy cream. Cover and simmer for 1 hour, taking care to stir occasionally so meat won't stick. Add water if necessary. Remove meat to a hot platter, skim fat from sauce, and scrape sides and bottom of pan so that none of the delicious brownings will be lost. Whirl smooth in a blender or press through a fine sieve. Reheat and pour over meat. Makes 6 servings.

HAMBURGRYG MED RIBSGELÉ
(Bacon with Currant Jelly)

Slice 1 pound Danish Canadian-style bacon ¼ inch thick and sauté in 1 tablespoon butter until brown. Remove from pan and drain. Keep hot. To the fat in the pan, add 2 tablespoons minced onion and cook until soft. Stir in ¼ cup currant jelly, 1 tablespoon prepared mustard, and 1 tablespoon sherry. Cook, stirring, for 3 minutes. Pour over bacon and serve with mashed potatoes. Makes 3 to 4 servings.

BENLØSE FUGLE
(Boneless Birds)

2 pounds round steak, sliced ½ inch thick
   Sliced bacon
   Salt and pepper to taste
¾ cup minced onion
   All-purpose flour
3 tablespoons butter
1 can (10½ ounces) beef bouillon

Cut meat into 12 uniform-size pieces and pound thin into approximate squares. Cover each piece with a thin slice of bacon (you'll have to cut the bacon to make it fit); then sprinkle with salt and pepper and a rounded tablespoon of minced onion. Roll up and tie firmly with white thread, making sure that the filling won't ooze out at the ends. Roll in flour and brown in hot butter on all sides. Add beef bouillon, cover, and simmer slowly for 1½ hours, or until tender, adding water if necessary and turning the rolls occasionally. Skim the fat and serve "birds" with their rich brown gravy. Potatoes or noodles go well here. Makes 6 servings.

FRIKADELLER
(Danish Meatballs)

1 large onion
1 tablespoon butter
¾ cup soft bread crumbs
¾ cup milk
¾ pound very finely ground beef or veal, ground 2 to 3 times
¾ pound very finely ground pork, ground 2 to 3 times
2 beaten eggs
1½ teaspoons salt
¼ teaspoon ground allspice
   Pepper
1 cup warm milk
2 tablespoons each of butter and oil
¼ cup all-purpose flour
1½ cups meat stock or consomme

Chop the onion and cook in the butter until soft. Soak the bread crumbs in the milk and combine with onion, meats, eggs, and seasonings. Mix well. Gradually beat in the warm milk. (This is easier if the beating is done in an electric mixer.) Add as much of the milk as the mixture will take. Chill, then form into about 12 meatballs. Flatten meatballs slightly. Heat together butter and oil. Brown meatballs. Drain off fat, sprinkle meatballs slightly with flour, and add stock to pan. Simmer for 5 to 10 minutes before serving. Milk may be used instead of stock, or 1 cup dairy sour cream may be added toward the end of the cooking. Makes 6 servings.

HVIDKAALSROULADEN
(Cabbage Rolls)

Put a head of cabbage in a pot of boiling water for 6 minutes, or until the leaves have softened. Peel leaves off carefully, one at a time. Cut out heavy part of stem

and put a large spoonful of meatball (*Frikadeller,* above) mixture on each leaf. Roll, and tie with thread or fasten with toothpicks. Arrange in a shallow pan such as a chicken fryer. Cover with bouillon or water and simmer for 30 minutes. Drain off liquid and season with salt and pepper to taste. Thicken slightly with 1 tablespoon each of butter and flour for each cup of liquid. Pour over cabbage rolls. Makes 6 servings.

VEGETABLES

BRUNEDE KARTOFLER
(Sugar-Browned Potatoes)

Boil small potatoes in salted water until just tender. Cool slightly and peel. For each pound melt together 2 tablespoons sugar and ¼ cup butter. Add potatoes and shake so that they are well coated with the mixture. Cook until glazed, shaking the pan occasionally.

STEGTE KARTOFLER
(Fried Potatoes)

Peel and slice 6 potatoes rather thin. Slice 2 large onions and brown in 6 tablespoons butter or margarine. Add potatoes, mix lightly, sprinkle with salt and pepper, and allow to brown on the bottom. Turn, using another pan or plate so that you can turn the whole panful together as a cake. Brown the other side, then add 2 tablespoons each of sugar and vinegar, mixed together. Cook for 4 minutes longer, and serve at once. Makes 4 to 6 servings.

Note: The trick is to turn them all at once.

BRAENDENDE KAERLIGHED
(Burning Love)

Make a batch of creamy mashed potatoes, seasoning them well with salt, butter, and pepper. Pile them in a great fluffy heap on a round platter. Around the outer edge make a wreath of crisply fried Danish bacon and fill the center with *Frisk Stegt Løg* (see page 538). Have all this very hot (you can slip it into the oven for a few minutes after it's arranged). Garnish the platter with slices of cold pickled beets before serving.

STEGTE TOMATER
(Fried Tomatoes)

Slice tomatoes ¾ inch thick. Dip into beaten egg and then into fine crumbs. Fry in hot fat (half butter and half cooking oil is best) until brown on both sides. Serve with *Varm Peberrodssovs* (page 542). Green tomatoes are particularly good prepared this way.

Agurkesalat   Frikadeller   Brunede Kartofler ▲

Gule Aerter   Wienerbrød   Medaljekager ▼

RØDKAAL
(Red Cabbage)

3 pounds red cabbage
¼ cup butter
½ cup water
2 tablespoons red-wine vinegar
1 tablespoon sugar
Salt and pepper
½ cup red currant jelly

Shred cabbage, discarding tough part. Cook in butter, stirring, for 3 to 4 minutes. Add water, vinegar, and sugar and cover. Simmer for 1 hour. Add currant jelly and salt and pepper to taste. Makes 6 servings.

Note: It's even better the next day.

SYLTEDE RØDBEDER
(Pickled Beets)

2 bunches small uniform beets (about 12)
½ cup sugar
1¼ cups vinegar
1 tablespoon whole pickling spice

Wash beets and cut off leaves an inch from the beets. Bake beets in preheated moderate oven (350°F.) for 40 minutes, or until tender. (Cook in water on top of range, if preferred.) Cool, rub off skins, trim, and slice. Combine remaining ingredients with spices tied in a cheesecloth bag. Simmer for 15 minutes, add beets, and bring to a boil. Discard spices, and chill before serving. Makes 6 servings.

Note: Store them in sealed jars to use as needed.

AGURKESALAT
(Cucumber Salad)

3 long thin cucumbers
1 tablespoon dillweed or 1 tablespoon dillseeds, crushed, or 2 tablespoons minced fresh dill
3 tablespoons each of water and cider vinegar
2 tablespoons sugar
1½ teaspoons salt

If skins of cucumbers are tough or waxed, peel them. Slice paper-thin. Mix together remaining ingredients. Pour mixture over cucumbers, mix gently, and chill thoroughly. Makes 6 to 8 servings.

SAUCES

SENNEPSSOVS
(Mustard Sauce)

3 tablespoons butter
1 onion, finely chopped
3 tablespoons all-purpose flour
1 tablespoon prepared mustard
1½ cups beef bouillon
2 tablespoons currant jelly
Salt and pepper

Melt butter. Sauté onion until wilted. Stir in flour. Stir in mustard. Gradually stir in bouillon. Add jelly. Cook, stirring, over low heat until smooth and

thickened. Season with salt and pepper if necessary. Serve with Fiskefrikadeller (page 539) or boiled codfish. Makes 2 cups.

Note: Try it on smoked tongue, too.

VARM PEBERRODSSOVS
(Hot Horseradish Sauce)

2 tablespoons butter
1½ tablespoons all-purpose flour
1 cup milk
2 teaspoons sugar
¼ teaspoon salt
3 tablespoons prepared horseradish

Melt butter. Stir in flour. Gradually stir in milk. Add sugar and salt. Cook over low heat, stirring constantly, until smooth and thickened. Stir in horseradish. Makes about 1 cup.

BREADS AND DUMPLINGS

RUGBRØD
(Rye Bread)

1 large potato, cut into chunks
Water to cover
1 package active dry yeast or 1 cake compressed yeast*
2 tablespoons molasses
1 teaspoon salt
1 tablespoon melted butter
3 cups rye flour (about)
½ cup rye meal (see Note)
½ cup whole-wheat flour (or more)

Cook potato until soft, drain, and reserve water. Force potato through a sieve, then measure ½ cup packed. Measure potato water and cool 1¼ cups of it to lukewarm. Add yeast to potato water. Let stand for a few minutes, then stir until dissolved. *Use very warm water (105° F. to 115°F.) for dry yeast; use lukewarm (80°F. to 90°F.) for compressed. Add potato, molasses, salt, butter, and enough rye flour to make a fairly stiff dough. Mix well, then turn out on a board lightly floured with rye meal and whole-wheat flour. Knead until smooth and no longer sticky, adding rye meal and whole-wheat flour as necessary. Put in a warm greased bowl, grease top lightly, cover, and let rise in a warm spot until almost doubled in bulk. Punch down, knead for about 6 minutes, and again allow to rise until the volume has increased by half. Form into a smooth oval and put in a greased loaf pan, pressing dough down to fill corners of the pan. Let rise until it reaches the top of the pan. Bake in preheated moderate oven (375°F.) for 40 to 50 minutes, or until it gives out a hollow sound when thumped. Cool before slicing. Makes 1 loaf.

Note: Rye meal is available in Scandinavian markets and at some health food

stores in the United States. If you can't find it, use crisp rye crackerbread. Roll or grind it, or whirl it in a blender until of the consistency of coarse meal.

AEBLESKIVER
(Danish Doughnuts)

1 cake compressed yeast or 1 package dry yeast
¼ cup lukewarm water*
1¾ cups milk
1 tablespoon butter
1 tablespoon sugar
1 teaspoon salt
2 cups sifted all-purpose flour
2 eggs
¼ teaspoon ground cardamom or nutmeg or 1 teaspoon vanilla extract

Add yeast to water. Let stand for a few minutes, then stir until dissolved. *Use very warm water (105°F. to 115°F.) for dry yeast; use lukewarm (80°F. to 90°F.) for compressed. Heat milk to lukewarm. Add yeast to milk; add butter, sugar, salt, and 1 cup of the flour. Beat well with rotary beater; cover and allow to rise in a warm spot until bubbly. Beat eggs, add with remaining flour and the flavoring; again let dough rise until bubbly. Heat *aebleskiver* pan and grease very generously so that a small amount of the shortening remains in the bottom of the pan. Spoon batter into individual depressions, having each one about three quarters full. Stand ready with a skewer or, as the Danes do, with a steel knitting needle, and as soon as the pancakes show signs of browning around the edges, turn them. Turn again if necessary to brown evenly on both sides. Serve at once with a shaker of powdered sugar or with jam or jelly. Makes 3 dozen, or 4 to 6 servings.

■ **Variations**—Often a cube of cooked apple, a couple of raisins, or a piece of cooked prune is dropped into the dough as soon as the depression is filled. (The literal translation of *aebleskiver* is "apple slices," so fond are the Danes of the addition of apples to their doughnuts.)

Note: You'll need a special *aebleskiver* or monk's pan for these delicate little pancake balls, or you can bake them in a muffin pan.

BRØDBOLLER
(Bread Dumplings)

Cut crusts from ¼ pound white bread and soak in ½ cup milk. Add 2 tablespoons melted butter and mix smooth. Beat 2 small eggs, add 2 teaspoons sugar, ½ teaspoon ground cardamom, and ¼ teaspoon salt. Beat until smooth, then drop by the spoonful into simmering fruit soup. Cover and cook for 10 minutes.

PASTRY

WIENERBRØD
(Danish Pastry)

1¾ cups milk
2 cakes compressed yeast or
2 packages dry yeast
¼ cup warm water*
⅓ cup sugar
1¼ cups butter
3 beaten eggs
1 teaspoon ground cardamom
1 teaspoon salt
6 cups sifted all-purpose flour

Heat milk to lukewarm.* Add yeast to water. Use very warm water (105°F. to 115°F.) for dry yeast; use lukewarm (80°F. to 90°F.) for compressed. Let stand for a few minutes, then stir until dissolved. Add yeast to milk with sugar, ¼ cup melted butter, eggs, seasonings, and 2 cups flour. Beat very well, then mix in remaining flour and knead until smooth. Let rise until doubled in bulk, about 1 hour. Punch down and roll into a rectangle. Knead 1 cup butter until smooth but not too soft; form into a flat square cake. Put in center of dough and fold each side over it, pressing down at the edges to seal. Give the dough a half turn, again roll into a rectangle, and fold as before. Repeat once more. Wrap in plastic or foil and chill for about 15 minutes. Don't let the butter get too hard or it will break through the dough when rolled. Roll, fold, turn, and chill three more times. The dough is now ready to be used. Roll it ⅛ inch thick, and cut as desired.

Crescents—Cut into 5-inch squares, cut into halves diagonally, and put a spoonful of jam, preserves, almond paste, or applesauce on each triangle; roll, starting at the long side. Turn ends in slightly to form a crescent and put on greased cookie sheet. To bake, see below.

Turnovers—Cut into 3½-inch squares, put a spoonful of filling in center, and fold into triangle. Put on greased cookie sheets.

Bear Claws—Cut into long strips about 5 inches wide. Put filling along center, the length of the strip, fold over, press edges, and cut into 3-inch widths. Slash each piece four times from folded edge to within an inch of the other edge. Arrange on greased cookie sheets.

□ **To Bake**—Chill for a couple of hours before baking. Brush with beaten egg, and put in preheated hot oven (425°F.), reducing heat at once to moderate (350°F.). Bake for 15 minutes, or until nicely browned. Makes about 2 dozen pastries.

DESSERTS

FLØDEBUDDING
(Cream Pudding)

2 envelopes unflavored gelatin
¼ cup cold water
2 cups light cream
3 egg yolks
3 egg whites
½ cup finely chopped blanched almonds
Frugtsauce

Sprinkle gelatin into water. Let stand for 5 minutes. Heat cream, add softened gelatin, and stir until dissolved. Cool. Beat egg yolks until thick and light. Gradually beat in the cream. Beat egg whites until stiff but not dry and combine mixtures, adding almonds. Pour into serving dishes, and chill. Serve with *Frugtsauce*. Makes 6 servings.

Frugtsauce (Fruit Sauce)

2 cups strawberry, raspberry, cherry, or currant juice
2 cups sugar
⅛ teaspoon salt
3 tablespoons cornstarch
½ cup water

Combine juice with sugar and salt. Cook over low heat, stirring occasionally, until sugar is dissolved. Mix cornstarch with water and stir gradually into the hot juice mixture. Cook over low heat, stirring constantly, until smooth and thick. Cover, and cool before serving.

RØDGRØD
(Red Pudding)

1 quart fresh red currants
1 pint fresh raspberries
5 cups water
1 cup sugar
½ cup cornstarch or potato flour
¼ teaspoon salt
1 teaspoon vanilla extract

Pick over currants and wash carefully. Wash raspberries. Combine berries. Add water, bring to a boil, lower heat, and simmer for 15 minutes. Strain. Mix sugar with cornstarch and salt. Gradually stir in strained juice. Cook over low heat, stirring constantly, until thickened. Taste and add more sugar if desired. Stir in vanilla. Pour mixture into a bowl, and chill. Decorate with blanched almond halves if you wish, and serve with cream, plain or whipped. When cream is served, the dish is called *rødgrød med fløde*. Makes 6 servings.

Note: Make it in July when currants are in season.

AEBLEKAGE
(Apple Cake)

Make fine crumbs from a good white or French bread, dried: you'll want 2 cups of crumbs. (Roll, or whirl in the blender, or put through the grinder.) Mix with 2 tablespoons sugar. Melt ½ cup butter in a heavy skillet. Add crumbs and cook, stirring, until browned and crisp; cool. Put a layer in the bottom of a serving dish. Cover with a layer of sweetened applesauce (2½ cups in all), repeating until the ingredients are used. The top layer should be crumbs. Chill; cover top with sweetened whipped cream with a few dabs of currant or raspberry jelly for garnish. Makes 6 servings.

Note: This dessert cake needs no baking.

MEDALJEKAGER
(Medal Cookies)

¾ cup butter
¼ cup sugar
2 egg yolks or 1 egg
2 cups sifted all-purpose flour
¼ teaspoon salt
Thick Custard Filling
Confectioners'-Sugar Frosting
Jelly

Cream butter. Gradually beat in sugar and egg yolks. Add flour and salt. Blend well. Chill 30 minutes. Roll out thinly; cut into 2-inch rounds. Put on greased cookie sheets. Bake in preheated moderate oven (350°F.) for 10 minutes, or until lightly browned. Cool. Put together in pairs with Thick Custard Filling, ice with Confectioners'-Sugar Frosting, and put a tiny dab of jelly in the center of each cookie. Makes about 15 to 18 two-inch double cookies.

Note: Keep cookies refrigerated or put together just before serving.

Thick Custard Filling

Scald 1 cup milk in top part of small double boiler over boiling water. Mix ¼ cup sugar, 2 tablespoons cornstarch, and ⅛ teaspoon salt. Stir into milk. Cook, stirring, until thick. Cover, and cook 10 minutes longer. Add small amount of mixture to 1 egg, beaten. Put mixture back in double boiler and cook, stirring, for 2 or 3 minutes. Add 1 teaspoon butter. Put in bowl, and sprinkle small amount of sugar over top to prevent skin from forming. Chill, and add ½ teaspoon vanilla extract. Makes about 1 cup.

Confectioners'-Sugar Frosting

Put 2 tablespoons hot milk, cream, or water in small bowl. Add a dash of salt and ¼ teaspoon vanilla extract. Gradually beat in 1½ cups confectioners' sugar, or enough to make frosting of spreading consistency. Makes about ½ cup.

VIKINGEKAFFE
(Viking Coffee)

In a stemmed glass pour 1½ ounces (3 tablespoons) Danish mead wine and ¼ cup strong hot coffee. Top with whipped cream.

Vikingekaffe

Roquefort Ost

Fiskebudding

Skinke med Madeira

Flødebudding
med Frugtsauce

Rødkaal

DASH—A small quantity or portion added to or put on a food with a quick stroke of the hand, i.e.: a dash of salt or pepper.

DASHEEN—A starchy root vegetable with large and small tubers side by side on one plant. It is a variety of taro and is grown in southern and tropical climates as a substitute for potatoes. The larger tubers (corms) weigh up to six pounds; the smaller tubers (cormels) are egg size. Both have brown, fibrous skins. When peeled and cooked, the flesh becomes cream-colored, mealy, and nutty-flavored.

The dasheen is thought to have come from China, as its name, a corruption of *de la Chine,* indicates. Dasheen and its first cousin, taro, are the staple food of millions of people in southeastern Asia, Polynesia, and the Pacific Islands, and are of paramount importance in Hawaii. Poi, a thin, pasty mass of cooked taro starch, is one of the principal dishes in the area.

Dasheens have been grown as a commercial crop in the southern United States since 1913. They are extremely wholesome and readily digested. They can be cooked like potatoes although it is preferable not to serve them mashed. They cook in a shorter time than potatoes.

Availability—Available year round in vegetable stores in Spanish neighborhoods.

Purchasing Guide—Buy firm, fresh looking vegetables, not those with wizened skin. Should be heavy and full-bodied.

Storage—Should be kept in a cool, dark, well-ventilated place. Will keep 4 to 5 days.

Nutritive Food Values—Dasheens have more carbohydrates and proteins than potatoes.

☐ 3½ ounces, raw = 98 calories

Basic Preparation—Scrub thoroughly with a brush. Do not peel before cooking as the raw juice is irritating to the skin. Cover vegetable with boiling salted water, bring to boil, cover, and cook for 15 to 30 minutes, or until tender. Peel and put through a ricer or vegetable mill. Season with salt and pepper and plenty of butter or margarine.

DATE—The fruit of the date palm, *Phoenix dactylifera,* a tree with a slender trunk which grows to a height of one hundred feet. It is a very long-lived tree, often reaching 200 years of age. It needs a hot climate with low humidity to thrive. The leaves of the palm tree grow in a stiff crown, to a length of ten to twenty feet.

The fruit, which is the date itself, is a one-seeded berry and it grows in thick clusters. Unripe, it is green; ripe, yellow or red, with thick and very sweet flesh. Depending upon the variety, dates can be soft, or hard and dry. Dates are ripened off the tree and dried before shipping.

Dates are one of the oldest and most valuable of food plants, with a history of more than 5,000 years. Supposedly they originated in Arabia and southwestern Asia, and were known of in Egypt before the Christian era.

Since date palms need less water than any other plant to produce fruit, they were of the utmost importance to desert peoples. Without dates, the populations of the Middle East and North Africa might not have survived. A handful of dates sustained them on their nomadic wanderings, and dates were their main cash and export crop.

Only those who have lived or traveled in arid countries can appreciate the blessing of the date palm and the shade it offers from the broiling sun. Mohammed called the date palm blessed, and Arab poets claimed that it was not created like other plants, but formed from the clods that remained after Adam's creation. They also said: "Bless the date palm trees, for they are your aunts."

Cleopatra of Egypt ate dates and drank the wine made from them, and so did the ancient Greeks. The Greeks thought of the date as a symbol of light, fertility, and riches, and dedicated it to Apollo, the god of music and poetry. There is a charming Hebrew legend that the female palm tree wept for her lover until a branch of the male tree was brought to her. And to Christians, palm branches are symbolic of Jesus' triumphal entry into Jerusalem on Palm Sunday.

In addition to the essential food and the wine made from dates, the date palm offers leaves to be woven into roofs, walls, and baskets; fiber to be made into rope, and the pits of the fruit to be roasted and brewed in the manner of coffee. It is indeed a tree of life.

The exact time at which date palms were first brought to America is unknown. Spanish missionaries planted date seeds around southwestern missions before 1800. The actual beginning of the date industry came in 1890. It was in this year that the Department of Agriculture had shipped from Egypt some of the better varieties of date palm, all carefully planted in tubs. Representatives of the Department and other commercial firms visited many date-growing countries in order to bring back shoots from the better trees.

Today, dates in America are grown principally in California and Arizona.

Availability—All year round.

Purchasing Guide—Dates are sold packaged, pitted and unpitted, and in bulk, unpitted. Good quality dates should be rich brown in color, with a whitish membrane between the flesh and the pit. Look for dates that are fairly plump and soft and that have a smooth, shiny skin.

Dates are also available chocolate-covered, stuffed, and rolled in coconut.

☐ Unpitted, 1 pound = 1¾ cups

☐ Pitted, 1 pound, cut = 2½ cups

Storage—Keep dates in a covered container in a cool, dry place or in the refrigerator.

☐ Kitchen shelf, packaged: 4 to 6 months

☐ Refrigerator shelf, opened and covered: 2 months

Nutritive Food Values—Dates are a good source of iron and sugar, as well as protein.

☐ 3½ ounces, pitted = 274 calories

Basic Preparation—To pit dates, make a lengthwise slit in the fruit using a small paring knife, and roll out the pit. To cut dates, use kitchen shears or a sharp knife and a cutting board. To prevent sticking, dip cutting implement frequently into water.

DATE AND NUT BREAD

½ pound dates
1 cup boiling water
¼ cup shortening
1 cup sugar
½ teaspoon salt
1 egg, well beaten
2½ cups sifted all-purpose flour
2½ teaspoons baking powder
½ cup walnuts or pecans, broken

Pit dates; cut into small pieces and pour boiling water over them. Add shortening, sugar, and salt; cool. Add egg, flour sifted with baking powder, and nuts; mix well. Turn into greased loaf pan (9 x 5 x 3 inches) and bake in preheated moderate oven (350°F.) for about 1¼ hours. Makes 1 loaf.

DATE-NUT MUFFINS

1 cup milk
1 egg, well beaten
2 cups sifted all-purpose flour
1 teaspoon salt
3 teaspoons baking powder
¼ cup sugar
½ cup chopped nuts
½ cup cut-up dates
¼ cup butter or margarine, melted

Mix milk and egg in bowl. Add sifted dry ingredients; mix well. Add nuts and dates, then butter, and mix only enough to blend. Half fill greased muffin pans; bake in preheated hot oven (400°F.) for 20 minutes, or until browned. Makes 9 large muffins.

SOUTHERN DATE PASTRIES

Butter (about 1 cup)
2¼ cups sifted all-purpose flour
½ teaspoon salt
½ cup flaked coconut
½ cup firmly packed brown sugar
1 cup (one 6-ounce package) pitted dates, cut fine
2 tablespoons light cream
Confectioners' sugar

Cut ¾ cup butter and the salt into flour with pastry blender. Roll out half to ⅛-inch thickness on floured board to form a 10-inch square. Brush with melted butter. Roll out remaining half to the same size on floured wax paper. Mix next 4 ingredients and spread on pastry on board. Top with pastry on wax paper. Press down slightly. Cut into strips 1 x 2½ inches and place on ungreased cookie sheets. Brush with melted butter. Bake in preheated hot oven (400°F.) for about 15 minutes. Cool and sprinkle with confectioners' sugar. Makes about 3 dozen.

INDIVIDUAL CARAMEL-DATE PIES

2 cups milk
¾ cup firmly packed dark brown sugar
¼ teaspoon salt
3 tablespoons all-purpose flour
3 tablespoons cornstarch
2 eggs, separated
2 tablespoons butter or margarine
1 teaspoon vanilla extract
1 cup chopped dates
8 4-inch tart shells, baked (2 cups flour recipe)
½ cup pecan halves
½ cup granulated sugar
¼ cup hot water

Scald milk in top part of double boiler over boiling water. Mix brown sugar, salt, flour, and cornstarch in a bowl. Add milk slowly. Return to double boiler and cook until thickened, stirring constantly. Beat egg yolks; add a small amount of cooked mixture and mix well. Add to remaining cooked mixture. Cook for 1 minute longer. Add butter, vanilla, and dates. Cool. Beat egg whites until stiff but still glossy; fold into cooked mixture. Pour into tart shells and arrange pecans on top.

■ **To Make Glaze**—Melt granulated sugar in small skillet over low heat, stirring constantly. Slowly add hot water and stir until sugar is dissolved. Cool slightly; pour over pies. Makes 8 servings.

Note: Filling may be put in baked 9-inch pie shell, if desired.

DATE-NUT PINWHEELS

½ cup soft butter
½ cup firmly packed light brown sugar
½ cup granulated sugar
½ teaspoon vanilla extract
1 egg
2 cups sifted all-purpose flour
⅛ teaspoon salt
¼ teaspoon baking soda
Date-Nut Filling

Cream butter and sugars. Add vanilla and egg and beat until light. Add sifted dry ingredients and mix well. Chill until firm enough to roll. Halve dough and roll each half on floured wax paper into a rectangle 12 x 9 inches. Spread with Date-Nut Filling and roll up tightly from narrow end. Wrap in paper and chill overnight. Slice ⅛ inch thick and arrange on lightly greased cookie sheets. Bake in preheated moderate oven (375° F.) for about 10 minutes. Makes about 6 dozen.

Note: If these are hard to slice, try freezing before baking. They're well worth a little extra work.

Date-Nut Filling

Cut 1 package (6½ ounces) pitted dates into small pieces and bring to boil with ¼ cup sugar, dash of salt, and ⅛ cup water. Simmer for 5 minutes, stirring often; add 1 cup minced nuts, and cool.

APRICOT-DATE BARS

3 eggs
1 cup honey
1 teaspoon vanilla extract
1½ cups sifted all-purpose flour
1 teaspoon baking powder
¼ teaspoon salt
1 cup finely cut dried apricots
1¼ cups (8 ounces) cut pitted dates
1 cup chopped nuts
Confectioners' sugar

Beat eggs until light. Add honey and vanilla; beat until blended. Stir in remaining ingredients except sugar. Bake in greased pan (13 x 9 x 2 inches) in preheated moderate oven (350°F.) for about 45 minutes. Cool in pan. Cut into bars 1 x 3 inches; roll in sugar. Makes 39.

STUFFED-DATE COOKIES

⅓ cup soft butter
1 teaspoon vanilla extract
¾ cup firmly packed light brown sugar
1 egg
1¼ cups sifted all-purpose flour
½ teaspoon salt
¼ teaspoon baking powder
½ teaspoon baking soda
½ cup dairy sour cream
36 pitted dates
36 California walnut halves
Icing

Cream butter and vanilla; gradually beat in sugar. Add egg and beat until light. Sift dry ingredients and add alternately with sour cream. Stuff dates with walnut halves and roll in dough. When well covered, drop from a fork onto well-greased cookie sheet. Bake in preheated hot oven (400°F.) for about 10 minutes. When cold, spread with Icing. Makes 3 dozen.

Icing

Melt 2 tablespoons butter; blend in 1 cup confectioners' sugar, 1 teaspoon vanilla, and 1 tablespoon sour cream.

DATE CHEWS

1¼ cups (8-ounce package) pitted dates
1 cup walnuts or pecans
1 can (3½ ounces) moist coconut
½ cup firmly packed brown sugar
1 egg

Force dates and nuts through food chopper, using coarse blade. Add ½ can coconut, brown sugar, and egg; mix well. Shape into 2-inch long finger-shape pieces; roll in remaining ½ can coconut. Place on greased cookie sheets and bake in preheated moderate oven (350°F.) for 10 to 15 minutes. Makes 2 dozen.

DATE STICKS

1 cup sifted all-purpose flour
1 teaspoon baking powder
½ teaspoon salt
2 eggs
1 cup granulated sugar
½ teaspoon vanilla extract
¼ cup melted butter
2 cups finely cut pitted dates
Confectioners' sugar

Sift flour, baking powder, and salt 3 times. Beat eggs and sugar; add vanilla, butter, and dry ingredients and mix well. Fold in dates. Bake in greased 9-inch square pan in preheated moderate oven (350°F.) for about 35 minutes. While warm, trim off crisp edges and cut into twenty-one 3-inch sticks. Roll sticks in confectioners' sugar, pressing down slightly while rolling to round off edges. Work quickly to avoid cooling cookies. Makes 21.

Rolled Fruit Sticks

Follow recipe above, using only 1 cup dates. Add ½ cup each of finely cut *soft* dried prunes and figs.

STUFFED SHERRIED DATES

1 cup sherry
1 pound pitted dates
Pecan halves (about 1 cup)

Pour sherry over dates in bowl; cover bowl and let stand in refrigerator for about 24 hours, or until most of sherry is absorbed, turning occasionally. Stuff each date with a pecan half. Store covered in refrigerator. Dates keep for about a month. Makes about 1 pound.

DAUBE—A classic French way of cooking meat, generally beef, in a slow manner with savory ingredients such as vegetables and spices. It resembles our braising. Meat *en daube* can be eaten hot or cold.

DAUBE DE BOEUF PROVENÇALE
(Beef Daube, Provence Style)

Every region in France has a *daube,* but since it is exceptionally popular in Provence this recipe has been chosen. The Provence *daube* is made in a *daubière,* a specially designed pot, quite deep, with a cover, and made from the native pottery. Any heavy braising pot or Dutch oven will do. The dish is usually cooked on top of the stove, but, if preferred, you can cook it in the oven. It's best when made a day in advance. Cool, and skim fat from the broth. Reheat or serve cold.

1 cup red wine
⅔ cup olive oil
1 tablespoon salt
1 teaspoon pepper
1 teaspoon each of dried oregano and rosemary
1 bay leaf
2 cloves
1 carrot, cut up
5 to 6 pounds bottom round or chuck, firmly tied
1 calf's or pig's foot, if available
½ pound salt pork
6 to 8 carrots, peeled
6 garlic cloves, peeled
1 bay leaf
1 teaspoon dried rosemary
½ teaspoon dried thyme
8 ripe tomatoes, peeled, seeded, and chopped
24 black Italian olives, pitted

Place first 9 ingredients for marinade in a pot and bring to boil. Lower heat and simmer for 5 minutes. Remove from heat and cool. Put beef and calf's foot in cooled marinade and let stand for 12 to 24 hours, turning fairly often.

Remove meat from marinade and put

in cooking pot. Add salt pork, carrots, garlic, and herbs. Strain the marinade and pour it over the meat. Cover pot tightly and bake in preheated slow oven (300°F.) for about 2½ hours. Add tomatoes and olives and bake for 35 to 40 minutes longer. Remove meat and let stand for a few minutes before slicing. Slice salt pork. Arrange meats on a platter and surround with vegetables. Mix a little of the liquid with some boiled noodles or macaroni. Pass rest of liquid in sauceboat. Makes 6 servings, with meat left over.

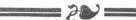

DECORATE—The word is used to describe the art of enhancing the appearance of food. Strictly speaking, it refers to decorations either applied directly to the food or arranged and served with it, but the latter types of decorations are more generally called "garnishes," with the word "decorating" reserved for additions to food: for example, canapés may be garnished, but a fudge cake is decorated.

There are elegancies in decorating that are the work of professionals and are not feasible in the home: among them are spun sugar, ice sculpture, and composite dessert presentations. Despite these limitations, there are many ways for the homemaker to decorate foods attractively. There is no hard and fast rule; experiment here and there, for it is your individual taste, imagination, and practice that will make your food decoration a work of art.

Decorations should be edible whenever possible. Among the many things used for decorations are frostings, glazes, fillings, sweetened whipped cream, and spoonfuls of jelly and jam; chocolate sprinkles, coconut, crumbled cookies, confectioners' or brown sugar and cocoa; candied fruits and ginger, dates, raisins, berries, angelica, mints and decorative candies, cherries, marshmallows, candied chestnuts, animal crackers, and sliced fruits.

A certain amount of special equipment is needed for decorating, and the most important skill to acquire is the proper use of this equipment.

■ **Pastry Bags**—These can be made from parchment, canvas, or fabric lined with plastic. For the person who does only a little simple decorating, very inexpensive plastic or metal plunger-type decorating syringes can be bought with the basic decorating tips.

■ **Tips for Pastry Bags**

Writing tip with a small round hole for simple piping or writing, stems of flowers, dots

Star tip for making small rosettes and borders

Large star tip for piping whipped cream, large rosettes; for shaping macaroons, French crullers, etc.

Rose tip for making flowers

Leaf tip to shape leaves

■ **Flower Nails**—These are large-headed flat-top nails on which to shape flowers

To use a pastry bag properly the tip should be placed into the bag before it is filled. Fill the bag only half full. Whatever is put into the bag should be without lumps to permit a smooth, even flow through the tip. The consistency should be medium soft to permit the food to pass easily through the tip opening, yet firm enough to hold its shape when the decoration is shaped. (Some decorations are made of frosting that hardens on exposure to air. These are shaped on a flower nail or wax paper and allowed to harden before being placed on the food they decorate.) Tint the filling the desired color before filling the bag. Liquid vegetable coloring or concentrated paste colors can be used.

Fold down the two top corners and then roll the top portion down to the level of the filling. Grasp the roll of fabric and squeeze from this section. Steady the hand which is holding the pastry bag with the other hand. Hold the tip of the bag about ½ inch above the surface being decorated. Work quickly and smoothly to achieve an even flow. If the design is a complicated one, first trace it with a toothpick on the food to be decorated.

Some manufacturers package frosting in tubes or pressurized cans with changeable tips; this eliminates the need for a pastry bag.

Decorating a Cake

■ Cool cake thoroughly on wire cake racks.

•1-Brush off all loose cake crumbs. Place 4 overlapping squares of wax paper on the platter on which the cake will be served. These will be pulled out after the cake is frosted, leaving the platter clean.

•2-Set bottom layer on wax papers on

serving platter. Spread a thin layer of frosting between cake layers, trimming the cake layers if necessary to keep cake as flat and even as possible.

•3-With a spatula cover the sides and top of the entire cake with a thin layer of frosting. Let dry for a few minutes. Cover with a second coat of frosting, smoothing the surface of the entire cake. The frosting used for the cake is generally a frosting that stays soft for easy cutting. The decorations may be made of buttercream or a decorator's icing which hardens on standing.

•4-Before decorating cake, let it stand for 30 minutes to allow the frosting to dry properly.

•5-Outline decorations with a toothpick.

•6-Fill pastry bag and decorate.

■ Chocolate-covered mints may be placed on top of a cake while it is still hot and allowed to melt. Spread melted mints over the top of the cake.

■ Spun sugar, pulled sugar, and molded sugar can also be used to decorate cakes. They are quite complicated to make and are often purchased from bakers' and confectioners' supply houses.

■ Gumdrops can be used for decoration by rolling them thinly on a board covered with granulated sugar and cutting the thin sheet into shapes desired; or cut them into small rounds and shape them into roses and leaves.

Decorating Cookies

■ Light-colored cookie dough for any type of cookie can be tinted with food coloring. Be careful not to overbrown cookies when baking since this will change the color.

■ Before baking ball cookies that are rolled in a mixture of cinnamon and sugar, put the sugar mixture in a plastic bag, drop 4 to 6 dough balls into the bag, shake it gently, and they are coated quickly and uniformly.

■ Decorations will stick better to unbaked rolled or refrigerator cookies if they are brushed before baking with egg white beaten until foamy.

■ Decorate unbaked drop cookies with

bits of candied fruit, coconut, nuts, semi-sweet chocolate pieces, or raisins before baking. Bits of raisins or fruit can be pressed into unbaked cookies to form funny faces.

■ Cut rolled cookie dough in fancy shapes such as animals, birds, or flowers. Bake cookies and outline edges and features with frosting of a contrasting color.

■ When making cookies in a cookie press, add chocolate shot; it will go through the press, and the result is like miniature chocolate-chip cookies.

■ Cut out large cookies with a cover or saucer. Bake as usual. Write names on cookies. Cookies can be used as place cards at a children's party.

■ Firm cookies can be coated with a glaze. To make enough glaze for about 3 dozen cookies, mix ½ cup each white corn syrup, sugar, and water. Boil without stirring until mixture thickens and spins a thread. Put glaze over a bowl of hot water. Dip cooled baked cookies in the glaze, decorate as desired, and let stand until firm.

■ After baking dip small drop cookies in a glaze, thin frosting, or melted semi-sweet chocolate. Sprinkle with tiny multicolored candies, colored sugar, plain or tinted coconut, or shaved chocolate. Or spread cookies with frosting and add decorations.

■ Put thin baked rolled or refrigerator cookies together to form sandwich cookies, for example: chocolate cookies with pink peppermint-flavored frosting, vanilla cookies with chocolate frosting, ginger cookies with yellow lemon-flavored frosting.

Decorating with Chocolate

■ Chocolate Curls—Use sweet or semi-sweet chocolate. Leave chocolate at room temperature. Run a vegetable peeler carefully over the length of a large piece of chocolate. Chocolate will curl as it is cut from the chocolate. Refrigerate until used.

■ Chocolate Wafer Designs—Melt semi-sweet chocolate in the top part of a double boiler over hot water. Chocolate can then be used to coat thinly the inside of cupcake papers. Chill; carefully tear away the paper and fill chocolate cup as desired.

■ Melted chocolate can also be used to glaze small cakes. It can be spread in a thin layer on wax paper, chilled, then cut into desired shapes with a cookie cutter. Work quickly or chocolate will melt. Chill decorations until serving time.

SIMPLE DECORATOR'S BUTTERCREAM
(For Frosting or Decorations)
1 cup butter or margarine
1 cup white vegetable shortening

3½ cups (1 pound) confectioners' sugar, sifted
2 teaspoons almond or vanilla extract
Food coloring

Have butter and vegetable shortening at room temperature. Cream butter and shortening until light and fluffy. Gradually beat in confectioners' sugar, extract, and coloring as desired. Beat until very light and fluffy. Fill pastry bag and decorate as desired. Chill after decorating. Decorations will become firmer after chilling. Makes about 4 cups.

DECORATOR'S OR ROYAL ICING
(For Decorations)
1½ cups sifted confectioners' sugar
1 egg white
1 teaspoon any desired flavoring
Food coloring as desired

Beat confectioners' sugar with egg white and flavoring until stiff enough to hold its shape. Tint as desired. Fill pastry bag and decorate as desired. If the decorations are to be stored until needed, shape them on wax paper and then remove after they are dried. Makes about 1½ cups.

Note: This icing hardens on exposure to air. Decorations made with it can be shaped ahead of time and stored in an airtight container until needed.

EASY FONDANT FROSTING
(For Frosting Cakes and Petits Fours)
½ cup Simple Syrup
1½ cups confectioners' sugar
1 teaspoon egg white
1 teaspoon melted butter

Mix syrup with confectioners' sugar in a saucepan and make a fairly stiff paste. It should be very thick. Place over low heat and stir constantly until mixture is lukewarm. Do not overheat or fondant will not be shiny. Beat in egg white and melted butter. If fondant is too thick, add more syrup or a little flavoring extract. If fondant is too thin, add a little more confectioners' sugar. This makes enough to frost the top of a 9-inch cake or 6 to 8 petits fours.

Simple Syrup
2½ cups sugar
¾ cup light corn syrup
1¼ cups water

Combine all ingredients in large saucepan. Stir over low heat until sugar is completely dissolved. When clear, wash down sides of pan with a brush dipped in cold water. Cover saucepan for 5 minutes to allow steam to dissolve any remaining sugar crystals. Uncover, and increase heat. Boil without stirring for 5 minutes. Cool, pour into jars, and cover tightly. Store at room temperature. Makes about 2⅔ cups.

STABILIZED WHIPPED CREAM
(For Decorations)
1 teaspoon unflavored gelatin
2 tablespoons water
2 cups heavy cream

Soak gelatin in water for 5 minutes. Heat over very low heat until gelatin is dissolved. Whip cream until it just begins to thicken. Beat in gelatin and whip until cream is stiff. Fill pastry bag and decorate as desired. Chill after decorating.
Note: This recipe should be used when cream will be pressed through a pastry bag.

BIRTHDAY CAKE CASTLE
It is in the realm of make-believe, but brought down to earth with ingredients that will delight the young and a simple method that will please the builder. On foil-covered cardboard place a loaf cake (13 x 9 x 2 inches) made with two packages of cake mix. Prepare 2 packages of frosting mix according to directions on package; frost loaf cake. Cut a bought poundcake (7 x 5 x 3 inches) into 2 pieces—one 4½ inches long; the other 2½ inches long—and place on loaf cake, as in picture; frost. Space unwrapped caramels around the edges of loaf cake and poundcakes to form battlements. Cut 2 pieces (one 4½ inches long, one 5½ inches long) from a cardboard tube from roll of wax paper or foil. Frost; then mount them on the smaller piece of loaf cake. Frost ice-cream cones, sprinkle with decorating candies, and invert on top of tubes. From two chocolate bars, cut doors and windows and press into frosting. Arrange candles, at an angle, between the battlements, for cannons; place a slice of gumdrop on each side for wheels. Plastic knights, direct from the five-and-ten, patrol the Cake Castle.

DECORTICATE—To "decorticate" is to remove a bark, husk, or coating. When this is done mechanically it is called decortication. The word "decorticated" is generally used only in the spice trade. White pepper bought in stores is actually decorticated black pepper made from peppercorns which have not been fully ripened.

Ground cardamom is also decorticated, that is, the pod is removed and the seeds ground for use as a condiment.

DEEP FRY or DEEP-FAT FRY—The term means to cook food in enough fat to cover the food completely. When food is properly deep fried, a thin coating forms on its outer surface, keeping its juices inside and preventing the fat from penetrating into the food.

Deep frying is one of the most delicious ways of preparing food and one of the oldest. Household records from ancient Rome show that the Romans cooked much of their food in deep olive oil, and their descendants in modern Italy still do. The French are masters at deep frying and the Chinese also stress it in their cookery.

Properly prepared deep-fried foods are crisp outside, moist and delicate inside. What is more, they have absorbed less fat than foods cooked in a smaller amount of fat. You must remember, however, that fat absorption increases with the length of frying time and the size of the surface exposed to the fat. Thus, foods to be deep fried should either take little time to cook, or should be precooked. Foods should also be cut into small pieces, not more than two to three inches in diameter, and the pieces should be uniform in size so that they will cook evenly.

Success with deep-fried foods depends largely on the heat of the fat. It must be hot enough to cause rapid browning of the food's surfaces but the fat should not be so hot that it smokes. The right temperature for most foods is 375°F., although some foods require a higher temperature. Recipes will generally specify the correct temperature when this is so.

Equipment—Equipment need not be elaborate. A deep heavy 3- to 4-quart kettle that will hold about 3 pounds of fat is a necessity. There must be enough fat in the kettle to cover the food completely and enough space for the food pieces to move around freely. The kettle should have a flat bottom so that it will sit firmly on the burner, and a short handle to avoid any danger of being overturned. Since the proper temperature is crucial to successful deep frying, an electric

fryer is desirable because the heat is thermostatically controlled.

A wire basket is almost a necessity when deep frying any quantities of food such as French-fried potatoes. The food is placed in it and then lowered into the fat. The basket makes it easier to get the food in and out and it insures even browning.

A frying thermometer is needed to measure the temperature of the fat. The importance of such a thermometer cannot be sufficiently stressed. While the fat is heating, keep the thermometer in a bowl of hot water to prevent its cracking when it is lowered into the hot fat. Be sure to wipe it very dry before using, because water makes hot fat spatter.

A slotted metal spoon and long-handled metal tongs are also useful for raising and lowering food into the hot fat. And you will need absorbent paper for draining the food.

Foods Suited for Deep Frying—Many foods, savory or sweet, may be deep fried. Fish, shellfish, chicken, veal, vegetables such as cauliflower, eggplant, and squash, potatoes, croquettes of all kinds, doughnuts, cakes, and fruits make excellent deep-fried foods.

Fats Best Suited for Deep Frying—Fats used in deep frying should have a high smoking point, i.e., heat to a high temperature before burning. Hydrogenated (solid) fats, lard, and oils, such as corn, cottonseed, peanut, olive, sesame, and soy, are suited for the purpose. Butter and margarine are not; they have a low smoking point and burn easily.

Basic Preparation—Foods may be fried naturally; or they may be coated with crumbs or a batter and then fried.

1. Dry foods well before frying. (Water causes fat to spatter.)
2. Have foods at room temperature.
3. Keep level of fat or oil 4 inches below top of fry pan to allow for bubbling. Heat fat gradually.
4. To keep temperature constant and prevent food pieces from being crowded, fry only a few pieces at a time.
5. Skim out food particles between fryings.
6. Salt foods after cooking.
7. Drain on absorbent paper.
8. Serve immediately. If not possible, keep hot in paper-lined pan in slow oven (300°F.).
9. After fat has cooled, strain it through several layers of cheesecloth. Use fat again for frying similar foods, such as fat used to fry fish for fish, etc.
☐ **To Coat**—Use fine crumbs or finely crushed cereals since they adhere during cooking and form a crisp coating. Dip foods into milk and egg before dipping

into crumbs. Flour mixed with seasonings can be used for coating foods. A thin batter may be used to coat the food.

☐ **To Deep Fry Frozen Foods**—They should be removed from their package and defrosted, then thoroughly drained and dried before being fried or coated and fried.

Caution—Keep a metal lid near kettle. In case fat should catch on fire, drop the lid on the kettle. The flame can also be smothered with salt. *Never* use water, since this will only spread the fire.

DEHYDRATE—The word means "to take away water" and refers to the process of drying foods in machines which use controlled heat. The nutritive value of the food is not impaired in the process.

DELMONICO—Delmonico's, a famous New York restaurant, was founded in 1834 by Lorenzo Delmonico, a Swiss chef. The restaurant was famed for certain of its dishes, especially diced or mashed potatoes baked in a rich cream sauce, and a steak or roast cut, now widely known as a Delmonico steak, which can be roasted, broiled, or cooked in a pan.

DELMONICO POTATOES
2 cups diced cooked potatoes
2 cups medium white sauce
  Salt and pepper
  Grated cheese
  Buttered bread crumbs

Combine potatoes, white sauce, and salt and pepper to taste. Pour into greased shallow casserole. Sprinkle grated cheese and buttered bread crumbs over top and brown in preheated hot oven (425°F.) for about 20 minutes, or until browned and thoroughly heated. Makes 4 servings.

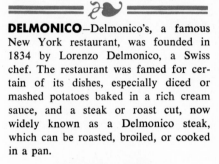

DEMITASSE—A French word which means "half a cup." It applies to a small cup for, or of, black coffee.

DESSERT—**By James A. Beard**—Dessert is the final course of a meal. The word comes from the French verb *desservir,* which means "to clear or take away," and in French gastronomy it includes the service of cheese, entremets (or sweets), and fruit.

I suppose that the idea of clearing the table completely before dessert, save for flowers, is as prevalent today as it was in the 19th century. In that era, an elaborate meal was likely to feature, in addition to a superbly set table, a spectacular buffet, which held the *pièces montées,* fabulous architectural decorations. These were flanked by beautiful baskets of fruit and surrounded by eye-filling arrangements of sweets. After cheese was passed at table and the table cleared, the guests were served with sweets and fruits from the buffet. Thus, the concept of "dessert."

The French love cheese as a course preceding the sweets, to be had with the last of their wine, or with a special wine, if the dinner is a large and formal one. The English prefer cheese after the sweet, and we independent Americans often combine the two when serving cheese with various fruit pies or with fresh fruit.

Entremets, or desserts (in American terminology), cover a variety of foods. There are pastries: pies, tarts, flans, torten, and small pastries. There are cakes of all descriptions: the layer cakes, as we have perfected them in this country, and the European cakes, which are generally of two types. One is the light *gênoise,* used with a range of fillings and icings and for the base of such rich desserts as *Zuppa Inglese* (and other variants of trifle), rum cakes, and Baked Alaska or *Omelette Norvégienne.* The second type includes the heavier Viennese torten and the British poundcakes, usually more suitable for tea than for a lunch or dinner dessert.

A third category of desserts is comprised of other baked items, such as éclairs and puffs, made from *pâte à chou* or, as it is known in America, cream puff paste. Also in this group is the delicate item baked in a skillet—crêpe, or what is wrongly described as a French pancake. It is equally popular in other countries. The most famous crêpe recipe is one made with butter, caramelized sugar, orange, various liqueurs, and cognac (the most authentic versions use Grand Marnier and cognac), and it is called Crêpe Suzette. (Who Suzette was, no one has ever been able to say for certain.) There are many other delicious kinds of crêpes, some extremely simple, filled with fruit or jam.

Puddings abound in the dessert repertory and range from simple milk puddings, such as rice pudding or custard, to cold soufflés and Bavarian creams. There are hot puddings, too—among them, charlottes and soufflés (I feel they must be classified thus), perhaps the most elegant of all; steamed puddings; and the mixtures of fruits and batter which one encounters in the cuisines of most nationalities with varying degrees of difference.

Ices and ice creams are among the most refreshing of desserts and include sherbets, water ices, *granités,* mousses, and *bombes.* This last combines several flavors and textures, some *bombes* having as many as five flavors and such ingredients as mousse, ice, ice cream, sherbet, and bisque. Ice cream is, of course, the most popular of the sweets in America. It is said to have originated in Italy and progressed through France to the United States. (Water ices, of course, were known to the ancients.) But surely we have made it into the varied and remarkable dessert it has now become. Ice cream can be made with pure heavy cream, with a custard mixture of eggs, milk, and cream, or with a pudding mix. When the cream is whipped before it is frozen, it becomes a mousse or a parfait, and when nuts or crumbs are added, it becomes biscuit, as in the famous Italian *tortoni.*

Fruit desserts have become increasingly popular in the United States over a period of years. There have always been fresh berries and cream on the menu, as well as fresh fruits in season, and the luscious shortcakes, which are characteristically American. But low-calorie eating has popularized fruit as never before. Not, of course, that fruit desserts are all low in calories. Many are exceedingly rich. Good fresh fruit, unadorned, is one of the best of desserts, and equally good is fruit flavored with a little liqueur or brandy. Cooked fruit is also much more in evidence than formerly. And cream and sour cream never cease to make fruits glamorous in another fashion.

Each country has its variations on the same theme. There may be subtle changes in the texture, flavor, or sometimes the appearance of a dessert, but basically the concept is the same. American pie, for instance, is an outgrowth of the English tart, with the addition of much fruit and a top crust. Both are related to Swiss tarts, the Scandinavian ones and the remarkably good *Tarte Tatin* of France: an upside-down apple tart, which is caramelized and delicious. One sees great similarity between the pastries in Vienna, Paris, Milan, London, and New York. Soufflés are the same the world over, and crêpes hide different fillings in Russian, French, and Chinese cuisine but are essentially the same.

Dinner-Party Desserts from a Jittery Cook

by Margot Sandler

Don't misunderstand me: I am a jittery cook, but I am a very good cook. Since experience has taught me that none of our qualities is unique, I conclude that the country is studded with other good, but jittery, cooks. When are we jittery? When we are giving a Dinner Party. Why are we jittery? I shall list a few reasons.

(1) There must be some small household god who arranges minor catastrophes to try our souls. You know the sort of thing; I almost hesitate to illustrate for fear of sounding trite. One of my afternoons before a dinner party ran so: the garbage disposer clogged, filling itself and the adjacent sink with garbage, with which I was trying to cope when a nervous neighbor appeared asking if I could drive her to the doctor, and as I put on my coat to do this, the telephone rang and my young daughter asked that I pick her and a friend up after their club meeting since her friend's mother's car had broken down. I guarantee that any one of you could top this story.

(2) My jitters-prone sisters and I suffer from what I shall call "opening-night syndrome." We may have gone calmly and sensibly through all our dinner-party preparations, cooking like angels, but just before the curtain rises we are suddenly overwhelmed with the enormity of what we have set in motion: mature adults are changing from perfectly good clothes into better clothes; expensive baby sitters are converging from all directions; TV dinners are being set before innocent children; husbands are being urged to shave for the second time in one day: no wonder we are temporarily unnerved. At this point we should not ask our trembling hands to create a chocolate soufflé; anyway, as all we good but jittery cooks instinctively know, the correct time to make a chocolate soufflé is when friends have dropped in and been asked to stay and take potluck for dinner. Such a soufflé will not be loaded with significance, and naturally it will be a masterpiece.

(3) My own third reason, and I hope for your sakes that it is rare, is that I personally have two left hands; am all thumbs; am butterfingered; have poor coordination; or possibly suffer from some deep-seated psychological problem that makes me drop things, particularly when under pressure.

Well, jittery or not, I like to give dinner parties, and I have learned to avoid some of the more common pitfalls. I have found, for instance, that there is nothing better for soothing the nerves than the thought of the good dessert waiting calmly in the refrigerator. To qualify, this gem should preferably be made on the previous day, and at most need only finishing touches no later than noon of the day of the party. It must also have some degree of inherent elegance: it should not, for instance, be likely to turn up with any regularity as a family dessert. It should also have a somewhat distinguished appearance: the staging should be such that no one could possibly mistake chocolate mousse for chocolate pudding. With all these virtues, surely no one will demur if the dessert takes a little extra fussing. But have no fear: I am not about to give you a recipe for *croquembouche;* while I have every confidence that you and I are capable of making ninety small cream puffs and sticking them together in a pyramid, I think that we should do this some weekend when everybody is out of town.

The recipes that follow are given in great detail. They may, in fact, sound like instructions for a class of backward girls, but this is not so: all these details appear in my own personal files. I always instruct myself on every particular, because for me last-minute thought is fatal: I am capable of standing transfixed for a half hour trying to remember whether or not I usually cover the *pot de crème* pots while baking.

All of the following desserts have been tamed and made docile by being put in exactly the right containers or pans. Some of our best writers about food have a bad habit of starting a recipe with some such comment as "Line a dish with ladyfingers." I have been rereading some of these recipes wistfully for ten years, unable to pick up my ladyfingers and begin, because I know that the size of that dish is all-important: if intuition selects the right dish, we have a masterpiece; the wrong dish, and we may have an undistinguished and expensive mess.

Not one of these recipes is a fly-by-night: all have given me and others good service. Some undoubtedly appear in your cook books, and my contribution may be largely the exact instructions which will ensure immediate success. Others have been changed: the Mexican Flan, for instance, has had its coating sauce changed, since I am congenitally unable to caramelize sugar. (I have in fact been trying annually since the age of twelve to caramelize sugar, and some of my latest effort is still stuck to the kitchen floor.) Now before we start, let me offer this helpful hint: several of these recipes use egg yolks only; if you freeze egg whites in individual ice-cube trays, you can store them individually and defrost as many as you need at a time.

CHERRY TORTE GLACÉ

This makes a flat, rather solid cake, but one that is handsome and unusual in appearance. There are no flavoring essences or spices used: it truly does not need them. This can be made the previous day, but it must be refrigerated because of the cream topping. Serves 12.

2¼ cups drained, sour pitted red cherries in syrup, for which you will need two 1-pound cans
1 cup walnuts, chopped
6 tablespoons butter
1½ cups sugar
2 eggs
1½ cups plus 2 tablespoons all-purpose flour, sifted before measuring
½ teaspoon baking powder
¾ teaspoon baking soda
⅛ teaspoon salt
1½ teaspoons unflavored gelatin
2 tablespoons cold water
1 cup whipping cream
1 cup cherry syrup drained from cans
½ cup sugar
2 tablespoons plus ½ teaspoon cornstarch
½ teaspoon red food coloring
Chopped green pistachio nuts

1. Preheat oven to 375°F. Grease a 10-inch-round, 2-inch-deep cake pan with margarine, line bottom with wax paper cut to fit, and grease the paper with butter.
2. Prepare cherries and walnuts. Drain the two cans of cherries in a sieve over a pan, so as to reserve syrup. Measure out 2¼ cups cherries, and return these to the sieve to drain again. Meanwhile chop one cup of walnuts coarsely. Chop cherries coarsely and place them back in the sieve to continue draining.
3. Cream butter, add the 1½ cups sugar gradually, creaming well. Beat two eggs until frothy and add to creamed mixture. Sift flour, measure and resift with baking powder, baking soda, and salt. Add to creamed mixture alternately with chopped cherries.
4. Fold in chopped walnuts.
5. Turn into pan and bake at 375°F. for about 30 to 35 minutes, or until top

is resilient when touched, and a toothpick inserted in center comes out clean. Cool in pan on a rack for 5 minutes; turn out on rack after loosening sides with knife, and immediately remove wax paper. Cool well. When cold, spread with topping.

6. Make topping: in small measuring cup soften gelatin in the 2 tablespoons water, then place cup in small pan of hot water, stirring until gelatin is dissolved, about 3 minutes. Cool a bit. Whip cream stiff and beat in dissolved gelatin gradually.

7. Turn cake onto a plate; if you plan to use a cake stand, make sure it will fit in your refrigerator. Spread cream topping over the top of the cake only, as smoothly as possible, not swirling. If you don't have a flat round serving dish and are using a dinner plate, the cake will sink in the middle: this is all right, just put more topping in the middle than at sides to even up. Put cake in refrigerator while making glaze.

8. Combine cherry juice, the ½ cup sugar, cornstarch, and food coloring in a saucepan and cook, stirring constantly, until thick and transparent. Cool, stirring frequently, until almost cold, which will take about 30 minutes. Then refrigerate it for about 5 minutes. When almost cold, spread on cake, being sure to cover most of the whipped cream. The sides of the cake are left plain, but you may let some glaze drip down decoratively. Arrange pistachio nuts around edge of cake.

9. Refrigerate cake: since this is a 10-inch cake, your cake cover may be too small: in which case insert toothpicks through the glaze around edges of cake, with one in center, and cover all with a plastic wrap, tucking it under the plate. The holes made by the toothpicks will not show later.

ORANGE FORM CAKE

This is a baking-powder version of Baba au Rhum; I love to make the yeast version, but everyone seems to prefer this. It makes 8 to 10 servings.

    2 egg whites
    4 egg yolks
    ½ cup sugar
    1 cup all-purpose flour sifted before
        measuring
    1 teaspoon baking powder
    ¼ teaspoon salt
    1 teaspoon vanilla extract
    ⅓ cup melted butter
    2 cups sugar
    2 cups water
    1 tablespoon grated orange rind
    1 tablespoon plus 1 teaspoon fresh
        lemon juice
    ½ cup rum
    ⅓ cup finely chopped walnuts

1. Preheat oven to 375°F. Grease a 9-inch round tube pan well, line the bottom with wax paper cut to fit, and grease that. You may use any round pan that will hold 1½ quarts, but a tube form

makes the most handsome cake.

2. Beat two egg whites until fluffy, gradually adding ¼ cup of the sugar, and then beating until stiff. In a smaller bowl and using the same beater, beat the egg yolks with the other ¼ cup of the sugar, then add all at once to the whites, stirring in lightly but well.

3. Sift the flour, baking powder, and salt together and fold into egg mixture gently.

4. Stir in melted vanilla and butter.

5. Pour into prepared pan and bake at 375°F. for about 30 minutes, until top feels springy when touched and toothpick inserted in cake comes out clean.

6. While cake is baking, make sauce. Dissolve the 2 cups of sugar in the 2 cups water in a pot, then add the grated orange rind and bring to a boil and boil for 10 minutes. Cool a bit at room temperature while cake is baking, then add lemon juice and rum.

7. When cake is done, turn out on rack, remove wax paper, and put immediately onto plate on which it will be served: a dinner plate is fine. Make holes all over the top of cake with a skewer, and spoon on all the warm sauce with a big spoon. Make more holes if necessary (right through to bottom of cake) and continue basting with any sauce that ends up in bottom of plate. When cake has absorbed nearly all sauce, sprinkle the top carefully with chopped nuts.

8. Refrigerate cake, covered. Serve plain, or with center filled with whipped cream or vanilla ice cream.

CHOCOLATE TORTE BURGUNDY

The easiest way to grate nuts is in a blender, so if you do not have one, it is worthwhile to visit a friend who does. This delicious torte makes 8 servings.

    6 ounces (1¾ cups) walnuts or pecans,
        grated; this will be about 1½ cups
        when grated
    ¾ cup dry red wine: an inexpensive
        California burgundy is fine
    ¾ cup sugar
    1 teaspoon fine dry bread crumbs
    6 ounces (1 cup) semisweet chocolate
        pieces
    6 eggs, separated
        Apricot or raspberry jam
        Sweetened whipped cream or dessert
        topping
        Shaved semisweet or unsweetened
        chocolate

1. Preheat oven to 325°F. Grease two 8 x 8 x 2-inch cake pans with margarine, then line bottoms with wax paper cut to fit, and butter the paper.

2. Grate nuts in blender, if possible, since you want them fine and fluffy. Combine nuts with wine, sugar, crumbs, and chocolate pieces in saucepan; cook over low heat, stirring constantly, until chocolate mixture is thick. This may take 10 to 15 minutes after chocolate is melted. Cool the mixture.

3. Separate eggs, and beat whites stiff

with rotary beater; with same beater, beat egg yolks until lemon-colored. Stir cooled chocolate mixture gradually into egg yolks; fold in egg whites.

4. Spread batter evenly in prepared pans and bake at 325°F. for 50 to 60 minutes, or until toothpick inserted in center comes out clean. Put pans on racks to cool for 10 minutes, then run knife around edges of cakes and turn out to cool completely on racks.

5. When cold, put one layer on serving plate, and spread rather thinly with apricot or raspberry jam (the exact amount does not matter). Put second layer on top. Decorate with whipped cream, forced through a pastry tube, and sprinkle with shaved chocolate.

SEVEN-LAYERED PRUNE TORTE

This pastry is impressive, and it is fun to make. It does take time, but it can be made days before the party. The dough is practically indestructible, and you cannot spoil it by overhandling, or by working very slowly. Makes 12 servings.

    1 cup butter
    1½ cups sugar
    2 eggs
    2 tablespoons cream or evaporated milk
    1 teaspoon almond extract
    4½ cups all-purpose flour, sifted before
        measuring
    1 teaspoon baking powder
    1 teaspoon ground cardamom
    ¼ teaspoon salt
    1 pound quick-cooking tenderized
        prunes
    1 cup sugar
    ½ cup juice from prunes
    2 teaspoons grated orange rind
    1 tablespoon brandy
        Aluminum foil
    2 tablespoons butter
    1 cup confectioners' sugar
    1 tablespoon fresh lemon juice
        Few drops of yellow food coloring

At least one day, and preferably two or three days before needed:

1. Preheat oven to 375°F. Using an 8-inch layer cake pan as a pattern, trace and cut out of wax paper seven 8-inch circles to fit the back of the pans.

2. Cream the cup of butter, and add the 1½ cups sugar gradually, and cream well together. Beat eggs in one at a time. Mix in cream and almond extract.

3. Sift flour with baking powder, cardamom, and salt. Add to creamed mixture gradually, finally working it in with your hands until smooth.

4. Grease the backs of 8-inch layer cake pans, cover with circles of wax paper, and butter papers. You will need 7 layers, so prepare as many pans as you have and as will fit in your oven at one time, or do 2 at a time, regreasing pans and putting on fresh wax paper. (This is a cookie-like dough, so must be baked on a flat surface and not inside pans; shiny pans are

Cherry Torte Glacé

Mexican Flan

Strawberry Bavarian Cream

Cold Chocolate Soufflé

Orange Form Cake

Chocolate Torte Burgundy

best so that rounds do not brown too quickly.)

5. Working with about ½ cup of dough at a time, pat it onto the paper on back of pans. Pat it out to edge: don't be afraid of handling the dough, but try to pat from the middle, and don't let the edges get ragged. You may patch, and smooth edges. Rounds should be ¼ inch thick. If you should end up with 8 rounds, so much the better, but 7 is fine.

6. Bake at 375°F. until golden, about 12 to 15 minutes. Don't let edges get too brown. If edges are brown, but you are in doubt as to whether center of round is golden enough, remove it from oven! Turn rounds out onto racks and remove paper. Rounds will become crisp and solid as they cool.

7. While you are baking, prepare filling. Cook the prunes as the package directs. Drain, reserving juice. Remove pits from prunes and chop fine, add 1 cup of sugar, ½ cup of the prune juice, and the 2 teaspoons of grated orange rind. Mix well and stir in the tablespoon of brandy.

8. When all 7 rounds are baked, tear off a 28-inch piece of aluminum foil that is 14 inches wide. Put one round on it, spread with filling to the edges, cover with another round, and repeat until all are used, leaving the top of the last round plain. Bring the foil up over the top and wrap to completely enclose torte. Put it in the refrigerator for one day at least, or for several days: this is to soften rounds and develop flavor: if you were going to freeze torte you would still let it mellow for a few days first.

9. On the day of serving, remove torte from refrigerator and undo foil. Reverse torte on your hand or a plate and then put right side up on a serving plate or cake stand. Do not be alarmed at the heavy weight of the torte!

10. Make icing: cream the 2 tablespoons of butter, sift the 1 cup of confectioners' sugar and work it gradually into butter; add lemon juice, and if desired add a few drops of yellow food coloring. Ice the top of torte only, doing it neatly.

11. At serving time, cut with a serrated knife into pie-shape pieces, about half the size you would ordinarily serve, as torte is rich and solid. If any is left over it will keep in the refrigerator wrapped in aluminum foil for two weeks or more, and can be frozen at any time during that period.

Note: Do not try to substitute for cardamom. It is a comparatively expensive spice, but can be used in many Scandinavian cookies, and you will surely remake this torte!

ORANGE CHIFFON REFRIGERATOR CAKE

This dessert, despite the whipped cream, seems light and refreshing. Many commercial bakeries make excellent orange chiffon cakes, so use one of those as a base, if possible; or you can make your own from a standard recipe or a mix. Failing an orange chiffon cake, use an orange spongecake. The aim is to start with a light airy cake as a base, so do not use a cake of the butter type. Makes 8 servings.

    1 orange chiffon cake, bought, made
      from a mix, or from a standard recipe
      for a 10-inch tube pan
      Grated rind of 1 large lemon
      Grated rind of 1 large orange
    3 tablespoons fresh lemon juice
    ½ cup fresh orange juice
    1 cup sugar
    2 eggs
    1 cup whipping cream
    1 can (11 ounces) of whole segments of
      mandarin oranges in syrup

1. Two days previously, make or buy cake. If you buy cake, the exact size does not matter; it may be smaller than a 10-inch round, but do buy a round one.

2. One day previously, cut cake with serrated knife into 4 layers. It does not matter if your slices are not exactly even, as you can restack the cake in its original form.

3. In top part of double boiler, mix lemon and orange rinds and juices with the sugar. Beat eggs lightly and add, mixing well. Then cook over boiling water until thickened, about 6 minutes, stirring constantly. (It will not get very thick.) Remove and allow to cool in the refrigerator.

4. Whip cream stiff, then stir completely cooled orange mixture into it.

5. Put bottom slice of cake on plate, spread with orange mixture, add the next slice, spread with orange mixture, and repeat until you have reconstructed cake and spread top and sides with remaining mixture.

6. Put cake cover or large bowl over cake and refrigerate until the next day.

7. On day of serving, drain can of mandarin orange segments, and then refrigerate drained orange slices, covered so that they will not dry out. Just before serving, space orange slices attractively around top edge of cake.

CHARLOTTE RUSSE

Charlotte russe can be made to look exceptionally handsome by making it in a springform pan lined with ladyfingers on the outside: on serving, remove the sides of the pan and place the charlotte russe, still on the bottom of the springform, on a cake stand. You may use either an 8-inch or a 9-inch springform: in the latter the pudding itself will come slightly below the edges of the ladyfingers, but this is of no consequence as you may fill the space with whipped cream. Makes 12 servings.

    12 ladyfingers
     2 envelopes unflavored gelatin
     1 cup sugar
     ¼ teaspoon salt
     4 eggs, separated
    2½ cups milk
     2 tablespoons brandy
     1 cup whipping cream
     ⅓ cup chopped maraschino cherries
     1 extra cup whipping cream for top,
       optional

1. Butter the sides of an 8- or 9-inch springform pan slightly. Split the ladyfingers, and stand them upright around the sides of the pan, with the rounded sides toward the outside of the pan.

2. Mix the gelatin, ½ cup of the sugar, and the salt together in a saucepan. Separate the eggs, and beat the yolks slightly, then add the milk to them, and then add this to the mixture in the saucepan. Put over simmering water, and stir constantly until the gelatin is dissolved and mixture coats a metal spoon.

3. Remove from heat and add brandy. Chill until mixture is beginning to set and mounds slightly when dropped from a spoon.

4. With rotary beater beat egg whites stiff and gradually beat in the remaining ½ cup of sugar. Beat until very stiff and shiny.

5. Fold gelatin mixture into the egg whites. Whip the cup of cream stiff and fold it in also. Pour into the prepared springform and chill until firm. Cover the whole pan with a plastic wrap and leave until next day.

6. To serve, remove sides of springform carefully but leave on bottom of pan. Drain the maraschino cherries carefully, and chop. Either arrange these carefully on top of pudding, or, if you wish, whip another cup of cream stiff, put it on top of the pudding, and arrange the cherries on the cream. Place on a cake stand or large plate.

STRAWBERRY BAVARIAN CREAM

A pleasant version of this favorite dessert, not too sweet. The amount is for a 5-cup mold; just see that it is a pretty mold, a sort of pleated or fluted effect is nice. Makes 6 to 8 servings.

    1 envelope unflavored gelatin
    6 tablespoons sugar
    ⅛ teaspoon salt
    2 eggs, separated
    ¼ cup water
    1 package (10 ounces) frozen sliced
      strawberries, thawed
    1 teaspoon grated lemon rind
    1 tablespoon plus 2 teaspoons fresh
      lemon juice
      Red food coloring
    1 cup whipping cream
      Fresh strawberries

1. In top part of double boiler mix thoroughly the gelatin, 4 tablespoons of the sugar, and salt.

2. Beat the egg yolks with the water and add to the gelatin mixture. Add the straw-

berries. Cook over boiling water, stirring constantly, until the gelatin is thoroughly dissolved and mixture coats a metal spoon, about 8 minutes.

3. Remove from heat and add lemon rind and juice. Pour into a dish and chill to the consistency of unbeaten egg whites. Stir in a few drops of coloring.

4. Beat egg whites until stiff, and beat in two tablespoons of sugar. Fold gelatin mixture into egg whites.

5. Whip the cream stiff and fold it into the mixture. Pour into a 5-cup mold. Chill until firm, or overnight.

6. If strawberries are in season, use for garnishing. Leave stems on fine-looking berries and wash. With sharp knife, loosen edge of dessert from mold slightly, dip mold in warm water for about 3 seconds, and turn out on plate; or reverse on plate and hold towel (wrung out in hot water) over it for a few seconds to loosen. Garnish around edge with strawberries.

COLD CHOCOLATE SOUFFLÉ
Everybody likes this, even the people who don't like whipped cream. I put it in either a 1½-quart soufflé dish, or in individual soufflé dishes. It could also be put into individual parfait glasses. Since it is so rich, it should not be heavily garnished with whipped cream. If whipped cream is used in addition, it should be just as small rosettes or puffs. Makes 6 servings.

    2 ounces (2 squares) unsweetened
      chocolate
    1 envelope unflavored gelatin, softened
      in 3 tablespoons cold water
    1 cup milk, heated
    ½ cup confectioners' sugar
    ¾ cup granulated sugar
    1 teaspoon vanilla extract
    ¼ teaspoon salt
    2 cups whipping cream

1. Start melting chocolate slowly over very low heat in a small heavy saucepan: a 3-cup size is good. Put gelatin in a small bowl with the 3 tablespoons of cold water. Heat the 1 cup of milk.

2. When chocolate is melted, add the confectioners' sugar to it, and then gradually add the hot milk, stirring constantly. Do not be alarmed if it lumps, just keep stirring, preferably with a small French whisk. Over low heat, stir until mixture reaches the boiling point, but do not boil.

3. Remove from heat; stir in softened gelatin, the granulated sugar, vanilla, and salt and mix well.

4. Pour into a large mixing bowl and refrigerate until slightly thickened; it usually takes a half hour before any thickening starts. Beat cream with rotary beater until whipped; with same beater beat chocolate mixture until light and fluffy. Fold cream into chocolate mixture and pour into serving dish. Chill, covered, for 4 hours or overnight.

Note: When putting soufflé in individual dishes, height can be raised above the level of dishes by making wax paper collars around tops of dishes before pouring in soufflé mixture. Cut strips of paper about 2 inches in width and long enough to fit around tops of dishes; grease papers on the inside and fit around dishes, overlapping ends. (Greasing holds ends together.) When ready to serve, gently peel off papers.

MEXICAN FLAN
Evaporated milk, which I understand Mexicans always use, makes a delicious flan. The brown sugar will melt and form a sauce; if you are a brave soul you may wish instead to caramelize 1 cup of white sugar in the pan before putting in the custard. However, everybody likes my version, and it certainly is easier. Use an ordinary bread pan (9 x 5 x 3 inches) and make sure that you have a small oval platter or rectangular dish on which to serve the flan. Makes 8 servings.

    8 eggs
    ⅔ cup granulated sugar
    ¼ teaspoon salt
    2 tall cans evaporated milk (this size is
      usually labeled as having weight of
      about 14 ounces and liquid measure-
      ment of about 13 ounces)
    2 teaspoons vanilla extract or
      1 tablespoon brandy
    ½ cup packed light-brown sugar (or
      substitute caramelized white sugar
      as directed above)

Make the day before needed.

1. Preheat oven to 350°F.

2. Beat eggs with rotary beater until yolks and whites are well blended. Add granulated sugar and salt and mix in well. Beat in the two cans of undiluted evaporated milk and add the vanilla.

3. Sift the brown sugar into the bottom of loaf pan, and pour the custard gently into the pan over it.

4. Place in a shallow baking pan containing hot but not boiling water. Bake in a 350°F. oven for 1 hour, or until a knife inserted in center comes out clean. Do not cover.

5. Refrigerate overnight. Before serving, run a knife around the edge of the pan and turn out onto a small platter.

Note: This particular custard gets a little crust on top when baked uncovered; to my mind this is all to the good, since you will be turning it over, and this makes a firmer base.

ORANGES À LA GRECQUE
Some dinners demand a fruit dessert. All that you need to make this beautiful and unusual compote is sugar, water, oranges, and quite a lot of fussy work. Always put fruit in glass: even a plain inexpensive glass bowl will display and reflect the glowing jewel tones of fruit as no other dish can, be it silver or gold. Try to use navel oranges when in season; they keep their shape so nicely. Makes 8 servings.

    6 large navel oranges
    4 cups water
    1½ cups sugar
      Red food coloring

1. With a sharp little knife cut all the yellow peel from the oranges in thin strips, taking care to include none of the white pith; then cut this peel into fine julienne strips not more than 2 inches long. Put peel in a large saucepan and pour a large amount of boiling water over it and boil for 2 minutes; drain, pour fresh boiling water over it, and boil another 2 minutes. Then repeat the whole process once more. You have now removed any bitter taste from the peel.

2. Dissolve 1½ cups sugar in 4 cups water and boil for 15 minutes. Add red food coloring, starting with under ⅛ teaspoonful, and adding it drop by drop until the syrup is a bright, light, clear red.

3. Meanwhile peel oranges, getting off every bit of white pith, even if you have to cut it off with a knife. Slice each orange across into 4 or 5 substantial slices, a good ½ inch thick, and remove any traces of membrane or seeds. Put in a dish with the juice.

4. Pour the hot syrup over the orange slices and let stand for 20 minutes; drain and boil the syrup for another 15 minutes. Combine the orange strips with the orange slices and pour the hot syrup over all. Let cool and refrigerate overnight or at least for 6 hours.

Note: Variations of this recipe give as much as 3 cups sugar to 4 cups water for the syrup; I prefer the less sweet proportions, but the other is admirable too.

PEARS IN RED WINE
This is also a very pretty dessert: its elegance depends mostly on careful handling of the fruit so that there is no bruising or marking, hence the use of wooden spoons. Makes 8 servings.

    2 cups dry red wine
    2 cups sugar
    8 medium-size pears, shapely, and of
      table quality
      Red food coloring
    4 thin strips lemon peel

1. Cook 2 cups dry red wine and 2 cups sugar for 5 minutes in a large pot.

2. Peel the pears very carefully, keeping whole and leaving the stems on. Gently poach the pears in the syrup until they are tender, usually about 15 minutes. However, after 5 minutes, if pears have not turned a beautiful rosy-red color, remove some syrup and add about ⅛ teaspoon of red food coloring to it, and then return it carefully to the pot, being sure not to pour it directly onto a pear. Stir with a wooden spoon and baste pears: if not sufficiently red yet, remove more juice and add food coloring as before.

3. Test pears for tenderness with a fork on the underneath or blossom end, so that marks will not show. Do not overcook; you do not want them to be mushy. When done, remove pears from syrup to dish with 2 wooden spoons.

4. With vegetable peeler remove 4 strips peel along the complete length of a lemon; add to syrup and simmer for 5 minutes. Pour syrup over pears and chill.

5. Next day serve pears standing upright in a glass bowl, also using individual glass fruit dishes if possible.

Note: I have tried decreasing the sugar in the syrup, but the results are best with this amount. The pears do not have to be completely ripe for this dish.

POMMES MERINGUÉES

This fruit dessert from Normandy looks delightful, the apples keep their shape and color, and the flavor is subtle and delicious: it is light, but satisfying. A flat-tish round glass dish is best for this, rather a problem since it must be able to go into the oven: the best solution I have found is to use the glass 10-inch pie pan that does not look too utilitarian. Makes 6 servings.

    4 or 5 good tart eating apples, of a
        variety that holds its shape well when
        cooked, such as Jonathan, Rome
        Beauty, or Winesap
    1 teaspoon vinegar
    1½ cups sugar
    1 cup boiling water
    1 tablespoon grated orange rind
    2 tablespoons fresh orange juice
    3 egg whites
    ½ teaspoon almond extract

1. Pare, quarter, and core the apples, cutting each quarter carefully into thirds; you should have 1 quart. Place in a bowl of water containing a teaspoon of vinegar so they will not discolor.

2. Put 1 cup of the sugar and the cup of boiling water in a skillet, and stir over low heat until sugar is dissolved. Add the orange rind and juice and boil for 5 minutes.

3. Drain the apples, and cook about half of them at a time in the syrup until they begin to become transparent: put them carefully into the skillet, on their sides, and do only one layer at a time. Watch them, and remove with a slotted spoon as they are done. Arrange the slices on their sides, all going the same way, in a circular pattern around the dish. (Because of the high proportion of sugar in the syrup they will keep their shape and not become apple sauce.) When all are done, pour syrup over, cover with plastic wrap, and refrigerate.

4. Next day, bring apples to room temperature. Baste them with the syrup with a small spoon. Beat egg whites stiff, beat in remaining ½ cup sugar gradually, and beat again until you can feel no granular quality in the meringue. Add the almond extract. Pile meringue on top of apple slices, and swirl it prettily around; do not bring it out to the edge of the dish, leave a little edge of apple showing. This meringue will stay high and not fall because of a rather high sugar content. Bake in preheated slow oven (300°F.) for 25 minutes to a half hour. Cool away from drafts, then refrigerate until very cold.

Note: This could, of course, be completely made on the day of serving, with the meringue put directly onto the warm apples. But don't make the meringue the day before: it just isn't as nice.

STRAWBERRIES ROMANOFF

This is a heavenly dessert; you must put it together at the last minute before you serve it, but the assemblage is simple, and I assure you that if I can do it without hysterics, so can you. It is worthwhile to buy strawberries out of season for this, and if you are being so extravagant, you may want to use the smaller amount given. Don't use the sliced strawberries frozen in syrup for this. Makes 6 to 8 servings.

    2 cups to 1 quart strawberries
    ¼ cup sugar
    1 cup whipping cream
    ½ pint vanilla ice cream
    ¼ cup Cointreau

1. Keep the berries whole; wash them, hull them, sprinkle with sugar and chill. (For some mysterious reason one uses the same amount of sugar with different amounts of berries.) Prepare berries at least 3 hours before needed.

2. Just before serving, beat the cream until very stiff. Beat the ice cream until fluffy and fold it into the whipped cream. Add the Cointreau, fold in the strawberries, and pour it into serving bowl and serve immediately. You may reserve some of the berries to float on the top at the last minute.

DEVILED—This culinary term refers to foods that have been highly seasoned with spices and other condiments. Deviled foods may be chopped finely or mashed and mixed with seasonings, or they may be cooked in a sauce that is seasoned, or they may be used whole sprinkled with the seasonings. In French, this kind of cookery is called *diable*, a word that means "devil."

The seasonings used for deviling foods are black pepper, cayenne, hot pepper sauce, Worcestershire sauce, powdered mustard, horseradish, hot paprika, and garlic.

Deviled or *à la diable* also indicates a way of cooking, which is especially suited to birds. The bird is slit open along the back, spread out flat, and pounded down to make it stay that way. It is then spread with butter or olive oil and broiled. After broiling, it is spread with a little more butter or olive oil, covered with fresh bread crumbs, and browned under the broiler. Poultry cooked this way is always served with *à la diable* sauce.

DEVILED ROUND STEAK

    1½ pounds round steak
        All-purpose flour
    1 onion, minced
    1 garlic clove, minced
    3 tablespoons fat
    2 teaspoons salt
    ¼ teaspoon pepper
        Dash of cayenne
    1 teaspoon prepared mustard
    1 teaspoon prepared horseradish
    1 teaspoon vinegar
    ½ cup tomato sauce
    1½ cups hot water

Cut steak into strips across the grain. Roll in flour; brown meat, onion, and garlic in hot fat. Stir in 2 tablespoons flour and the seasonings. Add remaining ingredients; cover and simmer for 1 hour, or until meat is tender. Good with rice, noodles, or mashed potatoes. Makes 4 servings.

DEVILED EGGS

    8 hard-cooked eggs
    4 teaspoons prepared mustard
    ½ teaspoon seasoned salt
        Dash of cayenne
        Dash of onion salt or ½ teaspoon
        instant minced onion
    1 teaspoon vinegar
        Mayonnaise or salad dressing

Cut eggs in half lengthwise. Mash yolks with remaining ingredients, except mayonnaise. Add enough mayonnaise to moisten and mix well. Fill egg whites and chill. Makes 16 halves.

DEVILED STUFFED POTATOES

Scrub 4 large baking potatoes and bake in preheated very hot oven (450°F.) for 45 to 50 minutes, or until done. Slice off tops. Scoop out potato pulp, mash, and season with salt and pepper, 2 tablespoons butter or margarine, 1 small can deviled ham, and ¼ cup hot milk. Beat until fluffy. Pile into potato shells and return to oven to brown lightly. Makes 4 servings.

DEVILED MUSHROOMS, CASINO

    20 large whole mushrooms
        Salt and pepper
    ¼ cup melted butter or margarine
        Toast
    1 cup chopped fresh mushrooms
    ¼ cup heavy cream
    1 teaspoon powdered mustard
        Few grains of cayenne
    ½ teaspoon paprika
    1 teaspoon Worcestershire

Wipe mushrooms with damp cloth; season; broil carefully, basting with melted butter, until tender. Put on 4 toast rounds.

Cook chopped mushrooms in butter until they are delicately browned. Season. Add cream and remaining ingredients. Reheat; pour over mushrooms on toast. Serve at once. Makes 4 servings.

À LA DIABLE SAUCE

¾ cup wine vinegar
1 tablespoon minced shallot or onion
1¼ cups brown sauce or canned beef gravy
2 tablespoons tomato puree
1 tablespoon Worcestershire
1 teaspoon hot pepper sauce
Cayenne

Combine wine vinegar and minced shallot and cook down to half the amount. Stir in brown sauce and tomato purée. Cook over medium heat, stirring occasionally, for 5 minutes. Add Worcestershire and hot pepper sauce and season to taste with cayenne. Use on broiled meats and poultry. Makes 1½ cups.

DEVIL'S FOOD—One of America's most popular chocolate cakes; with a true chocolate flavor, a deep rich color, and a light fluffy texture. Devil's food is probably so called to contrast it with the snowy-white angel food.

DEVIL'S FOOD CAKE

¾ cup cocoa
1⅓ cups sugar
1¼ cups scalded milk
2 cups sifted cake flour
1¼ teaspoons baking soda
1 teaspoon salt
⅔ cup shortening
3 eggs, unbeaten
1¼ teaspoons vanilla extract

Sift cocoa with ⅓ cup sugar. Pour in milk gradually and stir until smooth. Cool. Sift together flour, remaining sugar, soda, and salt. Add shortening and half of cocoa-milk mixture. Beat at medium speed of electric mixer or vigorously by hand for 1 minute. Add the eggs, vanilla, and remaining cocoa-milk mixture. Continue beating for 2 minutes in electric mixer at medium speed or by hand. Scrape bottom of bowl occasionally with rubber scraper. Pour into 2 deep 9-inch layer-cake pans lined on bottom with wax paper. Bake in preheated moderate oven (350°F.) for 25 to 30 minutes. Cool for 5 minutes. Turn out on racks

and peel off paper. Cool, and frost as desired. Makes 8 to 10 servings.

DEVIL'S FOOD CAKE WITH MARSHMALLOW FROSTING

½ cup soft butter or margarine
1½ cups sugar
1 egg
2 egg yolks
3 ounces (3 squares) unsweetened chocolate, melted and cooled, or 3 envelopes no-melt unsweetened chocolate
2 cups sifted cake flour
1 teaspoon baking soda
¾ teaspoon salt
1 cup milk
1 teaspoon vanilla extract
Marshmallow Frosting

Cream butter. Gradually add sugar and cream until light and fluffy. Add egg and egg yolks, one at a time, beating after each addition until smooth. Add chocolate and blend. Add sifted dry ingredients alternately with milk, beating after each addition until smooth. Add vanilla. Pour into two round 9-inch layer pans, lined on the bottom with wax paper. Bake in preheated moderate oven (350° F.) for about 30 minutes. Turn out on racks and cool. Spread Marshmallow Frosting between layers and on top and sides of cake.

Marshmallow Frosting

1½ cups sugar
⅓ cup water
¼ teaspoon salt
2 egg whites
1½ teaspoons light corn syrup
1 teaspoon vanilla extract
16 (¼ pound) marshmallows, quartered

Combine all ingredients, except vanilla and marshmallows, in top part of double boiler. Beat with rotary beater until mixed. Put over rapidly boiling water and beat constantly for 7 minutes, or until frosting forms peaks. Remove from heat and add vanilla. Add marshmallows and beat slowly until melted and blended.

DEVIL'S FOOD SQUARES

½ cup butter or margarine
1½ cups sugar
1 teaspoon vanilla extract
2 eggs
4 ounces (4 squares) unsweetened chocolate, melted
½ cup hot water
1¾ cups sifted cake flour
1 teaspoon baking powder
½ teaspoon salt
½ teaspoon baking soda
½ cup buttermilk
Fudge Frosting

Cream butter; add sugar gradually, beating until light and fluffy. Add vanilla and eggs, one at a time, beating well after each addition. Melt chocolate in water; cool and add to creamed mixture. Beat until smooth. Sift together dry ingredients and add to first mixture alternately with buttermilk. Turn into a bak-

ing pan (13 x 9 x 2 inches) lined on bottom with wax paper. Bake in preheated moderate oven (350°F.) for 35 to 40 minutes. Cool for 5 minutes. Turn out on rack and peel off paper. Cool, and frost with Fudge Frosting. Makes twelve 3-inch squares.

Fudge Frosting

2 cups sugar
2 tablespoons light corn syrup
⅔ cup milk
3 ounces (3 squares) unsweetened chocolate
¼ cup butter or margarine
1 teaspoon vanilla extract

Put the sugar, corn syrup, milk, and chocolate in large saucepan. Cook over medium heat, stirring until sugar is dissolved. Continue cooking until mixture forms a very soft ball when a small amount is dropped in very cold water (232°F. on a candy thermometer). Stir occasionally to prevent scorching. Remove from heat, add butter without stirring, and cool until bottom of pan feels lukewarm (about 1 hour). Then add vanilla and beat until frosting is creamy and barely holds its shape. Spread quickly on cake before frosting hardens. Makes about 2 cups.

DEVONSHIRE CREAM—This English country delicacy, from the county of Devonshire, is a thick, clotted cream made from nonhomogenized fresh farm milk. It is eaten with scones or toast, accompanied by jam (preferably wild strawberry jam), with fruit pies, or with fruit. It is a great treat, praised by all who have had the good fortune to taste it.

Take a gallon of the richest, freshest farm milk. Mix it, for a bigger yield, with 1 pint of heavy cream. Pour mixture into a large, shallow pan. Place pan over the lowest heat of your stove, or at the back of it. Warm the milk to a temperature of 175°F. Never let it become hot or boiling. When the top is covered with a shiny, crinkly yellow surface, remove the milk from the heat. Cool overnight in refrigerator or in a cool place. Skim off the cream with a slotted spoon. Place it on cheesecloth and set the cloth in molds or baskets so that any remaining milk can drain off. It is ready as soon as it is solid enough to keep its shape.

DEWBERRY—Closely related to the blackberry, dewberries differ from blackberries by growing on trailing rather than upright vines. There are many different species. Although grown commercially, both dewberries and blackberries are the most valuable wild fruit crop of the United States. Berry pickers should stake out their dewberry patches in the spring when the vines bear their lovely white flowers. Once the flowers are gone, berries and bushes become inconspicuous.

Dewberries can be used interchangeably with blackberries.

Availability—From June through August in some food stores in the localities where they are grown.

Purchasing Guide—Select berries that are bright in color, clean, well shaped, and fairly plump. They should have no green drupelets (the pulpy grains). Avoid overripe berries which are usually dull in color, soft, and sometimes leaky.

☐ 1 pint = 2 cups

Storage—Do not wash berries before refrigerating. Sort fruit and discard damaged berries. Store in moisture-proof container. Dewberries are perishable; plan to use as soon as possible.

☐ Refrigerator shelf: 1 to 2 days

Nutritive Food Values—Berries contain a fair amount of iron and vitamin C.

☐ 3½ ounces, raw = 58 calories

Basic Preparation—Wash berries in running water just before they are to be used. Avoid soaking fruit in water.

☐ **To Stew**—Cover bottom of saucepan with water to depth of ¼ inch. Add berries, cover, and simmer gently over low heat for 10 to 15 minutes, or until berries are cooked. Add more water if necessary. Remove from heat and add sugar to taste. Chill, and serve as dessert or sauce.

DEWBERRY FLUMMERY
2 cups dewberries or other soft berries
  Water
¼ cup cornstarch
¾ cup sugar
⅛ teaspoon salt
  Juice of ½ lemon

Simmer berries in 1 cup water for about 5 minutes, and sieve. Add enough water to make 2½ cups. Combine cornstarch, sugar, and salt and add to sieved berries. Cook over medium heat, stirring constantly, until mixture thickens. Add lemon juice. Cool, stirring occasionally. Chill. Serve with cream or dairy sour cream, if desired. Makes 4 servings.

DEWBERRY CRUMBLE
2 cups washed picked-over dewberries
⅔ cup sugar
  Juice of 1 lemon
3 tablespoons butter or margarine
⅔ cup sifted all-purpose flour
⅛ teaspoon salt

Put fruit in 1-quart baking dish with half of sugar. Sprinkle with lemon juice. Cream butter, remaining sugar, flour, and salt together. Sprinkle on berries. Bake in preheated moderate oven (350°F.) for about 40 minutes. Serve warm or cold with cream or hard sauce, if desired. Makes 4 servings.

DEWBERRY JELLY
4 cups dewberry juice (about 2½ quarts ripe berries)
¼ cup lemon juice, if needed
7½ cups (3¼ pounds) sugar
1 bottle liquid fruit pectin

Crush thoroughly about 2½ quarts fully ripe berries. Put in jelly cloth or bag and squeeze out juice. Measure 4 cups juice into very large saucepan. If juice lacks tartness, use only 3¾ cups juice and add ¼ cup lemon juice. Add sugar and mix well. Put over high heat and bring to boil, stirring constantly. At once stir in pectin. Then bring to a full rolling boil and boil hard for 1 minute, stirring constantly. Remove from heat, skim off foam with metal spoon, and pour quickly into hot sterilized glasses. Seal at once with paraffin. Makes 11 8-ounce glasses.

DICE, TO—As a culinary term, it means to cut into cubes with a sharp knife. First the food is cut into slices; then slices are cut into strips, and the strips are bundled and cut crosswise into cubes. Ordinarily size is assumed to be small, less than ½ inch. If size is important, it is generally indicated in a recipe by such expressions as "finely diced."

DIET—The word is derived from the Greek *diata,* meaning "manner of living," and when used about food refers in general to the food and drink regularly provided and eaten. It also means, more specifically, "to eat and drink sparingly or by prescribed rules."

Although we think of dieting in the second sense of the word as a comparatively modern development, this is by no means true. Demosthenes, in the 3rd century B.C., wrote, "Like the diet prescribed by doctors, which neither restores the strength of the patient nor allows him to succumb. . . ." The Roman poet Horace, in the 1st century B.C., was saying more positively, "Now learn what and how great benefits a temperate diet will bring along with it. In the first place you will enjoy good health." And Jonathan Swift commented, "The best doctors in the world are Doctor Diet, Doctor Quiet, and Doctor Merryman."

THE TRUTH ABOUT DIETS
by Fredrick J. Stare, M.D.,
Professor and Chairman of the Department of Nutrition, Harvard School of Public Health

My wife and I were driving home from an evening meeting, one that neither of us had wanted to attend, and we began talking about the plight of today's parents and, in fact, all adults. First, there are so many demands on their time, what with raising children, earning a living and doing professional or community work, and caring for an aging parent, that there's little time to relax before dinner or to enjoy good food and talk through a pleasant, leisurely meal. Many adults feel guilty if they don't arrive at the community or church meeting on time. Second, with the automobile, the outboard engine, electric golf cart, and now the motorized toothbrush, there seems to be a conspiracy against adults securing any physical exercise. Yet it is important to good nutrition and health, just as good food is. Nutritionally and healthfully speaking, things seem especially stacked against parents, although they are bad enough for any adult.

My wife and I decided that, along with the nutrition suggestions that I give new mothers, teen-agers, and the elderly, I should offer a few to adults. We decided firmly that parents are people, deserving of our approval and assistance! Kids, with their high spirits, can get exercise. Grandparents are inclined to ignore a suggestion from a son or daughter. But some adults, thank heaven, will listen.

These are exciting days in nutrition science and food technology. Things are happening of direct benefit and great promise to all adults. This article is about us, and what we adults can do for ourselves by making use of the latest nutritional knowledge and scientific developments. There are far more things working for us than against us. The picture is, in fact, bright. I even have some suggestions on how a busy person can get the exercise necessary for good health while going about regular duties.

As the result of recent nutrition research, there are several conclusions to be reached on what an adult can do (1) to feel his best, (2) to increase his output of useful work or achievement, (3) probably to live a longer and fuller life. We adults can now not only make the middle years, and those after the children have grown up, years of good health, high productivity, and pleasure, but we can also set a good example to the younger generation on sensible food habits. They gain most of their ideas from us, granted that getting ideas into youthful heads is often a laborious and trying process.

We are in the midst of unprecedented progress, a revolution in food and nutrition. This is evident in new products on food-store shelves: some 100 new products appear there each week. There are also new developments, not so easily observable, in the nutrition research laboratories, in the fields where new crops are growing, in the plants where foods are processed, packaged, and then distributed. Let me describe a few of these developments and their value to your health.

1. In the United States the nutritional deficiency diseases such as pellagra and rickets have largely disappeared. Many of the infectious diseases have been brought under control to a great extent. Research scientists are now devoting greater study to the attainment by men and women of optimum health. The chronic diseases, in which human metabolism plays an important role, are now receiving increased attention. Recent research shows that sound nutrition practices on the part of the adult man or woman can increase his or her span of years of maximum performance; this means a fuller, more productive life, greater enjoyment of daily living, and a longer life span. This is the first time in human history that these goals are within our reach.

2. Through current research we are rapidly increasing our knowledge of the relation of nutrition to heart disease and atherosclerosis, the main causes of death in our country. There is evidence that many adults can take steps to postpone, if not ward off, damage. Currently, there is much talk about cholesterol in relation to heart disease. Some restaurants list the cholesterol level in food, but this is not the only factor in determining the cholesterol level in the blood. It's much

more complicated than that. The research, clinical, and other scientific evidence indicates to me that there is insufficient data to designate blood cholesterol as the sole villain in the complex physiological and biochemical situation which results in atherosclerosis and heart disease. I believe that heredity, lack of exercise, excessive smoking, overweight, high blood pressure, possibly tension, and other factors are involved as well as cholesterol. Cut down or eliminate some of these factors and you will do yourself a good turn, for they act in a cumulative fashion.

Cholesterol is normally produced in the body and is always present in the blood. Actually, it is an essential body substance, for a number of hormones are made from it. However, excessive amounts of cholesterol in the blood, or foods that contain excessive amounts of cholesterol, are certainly to be avoided. Too much food of almost any kind (sugar, fats, or protein, and even alcohol) may result in excessive cholesterol being formed. In other words, calories do count not only in weight but also in cholesterol formation, regardless of what you may read. Only *you* can keep your weight at a desirable level and thus help avoid excess cholesterol formation: take regular exercise, eat a varied diet, and don't eat too much. Cutting down, not out, is the secret of proper dieting. No single food need be eliminated.

3. Meanwhile, I would advise any adult to avoid radical changes in diet or food habits. The best way to reduce, or to maintain proper weight, is to eat a balanced diet, including your regular favorite foods, but not as much of them. Each day your body and your brain need the nutrients to be found in meat, milk, poultry, and fish, cereals and cereal products, leafy vegetables, and fruits. Self-diagnosis, in deciding on a diet, can be dangerous, particularly if the diet is a little on the odd side. Consult your physician. You may get excellent help from a dietitian, too. Many hospitals, health departments, and community health facilities provide consulting dietitians or nutritionists. I find that adults are not as foolish as the young or old when it comes to crackpot diets; perhaps it's because they have work to do and know they must possess enough brain power and energy to do it.

4. During the past ten years I have taken part in many research studies of fat in the human diet. Fat is necessary, and a great energy producer. Yet, I constantly run into a few ill-informed adults who "try to cut out all fats." This is almost impossible to do because many foods contain fat. It is possible that many

Americans do have too high a fat intake of both the saturated and unsaturated fats. A recommended level in the human diet is about 30 to 40 per cent of the total calories depending on the height, age, weight, and work done by the individual person. The more we study fat metabolism, the more complex it becomes. It is not as simple as many self-styled nutrition authorities present it.

5. In finding new knowledge that will contribute to optimum health, it has been discovered that human beings require extremely minute amounts of mineral substances. These microelements or trace elements may be toxic or injurious to people in quantities beyond small amounts, yet they play an essential role in good nutrition and good health. It has been found, for example, that minute amounts of copper are necessary in the body for utilization of iron in forming red blood pigments. Also, fluorine is desirable in small amounts to form a dental enamel with maximum resistance to decay.

Recent research has also shown that the human body needs minute amounts of cobalt, molybdenum, manganese, zinc, selenium, chromium, in addition to copper and fluorine, and possibly more that we now know nothing of. Chromium helps regulate sugar metabolism in animals. Selenium helps regulate protein metabolism and liver functions in many animals and probably in man. Plants generally serve as regulators in balancing the uptake of trace elements from the soil, and thus offer protection to both man and animals. But this needs to be studied in each region or area. Research in trace elements enables growers to understand their soil better and to improve the yields, the safety, and the nutritional values in the foods and feeds produced.

How can an adult make sure he is getting all the trace elements his body needs? The answer is simple: by consuming a variety of foods, such as milk and its many products, cereals, meats, chicken, fish, leafy green vegetables, and tasty fruits such as strawberries, cantaloupes, apricots, and oranges. A reasonably balanced diet made up of foods purchased in the nearest supermarket or food store will provide all the trace minerals an adult needs.

6. In recent years, as editor of *Nutrition Reviews,* a scientific publication of The Nutrition Foundation, I have edited many articles showing the benefit of research in genetics. These can only be sketched, but let me mention a few.

A better understanding of genetics has enabled nutrition scientists to diagnose and treat anemias, also to diagnose and treat babies born with metabolic faults, such as the tendency to develop diabetes, or the inability to metabolize proteins or milk or sugars. Genetic research has enabled agriculturists to produce new varieties of tomatoes which will resist disease, give the processor a greater yield, and a longer period for good handling, and which possess a high nutritive value. A tomato has been developed which will grow well in hot climates, providing people in Mexico, for example, with a needed source of vitamin C. Genetic research is improving the quality, rate of growth, and egg-laying capacity of poultry. Through genetic research, more nutritious grains, fresh fruits, and dairy and beef cattle are also being produced. These developments help the food grower, the processor, and the consumer.

Such are some benefits of current research.

Here are some practical suggestions for adults on food habits. They are based on research in the university laboratories, in government programs, and the technical developments of the food industry with which I have been in personal contact. Industry is increasingly research-minded.

Don't be merely a calorie counter. It's fine to count calories once in a while, especially by weighing yourself, as long as one does not let this sobering pastime spoil good eating habits, and become a bore to one's friends. One should eat for pleasure and energy as well as for health, all in moderation. It is possible to eat positively and to enjoy it. Many of my friends approach the whole weight-control situation with an erroneous do-or-die attitude. They feel that if you want to lose weight you have to give up everything you like. This is simply not true. The most successful way to lose weight is to continue to eat many of the foods you like, but as I said before, less of them. Cut down, not out.

Enjoy your food. Good flavor appeals to the sense of taste and smell; good appearance to the eye. Both appeals whet your appetite. Adults lead busy lives these days and they need energy to maintain the pace. A wise selection of food can do wonderful things for your work output, for your enjoyment of daily life, and for being at your peak.

Conversely, an inadequate breakfast can reduce your morning work output by 25 per cent or more, and an inadequate lunch will do the same in the afternoon. Then, many of my friends make the mistake of eating a heavy dinner, which more than makes up in calories for their slighting of breakfast and lunch, and disturbs their sleep. How wrong can they get? Three reasonably balanced meals are always advisable, whether one is trying to lose, gain, or maintain a desirable weight.

Don't eat the same foods every day. Put some variety into your meals, both for good nutrition and for your pleasure. Experimentation both with animals and human beings shows the nutritional value of variety. Try at least one new dish every week. Monotony is the enemy of good nutrition and dulls the appetite. If you eat out occasionally, find some good new restaurants to try. Even your usual one will taste better to you with change. I am told that the proprietors of several famous restaurants advise their regular customers to eat elsewhere once in a while, and these men have science to back them up as far as the enjoyment and full utilization of food is concerned.

Don't be misled by food faddists. The normally healthy person is getting all the nutrients, minerals, and vitamins he needs in the food he buys at his store. Gimmick supplements will give him more of them than his body needs or can use. Most of them are not harmful per se, just harmful to the pocketbook. They may also lead to careless eating habits in general. I regret to report that some of my otherwise intelligent friends seem to be taken in by promoters who become "food authorities" overnight without bothering to study the subject for a few years at a university. They sell their products on the basis that the American food supply is lacking in essential nutrients because foods are grown on worn-out soils, are overprocessed, and so on. This is completely false.

Exercise regularly. I spoke earlier of the difficulty of adults getting sufficient regular exercise, a tremendously important factor in maintaining good health and possibly warding off or postponing vascular and heart disease. I, for one, have always found calisthenics dull, and there never seems to be time for them. But here is a good substitute: many of my scientist friends walk a great deal. On frequent trips to New York City I usually walk from the East Side Airlines Terminal on First Avenue and 37th Street to appointments in midtown, say at Fifth Avenue and 56th Street, or a little over two miles. At my rural home in Wellesley, Massachusetts, I plant shrubs, mow more than two acres of yard in summer, clean up scrub brush, and garden enthusiastically. In my university office, I climb at least two flights of stairs whenever possible. All these things help to keep one physically active. If one wants to lead a long and vigorous life, they will help. This is the opinion of every nutrition scientist I know.

If a person exercises regularly and has a medical check-up periodically, there is little danger of overdoing, certainly for most people. The great danger is not exercising enough; lack of exercise does great damage to the adult body.

My two sons are out of college and graduate school and working, and my daughter is thirteen years old. Mrs. Stare and I make it a point to enjoy an outing with any of them whenever we can, or to relax outdoors with a good hike or some skiing, skating, or tennis. Relaxation is also important to good health. With a little thought I find that parents and the younger generation can find many activities which they can enjoy together: kite flying, bird watching, bowling, and gardening, to name a few, excluding the Watusi.

Some of my adult friends ask me where they can secure reliable information on food and nutrition. One's personal physician is one good source, since he is familiar with one's medical history, mode of life, and so on. Dietitians are very good at solving practical nutrition problems.

• • •

The Nutrition Foundation, 99 Park Avenue, New York, New York 10016, has a number of pamphlets (at nominal cost) on such subjects as food fads, teenage nutrition, weight control, and low-sodium diets. A list will be sent to you upon request.

• • •

The U. S. Department of Agriculture has a series of pamphlets on food and nutrition. A list of the pamphlets can be procured from the Superintendent of Documents, Washington, D. C. 20402.

• • •

The American Dietetic Association, 620 North Michigan Avenue, Chicago, Illinois 60611, and the American Home Economics Association, 1600 Twentieth Street, N.W., Washington, D. C. 20009, are also good sources of information. Many of the life insurance companies have excellent pamphlets on the importance of nutrition to good health.

The point is, these people are authorities; you can rely on what they say.

DILL (Anethum graveolens)—This hardy, aromatic annual herb plant grows in temperate climates, reaching a height of about three feet. The branches have feathery leaves, and the flowers are yellow and very small. Dillseed is the dried fruit of the herb; dillweed, its dried leaves.

Dill is native to Asia Minor and Europe. It was one of the favorite herbs of the Greeks. The heavy air of Roman banquet halls, saturated with spices, was purified by the intensive freshness of decorative garlands of flowering dill.

Americans will agree with the remark of the 18-century English essayist Addison, who said: "I am always pleased with that particular time of the year which is proper for the picking of dill and cucumbers."

Dill is available as fresh leaves, dillweed, and as whole or ground dillseed. It is used in preparing and serving soups, cheese, fish, meats, poultry, vegetables, potatoes, breads, and apple pie.

SUGGESTIONS FOR USING FRESH DILL

■ Add some chopped fresh dill to mixed green salad or coleslaw.

■ Add chopped fresh dill or sprigs of dill to pot roast of veal or lamb while cooking.

■ Add chopped fresh dill to French dressing.

■ Moisten cream cheese with dairy sour cream, season with finely chopped fresh dill, salt, and pepper. Spread on long, thin slices of smoked salmon, roll up, and serve as an appetizer.

■ Add chopped fresh dill to butter and use as a spread for rye or pumpernickel.

Shrimps with Dill

■ Add chopped dill to hot melted butter to spoon over shrimps, vegetables, or baked potatoes.

SUGGESTIONS FOR USING DILLSEED

■ Sprinkle whole dillseed over cottage and cream cheese.

■ Add ½ teaspoon ground seed to the water in which turnips, cabbage, or fish is simmered.

■ Add dillseed to commercial salad dressings and use over coleslaw, cucumbers, potato salads.

■ Add dillseed to melted butter, or cream butter and beat in dillseeds. Spread over lamb chops, chicken, or steaks before broiling.

SHRIMPS WITH DILL

2 quarts water
1½ to 2 tablespoons salt
5 to 6 sprigs of dill
2 pounds raw shrimps
1 lemon, sliced

Bring water and seasonings to boil. Add shrimps and simmer for 5 minutes. Remove from heat, add lemon slices, and let shrimps cool in liquid. Pour off liquid and chill shrimps. Garnish with additional dill. Makes 8 servings.

SWEDISH BOILED LAMB WITH DILL AND DILL SAUCE

Breast or shoulder of lamb (2 to 3 pounds), trimmed of excess fat
Boiling water
1 tablespoon salt
3 to 4 peppercorns
1 bay leaf
5 dill sprigs or ¼ cup dillweed
Dill Sauce

Scald meat in boiling water. Drain, place in kettle, and add boiling water to cover. Bring to a boil and skim. Add next 4 ingredients. Cover and simmer over low heat for 1 to 1½ hours, or until meat is tender. Drain, and reserve stock. Cut meat into serving pieces. Serve very hot with Dill Sauce in separate dish. Garnish with additional dill sprigs, if desired. Makes 4 servings.

Dill Sauce

2 tablespoons butter or margarine
2 tablespoons all-purpose flour
2 cups hot lamb stock
2 tablespoons chopped dill or dillweed
1½ tablespoons cider vinegar
1 tablespoon sugar
Salt
1 egg yolk, beaten

Melt butter and stir in flour. Add hot stock gradually and blend thoroughly. Simmer over low heat, stirring occasionally. Add dill, vinegar, sugar, and salt. Remove and stir in beaten egg yolk. Do not boil again.

DILLED CRISSCROSS CARROTS

2 pounds carrots
1⅓ cups white vinegar
1⅓ cups water
½ teaspoon each of celery seed, caraway seed, and mustard seed

1 cup sugar
1 teaspoon salt
½ teaspoon crushed hot peppers
1½ teaspoons whole dillseed

Wash and scrape carrots and cut into thin crisscross slices. Cook in very little salted water until almost tender. Pack closely into hot sterilized pint jars. Make syrup of remaining ingredients. Bring to a full rolling boil; after boiling for 2 minutes, pour over carrots to overflowing, and seal jars. Serve chilled with salads or sliced cold meat. Makes 4 pints.

DILLED GREEN BEANS

4 cups (two 1-pound cans) whole green beans
1 garlic clove, split
¾ cup wine vinegar
¾ cup water
1 tablespoon salt
1 tablespoon crushed hot red pepper
¼ cup snipped fresh dill

Drain beans and pack into hot sterilized 1-quart jar; add garlic. Heat remaining ingredients to boiling, pour over beans, and seal jar. Let stand for several days before using. Serve as appetizers. Makes 1 quart.

DILL SAUCE FOR FISH

2 eggs
¼ cup salad oil
Dash each of salt and pepper
1 tablespoon minced fresh dill or dillweed
½ cup light cream
½ teaspoon fresh lemon juice or Worcestershire

Beat eggs; add remaining ingredients and beat until blended. Makes about 1 cup.

DINNER—The main meal of the day, eaten from noon onward. Country people usually eat their dinner at noon whereas city people, who can't get home in the middle of the day, eat theirs at night. The Norwegians eat dinner between four and five in the afternoon, the French between seven and eight, and the Spaniards after nine at night. There is no hard and fast rule for dinnertime.

Nor is there a rule as to the number of courses and dishes to be served at dinner. They have varied through the ages from the gustatory feasts of the ancient Romans, the Elizabethan English, and the French kings, to the calorie-counted meals of figure-conscious diners of our time. The number of diners, too, is a moot one. Hundreds may dine at state and other ceremonial dinners, and two, four, six, eight, or more in the home.

Dinner is so much part of living that at all times, and among all nations, the best way of celebrating a victory, a birth, a wedding, or an anniversary has been at the dinner table.

MUCH DEPENDS ON DINNER
Menus, recipes, and invaluable advice on the art of giving successful dinner parties
by Kay Shaw Nelson

One snowy winter evening, while plotting a menu, some lines of Byron came to mind. "All human history attests," observes Don Juan with some acuity, "That happiness for man—the hungry sinner—since Eve ate apples, much depends on dinner!"

The good Don probably based his remark on his own romantic experience, but the lines surely have broader application. For in the realm of hospitality dinner is the star, and the invitation to dinner implies more than an ordinary meal. If an extra amount of effort goes into the planning and preparation to create an atmosphere in which the enjoyment of good food promotes an aura of well-being among good company, the results are rewarding. Much does depend on dinner, the guests' pleasure and the hostess' pride.

Fashions in dining have, of course, changed radically "since Eve ate apples," but the witness of history confirms the importance attached to dinner in each age, as does the constant struggle for variety and interest, whether the dinner is regarded as meal, feast, or banquet.

Some 3,000 years ago, the ancient Egyptians, although somewhat limited in supplies, managed to dine rather well on such foods as spitted goose; salmon from the Nile; lettuce, radish, and cucumber salads; rolls sprinkled with sesame seeds; delicate lotus flowers; and dainty cakes and sweets. Gold and silver goblets held their wine, and their tableware was of alabaster and painted pottery. On gala occasions, musicians and dancers provided entertainment, although presumably without the aid of microphones.

Somewhat later, the Greeks and Romans placed such emphasis on ostentation and lavishness that fortunes were necessary to give an acceptable dinner. In fact, the Romans, reclining on expensive sofas, and dining on stuffed peacocks, ragouts of thrushes, tongues of flamingos, and elaborate pastries, spent so many hours at their tables that one cannot but suspect that the grandeur of Rome was strongly touched with gluttony.

The courts of Europe in the 15th century featured ordinary dinners comprising four courses, each of which was composed of ten pairs of dishes. For regal feasts, the royal chefs slaved to make such creations as a ship of confectionery, with guns charged with actual powder, and a castle of pies, containing live frogs and birds. So greedy did they become for spices, necessary for preserving and flavoring, that royal fortunes were spent on explorations to procure them, and thus the paths of empire were blazed. One of the adventurers, Columbus, in search, primarily, of black pepper, discovered America instead, as well as many previously unknown foods which delighted European palates.

In subsequent years, while wealthy Europeans marveled at the new tastes of pineapples, paprika, green peppers, and turkeys, the discontented poor fled to the New World. Dinner was frugal fare at first, featuring pumpkins, beans, and corn, but ingenuity at the stove led to variety in preparation. As the development of agriculture and industry filled the nation's coffers, however, supplies became more bountiful and tastes more lavish. By the late 19th century, in the twilight of an age, fashion decreed dinner parties both ornate and expensive. Hostesses vied with each other to offer new dishes and such delicacies as *artichauts farcis* (stuffed artichokes), pheasant under glass, truffled aspic, *crème parisienne,* and Italian mousse with macaroons. At fancy dinners, the dessert course alone might feature some twenty dishes, and centerpieces were created to resemble whole gardens or forests.

Two world wars and a new generation preaching informality have tended to simplify our concept of dining. Few could afford, nor would many appreciate, the elaborate and ornate trappings of the past. Yet the dinner party remains an occasion of significance. The presence of the family silver and china gleaming in candlelight, the shimmering crystal and tasteful linen, represent little additional effort, but they assure the guest that he is about to enjoy the best that hospitality has to offer. There is just and pleasurable anticipation of the meal to come.

In planning and preparing her dinner, today's hostess is fortunate in having the food products of the entire world at her disposal. With them she may be expected to prepare dinners that are simple with just a touch of elegance, interesting but not elaborate, some courses but not too many, seemingly expensive but not actually, and with just enough service to make the guests comfortable.

These five dinners were designed with all this in mind, and not forgetting that, whatever the occasion, "much depends on dinner."

SWORDFISH DINNER FOR EIGHT

BOURBON BLACK-BEAN SOUP
SKEWERED SWORDFISH
GREEN RICE
BROILED TOMATO HALVES
BACON AND GREEN-BEAN SALAD
COLD COFFEE SOUFFLÉ

BOURBON BLACK BEAN SOUP

2 cans (10½ ounces each) condensed black bean soup
2 soup cans hot water
2 tablespoons bourbon whiskey
Salt and pepper
⅛ teaspoon ground nutmeg
8 thin lemon slices
2 tablespoons minced onion

Combine soup, water, and whiskey. Mix well and bring to a boil. Season with salt and pepper to taste. Stir in nutmeg. Place 1 slice of lemon in each soup bowl. Pour in soup. Garnish each serving with a little minced onion. Makes 8 servings.

SKEWERED SWORDFISH

3 pounds fresh or frozen swordfish
1 cup cooking oil
⅓ cup fresh lemon juice
1 teaspoon crumbled dried oregano
2 medium onions, each cut into 8 wedges
2 bay leaves
Salt and pepper to taste

Remove skin from swordfish. Cut fish into 1-inch squares. Combine remaining ingredients and pour mixture over fish cubes. Let stand for at least 2 hours, stirring occasionally. Oil 8 skewers and thread with fish cubes and onion wedges. (There may be more than enough for 8 skewers.) Arrange on a piece of foil. Brush with marinade. Broil for about 15 minutes, turning once or twice, or until fish is tender. Serve on skewers. Makes 8 or 9 servings.

GREEN RICE

15 green onions with tops, chopped
3 tablespoons cooking oil
2 large green peppers, seeded and finely diced
2 cups uncooked long-grain rice
4 chicken bouillon cubes
4 cups water
¾ cup chopped parsley
1 cup grated Parmesan cheese
Salt and pepper to taste

Sauté onions in oil until tender. Add green peppers and rice. Sauté, stirring constantly, for several minutes, until rice is translucent. Add remaining ingredients and mix well. Pour into shallow baking dish and bake, uncovered, in preheated moderate oven (350°F.) for 40 minutes, or until rice is cooked and liquid is absorbed. Makes 8 servings.

BROILED TOMATO HALVES

Cut 8 large firm tomatoes into halves. Sprinkle each cut surface with salt and pepper. Dot with butter. Broil 5 to 8 minutes, or until cooked. Makes 8 servings.

BACON AND GREEN-BEAN SALAD

2 packages (10 ounces each) frozen French-cut green beans
½ cup salad oil
¼ cup wine vinegar
Salt and pepper to taste
Salad greens
5 slices of bacon, cooked and crumbled

Cook beans, drain, and cool. Add oil, vinegar, and seasonings and mix well. Chill. Serve on greens and sprinkle with bacon. Makes 8 servings.

COLD COFFEE SOUFFLÉ

1 envelope unflavored gelatin
¼ cup cold coffee
5 eggs, separated
1 cup sugar
¼ teaspoon salt
1 cup hot coffee
1 teaspoon vanilla extract
1 cup heavy cream

Soften gelatin in cold coffee. Let stand for 5 minutes. Beat egg yolks slightly. Add sugar, salt, and hot coffee. Cook in top part of double boiler over simmering water, stirring constantly, until slightly thickened. Remove from heat and stir in softened gelatin and vanilla. Cool. Beat egg whites until stiff but not dry. Whip cream until stiff. Fold egg whites and cream into gelatin mixture. Spoon into a 7- or 8-inch soufflé dish, or into individual molds. Chill for at least 8 hours. Top with additional whipped cream and a sprinkling of instant coffee, if desired. Makes 8 servings.

HAM DINNER FOR EIGHT

CHICKEN LIVER PÂTÉ
HAM À LA CRÈME
POTATOES IN FOIL
BROCCOLI AMANDINE
TOMATO-CUCUMBER SALAD
ORANGE AMBROSIA

CHICKEN LIVER PÂTÉ

1½ teaspoons unflavored gelatin
2 tablespoons cold water
½ cup chicken bouillon
1½ pounds chicken livers
1 garlic clove
Water
1 teaspoon salt
¼ teaspoon pepper
½ teaspoon each of ground nutmeg and ginger
⅛ teaspoon ground cloves
¼ cup minced onion
½ cup softened butter or margarine
2 tablespoons sherry

Soften gelatin in cold water. Let stand for 5 minutes. Heat bouillon and stir in gelatin. Pour mixture into 1-quart mold and chill until firm. Remove membranes from chicken livers. Add garlic and enough water to cover and cook for 10 minutes. Drain. While still warm, purée in a blender or force through the fine blade of a food chopper. Add remaining ingredients and blend until smooth. Carefully spoon into the mold over the gelatin. Level off, and refrigerate until ready to use. Unmold by setting in a pan of hot water and turning out onto a serving plate or platter. Garnish with lemon slices, if desired. Makes 8 servings.

HAM À LA CRÈME
- 4 medium onions, minced
- ½ cup butter or margarine
- ½ cup all-purpose flour
- 3 cups light cream
- 1½ cups milk
- 6 tablespoons tomato puree
- ¾ cup white wine
- Salt and pepper
- 2 ham steaks (about 2 pounds each)

In a large saucepan, sauté onions in butter until tender but not brown. Stir in flour. Gradually stir in cream and milk. Cook over low heat, stirring constantly, until smooth and thickened. Add tomato purée and wine. Put saucepan in larger pan filled with hot water and cook for 15 to 20 minutes, or until sauce is well blended and has the consistency of heavy cream. Season lightly with salt and pepper. Cut ham steaks crosswise into ¼-inch strips and heat in skillet. Arrange ham on a platter and cover with cream sauce. Makes 8 to 10 servings.

POTATOES IN FOIL
Drain 16 to 24 (two 1-pound cans) small potatoes. Arrange on a large sheet of foil. Sprinkle with chopped fresh parsley, salt, pepper, and paprika. Dot generously with butter. Fold foil over and close the edges so the juices do not escape. Heat in preheated moderate oven (350° F.) for 15 to 20 minutes. Makes 8 servings.

BROCCOLI AMANDINE
Cook 3 10-ounce packages frozen broccoli in a little water until tender. Melt 3 tablespoons butter or margarine. Add ⅓ cup toasted slivered almonds and salt and pepper to taste. Pour over the broccoli. Serve at once. Makes 8 servings.

TOMATO-CUCUMBER SALAD
Slice 3 tomatoes and 2 cucumbers (unpeeled and scored with a fork before slicing) and arrange on a plate. Sprinkle with fresh lemon juice and salad oil. Season to taste with salt and pepper. Let stand for at least 1 hour before serving. Makes 8 servings.

ORANGE AMBROSIA
- 8 oranges
- 2 tablespoons light rum
- 8 tablespoons flaked coconut

Peel oranges and slice crosswise. Arrange in a bowl and sprinkle with rum and coconut. Chill until ready to serve. Makes 8 servings.

STEAK DINNER FOR SIX
QUICHE LORRAINE
FLANK STEAK ROLL-UPS
POTATOES ANNA
GLAZED CARROTS
ROMAINE-AVOCADO-TOMATO SALAD
STRAWBERRIES A LA CHANTILLY

QUICHE LORRAINE
This pie is a famous specialty of Lorraine in northeastern France. Although there are many kinds, each town claiming its own, the basic formula is the same: a pastry shell filled with bacon or ham and an unsweetened custard. Sometimes the name *quiche* is also used for desserts. But the authentic Lorraine dish is always served as a first course or appetizer. After a long autumn drive through the Vosges Mountains, I was introduced to *quiche* in the charming city of Strasbourg in Alsace, a neighboring province of Lorraine. Since then I have encountered it many times. But nostalgia compels me to remember most fondly our first meeting.

- 1 package (10 ounces) piecrust mix
- ½ pound sliced bacon
- 1½ cups (6 ounces) grated imported Swiss cheese
- 1 small onion, minced
- 1 tablespoon bacon fat
- 3 eggs, well beaten
- 1 cup heavy cream
- ½ cup milk
- ½ teaspoon salt
- ¼ teaspoon pepper
- Dash of cayenne
- ½ teaspoon powdered mustard

Prepare piecrust mix according to directions on package. Line a 9-inch pie pan with rolled pastry and flute edges. Take 1 bacon slice and cook until limp. Cut into 1-inch pieces and set aside. Cook remaining bacon until crisp. Drain bacon and crumble into pastry. Sprinkle grated cheese over bacon. Sauté onion in bacon fat until golden, and drain. Sprinkle onion on cheese. Beat eggs with cream, milk, salt, pepper, cayenne, and mustard. Pour mixture into pastry. Decorate with reserved bacon pieces and bake in preheated moderate oven (375°F.) for 45 minutes, or until firm and browned. Cool slightly and cut into wedges.

FLANK STEAK ROLL-UPS
Sometimes flank steaks must be ordered ahead of time. Since each beef steer has just two, they are somewhat scarce. However, they are well worth seeking. Because of their lean flat flesh, without any bone, they are perfect for stuffing and rolling.

- 2 flank steaks (1½ pounds each)
- Water and meat tenderizer
- ¼ cup each of soy sauce, sherry, and tarragon vinegar
- ⅝ teaspoon pepper
- ⅔ cup each of minced onions and green peppers

- 3 tablespoons butter or margarine
- 1 cup chopped fresh mushrooms
- ¼ cup chopped parsley
- ½ teaspoon salt

Cut narrow ends from flank steaks and grind for hamburgers. Prick meat on both sides with fork. Sprinkle meat with water and meat tenderizer. Combine soy sauce, sherry, vinegar, and ½ teaspoon pepper. Pour mixture over steaks and let stand for 2 hours, turning occasionally. Sauté onions and green peppers in butter until tender. Add mushrooms, parsley, salt, and remaining pepper. Sauté for 5 minutes more. Transfer steaks to cutting board, reserving marinade. Arrange vegetable mixture lengthwise along centers. Roll, starting with the long, lower side, and hold securely with left hand. With right hand cut meat slightly on the bias into 1½- to 2-inch slices. Roll each folded slice tightly and string on skewers, being careful to lace them so stuffing won't fall out. Arrange on a sheet of foil. Brush with reserved marinade. Broil for 5 to 10 minutes, depending on the desired rareness. Turn once. Serve on skewers, or carefully remove to a hot platter. Makes 6 to 8 servings.

POTATOES ANNA
It took a long time for Europeans to learn to accept potatoes. In France they were introduced as ornamental plants around 1540 from Spain (after being brought from South America by early explorers). But it was not until the late 1700's that they were eaten at all. Due mainly to the efforts of food lover Antoine Parmentier, the vegetable soon became a staple and since then has been prepared in thousands of ways. One of these, Potatoes Anna, is also called potato cake with butter.

Peel 6 medium potatoes and slice thinly and evenly. Wash well and wipe dry. Butter the sides of a round 1½-quart mold or baking dish. Arrange one layer of potatoes over the bottom and sides. Dot with butter. Sprinkle with salt and pepper. Repeat until the dish is full. Spread more butter over the top. Cover with a lid or aluminum foil. Bake in preheated hot oven (400°F.) for 1 hour, or until potatoes are cooked. Carefully turn out on a warm plate or platter. Makes 6 servings.

GLAZED CARROTS
Cook about 18 small whole carrots until almost tender. Drain, and dry. Roll carrots in granulated sugar. Cook in melted butter in skillet, turning frequently until glazed. Makes 6 servings.

ROMAINE-AVOCADO-TOMATO SALAD
- 1 or 2 heads (depending on size) romaine lettuce

3 medium-size tomatoes, sliced
1 avocado, peeled and sliced
    Olive or salad oil and fresh lemon juice
    to taste
    Salt and pepper

Wash romaine, dry well, and tear into large shreds. Arrange in a salad bowl. Cover with tomato and avocado slices. Sprinkle lightly with oil and lemon juice and season with salt and pepper to taste. Or serve with French dressing if preferred. Makes 6 servings.

STRAWBERRIES À LA CHANTILLY

The charming town of Chantilly, not far from Paris, is now famous for its château and race track. But even when it was only a little village, it was known especially for its rich cream. Consequently, any dish made with stiffly beaten cream, sweetened and flavored, has been labeled Chantilly. This is a most delicious one.

2 pints fresh strawberries
2 cups heavy cream, whipped
½ cup grated sweet chocolate
2 tablespoons confectioners' sugar
2 tablespoons light rum

Hull strawberries and arrange in a bowl. Whip cream until foamy and just slightly thickened. Fold in remaining ingredients. Chill. At serving time, put strawberries in serving dishes and serve the whipped-cream sauce separately. Makes 6 to 8 servings.

━━ ━━ ━━ ━━ ━━ ━━

LAMB CHOP DINNER FOR SIX

CONSOMMÉ MADRILENE
CRABMEAT MOLDS
BAKED LAMB CHOPS
FRENCH PEAS
STUFFED BAKED POTATOES
CHEESE PLATE
MACEDOINE OF FRUIT

This dinner is somewhat more inclusive than the others and is intended for that special occasion when the hostess wants to spend a little bit more money and work a little harder. Five courses may seem like a formidable task. But with planning it is entirely possible, and for that "special dinner" well worth the effort. If you wish to serve each course at the dining room table the assistance of a servant or teen-age daughter would facilitate the procedure. However, I do it another way without the help of either. The consommé and crab, served several minutes apart, are eaten in the recreation room or on the porch, immediately after predinner conversation. Then we proceed to the dining room for the main meal, including the cheese plate. The fruit dessert and after-dinner coffee are passed later in the living room.

CONSOMMÉ MADRILENE

Combine 2 cans (13 ounces each) of consommé madrilene and ¼ cup sherry. Heat, and pour into small soup bowls or cups with a slice of lemon in each. Serve at once.

CRABMEAT MOLDS

1 pound fresh or canned crabmeat
½ cup mayonnaise
3 tablespoons sweet relish
1½ cups finely chopped celery
½ teaspoon salt
    Dash of pepper
    Lettuce leaves and pimiento strips

Remove shell and fibers from crabmeat. Do not break crabmeat into small pieces, but leave as large lumps as possible. Combine crabmeat with next 5 ingredients, pack mixture into 6 custard cups, and refrigerate. Just before serving, invert each on a large lettuce leaf. Garnish with strips of pimiento. Makes 6 servings.

BAKED LAMB CHOPS

6 loin lamb chops, 1½ inches thick
6 small slices of liverwurst or
    6 teaspoons liver pate
36 pine nuts or almond slivers
    Freshly ground pepper and nutmeg
    Onion juice or finely chopped onion
    Segments of navel orange (optional)

Cut a slit in the side of each chop where the meat is thickest without breaking into either surface. Into each slit insert 1 slice of liverwurst and 6 pine nuts. Fasten opening with toothpicks. Sprinkle both sides of each chop with pepper, nutmeg, and onion juice. Bake, uncovered, in preheated hot oven (425°F.) for 30 minutes. Remove toothpicks, and serve. If desired, garnish with orange segments. Makes 6 servings.

FRENCH PEAS

2 packages (10½ ounces each) frozen peas with onions
2 teaspoons sugar
¼ cup butter or margarine
¼ cup water
1 tablespoon chopped fresh parsley
6 lettuce leaves, chopped
2 teaspoons chopped chervil
    Salt and pepper to taste

Combine all ingredients and cook, covered, over low heat for 15 minutes, or until peas are tender. Makes 6 servings.

STUFFED BAKED POTATOES

7 uniform-size baking potatoes
    Light cream
    Butter or margarine
    Salt and pepper
    Paprika

Scrub potatoes. Bake in preheated very hot oven (450°F.) for 45 to 50 minutes, or until tender when tested with a fork. Cut a slice from top of each potato and scoop out pulp. Reserve 6 potato shells. Mash pulp, beat in enough cream to make fluffy, and season with butter and salt and pepper to taste. Pile into re-

served shells, rounding tops. Brush with melted butter and sprinkle with paprika. Put in oven to brown lightly for about 15 minutes before chops are done. Makes 6 servings.

CHEESE PLATE

Arrange 3 or 4 cheeses such as Roquefort, Bel Paese, Camembert, Gorgonzola, Edam, or Stilton on a plate with bread slices, and/or crackers, in between. Serve as a separate course just before the dessert and coffee.

MACÉDOINE OF FRUIT

Allowing ¾ cup for each serving, combine several fruits such as sliced bananas, oranges, peaches, and strawberries with pineapple cubes and melon balls. Arrange in alternate layers in a large glass or silver bowl. Sprinkle lemon or orange juice and sugar over each layer. Top with a few whole strawberries. Chill in the refrigerator for at least 1 hour.

━━ ━━ ━━ ━━ ━━ ━━

CHICKEN DINNER FOR FOUR

MOCK LOBSTER SOUP
CHICKEN MARENGO
RISI E BISI
BEET SALAD WITH ROQUEFORT DRESSING
SHERBET MOLD

MOCK LOBSTER SOUP

1 can (10½ ounces) pea soup
1 can (10½ ounces) tomato soup
2 soup cans light cream or milk
¼ cup sherry
1 teaspoon Worcestershire
    Dash of paprika
    Salt and pepper to taste

Mix all ingredients in a blender or with rotary beater. Serve chilled or hot. This recipe makes more than enough for 4. Save the rest for another meal, or freeze.

CHICKEN MARENGO

This dish was so named because it was prepared for Napoleon Bonaparte after the battle of Marengo in 1800 in which the French defeated the Austrians. After tasting it, Napoleon reportedly told his chef, Durand, "You must feed me like this after every battle." Since the supply wagons were somewhat distant and Napoleon was hungry, his chef had cooked whatever could be scavenged in the neighborhood. No white wine or mushrooms were used in the original dish. Durand revised the dish somewhat and added them at a later date.

4 small whole chicken breasts
    Salt and pepper
¼ cup cooking oil or butter
2 onions, thinly sliced
1 garlic clove, mashed
2 large tomatoes, peeled and chopped
    Paprika

¾ cup white wine
1 cup sliced fresh mushroom caps

Wash chicken breasts and wipe dry. Sprinkle with salt and pepper. Sauté in oil until golden brown on both sides. Remove to platter. Sauté onions and garlic until onions are tender. Add tomatoes and cook until mushy. Return chicken breasts to skillet. Season with salt, pepper, and paprika to taste. Pour in wine and cook, covered, for 30 minutes. Add more wine if necessary. Add mushrooms to mixture and cook for 7 to 10 minutes longer. Makes 4 servings.

RISI E BISI
(Rice and Peas)

2 cups water
2 chicken bouillon cubes
3 tablespoons butter
1 cup uncooked long-grain rice
1 package (10 ounces) frozen peas, thawed
3 tablespoons grated Parmesan cheese
4 slices of bacon, cooked and crumbled
1¼ teaspoons salt
⅛ teaspoon pepper

In a saucepan put water, bouillon cubes, and 1 tablespoon butter. Bring to a boil and stir in rice. Cook, covered, for 20 minutes. Add peas, remaining butter, the cheese, bacon, salt, and pepper. Increase heat and cook for 10 minutes, or until peas and rice are cooked and all the liquid has been absorbed. Mix lightly. Makes 4 to 5 servings.

BEET SALAD WITH ROQUEFORT
DRESSING

4 medium beets, cooked
1 carrot, shredded
2 tablespoons mashed Roquefort cheese
¾ cup French dressing
Salad greens

Skin and chill the beets, then slice. Sprinkle with carrots. Mix cheese with French dressing and spoon over beets. Serve on greens. Makes 4 servings.

SHERBET MOLD

1 pint lime sherbet
1 pint pineapple or lemon sherbet
1 cup (one 8½- to 9-ounce can) crushed pineapple, drained
2 tablespoons light rum
¼ cup chopped maraschino cherries
Whipped cream
Maraschino cherries

Soften lime sherbet slightly and spoon into 4½- to 5-cup mold, pressing with a spoon to line the bottom and sides evenly. Put in freezer until firm. Soften pineapple sherbet slightly. Fold in crushed pineapple, rum, and cherries. Spoon into mold cavity and level off with a knife. Again put in freezer until firm. Shortly before dinner, turn out of the mold onto a chilled plate or platter. Decorate with whipped cream and maraschino cherries. Return to freezer until just before serving. Cut into slices or wedges. Makes 8 servings.

DISSOLVE—In cookery, to dissolve means to add a solid to a liquid, hot or cold, and cause the solid to become one with the liquid. This is done, for example, when sugar is dissolved in hot coffee, gelatin in water, junket tablets in milk, a bouillon cube in hot water, salt in a sauce, and yeast in water.

DIVINITY—A creamy candy produced by cooking sugar, water, and corn syrup to the firm-ball stage (248°F. on a candy thermometer) and then slowly beating this hot syrup into stiffly beaten egg whites. The mixture is dropped by spoonfuls onto wax paper and allowed to harden and cool; or it is turned into a buttered pan, allowed to harden, and cut in squares. Melted chocolate, nuts, coconut, or candied fruits may be added for variety.

Divinity is usually made with white sugar but occasionally brown sugar is used. When Divinity is made with brown sugar, it is called "Seafoam."

DIVINITY

2⅓ cups sugar
½ cup water
⅔ cup light corn syrup
¼ teaspoon salt
2 egg whites, stiffly beaten
1 teaspoon vanilla extract

In saucepan mix sugar, water, corn syrup, and salt. Bring to boil and cook, stirring, until sugar is dissolved. Continue cooking without stirring until a small amount of mixture forms a very hard ball when dropped in very cold water (266°F. on a candy thermometer). Wipe away any crystals that form on side of pan with a damp cloth wrapped around a fork. Gradually pour mixture over egg whites, beating constantly. Continue beating until candy is very stiff and mixture will hold its shape when dropped from a spoon. Stir in vanilla. Pour into buttered pan (8 x 8 x 2 inches) and let stand until firm. Cut in squares. Or drop mixture by tablespoonfuls onto wax paper and let stand until firm. Makes about 1¼ pounds, or 16 pieces.

■ **Variations**—Dropped candy may be topped with a nut half or piece of candied cherry. If desired, sprinkle candy in pan with chopped nuts, chocolate shot, or flaked coconut.

DOLMA—This is an Arabic word, meaning "something stuffed." As a culinary term, it refers to grape leaves, vegetables, or fruits stuffed with well-seasoned combinations of meats, vegetables, and rice, eaten either hot or cold. Grape-leaf dolmas are probably the most famous ones.

Dolmas are a standard part of Near Eastern cookery and illustrate the triumph of making much from little. Where the dish comes from is open to debate, but for centuries it has been the favorite of Greeks, Turks, Syrians, Lebanese, Armenians, Arabs, Tajiks, Uzbeks, and Turkomans; all of the people who, at one time or another, were a part of, or were influenced by the Ottoman Empire.

There are many ways of preparing dolmas. Grape leaves, eggplant, squash, peppers, and cabbage leaves are used as dolma casings. In Iran, outstanding dolmas are made by stuffing quinces and apples with a savory filling.

Dolmas can be made in advance, stored in the refrigerator, and cooked when needed. Small ones make excellent appetizers.

DOLMADAKIA ME AVGOLEMONO
(Greek Stuffed Grapevine Leaves
with Lemon Sauce)

1½ pounds lean ground lamb
2 large onions, chopped
1 cup uncooked rice
1 teaspoon salt
¼ teaspoon pepper
½ teaspoon dried mint leaves, crumbled
Water
1 jar (1 pound) grapevine leaves
2 chicken bouillon cubes
2 tablespoons butter or margarine
3 eggs
Juice of 1 lemon

Mix first 6 ingredients and 1 cup water. Drain grapevine leaves, and wash well to remove brine. Separate largest and most perfect leaves and put a spoonful of the mixture in center of each. Roll up toward point of leaf, folding in edges. Tear some of the imperfect leaves, and put in bottom of large kettle or Dutch oven. Put rolls on torn leaves. Repeat until all ingredients are used. Dissolve bouillon cubes in 1 cup hot water and pour over leaves. Dot with butter. Cover and steam over low heat for about 1 hour. There should be some liquid in kettle. If necessary add a little more water. Beat eggs and lemon juice together. Add a little of the liquid from the kettle. Pour mixture over rolls, and serve. Makes 6 to 8 servings.

TURKISH GRAPEVINE LEAVES DOLMA

⅓ cup olive oil
4 medium onions, minced
1 cup uncooked rice
¾ cup hot water or bouillon, or more
3 tablespoons pine nuts
1½ tablespoons dry currants
1 teaspoon fresh or dried mint, chopped
½ teaspoon crumbled dried thyme
1 teaspoon each of sugar and salt
½ teaspoon pepper
2 tablespoons tomato paste
About 50 grapevine leaves, fresh or canned
Water
Juice of 1 lemon
Lemon wedges

Heat olive oil in deep pan. Cook onions in it until soft and golden. Add rice. Over medium heat cook rice, stirring constantly, for 4 minutes, or until glossy. Add hot water; the rice will sizzle. Cook, tightly covered, over low heat for 15 minutes. Add pine nuts, currants, mint, thyme, sugar, salt, pepper, and 1 tablespoon tomato paste. Cook, covered, for 10 to 15 more minutes, or until rice is just tender. (Amount of water and cooking time depend on kind of rice used.) At end of cooking time all liquid should be absorbed and rice should be dry. Cool rice.

Wash canned grapevine leaves in warm water. Or drop fresh leaves into boiling water for 3 to 5 minutes to make them soft. Place about 1 teaspoon of rice mixture in the center of each leaf. Fold bottom of leaf over stuffing. Then fold from each side to middle. Roll tightly to make a cylinder 2 inches long and 1 inch across.

Place 1 layer of dolmas in bottom of a heavy saucepan. They should be packed as tightly as possible. Cover with layer of grapevine leaves. Top with more dolmas and repeat process until all dolmas are packed. Finish with a layer of leaves. Combine lemon juice, remaining tomato paste, and ½ cup hot water. Pour over dolmas. Add more hot water to cover dolmas. Firmly press an inverted plate over dolmas to keep them down during cooking. Cover with lid. Simmer over lowest possible heat for 45 minutes. Allow dolmas to cool before removing lid and plate. When cold, drain off liquid and carefully remove dolmas from saucepan; place in rows on serving dish. Surround with lemon wedges. Serve cold, preferably the next day. Makes 4 servings as an entrée, 12 as an appetizer.

PERSIAN APPLE DOLMA

⅓ cup yellow split peas
  Water
1 medium onion, minced
3 tablespoons butter
1 pound beef round or chuck, ground
1 teaspoon salt
½ teaspoon ground cinnamon
¼ teaspoon pepper
8 to 10 firm tart apples
¼ cup cider vinegar (not wine vinegar)
3 tablespoons sugar

Cook peas in 1½ cups water until very soft and mushy. Sauté onion in 2 tablespoons of the butter until soft. Add meat and cook until golden brown. Add peas. Blend in salt, cinnamon, and pepper. Cool mixture. Cut a thin slice from stem end of each apple. Reserve slices. Hollow out apples with apple corer to about ½ inch from edge. Stuff apples with meat mixture. Replace stem slices and press down firmly so that filling won't ooze out during baking. Place apples in baking dish. Pour ½ inch of water into dish.

Bake in preheated moderate oven (350° F.) for 15 minutes. While apples are baking, combine remaining tablespoon of butter, vinegar, ¼ cup water, sugar. Bring to a boil. Remove apples from oven. Lift stem slice and baste apple stuffing with vinegar-water mixture. Return apples to oven and cook for 15 minutes longer, or until tender. Serve from baking pan. Makes 4 to 6 servings.

DOT, TO—"To dot" means to place small amounts of an ingredient over the top surface of food. It usually appears in recipes in such phrases as "dot with butter," "dot with melted chocolate," "dot with cherries," etc. The appearance and flavor of the food are improved by this procedure.

DOUGH—A mixture of flour or meal and liquid with other ingredients. Dough is thick enough to knead or roll and is partly plastic, partly elastic. (This is in contrast with a batter, a mixture of similar ingredients, but in different proportions, so that it is thin enough to pour or drop from a spoon.) A good dough is the foundation of much basic cooking and baking.

The plastic qualities of dough depend on the liquid (milk, water, etc.) used in it. The more liquid added, the softer the dough and the more carefully it must be handled.

The elastic qualities of dough depend on the flour used in it. All-purpose flour, when mixed with liquid and properly kneaded, produces elastic, or gluten, strands which, like millions of miniature balloons, stretch and hold gas during baking and form the structure of the dough. These elastic strands are tenderized during baking by the additional ingredients, and bake firm and dry so that the bread or roll or cake remains risen when taken from the oven. Since all-purpose flour forms the best gluten strands, it is generally used, in addition to any other type of flour called for, in making yeast breads.

To knead properly, mix the ingredients as specified by the recipe you are following. Place the dough on a lightly floured board. Dip hands into flour. Shape the dough into a small flat patty like a giant hamburger. With one hand fold the patty in half, pressing the edges of the dough together with the heel of the hand. Turn the half-patty lengthwise and repeat the folding and pressing process until the dough is smooth and plastic, yet yielding. Cover and let rest for 15 minutes to give the flour a chance to develop its gluten strands.

DOUGHNUT—A doughnut is a small cake, deep fried or baked and leavened with yeast or baking powder. Doughnuts are ring shape with a hole in the center. Crullers and fried cakes are closely related to them. Both are made of the same kind of dough and deep fried, but technically crullers are shaped in a twist, and fried cakes are made round or square, without a hole. However, in some parts of the country, the words "fried cake" are used for doughnuts, crullers, and solid cakes. And filled fried cakes are often called "doughnuts": for example, jelly doughnuts.

Doughnuts are more than a pleasant food. They are a national institution and a state of mind. The depth of popular sentiment for doughnuts has created a nationwide group of doughnut shops which sell more different flavored, frosted, or filled doughnuts than one would think possible.

All fried cakes can be made at home with simple equipment. They are really breads cooked in a kettle or skillet on top of the stove. This was an important consideration in the early days when oven cooking was not the easy thing it is today, but required long firing. Doughnuts, whatever their origin, are a genuine product of pioneer cooking.

The origin of the doughnut, or more particularly the doughnut hole, has caused considerable speculation. Some of our historians take great pleasure in tracing doughnut ancestry back to a tribe of prehistoric American Indians in the Southwest. Petrified fried cakes, complete with holes, have been unearthed. It is more likely that the secret of doughnut making came to this country with the colonists. Dutch settlers made a cake with a nut or raisin in the center instead of a hole. It was in New England that the first true "dough nuts" were made. Raised with yeast, they were spherical and a little larger than walnuts.

The most popular story regarding the hole in the doughnut centers around a New England sea captain named Hanson Gregory. In 1847, when Captain Gregory was a boy in Camden, Maine, he complained to his mother that fried cakes were never completely cooked in the center. To alleviate the problem of a doughy center he poked holes in them before they were cooked. Americans have enjoyed doughnuts with holes ever since. The boy Hanson Gregory also did a great service for American children. Traditionally, when homemade doughnuts are cut, the centers are reserved and fried separately for the children. To them the best part of the doughnut is the hole.

Caloric Values

☐ 1 baking powder or cake doughnut = 200 calories

☐ 1 yeast or raised doughnut = 168 calories

Basic Preparation—Keep dough as soft as possible, using just enough flour to make it possible to roll out dough. Chill well before rolling. Cut doughnuts with floured cutter. Let baking-powder doughnuts dry for 15 minutes before frying. Let yeast-raised doughnuts rise until doubled in bulk before cooking. Fry doughnuts in deep fat at a temperature of about 350° to 375°F., or when a bread cube dropped into fat browns in 50 seconds. Fry only a few doughnuts at one time. When doughnuts are first placed in the fat, they will sink, but they soon rise to the surface again. Turn at once with a fork and cook until nicely browned on the bottom. Turn again and cook until browned on the other side. Drain on absorbent paper.

Doughnuts are sometimes rolled in powdered sugar, granulated sugar, or cinnamon and sugar.

They may be spread thinly with any flavor frosting and dipped, while frosting is moist, into shredded coconut, chopped nuts, chocolate sprinkles, or finely minced candied fruits.

They may be filled with jelly, custard, or whipped cream.

☐ **To Freshen Stale Doughnuts**—Place in paper bag or covered dish. Reheat in moderate oven (350°F.).

DOUGHNUTS

2 tablespoons shortening
¾ cup sugar
2 eggs
4 cups sifted all-purpose flour
2 teaspoons baking powder
½ teaspoon each of ground cinnamon, mace, and nutmeg
½ teaspoon salt
1 cup milk
Fat for deep frying

Cream shortening and sugar until light and fluffy; add eggs, one at a time, beating well after each addition. Sift together dry ingredients and add alternately with the milk. Chill for 1 hour or longer. Roll out on lightly floured board to ½-inch thickness and cut with floured doughnut cutter. Fry in hot deep fat (370°F. on a frying thermometer) until golden brown on both sides, turning once. Drain on absorbent paper. Makes about 2½ dozen.

Doughnuts Filled with Applesauce

Roll out doughnut dough about ¼ inch thick and cut into rounds. Put a spoonful of thick applesauce or apple butter on each round, fold one half over onto the other, and press edges together. Fry in hot deep fat (370°F. on a frying thermometer).

CHOCOLATE DOUGHNUTS

2 eggs
1 cup sugar
2 ounces (2 squares) unsweetened chocolate
2 tablespoons shortening
1 cup mashed potatoes
⅔ cup milk
3½ cups sifted all-purpose flour (about)
6 teaspoons baking powder
1 teaspoon salt
¼ teaspoon ground cinnamon
Fat for deep frying

Beat eggs until light and beat in sugar. Melt chocolate and shortening together, and add. Add potatoes, milk, and flour mixed with the other dry ingredients. Use just enough flour to make a dough that can be handled. Chill dough, then roll it out on floured board; cut with a doughnut cutter. Fry in hot deep fat (370°F. on a frying thermometer) until brown on both sides, turning once. Drain doughnuts on absorbent paper. Makes about 3 dozen.

RAISED DOUGHNUTS

1 package active dry yeast or 1 cake compressed yeast
½ cup water*
¼ cup shortening
½ cup undiluted evaporated milk
¾ cup sugar
3 eggs
2½ teaspoons salt
1 teaspoon ground nutmeg
5 cups sifted all-purpose flour (about)
Fat for deep frying
Confectioners' sugar

* Use very warm water (105°F. to 115°F.) for dry yeast; use lukewarm (80°F. to 90°F.) for compressed. Sprinkle yeast or crumble cake into water in large bowl. Let stand for a few minutes, then stir until dissolved. Melt shortening in small saucepan; add milk and heat just to lukewarm. Pour into dissolved yeast. Add sugar and eggs, beat lightly, and add salt and nutmeg. Gradually beat in flour to make a soft dough. Cover and let rise until doubled. Knead for 5 minutes. Roll out ½ inch thick and cut with 2½-inch doughnut cutter. Let rise until doubled. Fry doughnuts in hot deep fat (370°F. on a frying thermometer) until golden brown on both sides, turning once. Drain on absorbent paper. Dust with confectioners' sugar. Makes about 2½ dozen.

DROPPED RAISIN DOUGHNUTS

4 egg yolks
¾ cup sugar
1 teaspoon grated orange rind
3 cups sifted all-purpose flour

4 teaspoons baking powder
¼ teaspoon salt
½ teaspoon each of ground nutmeg and cinnamon
¾ cup ground seedless raisins
1 cup milk
Fat for deep frying
Confectioners' sugar

Beat egg yolks with rotary beater until thick and lemon-colored; add sugar and orange rind. Sift together dry ingredients. Dredge raisins with ½ cup of flour mixture; then add remaining flour alternately with milk to egg mixture. Fold in raisins. Drop by tablespoons into hot deep fat (370°F. on a frying thermometer) and fry until golden brown on both sides, turning once. Drain on absorbent paper. Sprinkle with confectioners' sugar. Makes about 4 dozen.

DREDGE—To sprinkle a food with a dry substance, such as flour, cornmeal, or sugar.

The purpose of dredging is to add flavor, facilitate browning, or improve appearance. Veal cutlets are dredged with flour, and doughnuts and cookies with granulated or confectioners' sugar.

DRESSING—In culinary language, the word has three meanings. 1.) A sauce, usually cold, added to fish, meats, fruits, and, most commonly, salads. 2.) A solid, well-seasoned mixture used to stuff fish, poultry, or meats, or to be baked by itself. This type of dressing is often called a "stuffing." 3.) A method of preparing food for cooking. Fowl is dressed by plucking, drawing, singeing, trimming, and trussing; fish is dressed by scaling, gutting, and trimming.

SALAD DRESSINGS

Salad dressings are composed essentially of acid, fat, and seasonings. There are three basic types of salad dressings: French dressing, mayonnaise, and cooked salad dressing.

French dressing is a temporary emulsion made from oil, which may be corn, olive, peanut, soybean, or cottonseed oil, combined with vinegar or lemon juice and seasonings. The classic French formula of French dressing is three parts oil to one part vinegar, but this depends on personal preference, the flavor and strength of the oil and vinegar, and the use to which the dressing will be put. French dressing goes well with salad greens and with many vegetable and fruit salads. Always shake it well before using.

Dressings that spring from French dressing are vinaigrette, where herbs such as chives and/or chervil and/or parsley are added to the basic mixture; or chiffonade, which contains hard-cooked egg, parsley, pimiento, and scallion. Olives, herbs, and cheese are other ingredients that may be added to French dressing according to taste.

Mayonnaise consists of vegetable oil, vinegar or lemon juice, egg yolk or whole egg, and seasonings. At least 50 per cent of the combination must be oil, and the oil and egg in the dressing should equal not less than 78 per cent of it. The egg in mayonnaise acts as a stabilizer, causing a permanent emulsion.

Mayonnaise may be used with salad greens, meat, fish, chicken, certain fruit salads, and cooked vegetable salads. Use fruit juice, tomato juice, or cream to thin mayonnaise if desired.

Cooked dressings are made with milk or other liquid. They are thickened with starch and/or egg, and the acid is usually vinegar or lemon juice. Seasonings vary as in other dressings, and fat in the form of butter, margarine, or bacon fat may be added. Cooked dressing is often served with fruit salads and vegetables. It can be thinned with sweet or sour cream.

Salad dressing can also be as simple as orange juice poured over fruit. Yogurt or sour cream, sweetened if desired with honey, sugar, or fruit juices, can be served with vegetables.

Storage—Keep salad dressings tightly covered in the refrigerator. Do not freeze. At a very cold temperature mayonnaise may separate and French dressing may become cloudy.

Caloric Values

☐ French dressing, 1 tablespoon = 60 calories

☐ Mayonnaise, 1 tablespoon = 110 calories

☐ Cooked dressing, 1 tablespoon = 30 calories

POULTRY, MEAT, OR FISH DRESSINGS

Dressings, or stuffings, are usually a mixture of bread, bread crumbs, or rice or other starchy material, combined with a savory fat and seasonings. A dressing is one of the many recipes for which it is difficult to give a precise list of ingredients; just about any combination of foods may be used to suit the individual taste. Never use raw pork in a dressing. Cut bread into cubes or shred into large soft crumbs to keep it light.

Keep in mind that dressings will expand in the moist heat of cookery; the cavity of the poultry or meat should always be filled loosely without packing; otherwise the dressing will ooze out. Less-tender cuts of meat are cooked with dressing. They add flavor to the meat, they make the meat more tender, and they make the meat go further. Always

stuff meat, poultry, or fish immediately before cooking. Refrigerate stuffing separately until ready to use.

Amount of Dressing to Prepare
One cup of dressing for each pound of poultry, meat, or fish. If there is any excess dressing it can be baked separately, uncovered, in a greased baking dish.

SALAD DRESSINGS

SIMPLE FRENCH DRESSING
¾ cup salad oil
¼ cup vinegar
¾ teaspoon salt
⅛ teaspoon pepper or more to taste
1 small garlic clove, minced, or 1 tablespoon minced onion (optional)

Combine all ingredients in a jar. Shake well. Refrigerate covered. Shake before using. Makes about 1 cup.

Vinaigrette Dressing
To ¾ cup French dessing add:
1 teaspoon chopped chives or chervil or parsley, or a mixture of all three

Olive Dressing
To ¾ cup French dressing add ¼ cup chopped stuffed green or ripe olives.

Chiffonade Dressing
To ¾ cup French dressing add:
1 hard-cooked egg, chopped
1 teaspoon minced parsley
1 tablespoon minced pimiento
1 teaspoon minced green onion
⅛ teaspoon paprika

FRENCH DRESSING DE LUXE
½ cup fresh lemon juice or vinegar
1½ cups olive oil or other salad oil
Several garlic cloves, gashed
2 teaspoons salt
½ teaspoon pepper
1 teaspoon dry mustard
Dash cayenne
⅓ cup chili sauce
1 tablespoon horseradish
1 teaspoon paprika

Mix all ingredients in a 1-quart glass jar. Cover tightly, and shake until well blended. Refrigerate. Makes 2 cups.

RÉMOULADE SAUCE
1 teaspoon each of powdered English mustard and paprika
¼ teaspoon each of salt, pepper, and cayenne
2 teaspoons prepared horseradish
4 anchovies, minced
1 tablespoon minced capers
2 tablespoons minced celery
3 tablespoons wine vinegar
⅔ cup olive oil

Combine all ingredients and beat until thoroughly mixed and blended. Makes about 1½ cups.

RAVIGOTE SAUCE
8 fresh or 1½ teaspoons dried tarragon leaves
⅓ cup watercress leaves (stems removed)

1 tablespoon chopped chives
1 small garlic clove, minced
1 tablespoon chopped parsley
½ teaspoon prepared French mustard
2 tablespoons wine vinegar
¾ cup olive oil
Salt and pepper to taste

Pound together to a smooth paste tarragon, watercress, chives, garlic, and parsley. This is most easily done in a mortar, a blender, or with the back of a heavy knife on a cutting board. In a small bowl blend mustard, vinegar, and olive oil. Add herb paste and stir until smooth. Season with salt and pepper. Stir again before using. Makes about 1 cup.

SPANISH SALAD DRESSING
Mix ½ cup Spanish olive oil, ¼ cup each of fresh lime and lemon juice, ¼ cup red-wine vinegar, 4 teaspoons sugar, 4 teaspoons salt, ⅛ teaspoon pepper, ½ teaspoon curry powder, and 2 teaspoons crushed dried mint. Keep refrigerated. Makes 1⅓ cups.
Note: This is especially good with citrus fruits.

MAYONNAISE
2 egg yolks
½ teaspoon powdered mustard
½ teaspoon salt
2 teaspoons vinegar
½ teaspoon sugar
1 cup olive oil
2 tablespoons lemon juice

Start with all ingredients at room temperature. Beat egg yolks until lemon-colored. Beat in mustard, salt, ½ teaspoon vinegar, and sugar. Beat in very slowly, ½ teaspoon at a time, ½ cup olive oil. Mixture should thicken. Mix 1½ teaspoons vinegar and 2 tablespoons lemon juice. Alternately add another ½ cup olive oil and the vinegar-lemon juice mixture, drop by drop, until mayonnaise is thick and smooth. If dressing curdles, beat another egg yolk in another bowl and slowly beat in the curdled mayonnaise, drop by drop. If the dressing is too thick, thin it with cream. This may be prepared in an electric mixer using a small bowl and setting the speed at the one used for whipping cream. Makes 1½ cups.

Chantilly Mayonnaise
To one cup mayonnaise add ½ cup heavy cream, whipped. Makes about 2 cups.

Curry Mayonnaise
To 1 cup mayonnaise add 1 to 3 teaspoons curry powder. Makes about 1 cup.

Russian Dressing
To 1 cup mayonnaise, add:

1 tablespoon grated horseradish
¼ cup chili sauce or ketchup
1 teaspoon grated onion

Makes about 1¼ cups.

Thousand Island Dressing

To 1 cup mayonnaise add:
- ½ cup chili sauce or ketchup
- 3 tablespoons chopped stuffed olives
- 2 tablespoons chopped green pepper
- 1 tablespoon chopped onion
- 1 pimiento, minced

Makes about 2 cups.

Tartare Sauce

To 1 cup mayonnaise add:
- 1 teaspoon sharp prepared mustard
- 2 tablespoons chopped sweet pickle
- 1 tablespoon chopped drained capers
- 1 tablespoon chopped parsley

Makes about 1¼ cups.

COOKED SALAD DRESSING

- ½ cup sugar
- 2½ teaspoons all-purpose flour
- ¾ teaspoon salt
- 1 teaspoon powdered mustard
  Dash of cayenne
- ¼ teaspoon white pepper
- 2 teaspoons butter
- 2 eggs, slightly beaten
- 1 cup milk
- ½ cup cider vinegar

In top part of double boiler mix sugar, flour, and seasonings. Add remaining ingredients. Cook over boiling water until thickened, stirring constantly. Cool; then chill until ready to use. Makes 1½ cups.
Note: This dressing is good on potato salad, vegetable salads, or greens.

DRESSINGS FOR POULTRY, MEAT, OR FISH

SPANISH-RICE DRESSING

- 1 cup uncooked rice
- 3 tablespoons cooking oil
- 2 large onions, chopped
- 1 green pepper, chopped
- 1 garlic clove, minced
- 1 can (3 ounces) chopped mushrooms, drained
- 1 pimiento, diced
- 2 cups (one 1-pound can) tomatoes
- 1 egg, beaten
- 1 teaspoon salt
- 2 teaspoons seasoned salt
- ½ teaspoon monosodium glutamate
- ⅛ teaspoon pepper

Cook and drain rice. Add remaining ingredients and mix thoroughly. Makes about 6 cups.
Note: Use for veal, pork, or lamb.

APPLE AND ONION DRESSING

- 2 large yellow onions, chopped
- ¼ cup butter or margarine
- 2 cups diced peeled tart apples
- 4 cups soft stale bread crumbs
- 1½ teaspoons salt
- ½ teaspoon monosodium glutamate
- 2 teaspoons celery seed
- ½ teaspoon ground marjoram
- ¼ teaspoon pepper
- ½ cup apple cider or apple juice

Sauté onion in butter for 5 minutes. Add remaining ingredients and mix well. Makes about 4 cups.
Note: Use as stuffing for spareribs or pork shoulder.

Versatile salad dressings: Curry Mayonnaise, Simple French Dressing and Thousand Island Dressing

PINE-NUT DRESSING FOR CHICKEN

Chicken liver from roasting chicken
¼ cup butter or margarine
¼ cup pine nuts
2 cups packaged precooked rice
2¼ cups boiling water
¼ cup dried currants
Salt and pepper to taste

Chop chicken liver and cook lightly in 2 tablespoons butter. Cook nuts until golden in remaining butter. Cook rice with boiling water as directed on label. Mix all ingredients lightly. Makes about 5 cups.

OYSTER DRESSING FOR TURKEY

1 cup butter or margarine
1 cup minced onion
1 pint small oysters, drained and chopped
1 tablespoon crumbled poultry seasoning
1½ teaspoons salt
¾ teaspoon white pepper
⅓ cup chopped parsley
¾ cup chopped celery leaves
2½ quarts soft stale-bread crumbs or cubes
2 eggs, beaten (optional)

Melt butter in skillet; add all ingredients except crumbs and cook for 5 minutes. Add crumbs and beaten eggs, if desired. Use as stuffing for turkey. Makes about 10 cups.

RAISIN-WALNUT DRESSING

1½ cups chopped celery and leaves
1½ cups chopped onion
1 teaspoon each thyme and sage
½ teaspoon celery salt
1 teaspoon salt
¼ teaspoon pepper
¼ cup butter or margarine
½ cup water
3 cups soft stale-bread cubes
½ cup each chopped raisins and walnuts

Cook celery, onion, and seasonings in butter for 5 minutes. Add remaining ingredients and mix thoroughly. Use as dressing for chicken, duck, or other poultry. Makes about 5 cups.

SHRIMP DRESSING

9 slices firm white bread
6 tablespoons butter or margarine
½ pound raw shrimps
1 small onion, chopped
2 tablespoons chopped parsley
Juice of ½ lemon
1 egg, beaten
2 tablespoons milk
½ teaspoon ground thyme
1 teaspoon salt
⅛ teaspoon white pepper

Trim crusts from bread and spread slices with 3 tablespoons butter. Toast buttered side under broiler; then cut into cubes. Cook shrimps and cool. Peel shrimps, remove veins, and cut shrimps into small pieces. Cook shrimps, onion, and parsley in remaining butter for about 5 minutes. Mix bread, shrimp mixture, and remaining ingredients. Makes about 5 cups.
Note: Use to stuff sole, flounder fillets, or fish rolls.

Dried-Fruit Cook Book—

DRIED FRUIT—Fruits, of which the solids have been greatly concentrated by evaporating a large portion of the original water content, are called dried fruits. The purpose of drying is preservation, but the resulting decrease in bulk affords great savings in transportation and storage costs.

Dried fruits have a great variety of uses. They may be eaten as is, cooked and used as a sauce, used in pies, cakes, cookies, quick breads, puddings, and in stuffings, or served as meat accompaniments.

Availability—Dried apples, apricots, bananas, currants, dates, figs, nectarines, peaches, pears, prunes, raisins, and mixed fruits are available throughout the year in sealed packages of various weights and by the pound in bulk.

Purchasing Guide—All dried fruits are graded in at least three grades and some in as many as five. The terminology used is Extra Fancy, Fancy, Extra Choice, Choice, and Standard. The grades are based on size, color, condition, and water content. Size is the most important factor. "Tenderized," when it appears on the package, indicates that less cooking time is required.

Fruits should have no insects, dirt, molds, or musty odors. Packaged fruits generally list the size and grade of the fruit.

Storage—Store tightly covered in a cool, dry, well-ventilated place. In hot weather it is advisable to store in the refrigerator.
- [ ] Kitchen shelf: 6 to 8 months
- [ ] Refrigerator shelf: 6 to 8 months

Nutritive Food Values—In the drying, over 50 per cent of the water is removed, but practically all the food nutrients remain. Dried fruits contain a variety of vitamins and minerals. The caloric value per pound of dried fruit is four to five times that of the fruit when fresh. However, this is true only if the dried fruit is eaten as purchased. When cooked the fruit regains much of the water lost and approximates the fresh fruit in composition.
- [ ] Apples, 1 cup = 315 calories
- [ ] Apricots, 1 cup = 423 calories
- [ ] Currants, 1 cup = 536 calories
- [ ] Dates, 1 cup = 505 calories
- [ ] Figs, 1 cup = 453 calories
- [ ] Nectarines, 1 cup = 424 calories
- [ ] Peaches, 1 cup = 424 calories
- [ ] Pears, 1 cup = 405 calories
- [ ] Prunes (medium), 1 cup = 375 calories
- [ ] Raisins, 1 cup = 429 calories

Basic Preparation—Overly long soaking in cold water tends to make the fruit watery and tasteless. The dried fruit should be soaked for only 1 hour in hot water, then cooked for a short period of time. If sugar is needed, it should be added only in the last 5 minutes of the cooking period. If the sugar is added before cooking, the ability of the fruit to absorb moisture is affected and the tendering process is delayed. For "tenderized" dried fruits the cooking time is shortened appreciably. When cooking dried fruits to be used for purées, increase the amount of water, cook fruit longer, and then force through a sieve.

☐ **To Cook Dried Apples**—Dried apples increase to five times their original volume when cooked. Cover with water and simmer, covered, for about 40 minutes. Sugar may be added if desired: add about ¼ cup sugar to every cup of fruit.

☐ **To Cook Dried Apricots**—Apricots double in bulk during cooking. Cover with water and simmer, covered, for 40 minutes. Add about ¼ cup sugar to every cup of fruit.

☐ **To Cook Dried Figs**—Figs double in bulk when cooked. Cover with water and simmer, covered, for 20 to 30 minutes. Add 1 tablespoon sugar for each cup of fruit.

☐ **To Cook Dried Nectarines and Peaches**—These triple in bulk when cooked. Cover with water and simmer, covered, for 45 minutes. Add about ¼ cup sugar to every cup of fruit.

☐ **To Cook Dried Pears**—Pears triple in bulk when cooked. Cover with water and simmer, covered, for 35 minutes. Add ¼ cup sugar for each cup of fruit.

☐ **To Cook Prunes**—Prunes double in bulk when cooked. Cover with water and simmer, covered, for 45 to 60 minutes. Sugar is not necessary, but 1 tablespoon per cup may be added if desired.

☐ **To Cook Raisins**—Raisins double in bulk when cooked. Add 1 cup of water to every cup of raisins. Cover and simmer for 10 minutes. Sugar is not necessary.

Raisins, dates, currants, and figs combine better with other ingredients if they are first cooked in boiling water for 5 minutes and then drained.

DRIED- AND FRESH-FRUIT SOUP

¾ cup each of large dried prunes and seedless raisins
½ cup each of dried currants and apricots
6 cups water
½ orange (pulp and skin), chopped
1 apple, chopped
2 slices fresh or canned pineapple, cut into pieces
1 tablespoon butter or margarine
2 tablespoons light brown sugar
Juice of ½ lemon
1½ tablespoons cornstarch

Combine dried fruits and simmer in 2 cups water for about 30 minutes. Add fresh fruits, butter, brown sugar, and lemon juice; simmer for about 15 minutes longer. Add remaining 4 cups water and cornstarch mixed to smooth paste with a little more water; cook until slightly thickened, stirring constantly. Serve hot as a soup or dessert. Makes 6 to 8 servings.

FRUITED SPICED BEEF

5 pounds beef for pot roast
2 tablespoons cooking fat
2 cups water
2 tablespoons mixed pickling spice
2 teaspoons salt
1 pound dried mixed fruit

Brown meat on all sides in hot fat in large heavy kettle. Remove meat and pour off fat. Add water and bring to boil. Put meat on rack in kettle and add pickling spice. Cover and simmer for 2½ hours. Add salt and fruit and simmer for 1 hour longer, or until meat is tender. Slice meat and serve with the liquid poured over top. Garnish with dried fruit. Makes 6 to 8 servings.

PORK CHOPS WITH APRICOT STUFFING

1 cup dried apricots
1½ cups chopped onions
½ cup butter or margarine
4 cups soft stale bread crumbs
1 cup seedless raisins
1 teaspoon ground sage
Salt and pepper
8 loin pork chops, ½ inch thick

Cover apricots with water and soak for several hours; drain, and chop. Cook onions in butter for 5 minutes. Add apricots, crumbs, raisins, and sage. Season to taste with salt and pepper. Brown chops quickly on both sides. Put 4 in covered baking dish or casserole. Cover with apricot mixture and top with remaining chops. Cover and bake in preheated moderate oven (350°F.) for 1 hour, or until chops are tender. Makes 4 servings.

RAISIN-RICE-STUFFED VEAL BREAST

1 veal breast (about 4 pounds)
1¼ cups uncooked rice
⅓ cup melted butter or margarine
1 onion, grated
1 teaspoon salt
½ teaspoon poultry seasoning
1 tablespoon minced parsley
Grated rind of ½ orange
¼ cup raisins

Have butcher cut a large pocket in the side of the veal. Cook rice in boiling salted water until almost tender; drain. Mix with remaining ingredients; fill pocket in veal with stuffing and skewer or sew up opening. Place, rib side down, in an open roasting pan and bake in preheated slow oven (300°F.) for 2½ hours. Makes 8 servings.

CHICKEN WITH FIGS

1 frying chicken (about 3 pounds), cut up
2 tablespoons butter
2 tablespoons all-purpose flour
1 cup dairy sour cream
2 teaspoons seasoned salt
¼ teaspoon pepper
1 cup water
1 tablespoon fresh lemon juice

Dried Fruit Compote / Dried Apple Cake

8 dried California figs, halved
2 tablespoons sesame seeds, toasted

Wash and dry chicken pieces. Brown on all sides in hot butter. Remove chicken. Blend flour into drippings. Remove from heat and stir in sour cream, salt, pepper, water, and lemon juice. Add chicken, cover, and simmer for 30 minutes. Add figs and cook for 15 minutes longer, or until chicken is tender. Sprinkle with sesame seeds. Makes 4 servings.

SPICED APRICOTS AND PRUNES

1½ cups dried apricots
1½ cups dried prunes
3 cups water
1 cup cider vinegar
2 cups firmly packed dark brown sugar
4 cinnamon sticks
1 teaspoon whole cloves
1 teaspoon whole allspice

Put fruit and water in saucepan. Bring to boil, cover, and simmer for 20 minutes. Stir in remaining ingredients and simmer for 10 minutes longer. Cool. Store in refrigerator overnight before using. Makes about 5 cups.
Note: Good with almost any meat.

PRUNES IN SHERRY

Soak large dried prunes in enough sherry to cover. Store in a covered jar or crock. Serve them as they are or stuff with nuts or brandied fruits. Will keep for months. Good relish with poultry or game.

FRUIT TWIST COFFEECAKE

Yeast dough
2 tablespoons butter or margarine
¾ cup Tutti-Frutti (see page 579)
2 tablespoons water
¼ cup firmly packed light brown sugar

For yeast dough, use ½ package of roll or coffeecake mix, or make a sweet-roll dough, using 2 cups flour. When ready to shape dough, roll into a 12-inch square on a lightly floured board. Brush with melted butter and spread with mixture of fruit, water, and brown sugar. Roll up like jelly roll. Cut into halves lengthwise to within 1 inch of end, then twist one strip over the other, keeping cut side up. Pinch ends together. Let rise until almost doubled. Place on greased cookie sheet and bake in preheated hot oven (400°F.) for about 20 minutes. Makes 6 servings.

PINWHEEL BISCUITS

Biscuit dough (1½ cups flour)
¼ cup melted butter or margarine
½ cup Tutti-Frutti (see page 579)
2 tablespoons sugar
3 tablespoons hot water
2 tablespoons corn syrup

Roll out biscuit dough ¼ inch thick and about 10 inches long. Brush with 2 tablespoons melted butter. Combine Tutti-Frutti, sugar, and hot water; spread over dough. Roll as for jelly roll, making roll 10 inches long. Moisten edges of dough;

press together firmly and cut into 10 slices. Brush 10 muffin pans with remaining butter and add syrup. Put biscuits, cut side down, in pans. Bake in preheated moderate oven (375°F.) for about 30 minutes. Let cool for about 3 minutes before turning out of pan. Makes 10.

CHOCOLATE FRUIT PIE

¾ cup sugar
⅓ cup all-purpose flour
¼ teaspoon salt
2 ounces (2 squares) unsweetened chocolate, cut into pieces
2 cups water
1 teaspoon vanilla extract
9- inch pie shell, baked
1 tablespoon sugar
½ cup heavy cream, whipped
½ cup each of chopped pitted dates, chopped raisins, and chopped dried figs

Combine sugar, flour, salt, and chocolate in saucepan. Add water gradually and cook until thick, stirring constantly. Remove from heat; cool, and add vanilla. Pour into pastry shell. Fold sugar into whipped cream. Combine dried fruits; fold into cream and spread over chocolate filling. Chill. Makes 6 to 8 servings.

RAISIN-PINEAPPLE CUSTARD PIE

½ cup sugar
⅛ teaspoon salt
2½ tablespoons cornstarch
1½ cups milk
2 eggs, separated
¾ cup pineapple juice
2 tablespoons fresh lemon juice
1 cup seedless raisins
1 cup crushed pineapple, drained
1 teaspoon vanilla extract
9- inch pie shell, baked
Dash of salt
¼ cup shredded coconut

Combine ¼ cup sugar, salt, and cornstarch in top part of double boiler; add milk gradually and cook over simmering water, stirring constantly, until thickened. Beat egg yolks slightly; slowly add hot mixture and return to top part of double boiler. Continue cooking for about 3 minutes. Remove from heat and cool. Heat fruit juices; add raisins; simmer for 10 minutes and cool. Fold this mixture with pineapple into custard. Add vanilla. Pour into pastry shell. Beat egg whites until foamy. Add salt, then remaining sugar gradually, continuing to beat until stiff but not dry. Cover pie with meringue and sprinkle with coconut. Bake in preheated moderate oven (350°F.) for about 15 minutes, or until lightly browned. Cool. Makes 6 to 8 servings.

FRIED PIES

2 cups sifted all-purpose flour
½ teaspoon salt
1 teaspoon baking powder
3 tablespoons butter or margarine
1 egg, beaten
½ cup milk
2 cups dried apples, cooked
½ teaspoon each of ground cinnamon and nutmeg

1 tablespoon sugar
Fat for deep frying

Sift together flour, salt, and baking powder. Cut in butter. Add egg and milk and mix to a soft dough. Roll out thin and cut into 5-inch circles. In the center of each, place ½ cup dried apples sprinkled with spices and sugar. Fold over, wet edges with milk, and seal with a fork. Fry in hot fat (370°F. on a frying thermometer) until golden brown. Then drain. Serve warm with cream, if desired. Makes 4.

DRIED-FRUIT COMPOTE

½ cup each of dried apples, apricots, peaches, pears, and prunes
Juice of 1 lemon
Sugar to taste

Combine all dried fruits. Cover with water, add lemon juice and simmer, covered, until fruits are tender. To keep fruits whole, do not stir too vigorously. Add more water if necessary to keep from sticking. Add sugar to taste. Chill until ready to serve. Spoon mixture into compote dishes. Serve with cookies. Makes 8 to 10 servings.

APRICOT-RICE CUSTARD

⅓ cup uncooked rice
3 cups milk
¼ teaspoon salt
Grated rind of 1 orange
¾ cup sugar
2 egg yolks
2 cups cooked apricots
2 egg whites
⅛ teaspoon salt

Cook rice, milk, salt, and rind in top part of double boiler until rice is tender. Add hot rice gradually to ½ cup sugar and beaten yolks. Place apricots in baking dish; pour rice custard over fruit. Beat egg whites until foamy. Add salt, then remaining ¼ cup sugar gradually, continuing to beat until stiff. Bake rice and fruit in preheated moderate oven (350°F.) for 10 minutes; spread with meringue and bake for 18 minutes longer. Serve warm. Makes 4 servings.

APRICOT-COCONUT BALLS

2 tablespoons soft butter
½ cup light corn syrup
1 tablespoon water
½ teaspoon vanilla extract
⅔ cup nonfat milk crystals
2 cups finely chopped dried apricots
2 cups flaked coconut
Confectioners' sugar

Blend butter and corn syrup. Stir in water, vanilla, and milk crystals. Mix apricots and coconut. Add to first mixture and knead until well blended. Shape into ¾-inch balls. Roll in confectioners' sugar. Makes 42.
Note: These keep well.

DRIED APPLE CAKE

3 cups dried apples
1 cup molasses
1 cup butter or margarine

2 cups sugar
4 cups sifted all-purpose flour
2 cups raisins, finely chopped
2 cups nuts, finely chopped
1 pound dates, finely chopped
½ teaspoon salt
2 teaspoons each of baking soda, ground allspice, and nutmeg
1 teaspoon ground cinnamon

Soak dried apples overnight in just enough water to cover. In the morning, drain well and chop apples fine. Add molasses and simmer slowly until tender. Cool. Cream butter and sugar until light and fluffy. Sift a little flour over the raisins, nuts, and dates. Resift remainder of flour with salt, soda, and spices and stir into butter mixture, mixing well. Add raisins, nuts, and dates; when well blended stir in apples and molasses. Turn into two loaf pans (9 x 5 x 3 inches) lined on bottom with wax paper. Bake in preheated moderate oven (350°F.) for about 1 hour. Cool for 5 minutes; turn out on rack and peel off paper. Cool, and frost as desired. Makes 2 loaves.

RAISIN SPICECAKE

6 tablespoons shortening or sausage fat
¾ cup dark corn syrup
1 egg, separated
1½ cups sifted all-purpose flour
1 teaspoon baking powder
¼ teaspoon each of baking soda and salt
¾ teaspoon ground cinnamon
¼ teaspoon each of ground cloves and nutmeg
⅓ cup buttermilk or sour milk
⅓ cup raisins

Cream shortening; add syrup gradually, beating until mixture is light and fluffy. Add egg yolk and beat well. Sift dry ingredients together and add to first mixture alternately with buttermilk. Fold in raisins and stiffly beaten egg white. Pour into 8-inch square pan lined on bottom with waxed paper. Bake in preheated moderate oven (350°F.) for about 45 minutes. Cool for 5 minutes. Turn out on rack and peel off paper. Cool, and frost as desired. Makes 6 to 8 servings.

FRUIT-FILLED COOKIES

½ cup shortening
1 cup sugar
2 eggs
½ teaspoon salt
2½ cups sifted all-purpose flour
2 teaspoons baking powder
½ teaspoon ground nutmeg
Fruit Filling

Cream shortening and sugar. Add eggs, one at a time, beating until light after each addition. Add sifted dry ingredients and mix well. Roll dough out thin on a lightly floured board. Cut with 3-inch cutter, using doughnut cutter with hole for half of dough. Put rounds on greased cookie sheet ½ inch apart. Put a heaping teaspoon of Fruit Filling on each cookie and spread almost to edge; cover with circles cut with doughnut cutter and press edges with fork. Bake in preheated hot oven (400°F.) for about 10 minutes. Makes about 2 dozen.

Fruit Filling

¾ cup Tutti-Frutti (see recipe below)
½ cup sugar
¼ teaspoon salt
½ cup water
Juice and grated rind of 1 lemon
1 tablespoon butter or margarine

Mix all ingredients in saucepan; bring to boil. Cool.

EAST INDIAN DATE CHUTNEY

In saucepan mix 2 cups cider vinegar, 1 cup sugar, ½ cup water, and ½ teaspoon instant minced garlic. Bring to boil and cook for 3 minutes. Stir in 2 pounds coarsely chopped dates, ½ teaspoon cayenne, 1½ teaspoons ground ginger, and ¼ teaspoon salt. Cook, stirring, for 5 to 10 minutes. Pack in 4 hot sterilized ½-pint jars; seal.

Note: Good with curries, ham, and poultry.

TUTTI-FRUTTI

½ pound prunes
½ pound figs
2 packages (7¼ ounces each) pitted dates
1 package (15 ounces) golden or seeded raisins
½ pound apricots
1 cup nuts (optional)

Pit prunes and remove stems from figs. Force fruits through food chopper, using coarse blade. If fruit is alternated as it goes into chopper, it will come out already mixed. Put in covered jar or refrigerator dishes. Mixture will keep for several weeks on pantry shelf, for several months in refrigerator. It is not necessary to use this exact combination of fruits; others may be used because all dried fruits blend well. Grind 1 cup nuts with fruit if desired. Makes about 1 quart.

HOW TO USE TUTTI-FRUTTI

■ **Confection**—Roll mixture into 1-inch balls, or press into buttered flat pan and cut into bars or squares.

■ **Dressing**—Fill apples or pears to be baked; add a little to savory bread dressing for duck or goose.

■ **Filling for Tart Shells or Fried Pies**—Thin with fruit juice or water; sweeten. Add chopped nuts if desired.

■ **Sandwich Filling**—Thin with mayonnaise, top milk, or cooked salad dressing.

■ **Sauce**—Thin with fruit juice or water; sweeten. Heat if desired.

■ **Sprinkles**—Dress up cakes, puddings, biscuits, salads, pies, and cookies by sprinkling bits of Tutti-Frutti over them.

DRIP—This refers to a steady flow of liquid, drop by drop. The word is most often used in reference to making jelly: fruit juice is allowed to drip through several thicknesses of cheesecloth. It is also used when making mayonnaise or hollandaise: oil or butter is dripped into other ingredients to prevent curdling; or in cheese making: the whey drips out of the curd.

All of the following are done for flavor and appearance. Melted butter or other fats may be dripped over meats or strudel; frosting dripped over hot quick or yeast breads; melted chocolate dripped down the sides of a frosted cake.

DRIPPINGS—The term applies to any fat or juice that is drawn from food during cooking: i.e., bacon drippings, roast beef drippings, roast chicken drippings, salt pork drippings, ham drippings, lamb drippings.

Fat from drippings can be used as shortening in making gravies, sauces, piecrust, cookies, biscuits, breads, etc.

DROP—In reference to food and food preparation, the word has two meanings. In its first sense, it is a unit of measure for a minute amount of liquid which is usually measured out with an eye dropper or glass tube with a rubber squeeze-top. It is used for measuring flavoring extracts and food colorings as well as to indicate the rate of flow as in "add oil drop by drop."

In its second sense, the word "drop" describes a batter or dough of a certain soft consistency, which needs a spoon for shaping, such as in drop cookies, drop biscuits, drop dumplings, etc.

DRY—To dry food is to remove the moisture in it naturally by exposing the food to the sun or air. (All food has a considerable water content, whether we see it or not.) The reason for drying foods, a practice as old as history, is to preserve them by reducing water spoilage, such as molding, fermentation, or rotting. The small volume and weight of dried foods also makes them convenient to store and to transport.

Dry can also mean to remove moisture from the surface of a food by wiping it with a dry cloth, such as "wash chicken and pat dry."

In still another meaning, dry is used to describe wines lacking sweetness.

Duck Cook Book

DUCK—The duck is a dark-fleshed, web-footed water bird closely related to swans and geese. There are many species of this handsome and cosmopolitan fowl found on every continent except Antarctica. Primarily aquatic in their habits, the majority live in or near fresh water, although there are some that prefer the ocean, frequenting estuaries and seacoasts. The duck is well provided for his watery life by dense plumage that is kept constantly oiled and waterproofed by an oil gland at the base of the tail. Underneath lies a warm coat of down, offering protection against the cold.

Ducks have been hunted since the beginning of recorded time. Egyptians depicted them in their hieroglyphics, and were in the habit of drying and salting them in order to have a constant supply on hand.

The Chinese were the first people known to have bred ducks for food, and by the 1st century of the Christian era ducks had been domesticated in Europe. The Romans fattened their ducks on figs and dates and served them sprinkled with wine and perfumed with truffles. Apicius, the Roman gourmet, gives us a number of sauces suitable for crane or duck.

Among the various game birds, the duck is the most sought after. Duck hunters have many tales to illustrate the sagacity of the wild and wary black duck. This cautious bird is as tasty as he is intelligent, judging from the relish with which he was consumed by the lumberjacks in "The Great Black Duck Dinner" by Paul Bunyan. Another canny customer is the canvasback, with the green-winged teal and pintail not far behind. The flavor of wild duck depends on their diet. Those that feed on grains and greens are delicious throughout the season.

All domestic ducks are derived from either the mallard, *Anas platyrhynchos,* or the Muscovy duck, *Cairina moschata.* The mallard is a native of the Northern hemisphere. The Muscovy duck (the name is a corruption of "musk duck") is a native of Central and South America. It was known to the Mayans and most certainly domesticated before the 16th century. It was first introduced into Europe by the Spaniards after their conquest of Peru.

Long Island is the home of the largest duck-raising industry in the United States. Here, not seventy-five miles from New York City, live half of the ducks raised in this country. And they are all descended from three ducks and a drake which were brought from China in 1873. These White Pekin ducks were a variety of mallard and the pride of the imperial aviaries in Peking. There is some question as to who first brought them here. One version credits Captain James E. Palmer of Stonington, Connecticut, with first bringing the Pekin duck to America. The date is given as March 14, 1873. However, a Mr. McGrath of the firm of Fogg and Co., engaged in trade with China and Japan, claimed to have returned with the famous Pekin duck in the same year.

What there is no doubt about is the fact that the Americans knew a good bird when they saw one. In 1882, besides eastern breeders of the Pekin duck, there were breeders in Indiana, Kansas, Ohio, and Napa, California. Today about five million ducks are raised in this country each year. Since practically all the ducks sold in the United States are young birds, the words duck and duckling are used interchangeably.

In Europe, duck is prized as one of the greatest of all table delicacies and cooked in varied ways, especially in France. The most famous French ducklings come from Rouen. Another people excelling in duck cookery are the Danes. Danish duck is stuffed with apples and/or prunes, roasted, and served garnished with more apples and prunes.

Availability—The season for fresh duck is May through January. Frozen duck is available all year round. Duck livers are sometimes sold in bulk.

Purchasing Guide—Ducks come in two types: broiler or fryer duckling, a very young duck under 8 weeks of age, and roaster duckling, aged 8 to 16 weeks. Ducklings generally weigh 3 to 5½ pounds. Most come ready-to-cook, that is, fully eviscerated and without head and feet. When buying fresh duck, look for one which is well developed, moderately long and broad-breasted; well covered with flesh throughout the entire length of the bird, with breast and back well covered with fat; and practically free of pinfeathers. The skin should be unbruised and unbroken, soft and elastic rather than stiff or flabby.

Frozen ducklings should be well wrapped, to prevent exposure of skin to air.

Storage—Fresh duck should be loosely covered and placed in the coldest part of the refrigerator. Store giblets separately and use as soon as possible. Refrigerate cooked duck as soon as possible, with any stuffing removed, wrapped, and refrigerated separately.

☐ Fresh, refrigerator shelf, raw: 2 to 3 days
☐ Fresh, refrigerator shelf, cooked: 1 to 2 days
☐ Frozen, refrigerator shelf: 5 days
☐ Frozen, freezer: about 3 months
  Do not refreeze thawed duck.

Nutritive Food Values—Duck is an excellent source of high-quality protein and a fair source of iron. It is higher in fat and therefore higher in calories than other poultry.

☐ 3½ ounces, raw = 326 calories

Basic Preparation—Rinse duck, inside and out, under running water; pat dry. If duck is frozen, thaw in refrigerator, allowing 24 to 36 hours; or place packaged bird in cold water for 1 to 3 hours, until it is pliable. Use duck as soon as it has thawed.

If stuffing is prepared in advance, refrigerate separately until ready to roast.

☐ To Roast, Whole

1. Remove giblets and neck from duckling. Wash duckling and dry on absorbent paper.

2. To stuff for roasting, fill neck and body cavities with stuffing, about 1 quart.

3. To truss, fasten neck skin to back with skewer. Loop a cord around leg ends and bring together; tie.

4. Prick or score skin to allow fat to drain properly.

5. Rub outside of duck with salt. Pricking the skin and rubbing with salt helps to crisp the skin.

6. Put in shallow roasting pan on rack that is level with, or slightly higher than, top of pan. The range broiler pan with rack in place is excellent.

7. Roast in preheated slow oven (325° F.). A 4- to 5-pound stuffed duckling requires from 2½ to 3 hours. Pour off excess fat. This time can be shortened for those who like moister duck.

8. To glaze: About 30 minutes before duck is done, drain or spoon off drippings down to the brown meat juices. Increase oven temperature to hot (400°F.). Brush skin with mixture of 2 tablespoons honey and 1 tablespoon gravy sauce. Finish cooking, basting occasionally.

For added color and a crisper skin, increase the oven temperature to 425°F. for the last 10 minutes of roasting time. (Duck is so fatty that roasting in foil is not recommended.) Duckling is done when drumstick meat is soft when pressed between protected fingers.

☐ To Roast, Halves and Quarters

1. Roast halves or quarters, skin side up, on rack in shallow pan in preheated slow oven (325°F.) for 1½ to 2 hours.

2. Pour off excess fat. Increase temperature to hot (400°F.).

3. Brush with mixture of 2 tablespoons honey and 1 teaspoon gravy sauce.

4. Cook for 15 to 20 minutes longer, or until duckling is fork-tender and well browned.

☐ To Roast in Rotisserie

1. Wash duckling and dry on absorbent paper.

2. Score skin as for grilled duckling. Season inside and out with salt, pepper, paprika, and one of the following: chopped garlic, marjoram, or poultry seasoning. If desired, put 1 orange or 1 apple, quartered, in cavity.

3. Skewer neck skin to back; tie cord crisscross fashion around duckling beginning at neck and ending with legs. Insert spit rod through center of body cavity. Insert holding prongs firmly at both ends of duckling; tighten set screws, balancing duckling carefully.

(If using a charcoal rotisserie, arrange hot charcoal briquets at back of firebox. Put a foil drip pan in front of briquets. To make drip pan, use a double thickness of heavy-duty foil. Pan should be about 1½ inches deep and 5 inches longer than the duckling on the spit.) Pour in a few tablespoons of water. Attach spit with duckling carefully balanced and start motor as rotisserie manufacturer directs.

4. Cook in rotisserie for about 1½ to 2 hours for a 4- to 5-pound duckling. Pour off excess fat. If desired, brush with barbecue sauce occasionally during last 30 to 45 minutes of cooking. Duckling is done when drumstick feels very soft when pressed between protected fingers. (Cook 2½ to 3 hours in charcoal rotisserie.)

☐ To Broil

1. Wash duckling and dry on absorbent paper.

2. Split and remove backbone, using a sharp knife or poultry shears.

3. Put duckling, skin side down, on rack of broiler pan. Season, rubbing skin with herbs or cut garlic clove, if desired.

4. Put broiler pan 7 to 8 inches below heat to broil slowly. Turn at end of 30 minutes. Continue broiling, turning occasionally, until done.

5. A 4- to 5-pound duckling, split, will require 1 to 1¼ hours of broiling time. During last 10 minutes of cooking, brush with 2 tablespoons honey or syrup mixed with 1 tablespoon gravy sauce.

6. Broil until duckling is fork-tender and well browned.

☐ To Grill Outdoors—Duckling is partially roasted indoors before grilling. Wash duckling and dry on absorbent paper. With sharp knife, score skin over entire duckling at intervals of 1 inch. Quarter duckling, removing backbone. Remove first two joints of wings. Season quarters inside and out with salt, pepper, and paprika. If desired, rub skin and cut side with a garlic clove before seasoning. Arrange quarters in bottom of shallow baking pan. Toss 1 cup chopped celery and ½ cup chopped onion over duckling. Roast in preheated slow oven (325°F.) for 1½ hours. Drain drippings and wipe pieces of duck with absorbent paper. Refrigerate until ready to grill.

1. Start fire about 1 hour before serving time. After 45 minutes arrange duckling quarters directly on grill 3 to 5 inches above hot coals. Lighted briquets should be almost covered with a fine gray ash before putting duckling on grill.

2. Grill, turning occasionally, until well browned and thickest portions are fork-tender, 15 to 30 minutes. Test breast near shoulder joint for doneness.

3. If desired, brush duckling with barbecue sauce during grilling. Use your own recipe or bottled barbecue sauce.

☐ To Bone—Wash and pat dry. Remove wings. With a sharp, small pointed knife, cut the bird down the center back to the tail. Remove the tail section. Using the point of the knife against the bones of the bird, cut away the skin and flesh from the back and ribs. When the legs are reached, cut the joint at the hip to remove the leg, bone and all. Do the same with the wings. Continue cutting the meat away from the bones until the breastbone is reached. Carefully cut the skin away from the top of the breastbone. With the sharp knife, cut and scrape away the meat from the leg and wing bones. In doing this the wing and leg will be turned inside out when the bone is removed. Turn legs and wings right side out. Now the bird is ready for stuffing or rolling.

☐ To Quarter—Use poultry or kitchen shears. Cut duckling into halves lengthwise; with bird breast up, start from opening, cutting through skin, meat, and bone. Keep close to top of wishbone. Turn bird carefully over on breast and complete cutting, going through center of back. This splits duckling lengthwise. Divide each half into two pieces, cutting just above leg. Arrange on serving platter by pushing quarters together to resemble whole duckling.

☐ To Cook Giblets—Wash giblets and neck. Simmer in salted water to which celery stalks and onion have been added. Cook giblets (except liver) and neck for 1½ to 2 hours. Add liver for last 15 minutes of cooking. Chop giblets and add to gravy, casseroles, or rice. Use giblet broth as cooking liquid for rice.

Timetable for Roasting
Stuffed, Chilled Duck and Unstuffed Duck

READY-TO-COOK WEIGHT	AMOUNT OF STUFFING (Cups)	APPROXIMATE TOTAL COOKING TIME AT 325°F. (Hours)
3 to 4 pounds	2 to 3	2½ to 2¾
4 to 5 pounds	3 to 4	2¾ to 3

BRAISED DUCKLING

4- to 5-pound duckling, cut into serving pieces
1 tablespoon fat
½ pound mushrooms, sliced
3 tablespoons all-purpose flour
3 cups water
1½ teaspoons salt
¼ teaspoon pepper
1 bay leaf
Dash of ground thyme
1 onion, studded with 3 cloves
½ cup port

Wash duckling and dry on absorbent paper. Brown pieces on all sides in hot fat in skillet for at least 30 minutes. Remove duckling and pour off all but 3 tablespoons fat. Cook mushrooms in fat for 5 minutes and blend in flour. Stir in water and bring to boil. Return duckling to skillet and add remaining ingredients. Bring to boil, cover, and simmer for 1 to 1½ hours, or until tender. Remove bay leaf and onion. Add port, heat, and serve with rice if desired. Makes 4 servings.

ROAST DUCKLING À L'ORANGE

1 duckling, about 5 pounds
Salt and pepper
2 oranges
½ cup consommé
½ cup dry white wine or fresh orange juice
1 teaspoon cornstarch
Thin slices of unpeeled orange

Sprinkle body cavity of duckling with salt and pepper. Truss bird and put on rack in shallow roasting pan. Peel oranges and cut in quarters. Scrape white pulp from peel and cut enough peel in thin strips to make 1 tablespoonful. Add to duck with the consommé. Roast uncovered in preheated slow oven (325°F.) for about 3 hours, basting occasionally with some of the liquid in the bottom of the pan. When duck is done, remove to hot platter. Pour off all but ½ cup of the liquid. Add wine to ½ cup liquid. Blend cornstarch with small amount of cold water and stir into sauce. Cook, stirring, until thickened. Pour over duckling. Garnish with orange slices. Makes 4 servings.

BONED ROAST DUCKLING WITH SAVORY RICE

4- pound duckling
Onion salt, pepper, salt
½ bay leaf
1 small garlic clove
1 chicken bouillon cube
1 cup raw long-grain rice
1 onion, chopped
¼ cup each of chopped celery tops and parsley
¼ cup butter or margarine
1 teaspoon each of ground marjoram and sage
1 can (3 ounces) sliced mushrooms, undrained
1½ tablespoons all-purpose flour

Roast Ducks with Giblet Gravy

Wash duckling and sprinkle generously inside and out with onion salt and pepper. Put breast side up on rack in shallow pan. Roast, uncovered, in preheated slow oven (325°F.) for 2½ hours. Pour off fat after 1 hour.

Cover neck, giblets, and wing tips with water; add ½ teaspoon salt, bay leaf, and garlic. Cook, covered, for 10 minutes; remove liver. Continue cooking for 50 minutes more. Chop giblets, including liver and neck meat. Add bouillon cube and enough water to broth to make 2 cups. Bring to boil and stir in rice. Cover and simmer for 20 minutes, or until rice is tender. Sauté onion, celery, and parsley in butter for 5 minutes. Add giblets, neck meat, herbs, and mushrooms. Stir into rice with fork. Season with salt and pepper.

Cool duckling. Pour off fat and add 1½ cups water to pan. Cook over low heat, scraping brown bits from pan. Blend in flour mixed with a little cold water. Cook until slightly thickened. Season if necessary. Line shallow pan with foil. With sharp knife, split breast off duck into 2 long pieces, keeping skin in place. Slip larger pieces of meat off wing, drumsticks, and thighbone. Arrange in pile in pan and cover with 1 piece of breast, skin side up. Do the same with the other side. Cover with foil and reheat in slow oven (325°F.) for 25 minutes before serving. Remove foil and put under broiler to crisp skin. To serve, lift each portion with pancake turner to plate. Arrange reheated rice beside duck and serve with gravy. Makes 2 servings.

DUCKLINGS VARSOVIA

    2 ducklings (4 pounds each), cut into
        serving pieces
        Salt and pepper
    1 large head red cabbage
        Juice of 1 lemon
    1 onion, chopped
    2 ounces fat salt pork, diced
    1 tablespoon all-purpose flour
    ¾ cup red-wine vinegar
    ¼ cup water
    1½ tablespoons caraway seeds
    1 tablespoon light brown sugar

Wash ducklings and dry on absorbent paper. Put in shallow pan and season with salt and pepper. Roast in preheated moderate oven (375°F.) until well browned. Shred cabbage and blanch with boiling water. Sprinkle with lemon juice. In Dutch oven, sauté onion and pork until lightly browned. Blend in flour. Add remaining ingredients and salt and pepper to taste. Bring to boil, cover, and simmer for 20 minutes. Put browned ducklings on cabbage. Pour off fat from pan. Add ¼ cup hot water to pan and scrape up brown bits. Pour over ducklings; cover and simmer for about 1½ hours, or until duck is tender, adding a little water when needed. Serve ducklings on a hot platter

surrounded with the cabbage. Makes 4 to 6 servings.

DUCKLINGS IN CLARET

    2 ducklings (4 to 5 pounds each), cut
        into serving pieces
    2 cups claret
    ½ cup brandy
    2 onions, chopped
    1 garlic clove, slivered
    8 parsley sprigs, minced
    1 small bay leaf
        Pinch of ground thyme
    ¼ cup cooking oil
    2 cups sliced fresh mushrooms
        Salt and pepper

Wash ducklings and dry on absorbent paper. Put pieces in a deep dish. Mix next 7 ingredients and pour over duckling. Marinate for 5 hours, turning pieces occasionally. Drain ducklings and put marinade through a fine sieve or blender. Brown ducklings in hot oil; put in a heavy kettle and add marinade. Bring to boil, cover, and simmer for 1½ to 2 hours, or until ducklings are tender. Add mushrooms and cook for 15 minutes longer. Spoon off fat, and season to taste. Makes 6 to 8 servings.

DUCK CHOW MEIN

    1 cup sliced onion
    1½ cups sliced celery
    2 tablespoons butter, margarine, or
        cooking oil
    1 green pepper, sliced
    1 cup gravy or broth
    2⅓ cups (one 1-pound, 3-ounce can)
        bean sprouts, undrained
    1 to 2 tablespoons soy sauce
    1 teaspoon dark molasses
    1 cup slivered cooked duckling
        Salt and pepper
        Chow-mein noodles

Sauté onion and celery in butter for 5 minutes. Add green pepper and cook for 1 minute. Add gravy or broth. (If broth is used, thicken with 1½ teaspoons cornstarch blended with a little cold water.) Add bean sprouts, soy sauce, molasses, and duck, saving a few slivers for garnish. Heat to boiling, and season to taste. Garnish with reserved duck slices. Serve with noodles and more soy sauce. Makes 4 servings.

VIENNESE GIBLET FRICASSEE

        Necks, giblets, and livers from 2 to 3
        ducklings
        Water
    1 carrot
    1 leek
    1 celery stalk
    1 small parsnip
        Few parsley sprigs
    2 chicken bouillon cubes
    ½ cup sliced fresh or canned mushrooms
    2 tablespoons butter or margarine,
        melted
    2 tablespoons all-purpose flour
    1 tablespoon fresh lemon juice
        Salt, pepper, paprika to taste
    1 egg yolk
    2 teaspoons light cream

Cut necks and giblets into bite-size pieces. Cut livers into pieces, but keep

separate. Cover necks and giblets with water and add next 6 ingredients. Bring to boil, cover, and simmer for about 50 minutes. Add livers and mushrooms; cook for 15 minutes longer. Remove vegetables and pour off 2 cups broth, adding water if necessary to make the amount. Cream butter and flour and add paste to broth. Cook over low heat, stirring constantly, until smooth and thick. Add to giblets with lemon juice and seasonings. Bring to boil, remove from heat, and beat gradually into egg yolk beaten with cream. Serve over riced or whipped potatoes and garnish with minced parsley, if desired. Makes 2 to 3 servings.

Note: When serving ducklings, reserve the necks and giblets to make this delicious luncheon dish.

STUFFINGS

PRUNE-APPLE-RAISIN STUFFING

    ¼ cup each of chopped cooked prunes
        and seedless raisins
    1 cup chopped tart apples
    2½ cups toasted bread cubes
    2 tablespoons melted butter or
        margarine
    2 tablespoons dark brown sugar
        Grated rind of ½ lemon
    ¼ teaspoon each of paprika and ground
        cinnamon
    ½ teaspoon salt
    ⅓ cup apple juice or cider

Mix all ingredients. Stuff bird, truss, and roast as for Roast Duckling, page 581. Makes enough stuffing for 4- to 5-pound bird.

APPLE CORN-BREAD STUFFING

    1 small onion, minced
    ⅓ cup melted fat from duck
    4 cups crumbled corn bread
    1 cup diced unpeeled red apple
    1 teaspoon poultry seasoning
        Dash of pepper
    ½ cup hot giblet stock

Cook onion in fat until golden. Add to remaining ingredients and mix well. Stuff bird, truss, and roast as for Roast Duckling, page 581. Makes enough stuffing for a 5- to 6-pound bird.

APRICOT STUFFING

    3 cups toasted bread cubes
    ⅔ cup finely chopped dried apricots
    ¼ teaspoon salt
    ⅛ teaspoon each of white pepper and
        monosodium glutamate
    ⅛ teaspoon each of ground thyme,
        nutmeg, and cloves
    2 tablespoons butter or margarine,
        melted
    1 egg, beaten

Toss together bread, apricots, and seasonings. Combine butter and egg and add to first mixture. Stuff bird, truss, and roast as for Roast Duckling, page 581. Makes enough stuffing for a 5-pound bird.

Chicken with Dumplings

DUMPLING—A small amount of dough, usually shaped into a ball and cooked by boiling or steaming. Although dumplings are part of standard English and Scandinavian cooking, there is a "dumpling belt" in Central Europe, stretching from Alsace to Poland, and taking in southern Germany, northern Switzerland, and the whole of Austria and Czechoslovakia. Here the dumpling reigns supreme.

Dumplings can be made from bread or bread crumbs, potatoes, crackers, flour, and other cereal grains. They can be leavened with eggs, baking powder, or yeast. The liquid can be milk, stock, water, etc., and usually in only small amounts. To make them tender use butter, lard, shortening, meat drippings, suet, etc. Dumplings can be filled with meat, liver, cheese, or fruit, either separately or in savory or sweet mixtures.

Basic Preparation—Use a large pan to allow for the swelling of dumplings during cooking. Cook dumplings in liquid that just *simmers*. Cook uncovered until dumplings rise to the surface; then cover the pan until dumplings are done; test with a toothpick or cake tester. Drain well.

When cooking dumplings by placing them on a stew, cover the pan as soon as they are placed on the stew.

SOUP DUMPLINGS

BREAD DUMPLINGS

3 cups ½-inch cubes of white bread
¼ cup all-purpose flour
1 tablespoon each of finely chopped onion and parsley
¾ teaspoon salt
¼ teaspoon baking powder
¼ teaspoon pepper
1 egg, lightly beaten
½ cup milk
1 tablespoon melted butter
5 cups prepared soup or broth

Combine bread cubes, flour, onion, parsley, salt, baking powder, and pepper in a bowl. Combine egg, milk, and butter and add all at once to the bread mixture. Stir well and let stand for 10 minutes. Using the fingertips, shape the mixture firmly into 16 balls about the size of large walnuts. Bring the soup to simmering and lower the balls in gently. Cook gently, uncovered, for 7 to 8 minutes. Makes 6 to 8 servings.

BUTTERKLÖSSE
(Butter Dumplings)

2 tablespoons butter
2 eggs
6 tablespoons all-purpose flour
¼ teaspoon salt

Cream butter until soft. Beat in eggs. Stir

in flour and salt. Drop batter by teaspoonfuls into simmering soup and simmer, covered, for 8 minutes. Makes 3 to 4 servings.

KNAIDLACH
(Matzo Balls)

4 eggs
⅓ cup melted shortening
1 cup matzo meal
⅓ cup water
1 teaspoon salt
Dash of pepper

Beat eggs and combine with remaining ingredients. Let stand for 20 minutes. Shape mixture into balls about the size of a walnut and drop into simmering chicken soup or salted boiling water. Cover and boil for 20 minutes. If cooked in water, drain and then serve in clear soup. Makes 6 servings.

FARINA BALLS

2 cups milk
½ cup farina or cream of wheat
1 tablespoon butter
½ teaspoon salt
2 eggs

Heat milk to the boiling point. Stir in remaining ingredients except eggs. Cook over low heat, stirring constantly, until mixture becomes thick. Beat in eggs, one at a time. Let mixture rest for 1 hour. Drop batter by teaspoonfuls into simmering soup stock. Cover and simmer for 10 minutes. Makes about 24 to 26.

LIVER DUMPLINGS

½ pound beef, pork, or lamb liver
1 small onion
¾ teaspoon salt
    Dash each of pepper, ground nutmeg, and marjoram
1 egg, beaten
1 tablespoon melted cooking fat
1 cup soft bread crumbs
    Clear tomato soup or meat broth

Remove membrane and large tubes from liver; force liver and peeled onion through food chopper, using fine blade. Add seasonings, egg, fat, and crumbs; mix well. Drop by teaspoonfuls into boiling tomato soup. Cover and simmer for 15 minutes. Makes 20.

STEWS WITH DUMPLINGS

HAMBURGER STEW WITH DUMPLINGS

2 slices of dry bread
    Water
1 garlic clove, minced
1 pound ground beef
¼ teaspoon pepper
2½ teaspoons salt
2 cups each of diced carrots, potatoes, and turnips
    Dumpling Batter

Break bread into ½ cup hot water and soak for 5 minutes. Add garlic, beef, pepper, and 1 teaspoon salt; mix well and shape into 8 patties. Brown in heavy kettle. Add 1 quart water; cover and cook for 20 minutes. Add vegetables and remaining salt; cook for about 5 minutes. Drop Dumpling Batter by teaspoonfuls into gently boiling stew. Cover and cook for 15 minutes without removing cover. Makes 4 servings.

Dumpling Batter

2 cups sifted cake flour
1½ teaspoons baking powder
2 parsley sprigs, chopped
1 tablespoon shortening
½ cup plus 1 tablespoon milk
¾ teaspoon salt
¼ teaspoon celery seeds

Sift dry ingredients; add celery seeds and parsley. Cut in shortening and add milk all at once, mixing quickly and lightly just until flour is moistened.

BEEFSTEAK STEW AND DUMPLINGS

1½ pounds beef round steak
    Seasoned all-purpose flour
    Bacon fat
8 onions
2 cups water
6 to 8 each of small potatoes and carrots
    Flour-and-water paste
2 cups biscuit mix

Cut steak into cubes; dredge with seasoned flour and brown in a little bacon fat in Dutch oven. Add onions and water; cover and cook for 1 hour. Add potatoes and carrots and cook for 40 minutes. Thicken gravy with a flour-and-water paste. Make dumplings with biscuit mix as directed on package and cook on top of stew according to directions on package. Makes 4 servings.

CHICKEN WITH DUMPLINGS

1 frying chicken (about 2½ pounds), cut up
3 cups water
1 onion, chopped
½ bay leaf
2 lemon slices
    Salt and pepper
    Dumpling Batter

Wash chicken and simmer with all ingredients except dumplings for 35 minutes, or until tender. Remove bay leaf and lemon. Drop Dumpling Batter on top of chicken by teaspoonfuls. Cover tightly and simmer for 15 minutes without removing cover. Serve at once. Makes 4 servings.

Dumpling Batter

1 cup sifted all-purpose flour
1 teaspoon baking powder
¾ teaspoon salt
    Dash of ground mace or nutmeg
1 teaspoon minced onion
2 egg yolks
⅓ cup milk

Sift together dry ingredients and add onion. Beat egg yolks with milk and add to dry mixture. Mix lightly until blended.

BROWNED CHICKEN STEW WITH CORNMEAL DUMPLINGS

1 stewing chicken (4 to 4½ pounds), cut up
    Seasoned all-purpose flour
    Boiling water

1 teaspoon salt
    Cornmeal Dumpling Batter

Wash chicken and dry on absorbent paper. Roll in seasoned flour. Render some chicken fat in heavy kettle and brown chicken on all sides. Add 1 quart boiling water; cover and cook very slowly for 3½ to 4 hours, or until chicken is tender. (Seasonings such as onion, parsley, celery, and celery tops may be added if desired.) Add enough boiling water to barely cover chicken; add salt. Drop Cornmeal Dumpling Batter by teaspoonfuls onto gently cooking stew. Cover and cook for 20 minutes; do not remove cover for first 10 minutes. Serve at once. Makes 6 servings.

Cornmeal Dumpling Batter

1 cup cornmeal
1 cup sifted all-purpose flour
1 teaspoon baking powder
½ teaspoon baking soda
1 teaspoon salt
½ teaspoon poultry seasoning
1 tablespoon shortening
1 egg, well beaten
1 cup buttermilk
¼ cup chopped parsley

Sift dry ingredients together in a bowl; work in shortening with fork. Combine beaten egg, buttermilk, and parsley; add to dry ingredients, mixing only enough to moisten flour.

MAIN-COURSE DUMPLINGS

SPAETZLE
(German Egg Dumplings)

2 eggs, well beaten
1½ cups sifted all-purpose flour
½ cup water
½ teaspoon salt
¼ teaspoon baking powder

Beat all ingredients together well. Drop small bits from a teaspoon, press through a pastry bag or a colander, or use a special spaetzle cutter. Drop dough into salted simmering water. Simmer until done. Makes 4 servings.

Note: Try one dumpling before cooking all the batter. If dumplings are heavy, it may be necessary to add a little water to the batter.

FRANKFURTER-POTATO DUMPLINGS

1 egg, slightly beaten
4 cups cooked mashed potato
1 cup sifted all-purpose flour
1½ teaspoons salt
⅛ teaspoon pepper
3 frankfurters (about 6 ounces), cut into small cubes
1 small onion, chopped
2 tablespoons butter or margarine

Mix egg, potato, flour, salt, and pepper to make a smooth dough. Turn out on lightly floured board; roll out to ½-inch thickness. Cut with floured 2½- or 3-inch round cutter. Combine frankfurters and onion; place on half of rounds; cover with remaining rounds. Firmly press edges together. Boil for about 10 minutes in salted boiling water. Drain. Put a little butter on each; serve at once. Makes about 1 dozen.

POTATO DUMPLINGS

    6 medium-size potatoes
    2 eggs
1½ teaspoons salt
 ½ cup all-purpose flour
    1 slice of bread, crust removed, cut
      into ¼-inch cubes
  10 tablespoons butter
 ¼ cup dry bread crumbs
 ¼ cup chopped parsley

Scrub potatoes and place them in a saucepan. Cover with water and boil in their jackets, uncovered, until tender, about 30 minutes. Chill the potatoes well for 12 hours or longer. Peel and rice them. Add the eggs, salt, and flour to the riced potatoes. Beat the mixture with a fork until fluffy. Sauté bread cubes in 2 tablespoons butter. Roll potato mixture into 1-inch balls and place a bread cube in the middle of each. Roll the balls in flour. Drop the balls into 2 quarts salted boiling water, a few at a time. Cover when the dumplings rise to the surface and simmer for about 8 minutes. Remove from the pot with a slotted spoon and drain on paper towel. Pile in a serving dish. Melt remaining butter, stir in bread crumbs and parsley, and pour over dumplings. Makes 8 to 10 servings.

GNOCCHI ALL'ITALIANA
(Dumplings Italian Style)

2½ cups mashed boiled potatoes
    2 eggs, lightly beaten
      Salt
2¼ cups sifted all-purpose flour
    3 cups tomato sauce
    1 cup grated Parmesan cheese

Mix potatoes with eggs and ½ teaspoon salt. Add flour, about 1½ cups, until dough is stiff. Turn dough out on a board covered with remaining flour. Knead dough for 3 to 4 minutes. Add more flour if necessary to keep dough from sticking. Cut dough into 6 pieces. Roll dough into long sausagelike strips and cut each strip into 1-inch lengths. Sprinkle dumplings with flour. Boil 2 quarts of water with 2 tablespoons salt. Cook about ⅓ of dumplings at a time in simmering water. Remove with a slotted spoon as soon as they rise to the surface. Continue cooking remainder of dough, and place the gnocchi as they are finished in a hot serving dish. Heat tomato sauce mixed with two thirds of cheese, and pour over gnocchi. Sprinkle with remaining cheese and serve immediately. Makes 6 to 8 servings.

POT-CHEESE DUMPLINGS

    1 pound dry pot cheese
    2 eggs
    1 cup sifted all-purpose flour
    1 teaspoon salt
    3 quarts boiling water

Butter or margarine
    1 cup dairy sour cream

Mash cheese; add eggs and mix well. Stir in flour and salt. Drop by tablespoonfuls into rapidly boiling water; cover and boil for 15 minutes. Drain; serve with melted butter and sour cream. Makes 4 servings.

DESSERT DUMPLINGS

PEACH AND PLUM DUMPLINGS

    3 peaches
    4 plums, halved and pitted
 ½ cup sugar
 ¾ cup water
      Grated rind of 1 lemon
      Dumpling Batter

Peel peaches and slice into covered saucepan. Add plums, sugar, water, and lemon rind; bring to a boil. Drop Dumpling Batter by teaspoonfuls onto boiling fruit. Cover and boil gently for 25 minutes. Do not remove cover during cooking. Serve at once. Makes 4 servings.

Dumpling Batter

 ½ cup plus 2 tablespoons all-purpose
      flour
 ¾ teaspoon baking powder
2½ tablespoons sugar
      Few grains of salt
    2 tablespoons butter or margarine
2½ tablespoons milk
      Few drops of lemon extract

Sift dry ingredients into bowl; cut in butter. Add milk and extract, mixing lightly. Do *not* beat until smooth.

DUMPLINGS BAKED IN CARAMEL
SAUCE

 ⅓ cup sugar
    1 cup water
    1 cup pancake syrup
    1 teaspoon vanilla extract
      Dumpling Batter

Cook sugar slowly in large skillet with ovenproof handle, stirring constantly, until golden brown. Slowly add water, syrup, and vanilla. Boil for 2 minutes. Drop Dumpling Batter by tablespoonfuls into boiling sauce; make 8 dumplings. Bake in preheated hot oven (425°F.) for 15 minutes. Cool for a few minutes until syrup thickens slightly; turn out of skillet while warm. These dumplings are good cold as well as hot. Makes 8 servings.

Dumpling Batter

    2 cups cake flour
 ½ cup sugar
1½ teaspoons baking powder
 ½ teaspoon salt
    1 tablespoon melted shortening
 ½ cup milk

Sift dry ingredients together into a bowl. Add melted shortening and milk, mixing quickly and lightly until flour is moistened. Do *not* beat until smooth.

GRANDPÈRES
(Grandfathers)

    2 cups maple syrup
    2 cups water
    2 cups sifted all-purpose flour
    4 teaspoons baking powder
    1 teaspoon salt
    2 tablespoons shortening or butter
    1 cup milk

Combine maple syrup and water in a wide saucepan with tight-fitting lid. Bring to the boiling point. Sift and measure flour, sift again with baking powder and salt, and cut in shortening. Add milk all at once, mix rapidly, and drop by tablespoonfuls into the boiling syrup. Cover pan and cook over slightly lowered heat for about 15 minutes. Serve at once. Makes 6 servings.

DAMPFNUDELN
(Raised Dumplings)

 ½ package active dry yeast or ½ cake
      compressed yeast
 ¼ cup lukewarm water*
 ¼ cup milk, scalded
    3 tablespoons sugar
    9 tablespoons butter
 ½ teaspoon salt
    1 egg, well beaten
      About 1¾ cups sifted all-purpose flour
 ½ cup scalded milk or fruit juice

Add yeast to water. *Use very warm water (105°F. to 115°F.) for dry yeast; use lukewarm (80°F. to 90°F.) for compressed. Let stand for a few minutes, then stir until dissolved. Combine scalded milk, sugar, 1 tablespoon butter, salt, and egg. Cool to lukewarm and stir in yeast mixture. Add enough flour to make a stiff dough. Cover and let dough rise until doubled in bulk. Turn dough out on lightly floured board and knead lightly until smooth. Roll to ½-inch thickness and cut into 2-inch rounds. Let rise until doubled in bulk. Spoon remaining ½ cup butter into a Dutch oven. If dumplings are to be served with meat, add ½ cup scalded milk. If dumplings are to be served with fruit, use ½ cup juice from stewed fruit instead of milk. Add dumplings and cover tightly. Bake in preheated slow oven (275°F.) for 1½ hours. Serve immediately. Makes about 16.

DURUM WHEAT—This is a variety of wheat (*Triticum durum*), often called "hard" or "macaroni" wheat, with hard translucent kernels. In this country durum wheat is grown in the Dakotas and Minnesota. It is used chiefly for making macaroni and other pastas. Pasta products made from it do not disintegrate in cooking, but become tender while remaining firm.

dutch cookery

Holland is one of the loveliest, most efficient, and most civilized countries in the world. Architecture, flowers, sea, land, and sky blend into an enchanting picture. The Dutch have been fighting the sea for centuries, building dikes to prevent the waves from washing away their land. Equally admirable is the efficient way they make use of their land. Holland has the densest population (918) per square mile of any country in the world.

by C. Countess van Limburg Stirum

Every country has its own national food and Holland is no exception. The Dutch have their meadows with cattle, which means milk, butter, and meat; their canals and the sea, meaning fish. Vegetables and fruit grow extremely well in this not very cold but dampish climate. The basis of Dutch food is its freshness, and in Holland meals go with the seasons.

The Dutch are great soup eaters and often soup is the main dish of the meal. The famous Dutch pea soup is the best pea soup in the world, better warmed over than when first made, and a whole meal in itself.

Meat is eaten daily in Holland. The veal is excellent, and so is the pork, fresh or smoked. An interesting feature of Dutch cookery is the combination cooking of meat, vegetables, and fruit. Fish, though a popular food, is not as much a staple as it is in the Scandinavian countries.

Dutch vegetables are remarkably succulent and flavorful. They are eaten in large quantities and varieties. Potatoes, a national dish, are delicious, whether plain boiled, or eaten out-of-hand as French-fries, which are sold from street stands. Cabbage is the king of winter vegetables, cooked with meat and potatoes. The tender white asparagus and the frail young green beans make gourmets speechless with delight.

Another Dutch specialty is the thin pancake, which is made large or small, plain or with bacon or apples.

The Dutch are great bread eaters and various kinds of delicious light and dark breads are found on every table. So are the cheeses: wonderfully good and varied and eaten at every meal, including breakfast.

Much fruit is grown in Holland. Cherries, strawberries, apples, and grapes (these grown under glass) are as much a joy to the eye as to the palate.

The Dutch are dessert eaters. They serve simple puddings and fruits, fresh or cooked. Cookies are another Dutch delight. They are baked at home, especially at Christmas time, but many kinds are bought in the splendid bakeshops, which make them according to century-old recipes. Chocolate, for which Holland is famous, is a staple food; the children sprinkle it on their bread and butter.

The people of Holland are very attached to their traditions. At Christmas, they serve roast goose or roast duck. At Easter, they color eggs for the children and serve a special salad. The greatest fun is had all over Holland on Saint Nicholas Day, December 6th, when the Saint enters the towns, and asks the children if they have been good or bad during the year. He brings presents and the children are treated to an astonishing variety of sweets from gingerbread men and women, marzipan and apple fritters, to fried Dutch doughnuts.

APPETIZERS AND SOUPS

KAASTRUFFELS
(Cheese Truffles)

½ cup butter
3 tablespoons grated cheese
  Pepper, salt, celery salt,
  or paprika to taste
  Slices of stale pumpernickel,
  crumbled into fine crumbs

Cream butter until light and fluffy. Mix in cheese and desired spices. Roll mixture into small balls about the size of a large olive. Roll balls in bread crumbs. Makes about 12.
Note: These are very easy to make and do not need any cooking.

NIER SOEP
(Kidney Soup)

1 veal kidney
4 cups boiling chicken stock or 4 cups water and 4 chicken bouillon cubes
1 tablespoon minced onion
3 tablespoons butter or margarine
3 tablespoons all-purpose flour
1 cup light cream
1 can (3 ounces) chopped mushrooms, undrained
2 tablespoons Madeira

Remove any outer membrane from kidney. Split kidney in half lengthwise. With scissors, remove fat and white veins and wash kidney. Add to stock, cover and simmer for 15 minutes, or until kidney is tender. Remove, cool slightly and cut in dice. Sauté onion lightly in the butter and blend in flour. Add hot stock and cook, stirring, until thickened. Add cream, mushrooms, and kidney. Heat and serve. Makes 6 servings.

ERWTENSOEP
(Pea Soup)

3 cups split green peas
3 quarts water
2 pig's feet
1- pound piece of bacon
3 leeks
2 onions
2 tablespoons butter
2 tablespoons chopped parsley
1 cup chopped celery stalks with leaves
1 celery root or celeriac, peeled and cubed
½ pound skinless frankfurters
  Salt and pepper to taste
  Pumpernickel

Cook peas in the water until tender.

When peas are tender press mixture through a sieve or whirl in blender. To this, add pig's feet and simmer for 2 hours. Add extra water when necessary. Remove pig's feet, bone and cube meat, and add to soup. Add bacon. Clean and slice leeks and onions. Melt butter and sauté leeks and onions until tender but not brown. Add to soup with parsley, celery, and celery root. Simmer, covered, for 1 hour. Cut frankfurters into crosswise slices and add to soup. Remove from heat and let stand overnight. Reheat the next day. Add salt and pepper. Stir well since standing will make it thicker, and add a little more water if necessary. Remove bacon and cut into slices. Serve bacon slices on pumpernickel with the soup which has been reheated until piping hot. Makes 6 generous servings, for this is served as the whole meal.

GROENTESOEP MET BALLETJES
(Vegetable Soup with Meatballs)

3 cups diced fresh vegetables (leeks, carrots, beans, peas, parsley, celery, etc. **No** tomatoes)
3 tablespoons butter
6 cups water
1 teaspoon salt
2 tablespoons uncooked rice
  Soepballetjes

Sauté vegetables in hot butter until golden brown. Add the water, salt, and rice. Cover and cook at a simmer until vegetables are tender. Add Soepballetjes and simmer for 10 minutes. Makes 6 to 8 servings.

Soepballetjes (Soup Meatballs)

2 slices of white bread without crusts, soaked in a little milk
½ pound ground beef or veal
1 egg, well beaten
½ teaspoon salt
¼ teaspoon ground nutmeg

Combine all ingredients and roll into small balls. Makes about 16.

FISH

GESTOOFDE KABELJAUW OF SCHELVIS
MET AARDAPPELEN
(Baked Fillets of Haddock or Cod
with Potatoes)

2 onions, chopped
3 tablespoons butter or margarine
6 fillets of haddock or cod
1 pound potatoes (3 medium), peeled
3 eggs
½ teaspoon salt
1 cup dairy sour cream
  Soft bread crumbs

Sauté onions in butter until golden brown. Flatten the fish into thin pieces. Boil potatoes for 10 minutes. Drain and slice. In a greased ovenproof dish layer fish with potatoes, sprinkling each layer with browned onions. End with a layer of potatoes. Beat eggs with salt for a few minutes. Add sour cream and pour over the fish. Sprinkle with bread crumbs. Bake in preheated moderate oven (350°F.) for about 45 minutes. Makes 6 servings.

SNOEK IN WITTE WIJN SAUS
(Pike with White-Wine Sauce)

1 pike (about 4 pounds)
½ cup butter
1 tablespoon chopped parsley
1 medium onion, chopped
1 tablespoon chopped celery
1 teaspoon salt
¼ teaspoon each of pepper, ground
  nutmeg, and mace
1 cup white wine
1 cup water
  Soft bread crumbs
1 lemon, sliced
¼ cup all-purpose flour
1 tablespoon drained capers
2 egg yolks, beaten

Cut cleaned pike into pieces and arrange these in the original shape of fish in a greased ovenproof dish. Melt half of butter and sauté parsley, onion, and celery until transparent. Add spices, wine, and the water. Pour mixture over fish. Sprinkle with bread crumbs and put slices of lemon on top. Bake in preheated moderate oven (375°F.) for about 30 minutes, or until fish is tender. Melt remaining butter and stir in flour. Stir in 2 cups of liquid drained from fish. Cook over low heat, stirring constantly, until sauce is smooth and thick. Add capers and stir hot sauce gradually into beaten egg yolks. Serve the sauce with the fish. Makes 8 servings.

HARINGSLA
(Herring Salad)

1 head lettuce
3 pickled herrings, chopped
3 apples, diced
3 hard-cooked eggs, chopped
2 boiled beets, diced
8 cold boiled potatoes, peeled and
  mashed
3 dill pickles, sliced
½ medium onion, minced
  Salt and pepper to taste
  Salad oil
  Vinegar
  Mayonnaise

For Garnish

2 hard-cooked eggs
  Dill-pickle slices
  Fresh parsley

Place lettuce leaves on an oblong dish. Mix the next 9 ingredients with enough oil and vinegar to make a solid mixture. Spread mixture on the lettuce leaves like a pudding. Cover with a thick coating of mayonnaise.

For garnish, chop the whites of the eggs and rub yolks through a sieve. Use with pickle slices and parsley. Makes 8 servings.

GARNALEN CROQUETTEN
(Shrimp Croquettes)

3 tablespoons butter
¼ cup all-purpose flour
½ teaspoon salt
⅛ teaspoon pepper
1 cup milk
2 cups minced cooked shrimps
1 tablespoon chopped parsley
¼ teaspoon nutmeg
1½ cups fine, dry bread crumbs
1 egg
2 tablespoons water
  Fat for frying

Melt butter and blend in flour, salt, and pepper. Gradually add milk and cook, stirring constantly, until smooth and thickened. Stir in shrimps, parsley, and nutmeg. Spread mixture on a flat dish and cool. Divide mixture into 12 equal parts. Shape each into a roll about 2 inches long. Roll in crumbs, then in egg beaten with the water. Roll again in crumbs. Let stand for 30 minutes. Then fry in hot deep fat (390°F. on a frying thermometer) until golden brown. Drain on absorbent paper. Makes 12 croquettes, or 4 servings.

OSSENHAAS À LA JARDINIÈRE
(Filet of Beef with Vegetables)

1 Filet of beef (about 2 pounds)
  Suet
6 tablespoons butter
  Salt and pepper to taste
  Various vegetables:
    cauliflower, asparagus, peas,
    small carrots, mushrooms,
    Brussels sprouts, small tomatoes
    stuffed with spinach, etc.
2 tablespoons butter
2 tablespoons all-purpose flour
¾ cup beef bouillon
¼ cup Madeira

Remove surplus fat and skin and pound the filet with the back of a knife, against the grain. Lard meat with strips of suet. Put meat in a colander and pour a kettle of boiling water over it. Melt butter in a roasting pan and brown meat on all sides. Bake filet in preheated moderate oven (350°F.) for about 20 minutes to the pound, basting meat with the pan juices during entire cooking period. Never cook the filet longer than 80 minutes. Remove meat from oven and season with salt and pepper. Cut filet into thin slices and arrange slices on a heated platter.

Cook vegetables separately and arrange them around the meat in a pretty pattern. Melt butter and stir in flour. Gradually stir in bouillon and drippings from pan. Cook over low heat, stirring constantly, until smooth and thickened. Just before serving, stir in Madeira and ¼ teaspoon salt. Spoon some of the sauce over meat and serve remaining sauce separately. Serve with mashed potatoes. Makes 6 servings.

HÂCHÉ
(Stewed Meat)

4 medium onions, chopped
¼ cup fat

2 pounds beef round steak, cut into
  1-inch cubes
3 tablespoons all-purpose flour
2 cups water
2 tablespoons vinegar
2 bay leaves
5 whole cloves
1 teaspoon salt
1 tablespoon Worcestershire

Brown onions in fat in a heavy pan. Remove browned onions from the pan and sauté meat in the same fat. Add onions and sprinkle with flour. Add water and all other ingredients. Cover pan and simmer for about 2 hours, stirring occasionally. Serve with boiled potatoes and red cabbage. Makes 6 servings.

BLINDE VINKEN
(Stuffed Fillets of Veal)

6 slices of veal cut from the round
¼ pound ground veal
1 egg
1 slice of white bread, soaked in milk
  Pinch each of salt, pepper, and ground
  nutmeg
¼ cup butter
1 tablespoon water
2 lemon slices

Pound veal slices until very thin. Combine ground veal, egg, bread, salt, pepper, and nutmeg. Cut mixture into 6 pieces and place 1 piece on each slice of veal. Roll up meat to enclose filling and tie with string. Melt butter and brown meat on all sides. Add water and lemon slices. Cover and simmer until tender, about 45 minutes. Remove string. Serve with the pan juices. Makes 6 servings.

Note: Instead of meat stuffing, the veal slices may be stuffed with a hard-cooked egg or with a filling of fried onions mixed with chopped parsley.

VARKENSSCHIJF
(Rolled Pork Rib)

4 pounds rolled rib (boned pork loin)
½ cup butter or other fat
1 apple, peeled and sliced
1½ teaspoons salt
1 teaspoon marjoram or oregano
½ teaspoon pepper

Cover meat with boiling water; drain. Brown the butter in a shallow roasting pan in preheated moderate oven (350°F.). Put meat in pan and roast for 1 hour. Add apple and seasonings. Roast about 1½ hours longer, or until meat thermometer registers 185°F. Add a little water during roasting if necessary and baste meat several times. Serve warm with cabbage or Brussels sprouts. Or serve cold with fried potatoes and a green salad. Makes 8 servings.

GEVULDE LAMSBORST
(Roast Cushion Shoulder of Lamb)

1 cushion shoulder of lamb
1 onion, chopped
  Butter
2 tablespoons flour
1 teaspoon curry powder
½ cup each milk and water
½ medium apple, peeled and diced
  Few sprigs parsley, chopped

Stoofperen

Aardappel-Purée
Met Ham en Uien

Ossenhaas à la Jardinière

¾ cup cooked rice
1 garlic clove, split

Have butcher leave one side of lamb open so that meat can be filled with stuffing. Cook onion in 2 tablespoons butter for 2 or 3 minutes. Blend in flour and curry powder. Gradually stir in liquids and cook, stirring, until smooth and thickened. Add apple and cook, stirring occasionally, until apple is softened. Add parsley and rice. Rub meat with garlic and fill pocket with stuffing. Fasten opening with skewers or sew up. Put meat on rack in shallow roasting pan and pour ½ cup melted butter over top. Roast in preheated slow oven (300°F.) for 40 minutes to the pound, basting often with drippings in pan. Meat thermometer should register 175°F. to 180°F. when meat is done. Serve with fried bananas and a green salad. Makes 6 to 8 servings.

VEGETABLES

SPINAZIE
(Spinach)

6 pounds fresh spinach
1 tablespoon salt
6 tablespoons butter
3 slices of white bread, cut into strips
3 hard-cooked eggs, quartered
Lemon quarters

Clean spinach and wash with several changes of water. Add salt, cover, and cook over low heat until spinach is tender. Drain and chop very finely. Add ¼ cup butter and reheat. Fry strips of bread in remaining butter and place them upright on the spinach. In Dutch these are called "little soldiers" or *soldaatjes*. Put the egg quarters in between bread strips on the dish. Serve lemon separately. Makes 6 servings.

BRUSSELS LOF
(Belgian Endive)

8 endives (1½ pounds)
1 teaspoon salt
2 tablespoons melted butter
¼ teaspoon ground nutmeg

Cook whole endives in water with the salt until tender, about 30 minutes. Drain well. Place endives in a shallow baking dish, cover with melted butter, and sprinkle with nutmeg. Bake in preheated very hot oven (450°F.) for 10 minutes. Makes 4 servings.

SPRUITEN PURÉE
(Purée of Brussels Sprouts)

4 cups Brussels sprouts
1 cup water
Salt
1 teaspoon grated nutmeg
½ cup heavy cream

Trim and wash Brussels sprouts. Cook until tender in salted water. Press Brussels sprouts through a sieve or whirl in a blender. Add 1 teaspoon salt and the nutmeg. Stir in cream. Reheat if necessary,

and serve with duck or pork. Makes 4 servings.

STAMPPOT WITTE KOOL
(White Cabbage with Potatoes)

1 head white cabbage
Salt
4 cups quartered peeled potatoes
2 cups water
½ cup bacon fat or butter

Remove outer leaves and core from cabbage. Cut cabbage in pieces. Wash thoroughly and cook in small amount of boiling salted water for about 15 minutes. Drain. Cook potatoes in 2 cups water with the fat and a little salt. When done (do not drain), add cabbage and mix well. This dish is eaten as a whole meal and is a typical winter dish. Makes 4 servings.

Note: Meat is not necessary, although frankfurters or pork chops go very well with this dish.

GESTOOFDE PREI
(Braised Leeks)

2 pounds leeks
2½ tablespoons butter
2 tablespoons all-purpose flour
1 cup milk
1 tablespoon vinegar
¼ teaspoon salt

Cut off roots from leeks and remove wilted outer leaves. Cut into 2-inch lengths. Cover with water, bring to a boil, and simmer for 30 minutes. Drain well. Melt butter. Stir in flour. Gradually stir in milk. Cook over low heat, stirring constantly, until thick and smooth. Add vinegar and salt. Simmer the leeks in the sauce for about 10 minutes. Makes about 4 servings.

STAMPPOT VAN BOERENKOOL
MET WORST
(Kale with Potatoes and Sausage)

4 pounds kale
4 pounds potatoes (12 medium), peeled and quartered
5 tablespoons fat or lard
1 teaspoon salt
1 pound knackwurst or frankfurters, heated

Strip the kale, wash, and boil for about 1 hour. Drain, and mince very fine. Use a large pot; place potatoes in it and half cover with water. Add kale, fat, and salt. Simmer. Cover and cook for 30 minutes, or until mixture is rather dry. Serve with knackwurst on top of kale and potatoes. Makes 6 to 8 servings.

AARDAPPEL-PURÉE MET HAM EN UIEN
(Purée of Potatoes with Ham and Onions)

6 medium potatoes
Salt
1 cup milk
2 medium onions, minced
Butter
¼ pound cooked ham, diced fine
1 tablespoon fine, dry bread crumbs

Peel potatoes and cook in small amount of boiling salted water until tender. Drain and force through a food mill or ricer.

Or mash in electric mixer. Beat in ½ teaspoon salt and the milk. Cook onions in 2 tablespoons of butter for 2 or 3 minutes. Butter a shallow 1½-quart baking dish. In dish, arrange alternate layers of mashed potato, onion, and ham, ending with potato. Sprinkle with the crumbs and dot with 1 tablespoon butter. Bake in preheated moderate oven (350°F.) for about 30 minutes. Makes 4 servings.

HUTSPOT MET KLAPSTUK
(Hodgepodge with Boiled Meat)

2 pounds of flank steak
2 teaspoons salt
4 cups boiling water
3 pounds carrots, peeled and diced
9 medium potatoes, peeled and quartered
9 large onions, peeled and quartered
Pepper

Put meat, salt, and water in large kettle. Bring to boil, cover and simmer for 1½ hours, or until meat is almost tender. Add carrots, bring to boil again and simmer for 30 minutes. Add potatoes and onions and simmer until vegetables are tender and liquid is nearly evaporated. Remove meat and serve separately. Stir vegetables until mixture is of stew consistency. Add pepper to taste. Makes 8 servings.

SPEKKIE SLA
(Bacon Slaw)

6 medium potatoes
Salt
1 cup milk
½ pound escarole
½ pound fat bacon, diced
Vinegar
Pepper

Peel potatoes and cook in small amount of boiling salted water until tender. Drain and force through a food mill or ricer. Or mash in electric mixer. Beat in 1 teaspoon salt and the milk. Wash escarole and drain well. Chop fine. Cook bacon until crisp; do not drain. When ready to serve, heat potato and add escarole. Put in individual soup dishes and pour fat and bacon over top. At the table make a hole in the center of each serving and add a little vinegar. Grind pepper over top. Makes 4 servings.

GEBAKKEN EIEREN MET UIEN
EN KAAS
(Baked Eggs with Onions and Cheese)

1 onion, grated
¼ cup butter or margarine
¼ cup grated Cheddar cheese
6 eggs
½ cup medium cream

Sauté onion in the butter until golden brown. Sprinkle in shallow baking dish. Top onion with 2 tablespoons cheese. Break eggs into baking dish, being careful to keep yolks whole. Cover with the cream and sprinkle with remaining cheese. Bake in preheated moderate oven (350° F.) for 15 minutes, or until eggs are of desired doneness. Makes 6 servings.

PANCAKES

SPEKPANNEKOEKEN
(Pancakes with Bacon)

1¼ cups all-purpose flour
2 eggs, beaten
2 cups warm milk
1 tablespoon cooking oil
6 slices bacon, halved
Molasses

Make a well in the flour and pour in eggs. Mix well. Add milk gradually, stirring constantly to keep mixture smooth. Stir oil into the batter. For each pancake fry 2 pieces bacon in a 6- or 7-inch skillet until crisp. Rotate pan so that bacon fat coats the entire bottom. Pour one sixth of batter into pan and tilt pan so batter coats entire bottom of pan and covers the bacon. Brown on one side, turn, and brown on the other side. Serve with molasses. Makes 6 pancakes.

FLENSJES
(Very Thin Pancakes)

¾ cup all-purpose flour
3 eggs
Pinch of salt
2 cups milk
Butter
Confectioners' sugar

Make a well in the flour. Beat eggs with salt and pour into well in flour. Beat until thoroughly blended. Add milk slowly. Beat until mixture is very smooth. Heat a 6-inch skillet and lightly grease bottom with a little butter. Spoon in about 2 tablespoons of batter. Tilt pan quickly so that entire bottom is coated. Brown on one side only. Sprinkle with sugar, roll up, and place on a warm dish. Makes 24 pancakes.

Note: *Flensjes* can also be eaten with all kinds of jam and marmalade.

DESSERTS

BROODSCHOTELTJE MET SINAASAPPELS
(Bread Dish with Oranges)

½ pound (about 7 slices) white bread without crusts
2 cups fresh orange juice
½ cup butter
2 egg yolks
¾ cup sugar
½ teaspoon grated lemon rind
2 egg whites, stiffly beaten

Mash bread with orange juice until mixture is very smooth (preferably use an electric blender). Cream butter until light and fluffy. Stir in egg yolks, sugar, and lemon rind. Beat until mixture is light and creamy. Mix into bread. Fold in stiffly beaten egg whites. Put in a greased 1½-quart casserole and bake in preheated slow oven (325°F.) for 1 hour. Makes 6 servings.

APPELSCHOTELTJE
(Zwieback with Apple in the Oven)

8 tart apples, peeled and sliced
Butter

⅔ cup sugar
½ cup flour
1 cup milk
¼ teaspoon grated lemon rind
Dash of salt
3 eggs, separated
8 zwieback, crumbled

Simmer apple slices with 1 tablespoon butter and ⅓ cup sugar for 10 minutes. Melt ½ cup butter and blend in flour. Gradually add milk and cook, stirring constantly, until smooth and thickened. Add remaining sugar, lemon rind, and salt. Beat into milk mixture. Stir in egg yolks. Add apples and fold in stiffly beaten egg whites. Butter a shallow 1½-quart baking dish. Alternate layers of apple mixture with crumbled zwieback in dish, ending with zwieback. Dot with 1 tablespoon butter. Bake in preheated slow oven (325°F.) for about 45 minutes. Makes 6 servings.

RIJSTPUDDING
(Rice Pudding)

1 cup uncooked rice
1 cup water
3 to 4 cups milk
1 teaspoon salt
¼ cup sugar
2 eggs, beaten
Grated rind of ½ lemon
⅓ cup raisins
1 teaspoon vanilla extract
Fine dry bread crumbs
1 tablespoon butter

Heat rice in the water. Add 3 cups milk, salt, and sugar. Simmer, covered, for 40 minutes, or until rice is tender. Add more milk if necessary to keep rice from becoming dry. Stir frequently during cooking. Remove from heat and stir into eggs. Add lemon rind, raisins, and vanilla. Butter a 1½-quart casserole and cover bottom and sides with bread crumbs. Pour in rice mixture. Dot with the butter and sprinkle with crumbs. Bake in preheated slow oven (325°F.) for 30 minutes, or until set. Cool, and unmold. Serve with strawberries or raspberries or with stewed fruit. Makes 6 servings.

KARNEMELK PUDDING
(Buttermilk Pudding)

2 envelopes unflavored gelatin
½ cup cold water
2 cups sugar
1 cup fresh lemon juice, heated
2½ cups buttermilk
1 cup heavy cream, whipped

Soak gelatin in the water. Let stand for 5 minutes. Place over low heat and stir until gelatin is dissolved. Dissolve sugar in hot lemon juice. Add to buttermilk. Stir in dissolved gelatin. Blend well and pour mixture into a 1-quart mold. Chill until firm. Serve with whipped cream. Makes 8 servings.

STOOFPEREN
(Stewed Pears)

1 cup water
1 cup dry red wine
1 cup sugar

12 pears, peeled, cored, and quartered
2 cinnamon sticks
½ teaspoon grated lemon rind

Bring first 3 ingredients to boil and cook, stirring, until sugar is dissolved. Add pears and simmer until almost tender. Add cinnamon and lemon rind and simmer until fruit is tender. Cool. Makes 8 servings.

SPECULAAS
(Spiced Cookies)

⅓ cup shelled almonds, or enough for each cookie, depending on number
4 cups all-purpose flour
1 cup softened butter
1 cup firmly packed light-brown sugar
4 teaspoons baking powder
1 teaspoon salt
1 tablespoon ground cinnamon
1 teaspoon each of ground cloves and nutmeg
½ teaspoon each of pepper and ground aniseed
⅓ to ½ cup milk

Pour boiling water over almonds. Let stand for 5 minutes and rub off skins. Combine all other ingredients and knead into a soft dough. Add more milk if necessary. Roll dough on lightly floured board to ½-inch thickness. Cut fairly large cookies, about 2½ inches in diameter, and press an almond into each cookie. Put on greased cookie sheets. Bake in preheated moderate oven (350°F.) for 25 minutes. Remove cookies when they are golden brown. Makes 3½ to 4 dozen.

DUXELLES—A preparation of dry, cooked mushrooms used as a flavoring in French cooking for sauces, stuffings, meat, fish, and vegetables; in short, wherever the flavor of mushrooms is desirable. Since the preparation is dry, it will keep for several weeks in the refrigerator and may be frozen.

DUXELLES

½ pound fresh mushrooms, minced
1 tablespoon cooking oil
2 tablespoons butter
2 tablespoons minced scallions
¼ cup beef bouillon
Salt and pepper

Place mushrooms, one handful at a time, into clean kitchen towel. Over a bowl twist towel into a ball to extract as much mushroom juice as possible. (Use mushroom juice for sauces, soups, stews, etc.) Heat oil and butter in skillet; over moderate heat sauté mushrooms and scallions in it, stirring frequently. Cook for about 7 minutes, or until mushroom pieces are browned and separated from each other. Add bouillon. Cook over high heat, stirring constantly, until bouillon has evaporated and mixture is dry. Season with salt and pepper to taste. Makes about ¾ cup.

ÉCLAIR—A cream puff in an oblong shape is called an éclair. The name is French and literally translated means "lightning." Though cream puffs and éclairs are made from the same ingredients, éclairs are considered more festive and elegant than cream puffs; why, no one knows.

Éclairs are made with a *chou* pastry, filled with cream fillings, whipped cream, or ice cream, and glazed with chocolate, vanilla, or coffee icing. They can be frozen, but most devotees prefer fresh éclairs.

ÉCLAIRS

- 1 cup water
- ½ cup butter or margarine
- ¼ teaspoon salt
- 1 cup sifted all-purpose flour
- 4 large eggs, beaten
  Vanilla Cream Filling
  Chocolate Glaze

In saucepan heat water, butter, and salt to full rolling boil. Reduce heat and quickly stir in flour, mixing vigorously with wooden spoon until mixture leaves the sides of the pan in a ball. Remove from heat and add eggs in 6 additions, beating after each addition until mixture is very smooth. (An electric mixer at a low speed makes this procedure easier.) Force mixture through pastry tube, or shape with spatula into 16 fingers 1 x 4 inches. Bake on greased cookie sheets in preheated hot oven (400°F.) for 40 to 45 minutes. Remove at once to racks and cool away from drafts. Split; fill with Vanilla Cream Filling. Top with Chocolate Glaze. Store in refrigerator. Makes 12 large or 16 medium éclairs.

Vanilla Cream Filling

- 3 cups milk
- ¾ cup sugar
- 6 tablespoons cornstarch
- ½ teaspoon salt
- 3 eggs, beaten
- 1 tablespoon butter
- 2 teaspoons vanilla extract

Scald milk in top part of double boiler over boiling water. Mix sugar, cornstarch, and salt. Stir into milk. Cook, stirring, until thick. Cover; cook for 10 minutes longer. Add small amount of mixture to eggs; return to double boiler; cook for 5 minutes. Add butter. Put in bowl and sprinkle small amount of sugar over top to prevent skin from forming. Chill; add vanilla.

Chocolate Glaze

Melt 3 ounces (3 squares) unsweetened chocolate; cool. Boil ⅓ cup sugar, dash of salt, and ¼ cup water until sugar is dissolved. Cool. Stir into chocolate; blend well. Let stand until of spreading consistency.

EEL—A long, snakelike fish with a smooth skin and no scales. There are several varieties of eel, each with a different number of vertebrae. Some eels live in fresh water; others in salt water. Their flesh is tender, delicate, and rich. Young eels are called elvers. Eels are a highly appreciated delicacy in Europe and many other parts of the world.

Eels are among the strangest of fish. Unlike salmon, they spawn at sea and migrate to fresh waters to live. They travel enormous distances across oceans and far up inland waters, and their ways of living, traveling, and reproducing fascinate the scientific world as one of the mysteries of nature.

Eels turn up in the folklore of many countries. A 4th-century Greek manuscript, the *Hexameron* of Basil, claims they are generated by mud. Some tribes in Madagascar believe that eels are the souls of the dregs of the population, but to certain Philippine tribes they represent the souls of all of the dead. In some parts of Europe it is believed that a person oiled with eel fat will see fairies, and live eel put into a drunkard's tipple will cure him of the habit.

Availability—Fresh eels are most abundant in the fall. However, in some food stores they are available throughout the year. Smoked eels are available all year. Several varieties of canned eel in jelly are sold in gourmet food departments.

Purchasing Guide—Be sure eels are alive when purchased. Fish dealer will skin and clean them. Or follow Basic Preparation.

Storage—Refrigerate fresh eel. It is very perishable and should be used as soon as possible.

☐ Fresh, refrigerator shelf, raw: 1 to 2 days
☐ Fresh, refrigerator shelf, cooked: 3 to 4 days
☐ Fresh, refrigerator frozen-food compartment, prepared for freezing, raw: 2 to 3 weeks
☐ Fresh, freezer, prepared for freezing, raw: 1 year
☐ Smoked, refrigerator shelf: 2 to 3 months
☐ Canned, kitchen shelf, unopened: 1 year
☐ Canned, refrigerator shelf, opened: 3 to 4 days

Nutritive Food Values—Eel is classified as a fat fish. It is a good source of protein.

☐ 3½ ounces, raw = 233 calories

Basic Preparation—Eels must be skinned before cooking. To skin eel, cut the skin around the head. With a sharp knife, cut under skin slowly to loosen a small flap. Hold the head in one hand and grasp the skin with the other hand. Or use a pair of pliers. Strip the skin off in one motion. Cut off head. Cut eel into desired lengths. Remove entrails, wash eel, and

cut into pieces.

Eels may be broiled, baked, fried, poached, or marinated. They may be served hot or cold in a salad or as an appetizer.

Smoked eel should be sprinkled with lemon juice and black pepper before serving. Canned eel may be served on greens with a mayonnaise dressing.

EEL STIFLE

3 pounds of eel
4 potatoes
4 onions
  Butter
  All-purpose flour
  Pepper to taste
  Salt pork

Cut eels into 3-inch pieces. Wash the pieces thoroughly. Peel and slice the potatoes and onions. Butter a 3-quart casserole or baking dish and place a layer of potato slices in the bottom; add a layer of onions and then a layer of pieces of eel. Sprinkle each layer with a bit of flour and pepper. Top with small pieces of salt pork and dots of butter and fill with just enough water to cover the vegetables and fish. Cover the casserole and bake in preheated moderate oven (375°F.), or cook slowly on top of the stove for about 1 hour, or just until the eel and vegetables are done. Makes 6 servings.

MATELOTE OF EELS, NORMANDY

2 pounds eel
3 onions
2 carrots
3 celery stalks
  Salt and pepper to taste
  Tarragon, parsley
1½ cups cider
12 small white onions, peeled
3 tablespoons butter
3 tablespoons all-purpose flour
2 egg yolks
½ cup heavy cream
  Chopped fresh sorrel or dash of lemon juice
  Fried croutons

Skin the eels, cut them into 3-inch sections, and remove the intestines (see Basic Preparation at left for proper method of skinning eels). Peel onions and carrots and cut these and the celery stalks into very fine strips. Put the strips of vegetables in the bottom of a kettle and top with pieces of eel. Season with salt, pepper, a bit of tarragon, and a sprinkling of minced parsley. Pour cider over all and simmer gently until eel is tender. Meanwhile, cook the onions in salted water.

Remove cooked eel to a hot dish and keep it hot. Reduce broth to about 1 cup and strain. Melt butter and blend in flour. Slowly add the reduced broth and stir until smooth and thickened. Beat egg yolks with cream; add sauce slowly to egg mixture. Replace on heat. Blend and heat through but do not boil or the

sauce will curdle. Add a few leaves of chopped sorrel. Pour over the eel, surround with the white onions, and serve with fried croutons. Makes 4 to 6 servings.

PAUCHOUSE BOURGUIGNON
(Fish Stew from Burgundy)

4 cups court bouillon (see below)
2 slices of salt pork
  Butter
8 small white onions
  Confectioners' sugar
2½ to 3 pounds fish (in addition to eel, use any fresh-water fish available, i.e., pike, perch, whitefish, carp, lake trout, etc.)
  Beurre manié
½ cup heavy cream
¼ cup brandy or Armagnac
  Fried toast
  Garlic

☐ **To Prepare Court Bouillon**—You may use 4 cups of water, or water and white wine combined. Flavor it with 1 or 2 slices of lemon, 1 small onion stuck with 1 clove, a few parsley sprigs, 1 celery stalk, 1 carrot, 1 teaspoon crumbled dried thyme, and 1 garlic clove. Simmer this gently and season to taste with salt as it cooks. After it has simmered for about 20 minutes, strain the broth and return it to the kettle.

While broth is cooking, cut salt pork into bits. Fry these in 1½ teaspoons butter. Peel onions and cook them gently in a small amount of water until they are just tender. Then drain and brown them in a bit of butter. As they brown, sprinkle the onions with a little confectioners' sugar to give them a nice glaze.

When the broth is cooked and strained, add the fish cut into serving pieces and cook it gently until just tender. This should take no more than 15 minutes. Remove fish to a hot dish and keep it hot. Strain broth again and put over high heat for 10 minutes to reduce it to about 1½ cups.

Prepare *beurre manié* by kneading 2 tablespoons butter with 3 tablespoons flour. Use the tips of your fingers. Roll butter and flour mixture into tiny balls the size of peas and sprinkle these over the surface of the broth, stirring constantly. Continue stirring and cooking gently until the sauce thickens and is smooth. Add the bits of salt pork, the browned onions, and heavy cream. Stir and blend well.

Pour brandy over the fish and ignite it. Pour the sauce over the fish and serve with fried toast rubbed with garlic. Makes 4 servings.

Note: This famous fresh-water fish stew resembles bouillabaisse in the great variety of fish used in its preparation. You may use any local fish providing you always include eel.

EGG—An egg is the reproductive body of certain species of living creatures, such as birds and reptiles. It is encased in a shell or membrane which protects the soft inner parts which are the ones that do the reproducing in a highly complex manner. The word "egg" comes from the Middle English *egge*. The Latin word for egg is *ovum*.

When we speak of eggs as food, we usually mean hen's eggs and sometimes the eggs of other fowl, such as duck, goose, plover, quail, etc.

Eggs are a basic food. Their taste, their nutritive values, and their availability are matched only by their versatility. Eggs are also a part of the folklore of people all over the world, standing as symbols of fertility. There are many old sayings connected with the egg; to wit: "A kiss without a moustache is like an egg without salt" (old Spanish saying). "No wonder, Child, we prize the Hen, Whose Egg is mightier than the Pen" (Oliver Herford).

In addition to their use as a food in their own right, eggs are used in cooking to thicken, as in custards and puddings; to leaven, as in soufflés, angel food, spongecake, and puffy omelets; to coat for proper adherence of breading; to bind, as in meat loaves and casseroles; to emulsify, as in mayonnaise and salad dressings; to clarify, as in consommé and boiled coffee; to add color, as in sauces and cakes; to hinder crystallization, in candy making; and to garnish as in canapés, salads, and soups.

Availability—Eggs are available throughout the year, although they are more plentiful, and consequently less expensive, in the spring and summer.

They may be purchased fresh in the shell, frozen whole or with whites and yolks separated, or dried whole or with whites and yolks separated.

Eggs are especially packed in jars for babies: strained egg yolks, strained cereal, egg yolks, and bacon breakfast, and junior cereal, eggs, and bacon breakfast.

Purchasing Guide—Eggs in cartons are sorted for size, which is determined by weight per dozen as follows:

WEIGHT PER DOZEN			
Jumbo	30 ounces	or	more
Extra large	27 "	"	"
Large	24 "	"	"
Medium	21 "	"	"
Small	18 "	"	"
Peewee	15 "	"	"

TO FILL A STANDARD 1-CUP MEASURE		
Whole Eggs	Egg Whites	Egg Yolks
4	6	12
5	7 to 8	12 to 14
6	8 to 9	14 to 16
7	9 to 10	15 to 19

Buy eggs to suit family needs. Smaller eggs may be an economy when used for cooking.

Eggs in cartons are graded according to freshness by standards established at the Poultry Division of the Agricultural Marketing Service.

Grade AA and Grade A eggs are top quality. They have a small air cell and a large proportion of thick white which stands up well around the firm yolk. Their appearance and fine flavor are most appreciated for poaching, frying, and cooking in the shell.

Grade B and Grade C eggs have a larger air space, thinner whites, and rather flat yolks which may break easily and show up off center in hard-cooked eggs. These eggs are less expensive and good to use for scrambling, baking, thickening sauces, and combining with other foods. (Exception: Angel-food cakes are better flavored with higher grade eggs.)

Shell color, brown or white, depends on the breed of the hen and is a matter of personal preference. The eggs inside the shell have the same nutritive food value. The yolk in the brown egg may be yellower than the yolk in the white egg.

Storage—Eggs should be refrigerated when you buy them as quality deteriorates with higher temperatures as well as with longer storage times. Since egg shells are porous and absorb strong flavors, store eggs, broad end up, in carton in refrigerator and remove only the number of eggs needed. Leftover whites should be tightly covered and refrigerated; leftover yolks should be covered with cold water and refrigerated. Drain before use.

☐ Yolks and whites, refrigerator shelf, raw and separated: 1 or 2 days

☐ Yolks and whites, refrigerator frozen-food compartment, raw and separated and prepared for freezing: 3 to 4 weeks

☐ Yolks and whites, freezer, raw and separated and prepared for freezing: 1 year

☐ Whole eggs, refrigerator shelf: 10 days (use older eggs for cooking)

☐ Whole eggs, refrigerator shelf, cooked, shelled or unshelled and wrapped: 10 days

Nutritive Food Values—In quantity (two or more), eggs are a good source of high-quality protein. The yolk is a fair source of iron, vitamin A, and riboflavin.

☐ 1 large egg = 80 calories

Basic Preparation

☐ **To Separate Eggs**—Separate eggs while cold (yolks are less likely to break).

Crack the shell with a sharp tap at the center; pull apart, retaining the yolk in one half while letting the white pour out of the other half into a bowl. Pour the remaining egg from one half of shell to the other half, until only the yolk is left. If any yolk should get into the white part, remove with the corner of a paper towel. (Even just a trace of yolk will prevent whites from beating to full volume.)

☐ **To Beat Eggs**—When beating eggs, whole, yolks, or whites, they will beat to greater volume when at room temperature.

☐ **To Beat Egg Whites**—Egg whites should be beaten in a bowl with a small rounded bottom. (Volume will increase 2½ to 4 times.) Use a rotary beater, a whip, a fork, or set electric beater at high speed. Do not beat egg whites in blender. Be sure the beater and bowl are very clean with no trace of fat. Acids such as cream of tartar, lemon juice, or vinegar should be added after the egg whites have been beaten until foamy. The addition of these acids results in a stiffer beaten white with larger volume and greater stability. Use ⅛ teaspoon cream of tartar to every 3 egg whites or ½ teaspoon vinegar or lemon juice to every 3 egg whites. Egg whites must be beaten to different stages for various uses:

SLIGHTLY BEATEN (foamy)—Frothy or foamy; large air bubbles; transparent; flows easily. **Use**—Clarifying, coating, emulsifying, and thickening.

STIFF (drier peak)—No longer foamy; air cells very small and very white; may slip slightly if bowl is tipped; still glossy, smooth, and moist in appearance. **Use**—Cakes, tortes, omelets, soufflés, marshmallows, hard meringues*, ice creams, and sherbets.

* When beating meringues, beat egg whites to the stiff-foam or stiff stage. Then beat in sugar, 1 tablespoon at a time, until very stiff and glossy.

☐ **To Beat Egg Yolks**—Use a small bowl of narrow diameter. Beat until thick and pale lemon-yellow in color.

☐ **To Use Leftover Yolks or Whites**—Use yolks for custards, biscuits, bread, rolls, muffins, cakes, cookies, tarts, French toast, scrambled eggs, salads, sauces, croquettes, vegetable and noodle rings, cream pies, puddings, eggnog.

Use whites for soufflés, fruit sherbet, candies, frostings, cakes, cookies, custards, puddings, meringues, foamy sauce, Mexican hot chocolate, fruit or coffee flip, glazes for breads, cookies, nut meats.

☐ **To Add Eggs to Hot Mixtures**—Beat eggs or egg yolks just enough to blend. Add small quantity of hot mixture to beaten eggs or egg yolks; mix well and gradually add to remaining hot mixture, stirring constantly. If eggs are first mixed

with an equal amount of cold liquid (if it is an ingredient), this mixture may be added *very carefully* to a hot mixture; add gradually, stirring constantly.

☐ **To Cook Eggs**—Eggs can be boiled, soft cooked or hard cooked, poached, scrambled, fried, baked, or shirred. For step-by-step directions for these methods see *How to Cook Superbly: Eggs and Omelets,* below.

☐ **To Freeze**—Raw eggs may be broken and frozen in moisture-proof vapor-proof containers. When freezing whole eggs and egg yolks, add 1 teaspoon salt per cup or 1½ tablespoons sugar per cup; label accordingly. Freeze egg whites as is. Freeze in small containers as you will use them, so that you don't have to defrost a large amount.

How to Cook Superbly: Eggs and Omelets

By Helen Evans Brown

Anyone can boil an egg, but everyone can't do the job perfectly. The same is true of other supposedly easy ways to cook eggs, such as frying, poaching, and scrambling. Here I will try to give exact directions for doing these simple egg dishes, as well as a few ways to fancy them up.

EQUIPMENT

Most kitchens will have all the necessities for egg cookery: saucepans, bowls, and skillets, a perforated spoon for draining, a wooden spoon for stirring, a whisk for beating. Of course, it's nice to have some special little dishes for shirring, and molds for eggs in aspic, but saucers and custard cups will do in a pinch if nothing else is available to you.

Cooked on top of the stove or in the oven, eggs provide varied and wonderful eating. Shown here: Shirred Eggs with Bacon Strips, Eggs Florentine with Mornay Sauce, Scrambled Eggs, Boiled Eggs, Eggs Benedict, and Eggs Provençale.

BOILED EGGS

"There is always a best way of doing everything, if it be to boil an egg," Ralph Waldo Emerson said. Almost everyone knows that the right way to boil an egg is *not* to boil it, which is why today's food writers usually say a hard- or soft-"cooked" egg. But as eggs can be hard-fried, poached, or even scrambled, this is not an exact description. The French term *oeufs à la coque,* or "eggs (cooked) in the shell," is much more descriptive, I think. But I'll go along with the crowd this time, and I'm sure you'll know what I'm talking about.

There are several ways to cook eggs in the shell, but I think the most reliable is to lower the egg or eggs carefully into rapidly boiling water, immediately lower the heat to just under the boil, and cook for the required length of time. But remember that cooking time will vary greatly depending upon the size and temperature of the egg, and the amount of water used. In these recipes I use so-called "large" eggs (not extra-large or jumbo), at room temperature, about 70° F. I also use plenty of water so it won't cool off too much when the eggs are added: a pint to an egg is a good rule, but remember that the eggs have to be well covered so if you cook but one egg in a pint of water, it has to be in a small (3-cup) saucepan. Eggs should be fresh, of course, but a very fresh egg is difficult to peel (see below). Timing is up to how you like your eggs. Cooked as above for 3 minutes, they will be very soft, the yolk runny and the white jelly-like. At 4 minutes the yolk will still be soft and the white barely set. At 5 minutes the white will be completely set and the yolk still soft. A 6-minute egg, known in France as an *oeuf mollet,* has a white that is set and a yolk that is just beginning to set around the outside. These eggs are plunged into cold water the minute they are done, then carefully peeled. Like hard-cooked eggs (10 minutes), these are more easily shelled if the small end is pricked with a needle before cooking. Crack them by tapping very gently all over, and start shelling at the large end where there is an air space. Hard-cooked eggs and eggs *mollets* used for aspic can be allowed to cool before shelling.

POACHED EGGS

Poached eggs are a great breakfast favorite, on toast or in eggs Benedict, but they can also be used for eggs in aspic and other more elaborate dishes. The fresher the eggs, the better they poach. This is because the white does not spread when the egg is broken but remains around the yolk. Also cold eggs poach better than eggs at room temperature. To poach eggs the American way, put enough water to cover the eggs in a shallow pan or skillet; 1¼ inches will cover even an extra-large egg. Add salt, 1 teaspoon for a 10-inch skillet, and bring the water to a boil. Break the first egg into a cup, turn heat low so that the water is just simmering, and slip the egg gently into the water. Repeat until all the eggs are in; don't crowd them! When they are done to your liking (probably in 2 or 3 minutes, but you can tell by their looks), remove with a perforated spoon and, if they are to be used for a fancy dish, trim them. Do this with a 2½- to 3-inch round cookie cutter, depending upon how much they've spread. Or, you could trim them carefully with a knife. If you've used an egg poacher or muffin ring, you won't need to trim them. Muffin rings are greased lightly and put into the pan of water; an egg is dropped into each ring. If the poached eggs are to be used cold (see below), slip them into cold water. If hot, either serve at once, or undercook slightly and slip into water as hot as your hand can stand comfortably. They will not cook much more this way, and can stand as long as the water remains warm. For a really large party, when the eggs have to be poached way in advance, undercook them slightly, put in cold water and, at serving time, reheat in boiling water for half a minute or so.

Another way to poach eggs and have them very attractive looking is to use only ½ inch of salted water. Done this way, the yolks will stand high above the whites. These are called bull's-eye eggs and when you see them, carefully trimmed with a round cookie cutter, you'll know why. They are especially effective floating in consommé or peering through aspic.

If you have wondered how the French poach their eggs so that they are oval, the yolks completely surrounded by the whites, this is the secret: add 1 tablespoon vinegar and 1 teaspoon salt to each quart of water, and bring it to a boil in a small deep saucepan. Cook 1 egg at a time. Break it into a cup and hold the cup in one hand. With the other hand stir the boiling water around and around until a deep whirlpool forms in the center. Slip the egg into the whirlpool and turn the heat low. The egg will spin just long enough to wrap the white around the yolk. If it isn't absolutely fresh, you may have a little tail that meanders off into the water, but this can be trimmed away. When done, lift out with a perforated spoon and use in any number of ways.

FRIED EGGS

My husband fries a superb egg! It's tender, yet firm, just golden on the bottom and shiny on top. No hard edges or tough whites. This is the way. Put butter, olive oil, or bacon fat into a frying pan, using 1 tablespoon for a small 1- or 2-egg pan, up to 3 tablespoons for a 10-inch skillet. Heat gently. Carefully break fresh eggs (here, again, it is better to break them into a cup first to be sure the yolks hold together) and slip them into the hot, but not too hot, fat. Turn heat as low as it will go, put a lid on the pan, and cook slowly until done to your liking. (Oh, yes, you'll have to peek!) Turn if you like your eggs that way. Season, and serve at once.

SCRAMBLED EGGS

James Beard and I love to fight about the best way to scramble eggs. Although we are too stubborn to admit it, each method is good, they're just different. Jim's way allows 2 eggs per person, with an extra one "for the pan." Beat them slightly, add salt and pepper to taste, and 1 tablespoon of either water or light cream for each egg. Melt butter, 1 scant tablespoon for each egg, in a skillet, or in the top part of a double boiler over boiling water. When the butter is hot, add the eggs all at once, turn down the heat, and as soon as they begin to set stir them constantly, scraping from the sides and bottom. As soon as they are set, but still soft and fluffy, serve. My way is this: allow 2 eggs per person, plus 1 extra for any number of eggs up to 6; season to taste and beat just enough to mix whites and yolks, no more. Melt butter in a frying pan, allowing 1 tablespoon for each 2 eggs. As soon as the butter is hot and just beginning to color, turn the heat low, give the eggs a final beat, and pour all at once into the pan. Allow to set just slightly at the bottom; then, using a wooden spoon, stir, drawing the spoon completely across the bottom, forming large soft curds. Continue this, covering bottom and sides completely. When the eggs are barely set, still shiny and soft looking, remove from the heat and add either 1 tablespoon hot heavy cream for each four eggs, or the same amount of melted butter. Serve at once, garnished with parsley and pimiento if you wish, on warm, not hot, plate so that the eggs won't continue to cook.

BAKED OR SHIRRED EGGS

The only difference between baked and shirred eggs is that, technically, shirred eggs are started on top of the stove and finished in the oven. In France they are called *oeufs sur le plat* or *oeufs au miroir*. Baked ones are cooked entirely in the oven. Recipes using the two are usually interchangeable. To shirr eggs put 1 teaspoon melted butter in a shirred-egg dish or a flameproof saucer, break 2 eggs into it, and cook over low heat on top of the stove until the white just begins to set on the bottom. Pour another teaspoon melted butter over the yolks, sprinkle the whites with salt and pepper, and put in preheated moderate oven (350°F.) for 5 minutes, or until the whites are milky-looking but still soft. Serve at once in the dish they've been cooked in. Do baked eggs exactly the same way, but skip the cooking on top of the stove. They will take longer, probably 8 to 10 minutes.

OMELETS

A truly fine cook is not judged by elaborate, exotic, and costly dishes, but by his skill in producing such essentially simple ones as a perfect soufflé, a tender French pancake, a suave cream sauce, or even a lowly sole with its amber outside hiding the delicate moist flesh within. These and many other dishes are so very easy to master and so excellent to eat that even the busiest housewife will count her time in learning them well spent.

An omelet is a cook's best friend. It's quick, inexpensive, versatile, and impressive. It's elegant enough to serve to your fanciest friends, and nutritious enough for a family meal. It is also a wonderful way to use up dabs of leftovers (see Hints, page 602).

Making a perfect omelet may be an art, but it's one that anyone can learn easily. When you can produce, in a matter of a minute or two, beautifully formed tender omelets, creamily moist in the middle and with an outer coating tinged with topaz, you will be well on the way to being an expert cook. All it takes is self-confidence, the right pan, eggs, water, salt and pepper, butter, and a table fork—plus a bit of practice.

EQUIPMENT
The Proper Pan—The pan should be of

To make the perfect omelet you need the right pan, eggs, water, salt, pepper, butter, a fork, plus self-confidence.

thick cast aluminum or iron, but not too heavy for you to handle easily with either hand. It should have a perfectly flat bottom and curving sides, and should be porous enough so that it absorbs and holds a patina of butter.

Many people who make a lot of omelets (and you will too, once you've mastered the trick) never use the pan for anything else and never wash it. I personally think this is unnecessary, although I am willing to admit that the pan should have proper treatment before using and again after it has been necessary to wash it.

To Treat a New Omelet Pan—Wash and dry the pan, fill it with cooking oil, and heat it very slowly until the oil seems to move around at the bottom. Turn off the heat and allow the oil to stand in the pan until cooled (you can use the oil again). Wipe the pan thoroughly with a paper towel. The inside of the pan should be perfectly smooth with a slick, slightly greasy feeling.

Re-treating a Pan—If the pan has been used for something else and needs washing, do so, using hot water but not scouring powder or steel-wool pads. If the pan needs scouring, rub it clean with salt and paper towels and give it the oil treatment described above. Your pan will then be just as good as ever.

Cleaning the Pan—After you've made your omelet, simply wipe out the pan with a paper towel. If the omelet should stick (it won't after you've become practiced), just scour it with salt and paper towels.

The Size of the Pan—The easiest omelet to make, and therefore the best one to practice on, is one using 2 or 3 eggs. For this a pan with a top diameter of 7 or 8 inches is right. A 10-inch pan is good for a 6-egg omelet, and as any omelet larger than this is difficult to make, pans in these two sizes should suffice. A 2-egg omelet serves one person. A 3-egg one, made in the same pan, can serve two people; a 6-egg omelet is enough for three or four.

Other Utensils—Besides the pan you will need a bowl for the eggs, an ordinary 4-pronged table fork for beating the eggs and making the omelet, and a warm plate or platter on which to turn it out. (If you'd rather beat your eggs with a French whisk or rotary beater, you'll need that, too.)

FOR A 2-EGG OMELET

2 eggs
2 teaspoons cold water
A few grains of pepper
A generous pinch of salt (⅛ teaspoon)
1 tablespoon butter

FOR A 6-EGG OMELET

6 eggs

2 tablespoons cold water
A pinch of pepper
A scant ½ teaspoon salt
1½ tablespoons butter

Just keep in mind that you allow 1 teaspoon cold water, a few grains of pepper, a pinch of salt, and about 1 teaspoon butter for each egg (a little more for a small omelet, a little less for a bigger one), and you have the recipe memorized. **Note:** Some cooks don't add pepper until after the omelet is cooked, believing it toughens the eggs. Ideally, the pepper used should be white and freshly ground.

HERE'S HOW

Read these directions before you start, then read them again to make sure you'll remember. The secret of a good omelet is speed, so you can't stop in the middle and look at the directions again.

1. Break eggs into the bowl; add water, pepper, and salt.

2. Put pan on to heat.

3. Have butter measured and ready to pick up on the end of a fork (see Hints, at right).

4. Have plate or platter warming on the stove's pilot light or in a cool oven.

5. Beat eggs, using fork or your favorite method. The eggs should be beaten just enough to be thoroughly mixed, with a very slight froth on top. Two eggs and brisk beating with a fork will take about 30 seconds (that's as long as it takes me to count to 60!); 6 eggs will take longer.

6. Put butter on the end of a fork and test your pan with it. It should sizzle but not brown. (If the butter is too hot, remove it quickly, wipe the pan out with a paper towel, and try again.) Adjust heat so that pan stays hot. (Although eggs are usually cooked at a low temperature, this does not apply to omelets.) Tip and roll the pan so that the butter flows over the bottom and part way up the sides. As soon as the butter foams, which should be almost at once:

7. Add the eggs. Now, working quickly, shake the pan with your left hand, sliding it vigorously back and forth; at the same time stir the eggs once all around with the fork, then a few times in the middle, stroking the mixture toward the center. You should still be shaking the pan with the left hand and the omelet should be sliding free. Now smooth the top of the omelet with your fork, and let it rest for a second or two. As soon as the edges appear done and the top is still moist and creamy-looking, you can start folding.

8. Using your fork and, if you're right-handed, starting at the right side, begin folding the omelet toward the center, nudging it until about one third of it is folded to the center. Hold the warm plate under the pan, using your left hand.

Now slide the unfolded part of the omelet onto the plate, to within a third of the plate's farther edge. With a quick flip of the wrist, turn the pan upside down. This will give the omelet another fold and will leave it, just slightly tinged with gold, neatly in the middle of the plate. Congratulations! You have just made a perfect omelet.

HINTS

Practice—If you're afraid your omelet won't be perfect the first time—and it's quite likely it won't—practice alone. Either eat your less-than-gorgeous creations (they will still taste good), or let them get cold and chop, mix with mayonnaise and chopped olives, and use for a sandwich filling.

Timing—If at first you have difficulty in having the pan too hot or not hot enough, correct the heat after the eggs are beaten, then give eggs two or three extra strokes to restore their liveliness.

Measuring Salt—Measure your own "pinch" of salt. Chances are that four of them will equal ¼ teaspoon. If so, use a pinch for each egg and don't bother with a measuring spoon again.

Measuring Butter—Mark a ¼-pound bar of butter in the middle, then mark each half into 4 slices. Each slice is 1 tablespoon. Next time you'll know just how thickly to slice the butter and you'll never have to measure a tablespoon again.

Sticking Omelet—If your omelet doesn't slide freely in the pan, don't despair. You can free it with a spatula and slip a little extra butter under it for lubrication.

Warm Plate or Platter—Don't have the plate sizzling hot, or it will cause the creamy center to dry out.

Variations—These are so numerous that a book could be written on the subject. The simplest is a French *Omelette aux Fines Herbes*. Just add 1 tablespoon finely minced herbs (parsley and chives are usual, tarragon and/or chervil good) to the 2-egg mixture before cooking. A cheese omelet is easy too: just before folding, sprinkle top with grated cheese, allowing 1 tablespoon for each egg. Other kinds of omelets are usually made by putting some of the filling (if cooked, it should be warm) in before the folding, and then pouring the rest over or around the finished omelet on its plate.

Leftovers—Small amounts of many leftovers can be used up with omelets. Little nubbins of cheese can be diced and used as above; jelly can be whipped and spread over before folding; bits of warmed meat, fish, or vegetables can be combined with sour cream, warmed cream sauce, mushroom sauce, or brown gravy and used in and around the omelet. Or, very small amounts can be minced and added to it before cooking. Before you know it, you'll be creating variations of your own!

EGG COOK BOOK

Delicious, nutritious dishes featuring the tender versatile egg: hard-cooked, poached, fried, scrambled, shirred or baked, and in omelets

HARD-COOKED EGGS

EGGS IN ASPIC

4 hard-cooked eggs, halved lengthwise
Anchovy fillets
Chopped parsley and chives
1 envelope unflavored gelatin
¼ cup cold water
1½ cups hot well-seasoned chicken bouillon
¼ cup dry white wine

Put eggs, flat side down, in serving dish. Make a cross of anchovy fillets on each. Sprinkle with herbs. Soften gelatin in cold water. Dissolve in hot bouillon. Add wine; cool. Chill until slightly thickened. Spoon over eggs. Chill until firm. Makes 4 servings.

EGG AND POTATO CASSEROLE

6 medium potatoes, boiled
6 hard-cooked eggs
6 slices of bacon, chopped
Salt and pepper to taste
2 tablespoons chopped parsley
½ to ⅔ cup dairy sour cream

Slice potatoes and hard-cooked eggs. Cook bacon until crisp. Drain; reserve fat. Place alternate layers of potatoes, eggs, and bacon in greased 1½-quart baking dish. Season with salt and pepper and sprinkle with parsley. Stir remaining bacon fat into sour cream. Pour over other ingredients. Bake in preheated moderate oven (350°F.) for 15 to 20 minutes, or until golden. Makes 6 servings.

RAGOUT OF EGGS AND MUSHROOMS

2 tablespoons olive oil
1 tablespoon minced onion
1 tablespoon chopped parsley
1 pound mushrooms, sliced
1 tablespoon all-purpose flour
½ cup dry white wine
Salt and pepper to taste
6 hard-cooked eggs, coarsely chopped

Heat olive oil over medium heat and cook onion and parsley in it for 2 minutes. Add mushrooms; cover and cook over low heat for 10 minutes. Stir in flour and add wine. Cover and simmer for 5 minutes. Season with salt and pepper. Add eggs and simmer, covered, for 5 more minutes, stirring occasionally. Serve as an entrée with hot garlic bread, or with broiled ham or sausages, or with game. Makes 6 servings.

ENGLISH THIN YELLOW BOYS

6 hard-cooked eggs, chopped fine
2 tablespoons butter, melted
1 tablespoon prepared Dijon or French mustard
1 tablespoon steak sauce or Worcestershire
1 tablespoon wine vinegar
1 tablespoon chopped tarragon, fresh or dry
1 tablespoon minced fresh chervil
1 tablespoon minced parsley
1 tablespoon minced shallot or finely minced onion
Salt and pepper to taste
8 slices of hot buttered toast

Combine all ingredients except toast and heat through thoroughly, mixing well. Spread between toast slices and serve very hot. Makes 4 servings.

BAKED EGGS AND ONIONS

2 large onions
¼ cup butter
6 hard-cooked eggs, sliced
Salt and cayenne to taste
For the sauce:
2 tablespoons butter
2 tablespoons all-purpose flour
1⅔ cups light cream, heated
1 teaspoon prepared Dijon or French mustard
2 tablespoons grated Swiss or Parmesan cheese
1 egg yolk
2 tablespoons milk

Slice onions thinly. Heat butter, but do not let brown. Cook onions in butter over medium heat for 5 to 7 minutes, or until soft. The onions must remain pale. Butter a shallow baking dish. Arrange alternate layers of eggs and onions. Sprinkle with salt and a little cayenne. Add sauce.

Melt butter and stir in flour. Blend in hot cream and cook over medium heat until sauce is thickened, stirring constantly. Add mustard and cheese and cook for 2 to 3 minutes longer. Beat together egg yolk and milk. Remove sauce from heat and stir in egg and milk. Pour sauce over sliced eggs and onions and broil quickly under broiler until top is brown and bubbly. Or bake in preheated hot oven (425°F.). The broiler method is better, since it will not dry out the dish. For luncheon, serve with fried chick-peas and a tomato salad. Makes 4 to 6 servings.

◄ PICTURED AT RIGHT ▶

SPINACH SOUFFLÉ

- 3 tablespoons butter or margarine
- ¼ cup all-purpose flour
- 1 teaspoon salt
- ¼ teaspoon pepper
- ⅛ teaspoon nutmeg
- 1 cup light cream or milk
- 1 cup (¼ pound) grated Swiss cheese
- 1 cup well-drained finely chopped cooked spinach
- 3 eggs, separated

Melt butter and blend in flour, salt, pepper, and nutmeg. Gradually add cream, stirring until well blended. Cook over low heat, stirring constantly, until mixture is thick and smooth. Add cheese and spinach, and cook until cheese is melted. Cool. Beat egg whites until stiff, but not dry. Then beat egg yolks until thick and lemon-colored. Add yolks to spinach mixture. Fold in whites. Pour into buttered 1½-quart soufflé dish or straight-sided casserole. Bake in preheated slow oven (325°F.) for 45 to 50 minutes. Makes 4 to 6 servings.

STEAMED EGG-PARMESAN PUDDING

- 6 eggs, separated
- ¼ cup all-purpose flour
- 1 cup milk
- ¼ teaspoon each of salt and pepper
- 1 cup (¼ pound) coarsely grated Parmesan cheese
  Hot tomato sauce

Beat egg whites until stiff, but not dry. Set aside. Beat yolks until blended. Blend flour with some of the milk until smooth. Stir in remaining milk. Cook, stirring constantly, until thickened. Stir mixture into eggs, put back in saucepan and cook, stirring, for a few minutes longer. Remove from heat and stir in salt, pepper, and cheese. Fold in egg whites. Pour into well greased 1½-quart pudding mold. Grease lid and cover mold. Put on rack in kettle, and add enough boiling water to come half way up sides of mold. Cover kettle and steam for about 45 minutes. Unmold and serve with tomato sauce. Makes 4 servings.

EGGS AU GRATIN

- 4 hard-cooked eggs, halved
- 3 slices of bread, soaked in milk
- ¾ cup grated cheese, half Parmesan, half Swiss
- 2 raw egg yolks
- 3 tablespoons heavy cream
  Salt and pepper to taste
- 2 tablespoons fat
- 1 cup Béchamel sauce flavored with nutmeg
- ⅓ cup bread crumbs

Mash hard-cooked egg yolks and mix with bread, half of cheese, the raw egg yolks, cream, seasonings, and fat. Fill the halved hard-cooked whites with mixture. Put in baking dish; place any left-over filling between eggs. Cover with

Spinach Soufflé

Steamed Egg-Parmesan Pudding

Béchamel sauce (use 2 tablespoons butter, 2 tablespoons all-purpose flour, 1 cup milk or light cream, and a dash of grated nutmeg), crumbs, and rest of cheese. Bake in preheated hot oven (400° F.) until brown. Makes 4 servings.

SKILLET EGGS AND POTATOES

4 cups diced raw potatoes
2 cups boiling water
1½ teaspoons salt
1½ teaspoons white pepper
1 onion, minced
¼ cup butter or margarine
6 hard-cooked eggs, cut into chunks
¾ cup milk
Chopped parsley

Put first 3 ingredients in skillet, cover, and cook for 10 minutes. Uncover and cook until water is evaporated. Add next 3 ingredients and cook, stirring occasionally, until lightly browned. Add eggs and milk; heat. Top with parsley. Makes 4 servings.

MADEIRA EGGS, FUNCHAL

1 onion, minced
½ pound mushrooms, chopped
2 tablespoons butter
¼ cup Madeira
Salt and pepper
12 hard-cooked eggs, shelled

Sauté the onion and mushrooms in the butter until they are just golden, not brown. Add the wine, stirring well. Season to taste with salt and pepper. Cut the eggs into halves and put in a serving dish. Pour the sauce over the eggs. Makes 6 servings.

EGGS MORNAY

6 tablespoons butter or margarine
6 tablespoons all-purpose flour
1¾ cups milk
1 cup chicken bouillon
4 ounces (about ¾ cup) sharp Cheddar cheese, diced
½ cup grated Parmesan cheese
¼ cup sherry
½ teaspoon Worcestershire
Salt and white pepper
12 eggs
Croutons
Chopped parsley

Make a sauce with first 8 ingredients: Melt butter. Stir in flour. Gradually stir in milk and bouillon. Cook over low heat, stirring constantly, until smooth and thickened. Stir in cheeses, sherry, and Worcestershire. Stir until melted. Add salt and pepper to taste. Hard-cook eggs, or cook for less time if preferred. Shell while warm and put in shallow baking dish. Surround with the sauce and sprinkle with croutons. Reheat, if necessary, in slow oven (300°F.). Just before serving, sprinkle with parsley. Makes 6 servings.

EGGS HONGROISE

1 small onion, minced
6 tablespoons butter
¼ cup all-purpose flour
2 tablespoons paprika
1½ cups milk
1 cup heavy cream
½ cup chicken bouillon
Salt and pepper
6 hard-cooked eggs, sliced
Hot buttered toast points

Cook onion in the butter for 5 minutes. Blend in flour and paprika. Gradually add liquids and cook, stirring, until thickened. Season to taste. Add eggs, and heat. Serve on toast. Makes 4 servings.

INDIAN EGG CURRY

8 hard-cooked eggs, shelled
2 onions, minced
2 tablespoons butter or margarine
2½ teaspoons salt
1 teaspoon ground turmeric
1 teaspoon curry powder
½ teaspoon chili powder
2 cups (one 1-pound can) tomatoes
¼ cup buttermilk
Hot cooked rice

Cut the eggs into halves. Cook the onions in the butter. Add salt and spices and stir well. Add tomatoes and buttermilk. Simmer for a few minutes. Add the eggs and spoon some of the onion-tomato mixture over them. Simmer for about 10 minutes. Serve with rice. Makes 4 servings.

EGG AND OLIVE MOLD

1 envelope unflavored gelatin
½ cup cold water
½ teaspoon salt
Juice of 1 lemon
Dash of hot pepper sauce
1 cup mayonnaise or salad dressing
Small amount of grated onion
¾ cup diced celery
¼ cup chopped stuffed olives
4 hard-cooked eggs, chopped
Salad greens
2 hard-cooked eggs, cut in wedges (optional)
Pimiento strips (optional)

Soften gelatin in cold water. Dissolve over hot water. Add salt, lemon juice, and hot pepper sauce; cool. Stir mixture slowly into mayonnaise. Add remaining ingredients except salad greens and pour into 3-cup mold. Chill until firm. Unmold onto greens and garnish with hard-cooked egg wedges and pimiento strips, if desired. Makes 4 servings.

EGG-CHEESE SPREAD

6 warm hard-cooked eggs
½ cup crumbled Cheddar or blue cheese
Dash of garlic salt
Salt and pepper

Mash eggs and gradually blend in cheese. Season to taste with remaining ingredients. Store in covered jar in refrigerator until ready to use. Good on pumpernickel or whole-wheat bread. Makes 1¾ cups.

STUFFED EGGS

8 hard-cooked eggs
¼ cup salad dressing or heavy cream
½ teaspoon powdered mustard
Salt and pepper
Paprika

Cut eggs into halves. Remove yolks, mash, and mix with next 4 ingredients. Stuff egg halves with the mixture. Sprinkle with paprika. Chill before serving.

Stuffed Eggs with Dried Beef

Use Stuffed Egg recipe, adding 2 tablespoons pickle relish and ½ cup chopped dried beef to the egg yolks.

Stuffed Eggs with Anchovies

Use Stuffed Egg recipe, adding 1 can (¾ ounce) anchovy fillets, drained and crushed, or 1 tablespoon anchovy paste to egg yolks. Garnish with capers.

Stuffed Eggs with Deviled Ham

Use Stuffed Egg recipe, adding 2 or more tablespoons deviled ham to egg yolks. Garnish with chopped parsley.

Stuffed Eggs with Olives

Use Stuffed Egg recipe, adding 2 tablespoons chopped stuffed green or ripe olives to egg yolks.

Stuffed Eggs with Mushrooms

Use Stuffed Egg recipe, adding 2 or 3 tablespoons canned chopped mushrooms to egg yolks. Garnish with a bit of pimiento.

Stuffed Eggs with Caviar

Use Stuffed Egg recipe, adding 2 or more tablespoons caviar to egg yolks.

Curried Stuffed Eggs

Use Stuffed Egg recipe, adding 1 teaspoon curry powder to egg yolks. Garnish with chutney.

Stuffed Eggs with Herbs

Use Stuffed Egg recipe, adding chopped chives, chervil, parsley, savory, or other herbs to egg yolks.

PIQUANT EGG SALAD

8 hard-cooked eggs, chilled
¼ cup each of small pickled onions and chopped sweet gherkins
½ cup salad dressing
1 teaspoon prepared mustard
Salad greens

Cut eggs into large chunks. Mix lightly with remaining ingredients except greens. Serve on greens. Makes 4 servings.

SAVORY EGG SALAD

2 tablespoons butter
2 tablespoons all-purpose flour

1½ teaspoons salt
    Pepper
1 cup milk
4 cups diced cooked potato
1 onion, minced
1 pimiento, chopped
1 cup diced celery
⅓ cup minced ripe olives
6 hard-cooked eggs, chopped
⅔ cup salad dressing

Melt butter; blend in flour and seasonings. Gradually add milk and cook, stirring, until thickened. Add potato and heat gently. Just before serving, add remaining ingredients, reserving some of the chopped egg to garnish top. Mix lightly. Add more salt and pepper, if necessary. Serve hot. Makes 4 servings.

EGG, HAM, AND MACARONI SALAD
6 hard-cooked eggs, diced
1½ cups diced cooked ham
2 cups cooked macaroni, chilled
½ cup diced celery
1 sour pickle, chopped
¼ cup chopped stuffed olives
    Mayonnaise
    Salt and pepper
    Salad greens

Mix first 6 ingredients. Add mayonnaise to moisten, and season to taste. Serve on greens. Makes 4 servings.

POACHED EGGS

EGGS BENEDICT
Panfry 8 small thin ham slices until browned and done; keep warm. Split and butter 4 English muffins and toast under broiler. In large skillet poach 8 eggs in boiling salted water. Top each of 8 muffin halves with a ham slice, then with a poached egg. Serve at once with hollandaise sauce and a garnish of parsley. Makes 4 servings.

EGGS POACHED IN CREAM
½ cup heavy cream
    Salt and pepper to taste
8 eggs
    Hot toast

Heat cream, seasoned with salt and pepper, in large skillet. Break in eggs, cover, and poach until of desired doneness. Serve on toast. Makes 4 servings.

EGGS MAYONNAISE
Poach 4 eggs, cool, and trim. Put each egg on a slice of ham cut into a round. Mask with jellied mayonnaise. (Mix 1 teaspoon gelatin with 2 tablespoons water and melt over hot water; combine with ½ cup mayonnaise.) Decorate eggs with pimiento or sliced olives or truffles. Let set, and serve surrounded by a crown of tiny, crisp lettuce leaves. Makes 4 servings.

OEUFS MOLLET CHASSEUR
1 green onion with top, minced
3 mushrooms, chopped
1 tablespoon butter
¼ cup chicken bouillon
1 tablespoon sherry
    Salt and pepper
4 eggs, poached
2 tablespoons heavy cream
2 tablespoons grated Parmesan cheese

Mix onion with mushrooms and sauté in butter for 5 minutes. Add chicken bouillon. Cover and simmer for 10 minutes. Add sherry and salt and pepper to taste. Pour mixture into a 9-inch pie pan. Top with poached eggs. Pour heavy cream over eggs. Sprinkle with cheese. Broil until golden. Makes 4 servings.

OEUFS À LA MATELOTE
(Poached Eggs in Red Wine)
1 cup dry red wine
1 cup chicken bouillon
1 onion, sliced
1 garlic clove
    Salt and pepper to taste
⅛ teaspoon ground nutmeg
6 eggs
1½ tablespoons all-purpose flour
1 tablespoon butter

Combine wine, bouillon, onion, and garlic; season with salt and pepper and add nutmeg. Cover; simmer over low heat for 10 minutes. Strain, and bring again to boiling point. Drop eggs, one at a time, into the boiling liquid and simmer for 4 to 5 minutes. Remove from liquid and keep hot. Boil liquid until it is reduced to 1 cup. Mix flour and butter to a paste, and add, a little at a time, to hot liquid, stirring constantly. Serve eggs either on a hot purée of kidney beans or on slices of toast buttered on one side only, placing the eggs on the unbuttered side. Pour sauce over eggs and serve immediately. Makes 4 to 6 servings.

EGGS FLORENTINE IN MORNAY SAUCE
2 boxes frozen chopped spinach, cooked and drained
6 eggs, poached
⅓ cup butter or margarine
⅓ cup flour
¾ teaspoon salt
⅛ teaspoon cayenne
2 cups milk
⅓ cup heavy cream, whipped
⅓ cup grated Parmesan cheese

Divide spinach into 6 individual broiler-proof baking dishes or shallow 1½-quart baking dish. Make depressions in spinach and put 1 egg in each. Melt butter and blend in flour and seasonings. Gradually add milk, and cook, stirring constantly, until smooth and thickened. Fold in whipped cream and cheese. Pour over eggs and spinach. Put under broiler until

lightly browned and bubbly. Makes 6 servings.

FRIED EGGS

EGGS AU BEURRE NOIR
4 eggs
3 tablespoons butter
1 tablespoon lemon juice or vinegar
    Hot toast
    Salt and pepper to taste

Fry eggs gently in 2 tablespoons butter. Remove eggs and keep hot. Add remaining butter to skillet and brown. Add lemon juice, slowly so it doesn't spatter, and heat. Put eggs on toast, and season. Pour sauce over eggs. Makes 4 servings.

HOBO EGGS
Take 2 slices of bacon per person and brown in skillet. Over this, before the bacon is quite crisp, place a slice of bread with a hole in the center large enough to hold an egg. Drop in egg, let cook for a few minutes on one side, then turn bread, egg, and bacon together and cook for a few minutes on the other side.

HUEVOS RANCHEROS
(Ranchers' Eggs)
1 garlic clove, minced
2 large onions, chopped
3 tablespoons butter
1 or 2 dried hot peppers
1 pimiento, chopped
3½ cups (one 1-pound, 12-ounce can) tomatoes
    Salt
8 eggs

Cook garlic and onion in 2 tablespoons butter until lightly browned. Add crumbled hot pepper, pimiento, and tomatoes. Simmer for 45 minutes, or until thickened. Add salt to taste. Fry eggs in remaining butter. Serve with the sauce. Makes 4 servings.

JOCKEY CLUB EGGS
1 cup diced veal kidney
    Fat for sautéing
½ cup sliced mushrooms
½ cup tomato paste
¾ cup beef bouillon
    Salt and pepper to taste
1 tablespoon Madeira
1 tablespoon all-purpose flour
3 tablespoons mixed chopped herbs
    Parsley
    Eggs

Two pans are needed: one to cook in, the second to keep cooked things warm while the others are being cooked. Sauté the kidney lightly and quickly over high heat; put aside. Then sauté mushrooms and put with kidney. Dilute tomato paste with bouillon; add seasonings and Madeira and thicken with flour mixed with

a little cold water. Off heat, mix in kidney, mushrooms, herbs, and parsley. Put aside and keep warm. Fry 1 or 2 eggs per person; with a glass, cut them into circles. (The remaining irregular bits of whites can be chopped up and added to the sauce.) To serve, arrange nicely on a dish, the sauce in the center, the eggs around it.

EGG-AND-CHEESE BURGERS
6 sandwich rolls
6 thin slices of process American cheese
6 eggs
  Butter
  Salt and pepper to taste
6 thin onion slices
  Chili sauce, chopped pickle relish, or prepared mustard

Split rolls, and toast. Put a slice of cheese on top half of each roll. Fry eggs in small amount of butter, turning once. Put on bottom halves of rolls. Sprinkle with salt and pepper. Top with a slice of onion. Add relishes as desired, and serve at once. Makes 6 servings.

HUEVOS FRITOS
(Deep-Fried Eggs)
Cook eggs for 4 minutes. Run cold water over them for easier peeling, and peel very carefully. Roll eggs in flour, dip into beaten egg, and roll in fine dry bread crumbs which have been seasoned with salt and pepper. Fry them in hot deep olive oil at 375°F. for 1 to 2 minutes. Drain eggs carefully on absorbent paper, and serve with a well-seasoned tomato sauce.

EGGS PROVENÇALE
1 egg
1 tablespoon water
  Salt and pepper to taste
6 slices eggplant, ½ inch thick
  Fine dry bread crumbs
  Olive oil
½ garlic clove, crushed
6 thick slices tomato
6 hot fried eggs

Beat egg with water and season with salt and pepper. Dip eggplant in egg mixture, then in crumbs. Fry in a little hot olive oil until golden brown on both sides and tender. Keep warm. Add garlic to a little oil in same skillet. Add tomato slices and sauté lightly. Top each eggplant slice with a slice of tomato. Top tomato with a fried egg and sprinkle with salt and pepper. Serve at once as a luncheon dish. Makes 6 servings.

SCRAMBLED EGGS

CREAMY SCRAMBLED EGGS
WITH BACON
½ pound sliced bacon
2 tablespoons butter or margarine

8 eggs
½ cup cream
¾ teaspoon salt
  Dash of pepper

Cook bacon as desired and drain on absorbent paper. Keep warm. Pour off bacon fat and melt butter in same skillet. Beat eggs slightly and mix with cream, salt, and pepper. Pour into skillet and cook over low heat, stirring occasionally, until thickened but still moist, about 5 to 8 minutes. Pile on a hot platter and garnish with bacon strips. Makes 4 servings.

HUEVOS HILADOS
(Threaded Eggs)
2½ cups water
4 cups sugar
12 egg yolks, slightly beaten

In 12-inch skillet combine water and sugar and cook until sugar is completely dissolved. Remove from heat. Place eggs in top part of double boiler over hot water and stir until smooth and thinned, 2 to 3 minutes. Pour egg yolks through a fine sieve. Put a small amount of egg yolks into measuring cup. Over low heat, heat syrup to simmering point. Do not boil. Pour egg yolks in very thin stream into syrup, holding the measuring cup about 12 inches from the surface. Use a rotating movement, to keep strands separated and long. Cook for about 3 minutes. Remove eggs from syrup with slotted spoon and dip into cold water. Drain on absorbent paper. Use remaining egg yolks in the same manner, taking care that syrup remains at the same simmering point until all eggs are cooked. Serve with cold cuts or ham. Makes 8 to 12 servings.

Note: Instead of pouring the eggs from a cup, you might use a small tin can with the top removed and a hole the size of a pencil point punched in the middle of the bottom.

PIPÉRADE
(Basque Scrambled Eggs)
⅓ cup lard or bacon fat
4 medium onions, thinly sliced
4 medium tomatoes, peeled and coarsely chopped
3 large or 5 small green or red peppers, sliced
  Salt and pepper to taste
¼ teaspoon ground thyme or marjoram
6 to 8 eggs, beaten

Melt lard in heavy skillet. Cook onions in it over low heat for 5 to 10 minutes, or until very soft. They must not brown. Add tomatoes, peppers, salt, pepper, and thyme. Cover and cook over very low heat for about 15 minutes, or until the vegetables are almost a purée. Stir frequently. Pour beaten eggs into vegetables

and scramble gently with a fork until eggs are just set. The *pipérade* must be very soft and hot. Makes 6 to 8 servings.

SHIRRED OR BAKED EGGS

SHIRRED EGGS CARUSO
4 teaspoons melted butter
8 eggs
8 tablespoons heavy cream
  Salt and pepper to taste
  Sautéed chicken livers (about 1 pound)

Put 1 teaspoon butter in each of 4 individual baking dishes or ramekins. Break 2 eggs into each. Add 2 tablespoons cream and sprinkle with salt and pepper. Bake in preheated moderate oven (350° F.) for 10 to 15 minutes, or until of desired doneness. Garnish with chicken livers. Makes 4 servings.

CRÈME LORRAINE
6 slices of lean bacon
1½ cups grated Swiss or Gruyère cheese
1½ cups grated Parmesan cheese
2 cups heavy cream
2 eggs, well beaten
1 teaspoon salt
¼ teaspoon white pepper

Fry bacon until crisp. Drain, and break into small pieces. Mix with cheeses, cream, eggs, salt, and pepper. Pour into buttered 1½-quart baking dish. Bake in preheated moderate oven (350°F.) for 45 to 50 minutes, or until set. Makes 4 servings.*

* If more than 4 servings are needed, it is better to make up two *Crèmes Lorraine* and bake them in two dishes, rather than doubling the quantities for one large dish.

Note: The cheeses must be Swiss or Gruyère and Parmesan.

GOLDEN FLEECE
2 packages (3 ounces each) cream cheese
¾ cup milk
4 eggs
½ teaspoon salt
½ teaspoon powdered mustard

Heat cheese in top part of double boiler over hot water until softened. Remove from heat. Add remaining ingredients and beat until blended. Pour into individual baking dishes or custard cups and bake in pan of hot water in preheated moderate oven (375°F.) for 20 to 25 minutes. Makes 4 servings.

EGG-SALMON QUICHE
  Pastry for deep 9-inch pie, unbaked
1½ cups (one 1-pound can) flaked salmon
  Juice of ½ lemon
1 onion, minced
2 tablespoons butter or margarine

2 tablespoons chopped parsley
6 eggs, beaten
1½ cups light cream or milk
1 teaspoon seasoned salt
¼ teaspoon white pepper

Bake pastry in preheated hot oven (450° F.) for 5 minutes. Drain salmon liquid into bowl. Remove bones and skin, and flake salmon. Put in pastry-lined pie pan and sprinkle with lemon juice. Cook onion lightly in the butter. Sprinkle onion and parsley on salmon. Mix salmon liquid, eggs, cream, and seasonings. Pour over salmon. Bake in moderate oven (350°F.) for 50 minutes, or until firm. Cut into wedges and serve hot. Makes 6 servings.

BAKED CELERY EGGS

Mix 1 can (10½ ounces) cream-of-celery soup, ¼ cup milk, 1 teaspoon Worcestershire, and ⅛ teaspoon pepper. Put half into greased 9-inch pie pan. Break in 4 eggs and top with remaining soup. Sprinkle with paprika. Bake in preheated slow oven (325°F.) for about 30 minutes. Serve plain or on toast. Makes 4 servings.

EGG-STUFFED TOMATOES

4 tomatoes
8 eggs
1 garlic clove, minced
Chopped parsley
Salt and pepper to taste
¼ cup grated sharp Cheddar cheese
¼ cup browned bread crumbs
3 tablespoons butter or margarine

Halve tomatoes; scrape out center, pressing with spoon to extract most of juice. Put tomato shells in shallow baking dish and bake in preheated moderate oven (350°F.) for 10 minutes. Then break an egg into each. Add a little garlic and parsley; season. Sprinkle thickly with mixture of cheese, crumbs, and chopped parsley. Dot with butter. Bake in hot oven (425°F.) for 15 minutes, or until top is golden and eggs set. Makes 4 servings.

OMELETS

MINIATURE PUFFY OMELETS

4 eggs, separated
¼ cup sifted all-purpose flour
½ teaspoon salt
⅛ teaspoon pepper
¼ cup cold water

Beat egg whites until stiff. Beat egg yolks until thick and lemon-colored. Add flour, salt, pepper, and cold water to egg yolks; beat until smooth. Fold in egg whites. Drop from large spoon onto hot greased griddle and cook on both sides until

Eggs Florentine with Mornay Sauce ▼ **Egg and Olive Mold** ▲

browned. Serve at once. Makes 4 servings.

WESTERN OMELET

2 tablespoons butter or margarine
6 eggs
6 tablespoons each of finely chopped
  onion and green pepper
¾ cup milk
¾ cup chopped cooked ham
¾ teaspoon salt
  Dash of pepper

In a skillet melt butter. Beat eggs and stir in remaining ingredients. Pour mixture all at once into the skillet. Cook, stirring mixture to cook evenly. Serve while still moist and creamy. Can be used to make sandwiches with bread or toast slices. Makes 4 to 6 servings.

SPANISH OMELET

4 eggs, separated
¼ teaspoon salt
⅛ teaspoon pepper
1 tablespoon all-purpose flour
1 tablespoon softened butter
  or margarine
1 tablespoon water
  Spanish Sauce

Beat egg whites with salt until stiff but not dry. Beat egg yolks with pepper, flour, butter, and water until fluffy. Fold beaten yolks into beaten whites. Pour into a well-greased 8- or 9-inch skillet heated until a drop of water sizzles. Cover tightly. Reduce heat to low and cook for 8 to 10 minutes on top of range, until surface of omelet is dry when touched lightly with fingertip. Fold in half and serve promptly. Spoon Spanish Sauce over omelet. Makes 2 to 3 servings.

Spanish Sauce

1½ teaspoons butter
1 tablespoon each of minced onion and
  green pepper
1½ cans (use 8-ounce cans)
  tomato sauce
1½ teaspoons sugar
1½ teaspoons Worcestershire
  Pinch of cayenne

Melt butter and sauté onion and green pepper over low heat until vegetables are tender. Add tomato sauce and seasonings. Simmer for 20 minutes, or until sauce is thickened. Makes enough sauce for the Spanish Omelet.

ARTICHOKE OMELET HOLLANDAISE

2 tablespoons butter
3 artichoke bottoms, cooked and diced
  Equal amount of cooked mushrooms,
  diced
2 tablespoons tomato paste
  Salt and pepper to taste
  Pinch of red pepper
  Garlic
8 eggs

  Hollandaise sauce
1 small can flat anchovy fillets

Melt 1 tablespoon butter; lightly cook artichokes and mushrooms in it. Add tomato paste (dilute if too thick); stir well, season, put aside. Rub a bowl with garlic, break the eggs into it, and beat with a fork. Cook the omelet in remaining butter. When ready, slip onto a hot serving dish, top with artichoke mixture, and fold over. Put hollandaise sauce on top of omelet; garnish with anchovies. Serve at once. Makes 4 to 6 servings.

OMELET CHARENTIÈRE

8 slices of bacon, diced
2 tablespoons butter
8 green onions (white part), sliced
8 eggs, slightly beaten
3 tablespoons heavy cream
½ teaspoon salt
¼ teaspoon pepper
2 teaspoons prepared mustard
  Parsley

Cook bacon in large skillet until browned. Remove bacon and drain on absorbent paper. Pour off fat. Melt butter in skillet; add green onions and cook for 2 or 3 minutes. Add bacon to eggs with remaining ingredients except parsley. Pour into skillet and cook, lifting edges of mixture with spatula to let egg run under. When firm and browned on the bottom, fold over and turn out on a hot platter. Garnish with parsley. Makes 4 servings.

CHINESE EGGS FU YUNG

6 eggs
2⅓ cups (one 1-pound 3-ounce can)
  bean sprouts
2 tablespoons instant minced onion
1 teaspoon salt
½ teaspoon white pepper
1 cup crabmeat or shrimps
  Cooking oil
  Sauce

Beat the eggs well. Add the drained bean sprouts, onion, salt, pepper, and crabmeat. Fry in a little oil in a small skillet as you would pancakes. Turn the Eggs Fu Yung and fry on the other side. Serve with Sauce: Mix 1 tablespoon cornstarch and 1 tablespoon sugar. Add 3 tablespoons soy sauce and 1½ cups water. Cook until thickened, stirring. Makes 6 servings.

EGGNOG—An eggnog is a deliciously smooth cold drink containing beaten raw eggs, sugar, milk or cream, and flavoring. Often brandy, rum, or whisky is added. It is one of the traditional drinks served at Christmas time, especially in our southern states where eggnog parties are an established form of entertaining. Eggnogs are also served the year round to children, convalescents, and people suffering from malnutrition or disturbed digestion.

Eggnog is an American drink with English ancestors. The word eggnog (also egg-nog) is English in derivation. Nog is a shortened version of the word noggin, a small drinking vessel with an upright handle. Apparently the noggin was used for a strong ale which came to be known as nog. Thus, eggnog appears to have a close kinship with sack-posset, a milk-and-egg beverage known in England for centuries. The sack-posset was made with ale or with sack, a dry wine from the Canary Islands or Spain.

Since the earliest references indicate that eggnog was made with rum, and since the word "grog" is associated with rum, the term eggnog may also reflect a telescoping of sounds. In other words. eggnog may be an elision of the words egg 'n grog.

General confusion surrounds the nomenclature, ingredients, and technique used for milk-and-egg beverages. The beverage containing milk-and-eggs-and-flavoring which became known as eggnog appeared under many names and guises. It has been egg-pop, custard posset, syllabub, milk punch, egg-and-milk, flip, one yard of flannel, auld man's milk, and probably other things.

The recipes in the early cook books reflect the changing ingredients and techniques in mixing milk-and-egg beverages. There were no hard and fast rules. Sometimes milk punch was made with eggs, sometimes syllabub used egg whites to get a frothy top, and sometimes a posset had no eggs at all.

HOW TO MAKE SUPERB EGGNOGS

Use the finest ingredients obtainable: good fresh eggs, real vanilla extract or top quality flavoring, and fresh milk and cream. The flavor of nogs depends upon quality ingredients.

Be sure that cold eggnog is served *very* cold. This can be done by pre-chilling the ingredients as well as the mixing bowls, punch bowls, and serving cups. If possible, the bowl of cold eggnog should be set into a bed of crushed ice or into a large block of ice. Or, freeze part of the eggnog mixture as a block, then add to the punch bowl just before serving.

For the addition of "Christmas Spirits," use the kind you like, but be sure of excellent quality. The amount of the last-minute addition should be determined by the taste of the host and hostess. Gen-

erally ¼ to ½ cup of one's favorite rum, brandy, or whisky is right for each quart of eggnog.

EGGNOG

1 egg, well beaten
2 teaspoons sugar
1 cup milk or ½ cup milk and ½ cup light cream
¼ teaspoon vanilla extract
Nutmeg, grated

Beat together all ingredients, except nutmeg. Pour into tall glass and sprinkle with nutmeg. Makes 1 serving.

COLONIAL EGGNOG

¾ cup sugar
10 egg yolks, beaten
4 cups milk, scalded
½ teaspoon salt
10 egg whites
1 cup heavy cream, whipped
½ cup brandy
¼ cup light rum
Grated nutmeg

Blend ½ cup of the sugar and the egg yolks in top part of double boiler; stir in milk slowly. Cook over hot water until mixture coats spoon, stirring constantly. Chill well. Add salt to egg whites and beat stiff. Beat in remaining sugar gradually. Fold egg whites and whipped cream into mixture separately. Add brandy and rum. Chill for several hours. Pour into punch bowl; sprinkle with nutmeg. Makes thirty 4-ounce servings.

CHRISTMAS EGGNOG

3 egg yolks
¾ cup sugar
¼ teaspoon salt
3 cups milk
1 cup heavy cream
1 tablespoon sherry extract
3 egg whites
Grated nutmeg

Beat egg yolks; gradually add ½ cup of the sugar and the salt, beating constantly. Gradually add milk and cream. Cook over hot water, stirring constantly, until mixture is thick enough to coat a spoon. Cool. Add sherry extract; chill. Beat egg whites until stiff; gradually add remaining sugar, beating constantly until stiff. Fold into chilled custard. When ready to serve, pour into chilled punch bowl; sprinkle with nutmeg. Makes 2 quarts, or sixteen 4-ounce servings.

OLD ENGLISH SACK-POSSET

Adapted from a recipe in Sir Fleetwood Sheppard's 17th-century poem, "A Recipe for All Young Ladies That are Going to be Married: To Make a Sack-Posset"

¾ cup sugar
2 tablespoons all-purpose flour
½ teaspoon grated nutmeg
4 cups milk
3 eggs, beaten
¾ cup sherry

Mix sugar, flour, and nutmeg in top part of double boiler; gradually add milk, then eggs. Cook over hot water, stirring constantly, until slightly thick. Add sherry slowly; mix well. Serve immediately. Sprinkle with additional nutmeg. Makes sixteen 4-ounce servings.

FROTHY SYLLABUB

1½ cups sugar
2 cups white wine
5 tablespoons grated lemon rind
⅓ cup fresh lemon juice
3 cups milk
2 cups light cream
4 egg whites
Grated nutmeg

Stir 1 cup sugar into wine, lemon rind, and juice. Let stand until sugar dissolves. Combine milk and cream. Pour wine mixture into milk mixture; beat until frothy with rotary egg beater. Beat egg whites until stiff; gradually add remaining sugar, beating constantly until stiff. Pour milk mixture into punch bowl; top with spoonful puffs of egg white. Sprinkle puffs with nutmeg. Makes sixteen 4-ounce servings.

EGGPLANT—The eggplant is an erect branching plant (*Solanum melongena*) closely related to the potato. It is cultivated for its fruit, which we eat as a vegetable. The fruit, which in reality is a berry, varies in length from two to twelve inches. Its shiny surface may be dark purple, white, red, yellowish, or even striped, depending upon the variety. Eggplant is grown in different sizes and shapes; round, oblong, pear-shape, and long. Possibly the first variety known to Europeans was that resembling a hen's egg, hence the name eggplant. In this country the most common variety is the handsome large dark-purple variety. Eggplant requires a long growing season; it is cultivated in this country chiefly in Florida, New Jersey, and Texas.

The original home of the eggplant is believed to have been the East Indies although it is first mentioned as being used as a vegetable in India. A small-

fruited variety was developed in China. It was not until the Middle Ages that the eggplant was brought to Spain by the conquering Moors. To this day eggplants are a staple Arab food. First mention of the eggplant in northern Europe is made by Albert of Cologne in the 13th century; by the 16th century, a score of varieties were grown by the Germans. From Spain the eggplant journeyed to South America and was grown in Brazil about 1650.

Availability—All year round.

Purchasing Guide—Look for eggplants that are heavy, firm, smooth, and of a uniform dark glossy color. Select those of cylindrical or pear-shape that are about six to nine inches in diameter. Large, rough, spongy places indicate poor quality. Decay appears as dark-brown spots on the surface which will cause total loss in a few days.

Storage—Keep in a cool place with plenty of humidity. Use as soon as possible.
☐ Refrigerator shelf, raw: 3 days to 2 weeks
☐ Refrigerator shelf, cooked: 4 to 5 days
☐ Refrigerator frozen-food compartment, prepared for freezing: 2 to 3 months
☐ Freezer, prepared for freezing: 1 year

Nutritive Food Values—Little nutritive value can be found in eggplant. It tends to add variety to the menu.
☐ 3½ ounces, raw = 25 calories

Basic Preparation—Wash thoroughly in cold water; do not soak. Pare if desired. However, the skin is exceptionally flavorful, so if it is tender, do not hesitate to leave it on. Cut into slices, julienne strips, or cubes. Cut just before cooking as the flesh darkens rapidly.

☐ **To Boil**—Boil for 10 to 15 minutes in ½ inch of boiling salted water; season.

☐ **To Panfry, Plain or Cooked**—Panfry for 5 to 10 minutes in small amount of cooking oil.

☐ **To Deep Fry**—Deep fry for 5 to 10 minutes at 375° to 385°F. on a frying thermometer. It is usually breaded before frying.

☐ **To Bake**—Bake for 20 to 30 minutes at 350°F.

☐ **To Broil**—Broil for 10 to 15 minutes.

☐ **To Freeze**—Peel firm eggplants. Cut into ½-inch slices. Scald for 4 minutes in 1 gallon of boiling water with 2 teaspoons ascorbic acid added.

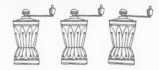

Italian Eggplant Parmigiana

The Elegant Eggplant

by Kay Shaw Nelson

When I lived in Turkey, while walking to the open-air street markets, I often whiled away the time by choosing adjectives for my favorite vegetables. As I remember there were cooling cucumbers, tantalizing tomatoes, aristocratic artichokes, caustic cabbages, and elegant eggplants. And as I purchased my daily supplies it was fun to peer at each one and wonder about my choice of words. Is a cabbage really caustic, I pondered. Perhaps not. But there was no doubt about the description of the long, pear-shape, purple vegetable. For the eggplant's appearance is "richness and refinement combined." And certainly when cooked it is "fastidiously tasteful."

Throughout the countries of the Middle East and along the Mediterranean I gained an appreciation of the eggplant's versatility in cooking. But more recently, while delving into the eggplant's past, I realized that years ago it would have been labeled eccentric rather than elegant. For at one time both in Europe and in the United States it was a suspect, unaccepted food.

How this wrong occurred to the eggplant is not absolutely clear. But possibly it was due to guilt by association. As a member of the nightshade family its relatives include not only the tomato and potato but also the poisonous belladonna (deadly nightshade). Tainted by the reputation of the latter, it took several centuries to convince our ancestors that the eggplant and the tomato were not infected too. Both acquired interesting nicknames: the tomato became known as the "love apple," whereas the eggplant was dubbed the "mad apple" (*malum insanum*).

Authors took great pleasure in inscribing warnings to their fellow countrymen about the possible perils of eating these "apples." One English botanist wrote: ". . . . doubtless these Raging Apples have a mischievous qualitie, the use whereof is utterly to be forsaken."

Fortunately some cooks never saw or heeded such warnings. While others fretted, they continued to prepare the dishes as they were enjoyed in ancient India some 2,000 years ago, and somewhat later at Lucullan banquets in Rome.

And eventually, when cleared of suspicion, eggplants and recipes for preparing them were introduced to the Western world.

Our grandparents deemed them culinary treasures. But then eggplants, grown only in warm climates, were rare in northern countries. Today we find them throughout the year in the food stores of every state. But autumn nostalgia compels me to prefer them when picked from a high pile of harvest vegetables at a roadside stand. Among the stoutish pumpkins, dark Hubbard squash, and dull-brown potatoes, the elegant eggplant truly displays its "refined gracefulness."

In preparing the following recipes do not worry about the worthy vegetable's name. For in years past, and even today in some countries, you would be preparing a small, oval, pale vegetable closely resembling an egg. Modern agriculture has developed the larger, richly colored specimen that we are privileged to use today.

SICILIAN EGGPLANT CAPONATA

1 large eggplant
Salt and pepper to taste
Cooking oil
2 medium onions, chopped
2 garlic cloves, crushed
3 celery stalks, chopped
1 can (1 pound) Italian plum tomatoes
10 large green olives, quartered and pitted
3 tablespoons pine nuts
¼ cup capers
¼ cup wine vinegar
2 tablespoons sugar

Wash eggplant. Do not peel. Cut into 1-inch cubes. Season with salt and pepper. Fry in heated oil until tender. Take out and set aside. Sauté onion in the same oil until tender. Add garlic, celery, tomatoes, and olives. Cook slowly for 10 minutes. Add eggplant, pine nuts, and capers. Heat vinegar and stir in sugar. Add to vegetable mixture. Season with salt and pepper. Cook for 5 minutes longer. Serve chilled as an appetizer or relish. Makes 6 servings.

BULGARIAN APPETIZERS

2 medium eggplants
3 tomatoes
2 to 4 garlic cloves, crushed
¼ cup chopped fresh parsley
¼ cup cooking oil (preferably olive oil)
2 tablespoons fresh lemon juice
Salt and pepper

Prick the eggplants in several places with a fork. Arrange on a cookie sheet and bake in preheated hot oven (400°F.) until soft, about 50 minutes. Peel and mash the pulp in a bowl. In the meantime bake the tomatoes until tender, about 10 minutes. Peel and chop. Mix with eggplants. Add other ingredients. (The Bulgarians prefer a strong garlic flavor and use 4 cloves. But 2 may be substituted if desired.) Chill; serve as a dip with crackers. Makes 8 servings.

EGGPLANT PUFFS

2 medium eggplants
1 cup grated Swiss cheese
1 egg, slightly beaten
6 to 8 tablespoons fine dried bread crumbs
1 teaspoon ground cuminseed
1 teaspoon garlic powder
1 teaspoon fresh lemon juice
Salt and pepper
All-purpose flour
Cooking oil for frying (preferably olive oil)

Cook the whole eggplants in boiling water until tender, 15 to 20 minutes. Peel; put the pulp in a bowl. Drain off any water. Mash finely with a fork and beat a little. Add the other ingredients except the flour and oil. Beat until well mixed with a whisk or in an electric blender. The final consistency may seem a little thin, but nevertheless shape into small balls and arrange on a plate. Let stand in the refrigerator for at least 1 hour. Roll in flour. Fry in hot oil until crisp. Serve hot with toothpicks. Makes about 24 small puffs.

DEEP-FRIED EGGPLANT

1 large eggplant
Salt and pepper to taste
¼ cup all-purpose flour
1 egg
2 tablespoons milk or water
¼ cup fine dry bread crumbs
Fat for deep frying

Peel eggplant and cut into sticks about ¼ inch thick. Sprinkle with salt and pepper, roll in flour, then dip into egg beaten with milk. Roll in crumbs and fry in hot deep fat (380°F. on a frying thermometer) until golden brown. Drain on absorbent paper, and serve at once. Makes 6 servings.

EGGPLANT CHIPS

This simple recipe shows the delicate flavor of the eggplant, particularly enhanced by oil. In the Middle East cooks always use olive oil with the eggplant, for they learned years ago that the two were most compatible.

Cut the eggplant crosswise into ¼-inch slices or cut into finger-size rectangles. Drop at once into hot olive oil (300°F. on a frying thermometer) in skillet. Fry until golden. Drain on absorbent paper. Serve as appetizers or as a vegetable.

EGGPLANT CLAM SOUFFLÉ

2 medium eggplants
½ cup light cream
Butter
1 can (10½ ounces) minced clams, drained
½ teaspoon ground nutmeg
1 teaspoon garlic salt
1 tablespoon fresh lemon juice
Salt and pepper to taste
2 eggs
3 slices of bread
¼ cup milk
2 tablespoons fine dried bread crumbs

2 tablespoons grated Parmesan cheese
¼ cup coarsely chopped pine nuts

Cook the eggplants in salted boiling water for 15 to 20 minutes, until tender. Peel off the skins. Mash the pulp. Add the cream, 2 tablespoons butter, clams, nutmeg, garlic salt, lemon juice, salt, and pepper. Separate the eggs. Beat the yolks slightly and add. Set aside the whites. Cut off the bread crusts and crumble the bread into the milk. Squeeze dry and add to the mixture. Beat the egg whites stiffly and fold in. Carefully spoon into a buttered casserole or soufflé dish. Combine the bread crumbs, cheese, and pine nuts and sprinkle over the top. Dot with butter. Bake in preheated hot oven (400° F.) until firm, 25 to 30 minutes. Serve at once in the same dish. Makes 8 servings.

THE SULTAN'S DELIGHT

2 medium eggplants
1 pound cubed lamb, from the leg
2 tablespoons cooking oil (preferably olive oil)
2 medium onions, chopped
½ cup red wine
2 cups (one 1-pound can) tomatoes
Salt and pepper to taste
1 tablespoon chopped fresh dill or 1 teaspoon dried dillseed
¼ cup milk
2 tablespoons melted butter
3 tablespoons grated Swiss cheese

Prick the eggplants with a fork. Bake in preheated hot oven (400°F.) for about 50 minutes, or until tender. In the meantime sauté the lamb cubes in oil until the redness disappears. Add the onions, wine, tomatoes, salt, pepper, and dill. Cover and simmer for about 30 minutes. Peel the eggplants and place the pulp in a bowl. Mash thoroughly. Add the milk, butter, cheese, and salt and pepper to taste. Whip smooth. Spoon onto a platter and cover with the lamb mixture. Makes 6 servings.

EGGPLANT-SAUSAGE CASSEROLE

1 pound pork sausage (not the hot variety)
3 tablespoons chopped fresh parsley
2 tablespoons chopped green onions
½ cup red wine
¼ cup ketchup
1 tablespoon curry powder
½ pound fresh mushrooms
1 can (10½ ounces) Cheddar cheese soup
1 large eggplant
Cooking oil (preferably olive oil)
1 large tomato
¼ cup soft stale bread crumbs

Sauté the sausage until the redness disappears. Pour off any accumulated fat and separate while cooking with a fork. Add the parsley, onions, wine, ketchup, and curry powder. Cook for 5 minutes, stirring often. Wash the mushrooms and snip off the stems if necessary. Slice and add to the mixture. Cook for another 5 minutes. Spoon in the soup. Mix well and remove from the stove. Remove the stem from the eggplant. Slice thinly lengthwise. Sauté in oil on both sides until tender. Drain on absorbent paper. Arrange one layer in the bottom of a shallow 1½-quart casserole. Cover with a layer of the sausage mixture, a layer of eggplant, another of sausage mixture, and lastly a top layer of eggplant. Peel and slice the tomato and arrange over the top. Sprinkle with the bread crumbs. Bake in preheated moderate oven (350° F.) for 30 minutes. Makes 8 servings.

BRAZILIAN STUFFED EGGPLANT
    2 medium eggplants
 1½ pounds cooked ham
    3 hard-cooked eggs
    2 cans (8 ounces each) tomato sauce
        Salt and pepper to taste
    1 teaspoon crumbled dried marjoram
  ¼ cup grated Parmesan cheese

Place the eggplants in a pan with ¼ inch of water. Bake in preheated hot oven (400°F.) for 20 to 30 minutes, or until soft. Remove stem ends and slice into halves lengthwise. Scoop out the insides,

leaving a ½-inch shell. Chop the pulp and whip with a fork. Chop the ham finely or force through a food chopper. Chop the eggs and add along with the eggplant to the ham. Mix well and spoon into the eggplant shells. Put into baking dish. Heat the tomato sauce. Season with salt, pepper, and marjoram. Cook for 5 minutes. Spoon over the stuffed eggplants. Sprinkle with cheese. Bake in preheated moderate oven (350°F.) for about 20 minutes. Makes 4 servings.

INDIVIDUAL BAKED EGGPLANT AND CHICKEN
    1 large eggplant
        Cooking oil (preferably olive oil)
    2 tablespoons butter
    2 tablespoons all-purpose flour
    1 cup milk
        Salt and pepper to taste
    1 teaspoon ground cuminseed
    1 tablespoon sherry
  ½ cup grated Romano cheese
    3 cups finely minced cooked chicken
    1 cup cooked peas
        Buttered soft bread crumbs

Remove the eggplant stem. Cut eggplant

in 6 thin slices crosswise from its thinner end. Slice the remaining eggplant thinly lengthwise. Fry all slices in oil on both sides until tender. Drain on absorbent paper. Line 6 small baking dishes, custard, or ovenproof glass cups with the longer slices. Reserve the rounds for later. Chop any remaining slices and set aside. Melt the butter in a saucepan. Add the flour and blend well. Gradually stir in the milk. Season with salt, pepper, cuminseed, and sherry. Cook for 5 minutes over low heat, stirring constantly, until sauce thickens. Add the cheese, chicken, and any chopped eggplant and cook for 5 more minutes. Lastly add the peas. Carefully spoon into the lined dishes. Sprinkle with bread crumbs. Top with an eggplant round. Cook in preheated moderate oven (350°F.) for 20 minutes. Makes 6 servings.

ITALIAN EGGPLANT PARMIGIANA
    1 large eggplant
        Salt and pepper to taste

Turkish Imam Bayeldi   *Deep-Fried Eggplant*

1 cup fine dry bread crumbs
2 eggs, lightly beaten
  Cooking oil (preferably olive oil)
1½ cups tomato sauce, heated
½ pound Mozzarella cheese, sliced
1 teaspoon crumbled dried basil
¼ cup Parmesan cheese, grated

Wash eggplant and cut crosswise into rounds ¼ inch thick. Do not peel. Season with salt and pepper. Dip into bread crumbs, dip into egg, and then again into bread crumbs. (Depending on size of the eggplant, more bread crumbs and egg may be necessary.) Place in refrigerator for 30 minutes. Heat about ⅛ inch of oil in a skillet. Fry eggplant slices until tender and golden on both sides. Add more oil when necessary. Drain on absorbent paper. Line a buttered shallow baking dish with some of the sauce. Arrange a layer of eggplant slices over the sauce. Cover with a layer of Mozzarella slices, more sauce, and a sprinkling of basil and Parmesan. Repeat in layers until the dish is full. Bake in preheated moderate oven (350°F.) for 25 to 30 minutes. Makes 6 servings.

EGGPLANT LASAGNA

2 quarts water
1 teaspoon cooking oil (preferably olive oil)
  Salt
½ pound lasagna macaroni
1 medium eggplant
1 can (6 ounces) tomato paste
1 cup red wine
½ cup hot water
1 garlic clove, crushed
1 teaspoon crumbled dried basil
1 teaspoon ground turmeric
  Pepper
2 cups chopped green peppers
10 black olives, pitted and chopped
½ cup grated Parmesan cheese

Heat the water, oil, and 1 teaspoon salt to boiling. Cook the lasagna for 12 to 15 minutes. Drain; arrange the lasagna lengths on a platter. Slice the unpeeled eggplant crosswise into ¼-inch rounds. Fry on both sides in heated oil until tender. (They cook quickly and absorb considerable oil which must be added constantly.) Drain on absorbent paper. Combine the tomato paste, wine, water, garlic, basil, turmeric, and salt and pepper to taste. Simmer for 5 minutes. Add the green peppers and olives. Cook for 5 minutes longer. Arrange a layer of lasagna in a buttered shallow baking dish. Cover with a layer of eggplant slices and several spoonfuls of the sauce. Sprinkle with cheese. Repeat until all the ingredients are used. Bake in preheated moderate oven (350°F.) for 30 minutes. Makes 8 servings.

TURKISH IMAM BAYELDI
(The Imam Fainted)

There are many stories about the origin of the name of this dish. One of them we heard while visiting Ankara, Turkey's capital. A long time ago a Turkish Imam

(Mohammedan priest), known for his love of good food, surprised his friends by announcing his engagement to the young daughter of a wealthy olive-oil merchant. The friends did not know about her ability to cook. But they presumed part of her dowry would include olive oil. They were right. For her father gave the groom twelve jars, each large enough to hold a person, of the precious oil. After her marriage the bride proved to be an excellent cook and each day prepared a special dish for her epicurean husband. One of them, eggplant cooked in olive oil, became his favorite. And he ordered that his wife prepare it each night for dinner. This she did for twelve consecutive days. On the thirteenth, however, the dish was missing from the meal. Queried about its absence, the bride replied, "Dear husband, I do not have any more olive oil. You will have to purchase some more for me." The Imam was so shocked that he fainted. And since that day, according to the story, his favorite dish has been known as *Imam Bayeldi*, The Imam Fainted.

2 medium onions, chopped
  Olive oil
2 garlic cloves, crushed
3 medium tomatoes, peeled and chopped
3 tablespoons chopped parsley
  Salt and pepper to taste
2 medium eggplants
2 teaspoons sugar
3 tablespoons fresh lemon juice

Sauté the onions in a little oil. Add the garlic, tomatoes, parsley, salt, and pepper. Cook until mushy. Cut the stem ends from each eggplant. Make 3 lengthwise slits, almost from end to end. With hand hold each slit apart and spoon the onion mixture into each cavity. Arrange eggplants in a baking dish. Sprinkle with sugar, lemon juice, and ½ cup oil. Bake, covered, in preheated moderate oven (350°F.) for 40 minutes, or until tender. Serve hot, or as they do in Turkey, cold with yogurt. Makes 4 to 6 servings.

FRIED EGGPLANT

Wash 2 medium eggplants. Slice into rounds about ¼ inch thick. Season to taste with salt and pepper. Dip into fine bread crumbs; dip into slightly beaten egg; dip again into bread crumbs. Heat about ⅛ inch of oil in a skillet. Fry the slices on both sides until crisp. Drain on absorbent paper. Serve, if desired, with sour cream. Makes 8 servings.

RATATOUILLE PROVENÇALE

1 medium eggplant
¾ to 1 cup olive oil
2 cups (one 1-pound can) plum tomatoes
1 jar (4 ounces) pimientos, drained
2 medium onions, sliced
1 garlic clove, crushed
2 tablespoons chopped fresh parsley
1 teaspoon capers
  Salt and pepper to taste

Remove the stem from the eggplant and

cut eggplant into cubes. Sauté in oil for a few minutes. Add the other ingredients and cook slowly, mixing occasionally, until the eggplant is cooked, about 20 minutes. Do not cook too long or the vegetables will become mushy. Makes 6 servings.

BALKAN STUFFED EGGPLANT

2 medium eggplants
2 medium onions, chopped
1 tablespoon butter
1 pound ground lamb
1 beef bouillon cube
½ cup hot water
3 tablespoons tomato purée
¼ cup uncooked rice
1 teaspoon crumbled dried oregano
2 tablespoons chopped parsley
½ teaspoon salt
¼ teaspoon pepper
½ cup soft bread crumbs
¾ cup tomato sauce

Slice eggplants in half lengthwise. Scoop out insides, leaving a shell 1 inch thick. Sauté the onions in butter until tender. Add the lamb and cook until the meat has lost its redness. Pour off any fat. Dissolve the bouillon cube in hot water and add with the tomato purée to the lamb. Cook for 10 minutes, separating the meat with a fork from time to time. Chop eggplant pulp and add to meat mixture; cook for 10 minutes. Remove from heat and mix in remaining ingredients, except bread crumbs and tomato sauce. Fill eggplant shells with the stuffing. Arrange in a shallow buttered baking dish. Sprinkle lightly with the bread crumbs. Streak the sauce over the tops. Bake in preheated moderate oven (375°F.) for 45 to 50 minutes, until the eggplant is tender. Serve hot. Makes 4 servings.

TURKISH EGGPLANT SALAD

2 medium eggplants
¼ cup olive oil
  Juice of ½ lemon
⅛ teaspoon salt
  Tomato slices
  Green-pepper slices
  Black olives

Place the eggplants under the broiler (not too close to the flame or the skins will break), turning eggplants occasionally, until the skins become charcoal black. (The blackness is necessary to impart the charcoal flavor to the pulp.) Peel off the skins while still hot. Place the pulp in a bowl. Cool and dice pulp. Mash finely with a fork. Add next 3 ingredients, a little at a time, beating after each addition. When mixture is light and fluffy, surround with tomato and green-pepper slices and black olives. Serve chilled. Makes 6 to 8 servings.

EGGPLANT-YOGURT SALAD

2 medium eggplants
1 cup plain yogurt
1 cup diced celery
2 carrots, diced

1 cucumber, scored and sliced
8 black or green olives, pitted
5 fresh mushrooms, sliced
3 tablespoons cooking oil
   (preferably olive oil)
2 tablespoons fresh lemon juice
   Salt and pepper to taste
   Tomato slices

Prick the eggplants with a fork. Place on a cookie sheet and bake in preheated hot oven (400°F.) for 50 minutes, or until tender. Peel; put the pulp in a bowl. Drain off any water. Mash with a fork until smooth. Cool. Add the other ingredients, except tomato. Mix well. Spoon onto a plate and shape into a mound. Chill. Decorate with tomato slices at serving time. Makes 8 servings.

ELDERBERRY—This is the fruit of the elder, a wild shrub of the *Sambucus* family, with white flowers and purple-black or red berries. There are several varieties of elder which grow wild in Europe, North Africa, western Asia, North America, and the West Indies. The flowers grow in saucerlike, flat clusters, and the berries grow in heavy clusters. Elderberries are among the most plentiful, useful, and healthful of wild fruits.

Elderberries lack acid and, eaten raw, they have a rank flavor and odor. When properly prepared with the addition of lemon juice, crab apples, or sour grapes, they are delicious. They are used for making jellies and jams; but they are best known as the basic ingredient for the most famous of homemade wines, a spicy brew as potent as the maker cares to make it.

Elderberries can also be dried or stewed and used for making muffins and pies.

The berry is not the only usable part of the wild shrub. The buds can be pickled. The clusters of white flowers, at the height of their bloom and without the coarse stems, make superlative fritters when dipped into batter and deep fried, and they too can be made into wine. The dried flowers make a tea used in cases of dyspepsia. The flowers are also used for making elderflower water, an ingredient in confectionery, perfume, and lotions. A hot poultice made from the crushed leaves of the plant is said to ease sprains and bruises. The Mahican Indians used the bark as a laxative and the flower tea as a colic medicine for infants.

Although the wood of the young shrubs or trees is brittle, the wood of the old ones is hard and close grained and very useful for making small wooden articles. People with a knowledge of the woods know that young elder twigs will make splendid blowguns, peashooters, water pistols, and whistles when their pith is removed so that only a thick hollow stem remains.

A surprising amount of folklore, both European and American, surrounds the elderberry bush. In Denmark the tree was under the protection of the Elder Mother who did not like its wood employed in household furniture. In England the elder attracted the devil, but in Scotland branches were hung in windows and doors to keep away the evil spirits. In some parts of the United States it was believed that an elder stick in the fire on Christmas Eve would reveal all the witches and sorcerers in the neighborhood.

Availability—Available in the late summer months in localities where they grow.

Storage

☐ Room temperature or refrigerator shelf: 1 to 2 days
☐ Refrigerator frozen-food compartment, prepared for freezing: 2 months
☐ Freezer, prepared for freezing: 1½ years

Caloric Value

☐ 3½ ounces, raw = 72 calories

To Freeze—Remove stems and wash berries. Freeze without sugar, or use 1 cup sugar to 6 cups berries, stirring until the sugar is dissolved.

ELDERBERRY JELLY

3 pounds ripe elderberries
½ cup strained fresh lemon juice
   (about 4 lemons)
7 cups (3 pounds) sugar
1 bottle fruit pectin

Remove large stems from elderberries. Put berries in kettle and crush. Heat gently until juice starts to flow, then simmer, covered, for 15 minutes. Put in jelly cloth or bag and squeeze out juice. Measure 3 cups into kettle. Add lemon juice and sugar and mix well. Put over high heat and bring to boil, stirring constantly. Stir in pectin at once. Then bring to a *full rolling boil and boil hard for 1 minute,* stirring constantly. Remove from heat, skim off foam with metal spoon, and pour quickly into hot sterilized jelly glasses. Cover at once with ⅛ inch of hot paraffin. Makes 11 medium glasses.

ELDERBERRY FRITTERS

   Elderberry flower clusters
1 cup sifted all-purpose flour
1 tablespoon sugar
1 teaspoon baking powder
2 eggs
½ cup milk
   Fat for frying

Dip washed and drained flower clusters into a batter made by beating next 5 ingredients together. Fry dipped clusters in deep fat or oil (375°F. on frying thermometer) for 4 minutes, or until they are golden brown. Drain on absorbent paper. Roll in additional granulated sugar. Serve hot. Makes 4 servings.

ELDERBERRY PIE

   Plain pastry (recipe made with 2 cups flour)
3 cups stemmed elderberries
½ cup sugar
⅛ teaspoon salt
2 tablespoons all-purpose flour
3 tablespoons fresh lemon juice

Line 9-inch pie pan with pastry. Fill with washed berries. Mix sugar, salt, and flour and sprinkle on berries. Add lemon juice. Adjust top crust and flute edges. Cut a few gashes in top to allow steam to escape. Bake in preheated very hot oven (450°F.) for 10 minutes. Reduce heat to moderate (350°F.) and bake for about 30 minutes longer. Serve slightly warm or cold.

ELDERBERRY WINE

12 quarts boiling water
4 quarts stemmed elderberries
6¾ cups sugar
3 teaspoons ground ginger
8 whole cloves
1 pound seeded raisins
   Brandy (optional)
   Active dry yeast or compressed yeast

Pour boiling water on berries and let stand for 24 hours. Strain through coarse bag or cloth, squeezing and breaking berries to extract all possible juice. Add sugar, ginger, cloves, and raisins. Bring to boil and simmer for 1 hour, skimming frequently. Cool to lukewarm. Measure, and if brandy is used, add ½ cup to each 4 quarts of mixture. Add 1 package active dry yeast or 1 cake compressed yeast to each 16 quarts of mixture. Let stand for 2 weeks to ferment. Then put in bottles and keep several months in a cool place before using. Makes about 8 quarts.

ELECTRONIC COOKING—In this type of cooking ultrahigh-frequency radio waves are used to produce heat. These waves pass back and forth rapidly, generating heat through the entire mass of the food at once. Only the food is cooked. The oven, a special electronic one, and the utensils in which the food is cooked remain cold. (In conventional oven cooking, heat is applied to the surface of a food; the surface heats up and the heat is conducted into the food until it is cooked to the degree of doneness desired.)

The principles of electronic cooking have been known for some time, and the method has been used commercially for several years. Today there are units available for homes with different combinations of conventional surface and oven units, plus the electronic unit. Food cooked electronically, although cooked through, does not brown on the surface. To accomplish this, electronic ovens include elements which supply normal, external heat needed for browning.

The particular advantage of electronic cooking is speed, especially when applied to large amounts of food. For example, a 12-pound turkey cooks in 1 hour electronically, whereas it would require 4 hours in a conventional oven.

ELIXIR—This word has a number of meanings. A sweetened and aromatic liquid containing more or less alcohol, used for its medicinal qualities or for flavoring; and, long ago, as a potion to instill love or hate. The other current meaning is "quintessence," the essential substance of a thing.

› Two additional meanings are now a thing of the past, although much used in their time. In the Middle Ages, an elixir was a substance that would change base metals into gold. And the words, *elixir vitae* or "elixir of life," were applied to a substance that would prolong life indefinitely, so that elixir came to mean a "cure-all." The medieval alchemists, in their laboratories crowded with brewing kettles, glass retorts, and other distilling paraphernalia, spent centuries trying to find *the* elixir that would solve mankind's financial and personal problems at one fell swoop, making people both rich and immortal.

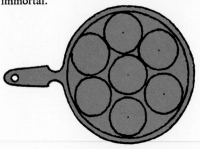

ENDIVE—This salad green is a member of the family of plants called *Cichorium,* to which chicory also belongs. The endive is a plant with narrow, finely divided, curly leaves and is often called "curly endive." It grows in a loose-leaved head.

Two other salad greens closely related to endive are escarole, which has broad waved leaves and a blanched heart, and witloof, or Belgian endive, which is four to six inches in length and one to two inches thick. The leaves of Belgian endive are white with light-green tips pressed close together to form a cylinder which tapers off to a point.

Endive appears to be native to the East Indies, but it was introduced to Egypt and Greece at an early period. The colonists first brought these greens to America.

Endive has a slightly bitter flavor and in America is used practically only in salads. Europeans cook it in broth and make composite dishes with it, which deserve recognition in the United States as a welcome change in cooked vegetables. Endive and escarole can be used interchangeably in salads and in cooking.

Availability—Curly endive is available from October through May. Main part of the crop comes from Florida and California.

Belgian endive is imported and is available from October to May.

Purchasing Guide—Look for crisp, fresh, tender plants. Avoid tough, dark-green outer leaves; look for a tightly packed head. Browning of the outer leaves indicates bruises.

Storage—Remove and discard any bruised outer leaves. Wash the heads thoroughly under cold running water. Drain; shake off as much of the water as possible; blot dry with a paper towel. Store in the refrigerator in the vegetable compartment or in a moisture-proof bag.

☐ Refrigerator shelf or vegetable compartment: 3 to 8 days

Nutritive Food Values—A good source of vitamin A and a fair source of iron.

☐ Curly endive, 3½ ounces, raw = 20 calories

☐ Belgian endive, 3½ ounces, raw = 17 calories

Basic Preparation—Remove from the refrigerator just prior to use in order to maintain maximum crispness. Cut away any tough segment of the stem. Use endive leaves whole for variety and texture in the salad; it may also be broken into bite-size pieces.

Serve endive with a salad dressing or combine it with chicory in a tossed salad. Use endive and chicory as a base for other salads or as a garnish.

BELGIAN ENDIVE APPETIZER

    12 endive leaves
    ¼   cup caviar
    4   lemon wedges
        Salt, pepper, Worcestershire
    2   packages (3 ounces each)
        cream cheese
        Mayonnaise

Fill endive with caviar and arrange 3 leaves on each plate, meeting at the center on a lemon wedge. Add salt, pepper, and Worcestershire to taste to cream cheese, and moisten with mayonnaise. Shape into balls and arrange 3 on each plate between endive leaves. Makes 4 servings.

BELGIAN ENDIVE AU GRATIN

    8   heads endive
        Salt
    ⅓   cup butter or margarine
    ¼   cup all-purpose flour
    2   cups milk
    ½   cup grated Parmesan cheese
        Dash of cayenne
    2   tablespoons soft bread crumbs,
        buttered

Cook endive in small amount of salted boiling water for 20 minutes, or until tender. Drain and put in shallow broiler-proof dish. Melt butter and blend in flour. Gradually add milk and cook over low heat, stirring constantly, until thickened. Add half of cheese, salt to taste, and cayenne. Pour over endive. Mix remaining cheese and crumbs and sprinkle over top. Brown lightly under broiler. Makes 6 to 8 servings.

CURLY ENDIVE STEWED IN BUTTER

Wash and trim 1½ pounds endive. Cut into ½-inch pieces. Melt 2 tablespoons butter or margarine in skillet. Add endive and cook, stirring, for 1 or 2 minutes. Add salt, reduce heat, cover, and cook for about 10 minutes. Add a little lemon juice, and serve. Makes 6 servings.

CURLY ENDIVE WITH BACON OR HAM

Prepare 1½ pounds endive as for Curly Endive Stewed in Butter. Just before serving, add ¼ cup diced bacon or ham cooked until lightly browned. Add a squeeze of lemon juice. Makes 6 servings.

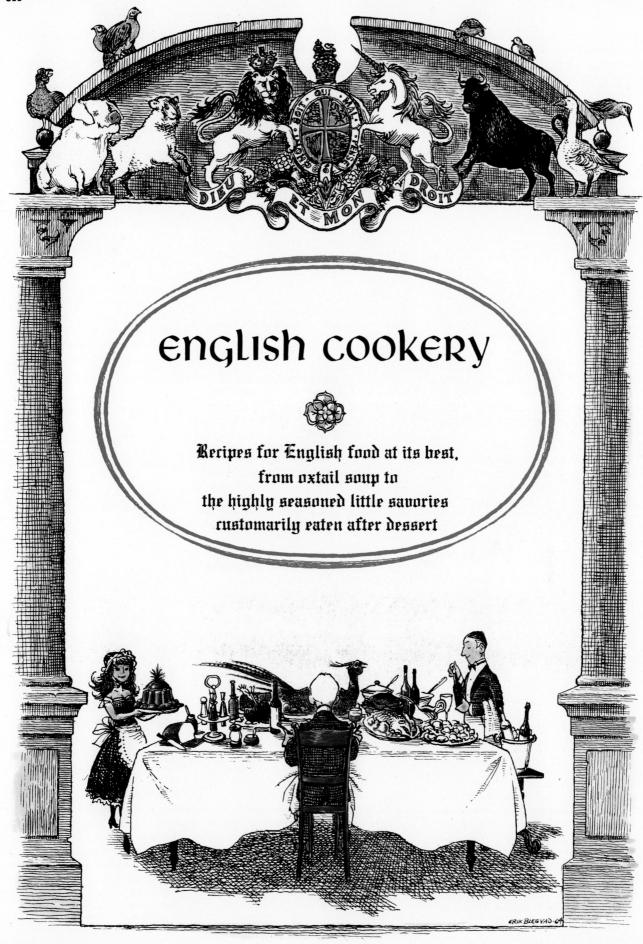

english cookery

Recipes for English food at its best,
from oxtail soup to
the highly seasoned little savories
customarily eaten after dessert

By James A. Beard

English cookery has been criticized so often and for so long that most Americans accept the notion that it is all dull and tasteless. Like most generalizations this is only partly true. English food can be bad or it can be delicious depending on where you are dining. Those who have had the opportunities and the time to explore the island, searching out good inns and restaurants and dining with English families who take pride in their tables, will contend that the English can and do serve great food. The specialties of England are expressive of a tradition of hearty satisfying foods. They are "rib-sticking" foods as my father used to call them. When they are properly prepared they are superb.

To begin with, the English have fine sources of basic foods. Their beef and mutton are excellent. Their country hams have the true old-fashioned flavor. English cheeses are famous throughout the world and practically every shire has a local cheese that is remarkably good. No spot in England is more than sixty miles from the sea so fresh fish is available all the time.

The island boasts an abundant variety of fresh fruits and vegetables in season and imported foods are in the markets all year. Also English and Scottish people have always made the most of the wild treasures such as berries, herbs, and game found in woods and meadows. This means that a traveler in the provinces encounters an amazing number of culinary treats.

In general, English cooking is rather simple and the emphasis is on bringing out the fine flavor of the basic ingredient. Fish and shellfish dishes, for example, have a fresh clean taste: potted shrimps made from the tiniest shrimps mixed with butter and mace and served cold for a first course; the fabulous chilled salmon served with good homemade mayonnaise and cucumber salad, or a fine salmon trout, both dishes elegantly simple and often served at the most formal parties. And of course there is that greatest of all fish, the fine Channel sole, meaty and delicately flavored. It is simply grilled or gently sautéed and served with lemon wedges and parsley.

The well known rare roast beef and the English mutton chop grilled rare are other examples of simple but elegant English cookery; and the utter delight of a steak and kidney pie with its savory seasonings can never be forgotten.

One of the world's great culinary treats is the traditional English tea. There is nothing quite like it in any other country. A tempting variety of tidbits is offered at this relaxing hour and it is mouth-watering just to recall them: pikelets, luscious moist buns like the crumpets found in some shops here; Devonshire scones made of rich biscuit dough, and often served with butter, fresh raspberry jam, and Devonshire cream. Utterly irresistible! The famous muffins which used to be delivered by the muffin man are, alas, seldom found in England today. In fact, as one traveled Englishman reported, the muffin is now available only in American chemist shops, meaning our drugstore counters!

The cakes for tea are known by such charming names as Madeira, Genoa, and Simnel. All of them are fruity, rich, and flavorful. Then there are tiny tarts and those incredible small cakes called Maids of Honour, and lemon cheese tarts, Chelsea buns, and treacle tarts, all equally satisfying with a good cup of tea and milk. If you want an egg tea, you may have a boiled egg or a dropped egg (poached) on toast. Or at a country tea you may be served a substantial dish of eggs and bacon.

Then there are tiny tea sandwiches made on thin, thin slices of fresh firm bread and filled with crisp cucumbers, tomato slices, sprigs of watercress, sardine paste, thin slices of chicken, or any number of things. For some reason the English make exceptionally good chicken sandwiches. It is a combination that is simple and depends on good quality: fine bread, fresh sweet butter, and moist flavorful chicken. Last summer I sat with friends in Brown's Hotel in London and lunched very well off thin well-filled chicken sandwiches and good champagne. Could anyone ask for better?

If you wander through London or other sizable English cities, you'll find shops with signs saying "Fresh Cut Sandwiches." The bread is generally good, the butter and fillings generously heaped, and these make hearty midday snacks.

The English breakfast is another great tradition, and travelers with hearty appetites are delighted when faced with the breakfast menu in a notable country inn. Such a lavish choice! Besides the usual bacon and egg dishes, there will be such items as grilled kidneys, grilled sausages served with small grilled tomatoes, eggs and perhaps a grilled mushroom cap or so; kippers, the smoky well-cured herring gently grilled; or finnan haddie poached in milk and drenched with butter; or kedgeree if you prefer it. All served with buttered toast, marmalade, and tea, of course. Each dish offers a distinctive blend of flavors that is definitely English.

Other traditions abound in English cuisine. *Crème Brûlée,* for example, a favorite at one of the colleges in Cambridge for over two centuries and never found in France despite its name. An old Dorset recipe for "Burnt Cream" is undoubtedly its origin.

Great pies, served cold, are another English specialty. They are often the *pièce de résistance* at buffets, suppers, and picnics. Filled with meats and savory jellied stock, they make good fare for a chilly day in the country. There are pork pies, veal and ham pies, and various game pies. Sometimes these pies are made in raised crusts. The crust is built up around a mold to form a rather deep rounded container, and the top crust is often decorated with bits of dough cut in various patterns: leaves, flowers, and so forth.

Then there is the great Christmas pudding, certainly completely English. There are many recipes for this dish, but all use suet, a stand-by in English cookery, and dried fruits. In times past, when the pudding was mixed each member of the household gave it a stir for good luck. These fruit puddings were rolled in cloth and dropped into a large boiler to cook for hours. On Christmas Day, the final product was arranged on a platter, wreathed with holly, and brought to the table flaming with brandy. Most certainly an impressive symbol of joy and well-being.

You gather, I'm sure, that I like English food. I do. I grew up on many of these dishes. I feel that they need to be discovered by more people, and discovery will lead to appreciation.

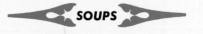

SOUPS

OXTAIL SOUP I (Clear)

1 oxtail, cut into sections
2 tablespoons butter
2 onions, stuck with 2 cloves
2 carrots, peeled
1 bay leaf
1 parsley sprig
6 whole peppercorns
2½ quarts water
1 teaspoon salt
1 cup cooked noodles or rice
Sherry, if desired

Place pieces of oxtail in baking pan. Dot with butter. Cook in preheated hot oven (425°F.) for about 30 minutes, or until oxtail is browned. Remove oxtail and juices to large heavy saucepan. Add remaining ingredients except last 3. Bring to a boil; skim. Reduce heat. Simmer, covered, for 3 to 4 hours. Remove pieces of oxtail. Trim off meat, chop it fine, and reserve. Return bones to broth and cook down to two thirds original volume; add salt. Strain broth; cool, and refrigerate for several hours to solidify fat on top. Remove fat. Broth beneath should be a rich jelly.

To serve, heat broth to boiling point; add more salt if desired. Add reserved meat; add noodles and simmer until tender. Often a little sherry is added at the last minute. Makes 1½ quarts.

OXTAIL SOUP II (Thick)

1 oxtail, cut into sections
  Butter or margarine
  All-purpose flour
1 carrot, peeled
1 turnip, peeled
1 celery stalk
1 onion stuck with 2 cloves
  Dash each of ground mace and nutmeg
1 teaspoon salt
¼ teaspoon pepper
2 garlic cloves
2 bay leaves
2½ quarts water
  Juice of 1 lemon (optional)
⅓ cup sherry or Madeira (optional)
  Lemon slices
  Chopped parsley

Place the pieces of oxtail in a shallow pan. Dot with 2 tablespoons butter and sprinkle with 2 tablespoons flour. Brown in preheated hot oven (425°F.) for about 30 minutes. Transfer meat and juices to a soup kettle. Add the vegetables, seasonings, and water. Bring to a boil, cover the kettle, and heat. Simmer for 3 hours. Remove the pieces of oxtail. Trim off meat. Discard bones. Chop meat fine and reserve.

Strain the stock, and taste for seasoning. Cool, chill, and skim off fat. At serving time, bring the stock to a boil again. Thicken it with small balls made of ⅓ cup butter and ⅓ cup flour kneaded together. If you like, add the lemon juice and wine. Use the finely chopped meat as a garnish. For a decorative touch, float a slice of lemon and a little chopped parsley on top of each bowl. Makes about 2¼ quarts, or 6 servings.

SCOTCH BROTH

2 to 3 pounds neck of lamb
½ cup pearl barley
2 quarts water
1 teaspoon salt
¼ teaspoon pepper
2 carrots
1 medium-size turnip
2 celery stalks, finely diced
12 tiny onions, peeled
  Chopped parsley

Put lamb and barley in large saucepan and add water. Simmer, covered, for 2½ hours. Strain soup and refrigerate broth to bring fat to top. Remove solidified fat and discard. Pick out bones and discard them. Cut meat into small pieces and

return with barley to broth. Add salt and pepper. Peel and dice carrots and turnip. Add with celery and onions to broth. Cook for 1 more hour, stirring occasionally, until vegetables are tender and soup well blended. If necessary, add salt and pepper to taste. Serve with chopped parsley. Makes about 2 quarts.

SPRING VEGETABLE SOUP

1 cup finely chopped onions (scallions or green onions are best)
2 cups green peas or 1 package (10 ounces) frozen peas
1 head lettuce, coarsely cut
1 pound spinach leaves or 1 package (10 ounces) frozen spinach
½ cup chopped parsley
1 teaspoon dried tarragon or 1 tablespoon fresh tarragon
  Few leaves of sorrel, if available
3 tablespoons butter
  Salt and pepper
2 quarts hot water
3 egg yolks
½ cup heavy cream

Sauté all vegetables and herbs in butter in large kettle for 2 minutes. Add 1 teaspoon salt, ⅛ teaspoon pepper, and water. Simmer, covered, until vegetables are just tender, stirring occasionally. Strain and reserve liquid. Put vegetables through a food mill or coarse sieve, or whirl in blender. Return to kettle. Add three quarters of liquid; reserve remaining liquid. At serving time, heat soup to a boil. Reduce heat. Beat egg yolks and mix with remaining liquid and the cream. Cook over low heat, stirring constantly; do not let it boil. When thickened, stir into soup. Mix well, season to taste, and serve at once. Makes about 2½ quarts.

 FISH

KEDGEREE

6 tablespoons butter
2 teaspoons curry powder
3 cups cooked rice
2 cups cooked flaked fish such as finnan haddie, salt cod, or fresh salmon
1½ tablespoons fresh lemon juice
4 hard-cooked eggs
  Dash of ketchup or Worcestershire
½ cup chopped fresh watercress, if available
  Salt and pepper

Melt butter in skillet. Stir in curry powder, blending for a minute over low heat. Add rice, fish, and lemon juice. Cook over low heat until heated through. Chop egg whites and add to mixture. Add ketchup and watercress and season to taste. Arrange on hot platter and garnish with chopped or sieved egg yolk. Makes 6 to 8 servings.
Note: This fish dish is excellent for brunch or supper. There are many versions of kedgeree, all of them good, but

I happen to find this recipe especially tasty.

FISH AND CHIPS

This is the Cockney's favorite meal. It is to him what the hamburger with French-fries is to us. He buys it at a fish-and-chips shop where it is handed to him in a cornucopia made of several thicknesses of paper. This absorbs the excess fat. He may carry it home or eat it en route.

The fish may be any kind of white fish. Allow about ⅓ pound per person. Cut the fish into narrow strips, flour them, and fry in hot fat (370°F. on a frying thermometer) until crisp and nicely browned. Sprinkle well with salt.

Serve with crisp French-fried potatoes. To save the trouble of having two fryers going at once, use frozen French-fries and heat them in the oven.

DRESSED CRAB

3 tablespoons salad oil
2 tablespoons vinegar
2 teaspoons powdered mustard
1 pound Maryland crabmeat or meat from 2 Dungeness crabs or three 6-ounce packages frozen Alaskan King Crab
2 tablespoons fresh bread crumbs
2 tablespoons chopped parsley
  Salt
1 teaspoon water
⅓ cup mayonnaise

Mix oil, vinegar, and 1 teaspoon mustard. Blend with crabmeat, crumbs, parsley, and salt to taste. Chill. Mix water and 1 teaspoon mustard. Add to mayonnaise and serve on crabmeat mixture. Makes 6 servings.
Note: The English usually serve dressed crab in the crab shell. If you don't have any, substitute a plate of greens or use small shell-shape pottery dishes.

LOBSTER SALAD, ENGLISH STYLE

Use a deep glass salad bowl and fill it half full with shredded lettuce. Marinate thinly sliced cooked potatoes and new peas in a good French dressing. Arrange these on top of the lettuce in a neat spiral pattern. Heap chunks of lobster meat on top and garnish with lobster claws, sliced hard-cooked egg, and chopped parsley. Serve with mayonnaise.
Note: If there is any pink coral from the lobster, blend it into the mayonnaise.

POACHED SALMON TROUT WITH TOMATO-MUSTARD HOLLANDAISE SAUCE

1 onion
1 carrot
  Parsley sprigs
1 celery stalk
1 teaspoon vinegar
1 teaspoon dried tarragon
½ teaspoon salt
¼ teaspoon pepper
  Water
1 salmon trout, about 4 to 5 pounds
  Lemon halves

ENGLISH COOKERY

Put vegetables, vinegar, seasonings, and enough water to cover fish in a large heavy skillet. Bring to boil and boil rapidly for 10 minutes. In the meantime, wrap fish in cheesecloth, leaving long ends of the cloth to use as handles. Lower fish into court bouillon and poach gently in barely simmering liquid. Cook for 5 to 6 minutes per pound, or until fish flakes easily when tested with fork or toothpick. Grasp handles and carefully lift out. Place on serving platter and unwrap. Garnish with additional parsley and lemon halves. Serve with hollandaise sauce flavored with 1 teaspoon prepared mustard and 1 teaspoon tomato paste. Makes 8 servings.

Note: This elegant fish, a great favorite in England, abounds in parts of this country as well. It is sometimes called landlocked salmon or lake trout. In Switzerland and France it is known as *omble chevalier*. It is indeed a delicacy.

Salmon trout vary in size from small fish that will serve two persons up to quite large fish that will serve eight.

BAKED SALMON WITH CAPER BUTTER

4 salmon steaks, about 1½ inches thick
⅓ cup fresh lemon juice
½ cup butter, melted
 Salt and pepper
¼ cup each of chopped parsley
 and capers

Rub the salmon steaks with lemon juice and brush them well with melted butter. Season with salt and pepper to taste. Arrange in a baking dish and bake in preheated hot oven (425°F.) for about 20 minutes, basting with a combination of melted butter and lemon juice every 5 minutes. Do not turn.

Arrange the cooked salmon steaks on a hot platter. Mix the pan juices with the chopped parsley and capers, and pour over the steaks. If additional liquid is needed, add a little dry vermouth or white wine. Good with new potatoes, dressed with butter and parsley, and a cucumber salad. Makes 4 servings.

POTTED SHRIMPS

2 cups cooked, shelled, and deveined
 shrimps
½ teaspoon ground mace
 Dash of ground nutmeg
 Salt and pepper
 About 1 cup butter, melted
 Lettuce leaves
 Parsley

If you can get the tiny shrimps from the Pacific or imported from Sweden, leave them whole. Large shrimps should be cut into pieces, some larger and some smaller; cut about ½ cup into small chunks and chop the rest coarsely. Mix shrimps with spices and season with salt and pepper to taste. Fill small pots or ramekins with the shrimp mixture; pour over them enough melted butter to cover. Chill. To serve, unmold the shrimp mixture on lettuce leaves and garnish with sprigs of parsley. Thin rye bread or whole-wheat bread sandwiches accompany this dish. Makes 4 servings.

GRILLED SOLE WITH MUSTARD SAUCE

English sole is the greatest fish from the northern seas; some people claim it is the greatest fish in the world. Our American flounder or lemon sole is the nearest we can come to it, and although it may not be quite the equal of the famed English fish, it is delicate and delicious. Allow 1 medium sole per person unless the fish are particularly small. Then allow about 1½ to 2 per person. If some of your guests or family have very hearty appetites, add an extra fish or two.

Brush the soles well with melted butter and season with salt and pepper. Grill under the broiler or over charcoal. The fish will take from 5 to 9 minutes to cook, depending on their size. Brush with butter several times during cooking. Brown them nicely on both sides. They are done when the flesh flakes easily with a fork or toothpick.

Remove to a hot platter, add a little melted butter, and sprinkle with chopped parsley. Serve with the following Mustard Sauce.

Mustard Sauce

Melt ¼ cup butter in a heavy saucepan over low heat. Add 3 tablespoons all-purpose flour and ½ teaspoon each of salt and pepper. Stir until blended. Gradually stir in 1 cup milk or light cream. Continue cooking and stirring until the sauce is smooth and thickened. Add 2 teaspoons, or more to taste, of Dijon mustard (bottled French mustard available in most food stores) and a drop of hot pepper sauce. Bring to a boil, and serve. Makes about 1⅓ cups.

English Specialties
1. *Stilton Cheese*
2. *Poached Salmon Trout*
3. *Five-Jam Tart*
4. *Trifle*
5. *Tomato-Mustard Hollandaise Sauce*
6. *Steak and Kidney Pie*
7. *The Roast Beef of England (English cut of beef with pan-browned potatoes)*
8. *Yorkshire Pudding*

MEAT

BOILED LEG OF LAMB WITH CAPER SAUCE

1 leg of young lamb, boned down to shank bone and tied
Salt and pepper to taste
Crumbled dried rosemary
Water
1 bay leaf
1 onion, stuck with 2 cloves
Parsley sprig
1 tablespoon peppercorns
Caper Sauce
Watercress

Rub meat with salt, pepper, and rosemary. Tie in heavy piece of linen. Put 2 cups water and rest of seasonings in heavy Dutch oven and boil for 10 minutes. Add lamb and more water, enough to cover. Bring to a boil; reduce heat so that liquid just bubbles. Cover and cook until meat is done, but it may be still pinkish, allowing 15 minutes per pound. A meat thermometer will register about 160° to 170°F. internal temperature. Unwrap and place on hot platter. Serve with Caper Sauce and garnish with watercress. Makes 6 to 8 servings.

Caper Sauce

3 tablespoons butter
3 tablespoons all-purpose flour
½ cup broth from the lamb
½ cup milk
3 tablespoons capers

Melt butter and stir in flour. Blend, and cook for 1 minute. Slowly stir in the broth and cook, stirring constantly, until sauce begins to thicken. Add milk and capers and continue cooking until well blended and hot through. Add salt and pepper if necessary.

ROAST LAMB WITH MINT SAUCE AND NEW PEAS

Simply roast a leg of lamb according to your favorite method. Serve it with new green peas, buttered new potatoes, and Mint Sauce. This is a classic of English cooking.

Mint Sauce

¾ cup vinegar
¼ cup water
2 tablespoons sugar
½ cup finely chopped mint

Combine the vinegar, water, and sugar and bring to a boil. Add the mint, and cool. Add more sugar if the sauce is too sharp for you. Makes about 1 cup.

STEAK AND KIDNEY PIE

2 beef kidneys
1 pound round steak, cut ½ inch thick
All-purpose flour
1 onion, minced
2 tablespoons margarine
Salt and pepper
2 cups water
1 bay leaf
Few sprigs of parsley
Few celery leaves
½ pound mushrooms, sliced
2 teaspoons steak sauce
Dash hot pepper sauce
Pastry (recipe made with 1½ cups flour)
1 egg

Remove outer membrane of kidneys. Split open and remove all fat and white veins. Soak in cold water to cover for 30 minutes. Drain and cut kidneys and steak in 1-inch pieces. Dredge with flour and brown with onion in margarine. Sprinkle with 2 teaspoons salt and ¼ teaspoon pepper. Add next 5 ingredients. Bring to boil, cover and simmer for 1 hour, or until meats are tender. Thicken with 2 to 3 tablespoons flour blended with a little cold water. Add remaining seasonings and salt and pepper to taste. Pour into 1½-quart casserole. Roll pastry to fit top, arrange on casserole, trim and flute the edges with a fork. Brush with egg, beaten with 1 teaspoon cold water. From remaining pastry, cut leaf and stem designs and arrange on pastry. Brush with the egg mixture. Bake in preheated very hot oven (450°F.) for about 20 minutes. Makes 6 servings.

THE ROAST BEEF OF ENGLAND

When one thinks of English food specialties, the first item that comes to mind is beef. The famed roast beef of England is the sirloin, a cut we use for steaks. It makes a delicious joint. Perhaps you can persuade your butcher to cut a sirloin roast for you. Do not buy top sirloin, but the section that is used for porterhouse and T-bone steaks. Have the butcher cut it with the fillet included. All the suet should be left on the roast so that it will be properly lubricated while cooking.

Rub the meat with salt, pepper, and a little flour and arrange it on a rack in the oven. Place a dripping pan underneath. Or if preferred, put meat on a rack in roasting pan. In former times, the roast was cooked directly in front of the open fire.

The English allow 15 minutes to the pound and 15 minutes extra for the roast. This is for rare meat. If you use a meat thermometer, it should read 130° to 140°F. Let the roast stand outside the oven for 15 minutes before carving.

This roast is usually served with potatoes browned in the pan and Yorkshire pudding. Other accompaniments are often buttered Brussels sprouts and mashed swedes (rutabagas).

Horseradish and mustard are passed and sometimes pickled onions.

YORKSHIRE PUDDING I

2 eggs
1 cup milk
Beef drippings
¾ cup plus 2 tablespoons unsifted all-purpose flour
½ teaspoon salt

Beat eggs well; add milk and 3 tablespoons beef drippings. Beat in flour and salt, blending well. Grease baking pan (11 x 7 x 1½ inches) or individual glass dishes with drippings. Pour in batter (individual dishes should be two thirds full). Bake in preheated very hot oven (450°F.) for 10 minutes; reduce heat to moderate (350°F.). Finish baking until pudding is crisp and golden brown, about 20 minutes longer. Makes 4 to 6 servings.

YORKSHIRE PUDDING II

2 eggs
1 cup plus 2 tablespoons milk
¼ teaspoon salt
¼ cup unsifted all-purpose flour
Beef drippings
1 tablespoon water

Beat eggs well, add milk, salt, and flour, beating thoroughly. Cover and let stand. Put drippings into 6 small glass dishes or individual pottery baking dishes and put in oven with roast to heat. Fold water into batter and fill hot containers. Bake in preheated very hot oven (450°F.) for 15 to 20 minutes, or until crisp and puffy and browned. Makes 6 servings.

COLD ROAST BEEF

The cold roast is cut into thin slices and served with pickled walnuts or chowchow. Accompaniments are salad, bread and butter, and sometimes potatoes, sautéed or fried.

BUBBLE AND SQUEAK

There are many versions of this dish. Sometimes it's made with all the vegetables left from the Sunday joint: potatoes, cabbage, rutabagas, carrots, all cooked together with beef drippings and bits of the meat mixed in. This should be cooked in a heavy skillet until brown and crispy, and served with slices of the cold roast: a hearty satisfying meal. Another version is made from leftover boiled beef. Slices of cold meat, cold boiled potatoes, cabbage and carrots are all cooked in beef drippings or butter until crispy and well mixed. Serve with pickles, bread and butter, and a good salad.

LANCASHIRE HOT POT

3 tablespoons butter
2 pounds sliced lamb neck
Salt and pepper to taste
2 medium onions, sliced
½ pound mushrooms, sliced
3 lamb kidneys, sliced
2 pounds potatoes, peeled and cut into ½-inch slices
3 tablespoons all-purpose flour
1½ cups stock or bouillon
1 teaspoon sugar

Melt the butter in a skillet. Brown the meat slices in it. Sprinkle with salt and pepper. Transfer meat to heavy casserole or baking dish with a tight cover. Use a casserole that can be brought to the table for serving. Brown the sliced onions in the same skillet that you used to brown the meat. Put them in a layer on top of the lamb. Add a layer of mushrooms and a layer of sliced kidneys. Arrange the sliced potatoes on top of kidneys, overlapping the slices and placing them in a neat spiral pattern.

Add the flour to the skillet in which you browned the meat. Blend it with the pan juices. Slowly stir in heated stock. Cook, stirring constantly, until thickened and smooth. Blend in sugar. Pour the broth over the contents of the casserole and cover tightly. Bake in preheated moderate oven (350°F.) for 2 hours. Remove the cover for the last 15 to 20 minutes to brown the potatoes. Makes 4 to 6 servings.

BOILED BEEF WITH CARROTS AND EGG DUMPLINGS
5 to 6 pounds cross rib, short ribs, or
    beef brisket
13 to 17 carrots, peeled
1 marrow bone
1 teaspoon crumbled dried thyme
1 parsley sprig
1 onion, peeled
1 teaspoon salt
Egg Dumplings

Put beef, 1 carrot, and remaining ingredients, except Dumplings, in kettle and add water to cover. Bring to boil, reduce heat and simmer, allowing 25 minutes per pound. One hour before meat is done, add rest of carrots. Ten minutes before end of cooking time, drop Egg Dumpling batter on top of liquid. Cover and steam without uncovering for 10 minutes. Serve beef with fresh horseradish, mustard, and good pickles. Have potatoes if you like, but they are not necessary with the dumplings. Makes 6 servings with beef left over.

Egg Dumplings
Mix 2 egg yolks, 1 tablespoon milk, and ½ teaspoon salt. Beat in 3 tablespoons unsifted all-purpose flour. Continue beating until light. Fold in 2 egg whites, beaten until stiff but not dry.

 POULTRY

ROAST TURKEY, ENGLISH STYLE
For the Stuffing
½ cup chopped onions
    Butter
2 cups puréed cooked chestnuts
2 cups soft stale bread crumbs
½ teaspoon dried thyme leaves
    Dash of ground nutmeg
    Salt and pepper to taste

Sauté onions in ½ cup butter until just transparent and soft. Combine with remaining ingredients and additional melted butter.

For the Turkey
1 turkey (8 to 10 pounds)

Strips of fat salt pork or bacon
    Butter
    Salt
2 pounds small pork sausages, cooked

Spoon stuffing into turkey. Sew up the vent and truss. Arrange on a rack in a roasting pan. Cover breast with strips of salt pork. Rub remaining skin with butter. Roast in preheated moderate oven (350°F.), basting every 25 minutes with pan juices and more butter if needed. Salt while basting. Allow 20 to 22 minutes per pound for roasting time. Remove turkey to hot platter and keep hot. Make Turkey Gravy. Put a garland of well-browned small pork sausages around turkey. Serve with gravy, mashed potatoes, mashed rutabagas, or a mixture of the two, and fresh green peas. Makes 8 to 10 servings.

Turkey Gravy
Pour off all fat from pan. Measure ¼ cup and put back in pan. Blend ¼ cup all-purpose flour with 1 cup water and 1 cup light cream. Beat until smooth and stir into fat in pan. Cook, stirring constantly, over medium heat until sauce is smooth and thickened. Add more salt and pepper as needed and a little chopped parsley if you like.

ROAST STUFFED CHICKEN
For the Stuffing
1 small onion, finely chopped
¼ cup butter
½ teaspoon crumbled dried thyme
    leaves
2 tablespoons chopped parsley
½ cup chopped cooked ham
1½ cups soft stale bread crumbs
1 egg, beaten
¼ cup light cream
    Salt and pepper

Sauté chopped onion in the butter for 2 or 3 minutes. Add thyme, parsley, ham, and bread crumbs. Stir in egg and enough cream to give moisture to the dressing. Season to taste with salt and pepper.

For the Chicken
1 roasting chicken (3 to 4 pounds)
½ lemon
    Butter

Rub inside of chicken with lemon. Spread giblets with 2 tablespoons of the butter. Place them inside the bird. Stuff with the stuffing and cover the vent with foil or sew it up. Truss the chicken, tying it securely. Rub it with butter. Place chicken on side on rack in a shallow roasting pan. Roast in preheated moderate oven (375°F.) for 20 minutes. Turn on the other side and baste well with pan drippings and melted butter. Roast for another 20 minutes. Turn the bird on its back and baste again. Continue roasting until tender. This will take about 30 more minutes. Serve with tiny crisp pork sausages, new potatoes, and young green peas. Makes 4 to 6 servings.

Note: This, served with green peas, is the traditional Easter dinner in England.

ROAST DUCK WITH SAGE AND ONION STUFFING
2 ducklings (4 to 5 pounds each)
2 cups water
1 teaspoon salt
6 tablespoons butter
2 large onions, chopped
½ pound ground veal
1 teaspoon ground sage, or more to
    taste
3 to 4 cups soft stale-bread crumbs
¼ cup chopped parsley
    Salt and pepper
2 eggs, beaten
    Heavy cream, if necessary
1 lemon, cut
3 tablespoons all-purpose flour

Put duck giblets in a pan with water and salt. Cook, covered, for about 30 minutes, or until tender. Drain, and reserve 1½ cups of the broth. Chop the giblets.

Melt 4 tablespoons of the butter and sauté the chopped onions gently until they are just soft and transparent. Add the veal and cook for 3 to 4 minutes, blending well. Remove from heat. Stir in remaining butter, the sage, and bread crumbs. Add parsley and season to taste with salt and pepper. Mix with beaten eggs. If the stuffing seems too dry, add a little cream or another egg.

Rub the cavities of the ducks with lemon. Rub the skin with lemon and season with salt and pepper. Stuff ducks and close the vents with foil, or sew them up. Truss the birds and arrange them on a rack in a shallow baking pan. Roast in preheated slow oven (325°F.) for about 2 hours. Increase the temperature to moderate (350°F.). Puncture the skin in several places with fork. Roast for 15 more minutes, until skin is crisp.

Remove the ducks to a hot platter and keep hot. Skim off all but 3 tablespoons of the fat in the pan. Place over medium heat and blend in flour. When the flour and juices are thoroughly mixed, slowly stir in reserved 1½ cups giblet broth. Cook, stirring constantly, until the sauce is smooth, thickened, and bubbling. Add the chopped giblets, if you like, and taste for seasoning. Pour into a sauceboat. With the ducks serve applesauce and boiled or mashed potatoes. An orange and watercress salad is sometimes added. Makes 6 servings.

ROAST STUFFED PHEASANT
1 medium onion, finely chopped
¼ cup butter
1 pound sausage meat or ground pork
1 pound ground veal
2 tablespoons chopped parsley
1 teaspoon dried thyme leaves
    Salt and pepper
1 cup soft stale bread crumbs
1 egg, beaten
2 pheasants
    Salt pork or bacon strips
    Bread Sauce

Sauté onion in butter. Add sausage meat and cook over medium heat, breaking up with fork and blending with onion. Add veal and mix well. Add the parsley and thyme and season to taste with salt and pepper. Mix with the crumbs and egg. Stuff birds and close the vents with foil. Truss; tie a piece of salt pork over the breast of each bird. Set in roasting pan, breast side down, and roast in preheated moderate oven (350°F.) for 25 minutes. Turn breast side up and roast for 20 minutes longer. Remove the salt pork and brown the breast skin. Young pheasants take about 1 hour to cook. Serve with Bread Sauce and gooseberry jelly. Makes 4 servings.

Note: This is a very common dish in England. If no one in your family shoots pheasant, you may be able to buy them in your area. Many specialty food stores across the country offer them. One bird will usually serve two persons. Pheasant can be very dry if not properly cooked. A moist stuffing helps.

Bread Sauce
1 small peeled onion
1 cup soft stale bread crumbs
  Dash of hot pepper sauce
½ teaspoon salt
1 cup milk
½ cup heavy cream
1 tablespoon butter

Combine all the ingredients, except the butter, in a saucepan and bring to a boil. Lower heat and simmer for 5 minutes. Add butter and let it melt. Remove onion. Serve hot with pheasant or other game birds.

CURRIED EGGS
3 onions, sliced
½ cup butter
¼ teaspoon salt
2 tablespoons curry powder
¼ cup all-purpose flour
2 cups chicken bouillon
12 small eggs, hard-cooked and peeled
2 to 3 cups cooked rice
¼ cup sultana or white raisins
¼ cup toasted almonds

Sauté onions in half of the butter until lightly brown; add salt. Remove from pan and reserve. Melt remaining butter in skillet. Stir in curry powder and cook for 1 minute; add flour and blend well. Gradually stir in bouillon. Cook, stirring constantly, until thickened and smooth. Add onions and eggs; add more salt if desired. Simmer, covered, over lowest possible heat for 30 minutes. To serve, make a ring of hot rice. Place eggs in center and pour sauce over them. Garnish with raisins and almonds. Makes 4 to 6 servings.

BACON AND EGG PIE
  Pastry for 2-crust 9-inch pie, unbaked
6 slices of bacon, partly cooked
3 tablespoons chopped parsley
6 eggs
  Salt and pepper to taste
1 egg beaten with 2 tablespoons water

Line 9-inch pie with pastry. Arrange bacon on bottom; sprinkle with parsley. Break eggs on top, keeping yolks whole. Sprinkle with salt and pepper. Cover with top crust, cutting an air hole in top. Brush with egg and water mixture. Bake in a preheated very hot oven (450°F.) for 10 minutes. Reduce heat to moderate (350°F.) and bake until crust is nicely browned. Serve hot or cold. When cold, it makes an excellent picnic dish. Makes 6 to 8 servings.

MAIDS OF HONOUR
1½ cups unsifted all-purpose flour
½ cup sweet butter, softened
1 teaspoon salt
1 hard-cooked egg yolk, sieved
1 raw egg yolk
2 tablespoons sugar
1 teaspoon grated lemon rind

Filling:
¼ pound pot cheese
¼ cup sweet butter
½ cup sugar
3 tablespoons ground blanched almonds
½ teaspoon salt
1 teaspoon grated lemon rind and juice of ½ lemon
4 egg yolks
  Nutmeg

To make pastry, put flour in a mound on board. In center, put the remaining pastry ingredients. Working with fingers, knead together to form a smooth mixture. Shape into a ball and wrap in wax paper. Chill while making the filling.

To make filling, sieve cheese. Cream butter until light and beat in cheese. Then beat in remaining ingredients, except nutmeg. Divide chilled pastry in 12 pieces. Press each piece into a 3-inch tart pan. Fill two thirds full with cheese mixture and sprinkle tops with nutmeg. Bake in preheated moderate oven (350°F.) for 25 minutes, or until tarts are lightly browned and filling is just set. Remove from pans while warm. Makes 12.

SIMNEL CAKE
  Butter
6 to 7 ounces canned almond paste
1 egg yolk
1 cup unsifted all-purpose flour
3 eggs
½ cup sugar
  Dash of salt
1 cup dried currants
⅓ cup chopped mixed candied fruit peel

Mix ⅓ cup butter, the almond paste, and egg yolk until thoroughly blended; set aside. Cream ¾ cup butter and the

flour together. Beat eggs until light and lemon-colored. Then beat in sugar and salt. Combine the two mixtures and add currants and peel. Butter and flour a 9-inch springform pan. Pour in half the cake mixture. Add a layer of almond-paste mixture, reserving remainder for the top. Add remaining cake mixture. Bake in preheated slow oven (325°F.) for about 1 hour. Remove from oven and, with a pastry tube, pipe reserved almond-paste mixture around edge of top of cake. Return to oven for 15 minutes to brown the topping. Remove from oven and cool. Makes 8 to 10 servings.

APPLE PIE
  Butter
  About 2½ pounds tart cooking apples (8 to 10 apples)
  Sugar
  Grated rind of 1 lemon
  Dash of salt
  Rich pastry for a top crust, unbaked, chilled
1 egg beaten with 2 tablespoons water

Choose a rather deep oval dish, about 9 to 10 inches long. A wide rim for the crust to rest upon is convenient but not necessary. Butter dish well. Peel and core apples and cut into quarters. Arrange in baking dish, building up in the center. Sprinkle with sugar according to the sweetness of the fruit; use at least 4 to 5 tablespoons. Dot with butter and sprinkle with lemon rind and salt.

Roll out crust ¼ to ⅜ inch thick. Cut 2 strips of dough about ¾ inch wide and long enough to go around rim of the dish; press around rim and brush with a little water. Fit the top crust on, pressing it to rim of dough. Seal edges with a fork and cut an air vent in top. Brush with beaten egg and water. Bake in preheated very hot oven (450°F.) for 10 minutes. Reduce heat to moderate (350°F.) and bake for 25 to 30 minutes longer, or until crust is golden brown and apples cooked. Sprinkle crust with sugar. Serve hot or cold, with heavy cream if you like. Makes 6 to 8 servings.

Note: English apple pie has only a top crust. Actually, it is what we call deep-dish apple pie. When the apples are flavorful and the crust is tender, it is one of the most satisfying desserts in the world. English country cooks used to add leaves from the peach tree or a few rose petals before putting on the crust. Each gave the pie a special flavor.

JAM TARTS
  Rich pastry dough for 2-crust pie, unbaked
  Jams of contrasting color and flavor

For a 4-jam tart, you might choose apricot, raspberry, pineapple, and strawberry. If you want to use 5, add currant jelly; and for a 6-section tart, add greengage plum jam or orange marmalade.

Roll out the dough and fit it into any flat pan you like. You could use a 9-inch pan, or a 12- to 13-inch pizza pan would be a good choice. For a 4-jam tart, cut a long strip of the dough and roll it into a rope. Use this rope of dough to divide your tart into 4 sections. Secure it to the bottom crust by brushing with a little water. Chill for 15 minutes. Fill the 4 spaces with the different jams.

If you are using 5 jams, mark off a circle in the center of the tart with a rope of dough. Then make 4 divisions around it. Fill the center with currant jelly and use the jams for the 4 sections.

Bake the tart in preheated hot oven (425°F.) for 10 minutes. Reduce the heat to moderate (350°F.) and bake for about 10 minutes longer, or until the crust is done. Serve cooled. Makes 6 to 8 servings.

Note: In the past, English hostesses and cooks took pride in making tarts in many different designs. Dorothy Hartley in her history of food in England says that if a hostess could design an open-face tart with six different jams, she felt she had achieved the height of elegance. The tarts were baked in round or square flat tins, and the various jams were separated by strips of pastry or small designs of pastry.

TRIFLE

6 thick slices of poundcake
1 cup sherry or port
⅓ to ½ cup raspberry jam
18 to 24 ladyfingers
Pastry Cream
½ cup heavy cream, whipped
Candied cherry halves

Arrange slices of cake in serving dish. Spoon over ½ cup of the sherry to saturate cake evenly. Spread jam on top. Dip ladyfingers into remaining wine and arrange on top. Cover with Pastry Cream and chill. Top with whipped cream and decorate with candied cherry halves. Makes 12 servings.

Pastry Cream

Beat 5 egg yolks thoroughly in bowl. Combine ⅔ cup sugar with ⅓ cup all-purpose flour and dash of salt. Beat into egg yolks. In heavy saucepan heat 2 cups milk just to a boil. Add hot milk slowly to egg mixture, beating constantly. Return to heavy saucepan and place over low heat. Cook, stirring constantly, until thick and smooth. Remove from heat. Beat in 1 tablespoon butter and 1½ teaspoons vanilla extract. (Or, heat milk in top part of double boiler and cook Pastry Cream over hot water to prevent scorching.) Cool to room temperature before putting on top of ladyfingers.

SUET PUDDINGS

The English make various puddings based on suet dough. Here is the recipe.

SUET DOUGH

1 cup all-purpose flour
2 cups dry stale bread crumbs
¼ cup sugar
1 cup finely ground or chopped suet
1 egg
  Milk to make a stiff dough (about 1 cup)

Combine all dry ingredients and suet. Mix in egg and enough milk to make a workable dough. Use the dough to make any of the puddings below.

Spotted Dog

Blend ½ cup each of currants, sultana raisins, and white raisins into Suet Dough. Roll mixture into a sausage shape on a floured damp cloth. Tie securely at the ends. Drop into boiling water and steam for 2 to 2½ hours. Serve hot with sugar, butter, and fresh lemon juice, or with a custard sauce. Makes 6 servings.

Jam Roly-Poly

Roll out Suet Dough on floured damp cloth and spread with jam up to 1½ inches from the edge. Damson plum, orange marmalade, raspberry, and black currant are best. Roll up the dough like a jelly roll and tie. Drop into boiling water and steam for 2 to 2½ hours. Serve in slices with heavy cream. Makes 6 servings.

Mincemeat Roly-Poly

Prepare as for Jam Roly-Poly, substituting mincemeat for the jam. Serve with hard sauce. Makes 6 servings.

 **SAVORIES**

Many English like a small savory served after the dessert to clean the palate of the sweet taste. Savories include such items as deviled kidneys, sardines on toast, and welsh rabbit—all served in small portions. In fact, they resemble hors-d'oeuvre. Here are two favorites:

ANCHOVIED MUSHROOMS

Melt 3 tablespoons butter and brush onto 12 mushroom caps; broil until just tender. Cut 12 thin slices of bread into small rounds and sauté them in butter until crisp and golden on both sides; or cut rounds from buttered toast. Chop 12 anchovy fillets and mix with ¼ cup dairy sour cream and a little chopped parsley. Top each toast round with a mushroom cap, fill it with a spoonful of anchovy cream, and garnish with a parsley sprig. (To serve as hors-d'oeuvre, put filled mushroom caps on toast under broiler for a few moments to heat through. Garnish with parsley and serve hot.) Makes 6 servings.

MARROW TOAST

Have your butcher cut about 6 or 8 sec-

tions of marrowbone. Poach these in boiling salted water for 3 or 4 minutes. Remove and scoop-out marrow. Arrange pieces of marrow on fried toast and sprinkle with salt, freshly ground black pepper, and lemon juice. Serve very hot.

ENGLISH MUFFIN—This English tea bread is a yeast-raised, unsweetened bread about three and one half inches in diameter and about one inch thick. Usually English muffins are cut and allowed to rise on a surface dusted with cornmeal, and then baked on a griddle. The baked muffins are then split and toasted and spread with butter or jam.

The wandering muffin man, who sold muffins fresh to every household, was a familiar figure on the streets of all English towns, and the cry with which he advertised his wares was one of the familiar street noises through the Edwardian era.

Commercially baked English muffins are sold packaged and ready for toasting.

ENGLISH MUFFINS

1 package active dry yeast or 1 cake compressed yeast
¼ cup lukewarm water*
¾ cup milk
2 tablespoons butter
1 teaspoon salt
3 cups sifted all-purpose flour

Add yeast to water. *Use very warm water (105°F. to 115°F.) for dry yeast; use lukewarm (80°F. to 90°F.) for compressed. Let stand for a few minutes, then stir until dissolved. Scald milk. Add butter and salt. Cool to lukewarm; add yeast mixture and 2 cups of the flour. Beat until smooth. Cover and let rise for 1 hour. Beat in remaining flour. Knead on a lightly floured board until smooth. Cover and let rise until doubled in bulk. The dough can be stored in the refrigerator for 1 week. Roll dough to ½-inch thickness. Cut out 3-inch rounds. Sprinkle surfaces with cornmeal. Let muffins rise until doubled in bulk. Place risen muffins on a lightly greased griddle over low heat and bake for about 7 to 10 minutes on each side, until they are lightly browned. Serve at once or cool and then split and toast. "Scotch them around the waist" is the phrase used to describe the proper method of splitting an English muffin, using 2 forks to tear the muffin apart. Makes about 12 muffins.

NUT-SPICED ENGLISH MUFFINS

4 English muffins
½ cup butter or margarine
½ cup firmly packed light brown sugar
¼ teaspoon ground cinnamon
⅓ cup chopped nuts

Split muffins; toast lightly under broiler. Combine remaining ingredients. Spread on muffins. Broil until bubbly. Serve hot.

Entertaining Cook Book

**BRUNCHES · BUFFETS · BARBECUES · LUNCHEONS
TEAS · DINNERS · COCKTAIL PARTIES
MENUS AND RECIPES · TABLE SETTINGS
TIPS ON SEATING AND SERVING**

The glory of the house is hospitality." These words come from a nineteenth-century fireplace motto extolling the virtues of the home, and they are as valid today as when they were written. We need to be reminded that the gathering of family and friends, the welcoming of strangers in our home is an essential part not only of family living, but also of all civilized life. Parties may be for few or for many, they may be simple or elaborate, but their purpose is always the same: they must create a mood of enchantment that will last long after the party is over. This mood is a mosaic of many pieces: the festive house, the flowers, the food, the service, the care to have them right for the occasion. In the pages that follow, you will find a guide to entertaining that will tell you how to assemble the various parts of a perfect party, and inspire you to add the touches that will make it unmistakably your own. A good party needs planning, and planning can be learned. It is a most rewarding assignment. For there is nothing more soul-satisfying to a hostess than guests who leave her house with the warm feeling of being far more attractive and brilliant than when they came.

Brunches

Leisure is perhaps the prerequisite to brunch, which is why we associate it primarily with the weekend. Brunch was first popularized in New Orleans during the last century, in a society where entertaining was both lavish and continuous. Late risers found the breakfast hour past and lunchtime imminent. The happy solution was a rather elegant combination of the two meals.

As for food, the hostess may serve what she wishes. A simple meal, such as cranberry juice, bacon omelet, blueberry muffins, and coffee, may be cooked by the hostess and eaten at a colorfully set table. Or it may be a sort of cook-it-yourself meal. Having covered a counter with various foods, some prepared and some not, the hostess invites the guests to choose what they wish: eggs to scramble, pancakes to fry, breads to toast. This requires careful planning, for everything must be displayed attractively and in easy-to-reach order. Also, there must be room for each cook to maneuver.

For the brunch featuring one main dish to be served from a chafing dish or electric skillet there are infinite possibilities: chicken livers and bacon, corned-beef hash with poached eggs, creamed chicken with water chestnuts, crabmeat and almonds in a sherry-flavored sauce, or curried eggs over Canadian bacon slices. Guests can serve themselves as the hostess pours the coffee and passes hot breads.

Buffet and dining-room brunches tend more to luncheon-type dishes, such as curried lamb with pilaf and salad; French crêpes filled with shrimps and an aspic; or eggs Benedict, accompanied by potato puffs or asparagus spears. As much of the preparation as possible should be carried out beforehand and service may be slightly more formal. Sometimes dessert is included but it is not necessary. Other beverages may or may not be served, but coffee is a must.

Brunch tables in the living or dining room can be set a little more formally, perhaps with solid-colored homespun mats, light-colored pottery, and a centerpiece of gourds and vegetables in a copper bowl. Porcelain dinnerware and silver flatware might be used with linen mats. Summer brunches in the garden or patio should feature gay cool colors, perhaps a mixture of dinnerwares, colored glassware, and, as a centerpiece, boxes or bowls of strawberries or grapes, or small vases of fresh flowers.

VIENNESE BRUNCH
(FOR 10)
GARNISHED PEARS
ALPINE EGGS   CARROTS WITH DILL
AUSTRIAN CRESCENTS   ALMOND TORTE
VIENNESE COFFEE

GARNISHED PEARS
6 cups (three 1-pound cans) pear halves, drained
2 cups (one 1-pound can) sweet cherries, drained

Arrange the pear halves in a large bowl. Garnish with the cherries. Chill in the refrigerator before serving. Makes 10 servings.

ALPINE EGGS
15 hard-cooked eggs, shelled
3½ cups diced cooked ham
3 cups diced cooked potatoes

3 cans (10½ ounces each) condensed
  cream-of-mushroom soup
½ cup milk
2 teaspoons Worcestershire
1 tablespoon fresh lemon juice
¼ cup chopped fresh parsley
  Salt and pepper

Cut the eggs into halves crosswise. Cut a slice from the bottom of each so it will stand level. Arrange in a large, shallow buttered casserole 1 or 2 inches apart. Spoon the ham (except 2 tablespoons) and potatoes in among the eggs, distributing evenly. Combine the remaining ingredients. Mix well and heat through. Pour carefully into the dish. Shred the reserved ham and spread over the top. Bake in preheated moderate oven (350°F.) for 20 minutes. This may be prepared beforehand. Refrigerate until ready to bake. Makes 10 servings.

Note: Hard-cooked eggs can be halved lengthwise, if preferred.

CARROTS WITH DILL

4 cups frozen carrot slices
3 tablespoons butter
1½ teaspoons snipped dill
  Salt and pepper

Cook the carrot slices in a little water until tender, about 10 minutes. Add the remaining ingredients. Mix well, and serve. Makes 10 servings.

AUSTRIAN CRESCENTS

Take out contents from 2 containers (8 ounces each) crescent rolls (the perishable kind that must be refrigerated). Stretch out flat. Place a spoonful of jam or jelly in the center near the top of each. Roll up. Bake according to directions. Brush with butter. Sprinkle with sugar. Serve warm. Makes 16 crescents.

ALMOND TORTE

¾ cup butter
1¼ cups sugar
4 eggs
1 cup cake flour
1 teaspoon baking powder
1 teaspoon almond extract

Topping

⅓ cup butter
2 teaspoons cornstarch
⅓ cup confectioners' sugar
2 tablespoons light cream
½ cup chopped almonds
1 teaspoon vanilla extract

Cream butter, add sugar, and blend well. Separate the eggs. Stir the yolks with a fork and add to butter and sugar. Set aside the whites. Sift flour and baking powder together, and add. Mix in the almond extract. Whip the egg whites until stiff and fold into the mixture. Pour into greased 8-inch square dish and bake in preheated moderate oven (375°F.) for 30 to 35 minutes.

In the meantime, make topping. Melt the butter in a saucepan. Add cornstarch, then the sugar and cream; cook until blended. Add the almonds and vanilla. Mix well and remove from heat. Spread over the top of the baked cake. Cut into squares and serve. Makes 10 servings.

VIENNESE COFFEE

Make coffee in any way preferred. But make it extra-strength (¼ cup coffee to each ¾ cup water). Sweeten to taste and top with whipped cream.

SUMMERTIME BRUNCH
(FOR 12)
CIRCLES OF MELON
CORNED-BEEF HASH WITH POACHED EGGS
BROILED TOMATOES
HOT MUFFINS   MARMALADE
SPECIAL COFFEE

CIRCLES OF MELON

Cut 3 cantaloupes or 1 large honeydew melon into halves crosswise. Remove the seeds and cut the fruit into circle-slices. Cut off the rinds. Arrange on a large platter. Place grapes in the centers of the slices. Sprinkle with fresh orange juice and confectioners' sugar. Refrigerate until ready to serve.

CORNED-BEEF HASH
WITH POACHED EGGS

3 tablespoons minced onion
¾ cup minced green peppers
2 tablespoons butter
5 cups (one 12-ounce can = 2 cups)
  diced cooked corned beef
4 cups diced cooked potatoes
½ teaspoon pepper
12 eggs
  Salt and pepper to taste

Sauté onion and green pepper in butter until tender. Mix with corned beef, potatoes, and pepper. Mash together until well mixed. Flatten out on a piece of wax paper to about 1-inch thickness. Cut into 12 large circles. Brown on both sides. Top each with a poached egg sprinkled with salt and pepper. Makes 12 servings.

Note: Hash circles may be prepared in advance and refrigerated until ready to cook.

BROILED TOMATOES

Cut out stem ends from 12 firm tomatoes. Cut each into halves crosswise. Sprinkle the cut surfaces with salt, pepper, and crumbled dried basil. Dot with butter. Heat under broiler for 3 to 5 minutes. Or bake in preheated moderate oven (350°F.) for 15 minutes. Makes 12 servings.

HOT MUFFINS

Make or buy 2 dozen cornmeal or graham muffins. Serve warm on a large plate or in a basket with small bowls of 2 or 3 kinds of marmalade nearby.

SPECIAL COFFEE

Prepare hot coffee. Pour into cups and top each with a spoonful of vanilla ice cream.

luncheons

At the White House our First Ladies have set interesting and imaginative precedents in planning their luncheons. In 1949, Mrs. Harry S. Truman invited her Spanish class to a Latin American repast which she and four friends, including the language teacher, prepared. The entrée was *picadillo* (four varieties of highly seasoned meat mixed with rice and garnished with almonds, pimiento, olives, and raisins), accompanied by a vegetable salad. Dessert was a combination of Mexican cheese and guavas in syrup. Wives of the official family served the luncheon, including Mrs. Dwight D. Eisenhower, whose husband was then Army Chief of Staff.

During Mrs. Eisenhower's own tenure as First Lady, her luncheons tended to evidence her fondness for pink, which was often the color of the tablecloths, flowers, and some of the foods. Perhaps the most discussed luncheon was given on Halloween in 1958. The lavish decorations included paper black cats and owls swinging from the elegant chandeliers; witches on broomsticks were centerpieces, while false and real pumpkins, as well as gourds and skeletons, were strategically placed around the room.

At Mrs. John F. Kennedy's first luncheon, to honor members of the Women's National Press Club, she established a precedent by having tables set up in the East Room, never before used for dining. A large buffet offered an array of choice foods: seafood Newburg with rice, galantines of turkey and ham, cold poached salmon with egg sauce, Hungarian goulash with noodles, *pâté de foie gras* with truffles *en gelée,* melon balls in a watermelon basket, finger rolls, *petits fours,* demitasse, salted almonds, and mints. The decorations were equally lavish: large Wedgwood jardinières with cherry blossoms, spun sugar baskets with lilies of the valley, and ice sculptures.

Not everyone, of course, can entertain on such a grand scale. But there are no limitations on the use of imagination and originality, which can achieve the same effect in much more modest surroundings with congenial company.

The congeniality is essential since women, and men too, of course, prefer to be with persons they like, with whom they can relax and enjoy themselves. Another important consideration is that the guests be comfortable. A small group which can be seated at the dining table is no problem. For a larger group the dining table can be used as a buffet, and side or tray tables can be arranged at convenient spots in the living room. Or card tables can be set up in the living room or in another area. It is important to plan it so that all guests can be seated.

If the weatherman's predictions are favorable, and if nature does not decide to disagree, luncheon may be attractively planned for the patio or garden. In the event that entertaining space is limited, however, it might be better to give more than one luncheon rather than a large one that is overcrowded.

Selecting the menu must be done with regard to the fact that a luncheon is generally a feminine affair. Since it is reasonably certain that some of the guests will be counting calories, the meal should be light. On the other hand, women delight in making culinary discoveries, so the menu should be as original and out of the ordinary as possible. Foods should be selected with an eye to color and particular attention should be paid to garnishes.

In any event the menu should include dishes that do not require a great deal of last-minute attention since the hostess manages this affair without the help of a host and she will wish to be with her guests as much of the time as possible.

At a sit-down meal, dessert plates and coffee cups and saucers may be placed on a low table or tea wagon next to the hostess' chair, where they will be ready to be passed when needed. The table or tea wagon may also be used for stacking the used luncheon plates.

The table should be set with a pretty, delicate cloth, immaculately clean and ironed (one crease down the center of the cloth). Attractive napkins, folded in oblong or triangle shape, may be placed in the center of the luncheon plate or to its left. If place cards are used, they should be put directly above the plates. A ladies' luncheon calls for the hostess' best china; mixing patterns if desired in order to achieve a more colorful setting. Both bread-and-butter and salad plates are customary, although the latter may be omitted. The silver may also be of mixed patterns. Dessert spoon or fork may be placed above the luncheon plate. Ashtrays, salts and peppers, and candy dishes with nuts or mints should be accessible to each guest.

A centerpiece should be compatible with and enhance the rest of the setting. Cut flowers in a wicker basket, blossoms in a silver bowl, or twin flower arrangements are generally attractive. If flowers are chosen, they should be so arranged as not to obstruct the view of any of the guests. Ornaments and figurines may be worked in to complement the selection. Candles are not appropriate.

INTIMATE LUNCHEON
(FOR 6)
SOUP ON THE ROCKS
CLAM COQUILLES
VEGETABLES VINAIGRETTE
FINGER ROLLS
COLD STRAWBERRY SOUFFLÉ
COFFEE

SOUP ON THE ROCKS
Heat to boiling 5 cups tomato juice, ½ cup each of minced celery and green pepper, 2 tablespoons vinegar, and dash of hot pepper sauce. Cool; chill. Serve in short glasses over ice cubes. Makes six 1-cup servings.

CLAM COQUILLES
- 2 cans (8 ounces each) minced clams
- 1 can (10½ ounces) condensed cream-of-chicken soup
- 1 cup herb-seasoned croutons, crumbled
- ½ cup minced green pepper
- 1 teaspoon curry powder
  Worcestershire, hot pepper sauce, salt, and pepper to taste
  Grated Parmesan cheese
  Soft bread crumbs

Drain clams, reserving 2 tablespoons liquid. Mix clams, liquid, and remaining ingredients, except cheese and bread crumbs. Cook for 5 minutes, stirring occasionally. Spoon into 6 coquilles or ramekins. Sprinkle with grated Parmesan and bread crumbs. Heat in preheated moderate oven (350°F.) for about 10 minutes. Makes 6 servings.

VEGETABLES VINAIGRETTE
Arrange 1 cup cooked tiny beets, 1 cup cooked cut green beans, and 1 cup cooked carrot circles on a bed of lettuce. Sprinkle with 1 tablespoon tarragon vinegar, 2 tablespoons salad oil, and salt and pepper to taste. Chill for at least 1 hour. Makes 6 servings.

COLD STRAWBERRY SOUFFLÉ
- 1 package (1 pound) frozen strawberries, thawed
- 1 envelope unflavored gelatin
- ¼ cup cold water
- 3 eggs, separated
  Dash of salt
- 1 tablespoon fresh lemon juice
- 1 teaspoon rum extract
- ½ cup sugar
- ½ cup heavy cream
  Colored sugar sprinkles

Mash thawed berries finely with fork or whip in a blender. Soften gelatin in cold water. Beat egg yolks slightly. Mix with salt, lemon juice, and rum extract in top part of a double boiler. Cook over hot water, stirring, until slightly thickened. Add gelatin. Mix well and remove from heat. When cooled slightly, add berries and mix well. Beat egg whites until stiff. Gradually add sugar and beat until mixture holds a peak. Whip cream until stiff. Fold egg whites and cream into the strawberry mixture, combining carefully until well blended. Rub a little oil over the inside surfaces of an 8-inch soufflé dish or straight-sided casserole. Carefully pour in the mixture. Sprinkle with colored sugar. Chill for about 2 hours, or until firm. Do not unmold, but serve in same dish. Makes 6 servings.

SPRING LUNCHEON
(FOR 8)
SHRIMP-CAVIAR CANAPES
SCALLOPED CHICKEN SUPREME
CRANBERRY SALAD
MINIATURE BRAN MUFFINS
TUTTI-FRUTTI MOUSSE   COFFEE

SHRIMP-CAVIAR CANAPÉS
Cut sixteen 2-inch rounds from slices of white bread. Spread lightly with mayonnaise. Place 1 or 2 (depending on their size) cooked shelled shrimps in the center of each round of bread. Surround with a border of black caviar. Refrigerate until ready to use. Serve before luncheon with any desired beverage.

SCALLOPED CHICKEN SUPREME
- 3 tablespoons butter
- 3 tablespoons all-purpose flour
- 2 cups chicken bouillon
- 1 cup milk
  Salt and pepper to taste
- 3 cups cooked rice
- 3 cups diced cooked chicken
- 1 cup sliced cooked mushrooms
- ½ cup slivered blanched almonds
- 1 can (4 ounces) pimientos, chopped
  Bread crumbs

Melt the butter in a saucepan and stir in the flour. Blend well. Add bouillon (or 2 chicken bouillon cubes dissolved in 2 cups hot water), milk, salt, and pepper.

Cook, stirring constantly, for a few minutes to make a sauce. Butter a 2-quart decorative casserole. Spread half of rice evenly over the greased bottom. Top rice with half each of chicken, mushroom slices, almond slivers, and pimiento. Carefully pour in half of sauce. Repeat the layers except pimiento and add remaining sauce. Sprinkle lightly with bread crumbs. Decorate with remaining pimiento. Bake in preheated moderate oven (350°F.) for 45 minutes. This may be prepared ahead of time. Refrigerate until ready to bake. Serve from the casserole. Makes 8 servings.

CRANBERRY SALAD
- 2 envelopes unflavored gelatin
- ¼ cup cold water
- 4 cups (two 1-pound cans) whole-berry cranberry sauce
- ½ cup sugar
- 1 cup diced peeled apples
- 1 cup chopped nuts
- ½ cup diced celery
  Lettuce

Dissolve the gelatin in cold water. Mix with cranberry sauce and sugar. Cook for 5 minutes. Remove from heat and add the apples, nuts, and celery. Pour into custard cups or muffin tins. Chill in the refrigerator for at least 1 hour, until firm. Remove by inserting a knife around the edges and dipping the bottoms into hot tap water for a second. Place on lettuce leaves. Refrigerate until ready to use. Makes 8 servings.

MINIATURE BRAN MUFFINS
Prepare 1 package (7 ounces) bran muffin mix according to directions, but fill muffin tins only one third full. Serve warm. Make beforehand and reheat just before serving. Makes 24 muffins.

TUTTI-FRUTTI MOUSSE
- 1 quart vanilla ice cream
- 1 cup maraschino cherries
- 1 cup chopped pecans

Let the ice cream soften. Add the other ingredients and mix well. Spoon into a loaf-shape mold. Freeze for at least 1 hour. Remove from the mold by loosening the edges with a knife and running hot water over the bottom. Place on a pretty plate. Return to the freezer. Take out 5 minutes before serving. Slice at the table. Makes 8 servings.

PARISIAN LUNCHEON
(FOR 12)
HORS-D'OEUVRE
FRENCH SHRIMP-MUSHROOM FLAN
ROMAINE SALAD
APPLE CREME   COFFEE

HORS-D'OEUVRE

Arrange the following on a platter or plate. Serve to guests during preluncheon conversation. All may be prepared beforehand and refrigerated until ready to use. Makes 12 servings.

Celery—Fill twelve 3-inch lengths of washed celery with turmeric-flavored cream cheese.

Cherry Tomatoes—Hollow out 18 cherry tomatoes and fill with a combination of salmon, mayonnaise, and chopped chives.

Cucumbers—Peel 2 medium-size cucumbers. Cut off a 1-inch piece from both ends of each and remove seeds with a knife, making a shell. Be careful not to cut shell. Stuff with deviled ham mixed with minced pineapple. Pack tightly. Leave in the refrigerator for 1 hour. Cut into ¾-inch slices.

Hard-Cooked Eggs—Mash yolks of 6 shelled hard-cooked eggs with a little sandwich spread. Spoon into the whites. Garnish each with a slice of stuffed olive.

Mushrooms—Stem 12 fresh mushrooms. Wipe the caps dry with damp paper towel. Fill with creamed Roquefort, or any other desired soft cheese.

FRENCH SHRIMP-MUSHROOM FLAN

2 sticks (one 10-ounce package) piecrust mix
40 medium mushrooms

½ cup butter or margarine
Juice of 1 lemon
2 tablespoons sherry
¾ teaspoon pepper
6 green onions, minced
2 celery stalks, minced
6 tablespoons all-purpose flour
1 teaspoon salt
¼ teaspoon cayenne
5 cups hot milk
2 pounds shrimps, cooked and cleaned
⅓ cup light cream
½ cup grated Parmesan cheese
6 eggs, well beaten

Prepare 2 baked 10-inch pie shells, using piecrust mix. Stem the mushrooms. Melt ¼ cup butter. Add lemon juice, sherry, ½ teaspoon pepper, and mushroom caps. Sauté for 4 minutes, turning once. Drain and set aside. Sauté onions and celery in remaining butter. Stir in flour, salt, ¼ teaspoon pepper, and cayenne. Blend well and slowly add milk, stirring. Simmer for 10 minutes, stirring often so it does not boil; strain. Discard vegetables. Add shrimps, cream, and cheese to the strained liquid. Cook for 1 minute, stirring. Spoon out some of the hot liquid to mix with the eggs. Add mixture to remaining hot sauce. Cook for 1 minute, stirring. Pour into pie shells. Spoon out the mushrooms and arrange, cap sides up, in circles over the filling. Bake in preheated very hot oven (450°F.) until a knife inserted in the center comes out clean, about 25 minutes. Let settle for 10 minutes. Cut into wedges. Each pie makes 6 servings.

ROMAINE SALAD

Arrange chilled washed small romaine lettuce leaves on individual plates. Place radish slices over them. Just before serving, top with French dressing.

APPLE CRÈME

3 eggs, separated
3 cups milk
3 tablespoons sugar
3 cups applesauce, chilled
1 teaspoon vanilla extract
Chocolate shavings

Beat egg yolks in top part of double boiler. Add milk and sugar and cook, stirring often, until mixture is slightly thickened and coats a metal spoon. Cool; add applesauce and vanilla. Beat egg whites until stiff and fold into mixture. Spoon into a large bowl or individual dessert dishes. Decorate with chocolate shavings cut from unsweetened chocolate. Chill but do not leave in refrigerator for more than 1 hour. Makes 12 servings

Afternoon Teas

In early 19th-century England there were many who felt the pangs of hunger in the late afternoon. It was Anna, the seventh Duchess of Bedford, however, who did something about it. Being of good appetite, she ordered that tea and cakes be served in her rooms each afternoon. Being also of a sociable and generous nature, she invited other ladies to share these goodies with her. Thus arose both a custom and a social occasion. Afternoon tea became a daily ritual which persists to this day, particularly in England, where it is an event characterized by charm and taste, imparting a sense of civilized well-being as well as gaiety and good cheer.

Termed in the Orient a "celestial bev-

erage," tea early became a favorite of Chinese philosophers. In Japan, it became the subject of a religious and artistic ritual, *cha-no-yu*, held in the highest esteem.

As a social event, afternoon tea follows the highest traditions of hospitality. Yet few occasions provide the hostess with such opportunities for gracious entertaining at such a modest expenditure of time and effort. The occasion is generally one for the distaff side. There is no reason of course why men should not be invited, but the hour, normally 4 o'clock in the afternoon, usually precludes their attendance, unless the tea is held on a Sunday or holiday or takes the form of a large formal reception. For a large tea, invitations may be extended by written cards, although a telephoned invitation is desirable in the case of a smaller affair.

Unusual opportunity for variety and attractiveness is provided in selecting the menu for a tea. There are some 1,500 blends of the delicious beverage available, ranging from the full-bodied, fermented black teas generally preferred in America, to the paler, more delicate, unfermented or partially fermented teas so loved in the Orient. These include the delightful "flower teas," so called because the leaves have been stored with gardenia or jasmine blossoms, imparting a perfumed flavor which makes the addition of cream, sugar, or lemon unnecessary. Iced tea may be offered in summer, and particularly in the case of a large affair an alternate beverage—chocolate, coffee, punch, or fruit juice—should be available.

In choosing foods for a tea, the hostess will seek those which complement the delicacy and lightness of the beverage itself. Dainty sandwiches and breads, small cakes, cookies, and pastries may be selected and attractively presented, supplemented by small bowls of candies, nuts, condiments, or candied fruits.

Tea must be prepared just before serving. At a small tea (eight or less) the hostess herself will serve from a low table, generally in the living room. Tea cups, saucers, spoons, pitcher or pot of hot water, creamer, lemon slices, bowl of lump sugar with tongs, small plates with a cloth napkin on each, forks (if other than finger foods are to be served) forks and knives (if needed to spread jams or marmalades), will have been placed on or near a large tray prior to the arrival of guests. Cold foods will also have been placed on a table beside the tray, or on an occasional table nearby. Tea and warm dishes may be brought in after the guests arrive. The hostess will pour the tea according to the individual preferences of her guests, plain or weak (adding hot water), and offering sugar, cream, or lemon.

At a larger tea, the service will take place in the dining room or area, customarily at the dining table. Prior to the arrival of guests the tea service is placed at one end of the table, with the alternate beverage or beverages at the other end. The cold foods may be arranged attractively along both sides of the table, leaving room for any warm dishes, together with appropriate plates, napkins, and silver.

It is customary for the hostess to ask two friends to pour for her, never a maid, so that she is free to greet and mingle with the guests and oversee the general arrangements.

The hostess will wish her table to reflect the grace and charm of the occasion. A cloth of organdy, lace, or embroidered cotton will provide a fitting background for her highly polished silver and finest china. An attractive centerpiece, such as a silver bowl of flowers, fresh buds and leaves in a porcelain compote, or a colorful arrangement of fruits on a crystal épergne, will complement the setting. Should the season and hour be such that lighting is in order, silver candlesticks or candelabra will also be appropriate.

ENGLISH AFTERNOON TEA
(FOR 10)
SCOTTISH SCONES
TINY SANDWICHES
OATCAKES   COCONUT COOKIES
CANDIES   NUTS
ENGLISH TEA

SCOTTISH SCONES
2 cups sifted all-purpose flour
4 teaspoons baking powder
½ teaspoon salt
¼ cup butter or margarine, softened
2 eggs, beaten
6 tablespoons milk

Sift flour, baking powder, and salt twice. Cut butter into flour mixture. Add eggs and then milk. Turn out on floured board and knead a little. Roll to ½-inch thickness. Cut into small rounds with cookie cutter or glass. Put on buttered cookie sheets and bake in preheated hot oven (400°F.) for 12 to 15 minutes. Serve with butter and marmalade or jam. Makes about 3 dozen.

TINY SANDWICHES
Make 20 tea sandwiches (see list on page 636) of various small sizes and arrange on a large plate. Chill until ready to serve.

OATCAKES
Old-fashioned rolled oats
1½ cups sifted all-purpose flour
½ cup sugar
1 teaspoon salt
½ teaspoon baking soda
¾ cup shortening
⅓ cup cold water (about)

Combine 1½ cups oats and next 4 ingredients. Cut in shortening. Add enough water to make a stiff dough. Separate into 2 balls. Roll each to ⅛-inch thickness. Dust on top with rolled oats. Press oats down into the dough with a rolling pin. Cut into small squares and put on buttered cookie sheets. Bake in preheated moderate oven (350°F.) for 15 minutes. Makes about 3½ dozen.

COCONUT COOKIES
½ cup butter or margarine, softened
1½ cups firmly packed dark brown sugar
All-purpose flour (about 1½ cups)
2 eggs
⅛ teaspoon salt
½ teaspoon baking powder
1¼ cups chopped nuts
1 cup flaked coconut

Cream butter. Add ½ cup sugar and 1⅓ cups flour. Mix. Press into buttered pan (11 x 7 inches). Bake in preheated moderate oven (350°F.) for 20 minutes. Mix eggs, salt, 1 cup sugar, 3 tablespoons flour, and baking powder. Mix well and add nuts. Spread evenly over the partially baked mixture. Sprinkle with coco-

nut. Bake for 20 to 25 minutes longer. Cut into bars while warm. Makes about 15.

ENGLISH TEA

Tea must be made in a china pot. Never, never try to make it in a teacup. Tea does not steep in the cup, and all the finest flavors and aromas escape. Fill the teapot with boiling water to heat it before you make the tea. Then empty it, and put in the tea leaves. The usual amount is 1 teaspoon of leaves per cup; some people who like very strong tea use a little more. If you like weak tea, don't cut down on the leaves, for you will sacrifice flavor and aroma. Instead, add a little hot water to the tea after you pour it into the cup. The water must be boiling, a round bubbling boil, when you pour it over the tea leaves in the pot. Clap the lid on quickly and cover the pot with a tea cozy. This holds in the heat while the tea steeps. Allow about 5 minutes for this process. Then pour it and drink!

ORIENTAL TEA
(FOR 16)
CHINESE ALMOND COOKIES
HAWAIIAN PINEAPPLE MUFFINS
AVOCADO SANDWICHES
KOREAN SESAME-SEED COOKIES
CHINESE FORTUNE COOKIES
TEA   JASMINE TEA

CHINESE ALMOND COOKIES
2¾ cups sifted all-purpose flour
1 teaspoon baking powder
½ teaspoon salt
1¼ cups shortening
1¾ cups sugar
1 egg
½ teaspoon almond extract
¼ cup water
Almonds

Sift flour, baking powder, and salt. Cut in shortening. Mix in sugar, egg, extract, and enough water to make a dough. Knead thoroughly. Let stand for a few minutes in a cool place. Form into balls the size of walnuts and press down to ¼-inch thickness. Put an almond in the center of each. Arrange on buttered cookie sheets. Bake in preheated moderate oven (350°F.) for 12 to 15 minutes. Makes about 5 dozen.

HAWAIIAN PINEAPPLE MUFFINS
4 cups sifted all-purpose flour
2 tablespoons baking powder
½ cup sugar
1 teaspoon salt
4 eggs, beaten
1½ cups milk

½ cup butter or margarine, melted
1½ cups drained crushed pineapple

Sift dry ingredients. Add eggs, milk, and butter. Stir until smooth. Add pineapple. Mix well. Spoon into greased 3-inch muffin pans, filling them three quarters full. Bake in preheated hot oven (425° F.) for 20 to 25 minutes. Makes 2 dozen.

AVOCADO SANDWICHES

Mash 1 or 2 (depending on the size) peeled ripe avocados with a silver fork. Add juice of 1 lemon, salt and pepper to taste, and crumbled crisp bacon (1 or 2 strips for each avocado). Spread on small rounds of bread. Makes 32. Refrigerate until ready to serve.

KOREAN SESAME-SEED COOKIES
2¼ cups sifted all-purpose flour
1 teaspoon baking powder
¼ teaspoon salt
½ cup butter or margarine
¾ cup sugar
1 egg
Toasted sesame seeds (about ½ cup)
2 tablespoons cold water

Sift flour, baking powder, and salt. Cream butter; add sugar, egg, and ⅓ cup seeds and blend well. Add flour mixture alternately with water. Mix well. Shape into an oblong about 2 inches wide and 2 inches thick. Wrap in foil and chill until firm. Cut into ⅛-inch slices and put on greased cookie sheets. Sprinkle with seeds. Press seeds down into the dough. Bake in preheated moderate oven (350°F.) for 12 to 15 minutes. Makes about 4 dozen. Store in a canister until ready to use.

■ **To Toast Sesame Seeds**—Put seeds in preheated moderate oven (350°F.) for 10 to 15 minutes.

CHINESE FORTUNE COOKIES

Fortune cookies, so popular in America, are not known in China. In fact they were not even created by the Chinese. It was Japanese immigrants on the West Coast who commenced the whole idea by putting messages in their rice cakes. However, these crumbled too easily. After considerable experimentation the present recipes have been devised by various firms who refuse to reveal them. Most important are the messages, which must not offend or upset the readers. Thus one of the most popular has been "God loveth a cheerful giver." Buy fortune cookies (available in food stores) and pass to guests during the tea so that they can read messages to each other.

JASMINE TEA

In the Orient, green (unfermented) and oolong (semifermented) teas are pre-

ferred. They are delicate drinks with pleasing aromas. A particularly pleasing one is Jasmine Tea, oolong leaves scented with jasmine petals. It is not customary to serve cream, sugar, or lemon with Jasmine Tea.

TEA FOR A CROWD
(FOR 24)
CHEESE ROUNDS   LINZER TORTE
ASSORTED SANDWICHES
DATE-NUT BREAD SLICES
CHOCOLATE CRISPIES   SALTED ALMONDS
FRESH STRAWBERRIES
TEA   COFFEE

CHEESE ROUNDS
1 cup butter or margarine
2 eggs
2 cups grated sharp Cheddar cheese
2¼ cups sifted all-purpose flour
½ teaspoon salt
Dash of paprika

Cream butter, add 1 egg, and mix well. Stir in next 4 ingredients. Form into a ball and chill for 1 hour. Roll out one fourth of the dough at a time about ¼ inch thick. Cut into 1¼-inch rounds. Put on buttered cookie sheets. Brush with remaining egg, beaten. Sprinkle with sesame seeds if desired. Bake in preheated hot oven (400°F.) for 12 minutes. Makes about 6½ dozen.

LINZER TORTE
1 cup unsalted butter
1 cup granulated sugar
2 egg yolks
2 hard-cooked egg yolks, sieved
Juice and grated rind of 1 lemon
1 tablespoon brandy
½ pound almonds, ground
2 cups sifted all-purpose flour
1 teaspoon baking powder
1 cup raspberry or apricot jam
Confectioners' sugar

Cream butter and gradually beat in granulated sugar. Add next 4 ingredients. Blend well. Stir in almonds, sifted flour, and baking powder. With fingers, work ingredients to a smooth dough. Press half of dough into greased loose-bottomed 9-inch layer-cake pan, making bottom layer thicker than sides. Cover bottom with ¾ cup jam. Chill remaining half of dough until easier to handle. Roll dough into ⅜-inch strips and arrange crisscross over jam-covered dough. Bake in preheated moderate oven (350°F.) for 45 to 50 minutes, or until pale gold in color. Before serving, fill spaces between strips with ¼ cup jam. Dust with confectioners' sugar. Makes 8 to 10 servings. **Note:** For 24 people do not triple recipe, but make three Linzer Torten.

ASSORTED SANDWICHES

Prepare 4 dozen tea sandwiches (see list at right) of various breads and fillings. Cover with wax paper and keep in refrigerator until ready to use.

DATE-NUT BREAD SLICES

Cut 2 cans (7 ounces each) date-nut bread into 24 thin slices. Stack slices and cut into halves. Spread with various marmalades or jams. Chill until ready to serve.

CHOCOLATE CRISPIES

¼ cup butter or margarine, softened
1 cup sugar
2 eggs, beaten
½ cup sifted all-purpose flour
2 ounces (2 squares) unsweetened chocolate, or 2 envelopes no-melt chocolate
½ teaspoon vanilla extract
1 cup finely chopped nuts

Cream butter, add sugar and eggs, and mix well. Stir in flour, chocolate, and vanilla. Spread thinly in buttered jelly-roll pan (15 x 10 inches) and sprinkle with nuts. Bake in preheated hot oven (400°F.) for 15 minutes. Cut into 2-inch squares while warm. Makes 2 dozen.

SALTED ALMONDS

Place salted almonds in 2 pretty bowls and place near the coffee and tea services.

FRESH STRAWBERRIES

Arrange on 2 large plates circles of un-hulled washed fresh strawberries. Put a small mound of confectioners' sugar, for dipping, in the center of each plate. Refrigerate until ready to serve. If strawberries are not available, use another fresh fruit that can be handled easily.

TEA FOR A CROWD

Pour 2 quarts boiling water over 1 cup tea leaves. Cover and let stand for 5 minutes. Strain into a teapot. For each cup of tea, pour in about 2 tablespoons brew and add hot water. Makes 40 to 50 cups of tea.

TEA SANDWICHES

Make early in the day. They should be varied in shape—round, square, triangular, or diamond. Use any kind of bread—white, rye, nut, or raisin. Remove crusts. Have them open or closed. To keep, put on plates, cover with foil, and store in the refrigerator. Estimate 3 or 4 for each guest.

Fillings

■ Cream cheese, minced cooked mushrooms, ground nutmeg.
■ Chopped watercress, softened butter, grated onion.
■ Strawberry marmalade, chopped pecans, cream cheese.
■ Minced crabmeat, mayonnaise, ground turmeric.
■ Mashed avocado, fresh lemon juice, hot pepper sauce.
■ Minced chicken, almonds, curry powder, dairy sour cream.
■ Creamed Roquefort cheese, cream cheese, sherry.
■ Sliced tomatoes spread with smoked cheese.
■ Minced cucumbers, dairy sour cream, capers.
■ Ginger marmalade and chopped walnuts.
■ Chopped cooked lobster, mushrooms, fresh lemon juice, mayonnaise.
■ Chopped walnuts, raisins, maraschino cherries, cream cheese.
■ Chopped hard-cooked eggs, crumbled bacon, minced sweet pickles, prepared mustard, mayonnaise.
■ Minced clams, grated onion, yogurt.
■ Chopped dried beef, hard-cooked eggs, minced celery, dairy sour cream.
■ Cottage cheese, chopped stuffed olives, onion juice, salt.
■ Deviled ham, minced sweet pickle, chili sauce.
■ Chopped dates, minced nuts, cream cheese, pineapple juice.
■ Mashed salmon, fresh lemon juice, mayonnaise.
■ Ground chicken, minced almonds, mayonnaise, cayenne.
■ Chopped mint, chopped parsley, minced onion, mayonnaise, paprika.
■ Guava jelly and cream cheese.

ICED TEA

Place 2 teaspoons tea leaves for each cup of cold water in a pitcher or glass container. Cover with water. Refrigerate, covered, for 24 hours. Strain, and serve in tall glasses over ice cubes.

FLOWER TEAS

To make flower teas at home, add fragrant petals such as roses, gardenias, or violets to leaves in canister. Or, as did the early American housewives, put a vanilla bean among the leaves. When brewed, the tea has a delectable flavor and aroma.

Buffets

Over 150 years ago restaurants, as we know them today, did not exist in France. A few innkeepers found it profitable to take pity on weary travelers, placing simple one-course meals on boards at one side of a dining room from which the grateful wayfarer served himself. If this buffet was rather plain, it did not long remain so.

With the emergence of the great restaurants in Paris, elaborate tables and cabinets were designed to display the elegant and attractive dishes produced by the master chefs. As the furniture for this purpose was dubbed a buffet, the name applied to any meal presented in this fashion, regardless of whether the diner served himself or was served from the buffet by waiters.

In these days when the number of guests who can be suitably accommodated at a sit-down dinner is limited by considerations of space and service, the buffet dinner is a boon indeed. It is no mere substitute, however, but a form of entertaining in itself, readily adaptable to a variety of occasions, and flexible as to the number of guests. Normally the number of guests will be upwards of eight, and may be limited only by the space available or the purpose of the evening.

Selection of the menu provides both challenge and opportunity to the hostess. If the buffet is to be a prelude to the theater or a dance, she will probably wish the meal to be fairly light, centering around a single casserole or chafing dish with a few supporting dishes, followed by a light dessert and demitasse. Particularly if it is a black-tie affair, she will stress a certain degree of elegance in the appointments and décor. Above all, the menu will be planned so that a minimum of effort on her part is required in the final stages of preparation and serving. The buffet in this instance is only the beginning of the evening, and her state of calm, to say nothing of dress, hairdo, and makeup, must be as unruffled at the end of the dinner as at its beginning if she and her guests are to enjoy themselves.

On other occasions, however, the buffet may be expanded considerably. A first course may be served, and the meal itself may be more elaborate. In any event

Shrimp Curry Buffet
features Curry, Indian Pilau,
assorted condiments,
Watercress-Tomato Salad
and Fresh Fruit Platter

the well-chosen menu will be "a show of choice edibles."

Placement of the buffet itself depends on the entertaining area. If the dining table is used it may be left in the center of the room or it may be pushed against the wall to provide more space in a small room. Guests should be able to move around it and foods should be within easy reach and in appropriate order. For very large affairs, a duplicate meal may be set on each side of the table for quicker, simultaneous service. Regardless of how it is arranged, the buffet should be decked with an attractive cloth and centerpiece with plates, napkins, and flatware conveniently placed prior to the arrival of guests. The sideboard, or another table, may be prepared beforehand for the serving of dessert and coffee so that only the dessert itself and the coffee need be brought in at the appropriate time.

The seating of guests should be planned. If the living room is to be used, tray-tables may be pressed into service to augment available space on coffee or end tables. It is possible to set up card tables in some cases, in which event they will be preset with cloth, napkins, silverware, glasses, ashtrays, and candles.

Greater latitude is possible, of course, if other entertaining areas are available. A recreation room or, in good weather, a patio or terrace can be a most attractive buffet locale.

Whenever possible, predinner conversation should be in an area other than that to be used for the buffet itself. Not only are the last-minute preparations carried out unobserved by the guests, but their anticipation is whetted and rewarded with pleasant surprise when they view the attractive arrangements of the buffet.

The roles of host and hostess should be carefully planned so that the necessary tasks of service and removal are smoothly accomplished and so that both are not absent from the guests at the same time. It is the hostess who does the planning in this regard, since she will be aware of the timing.

Attractiveness in appointments is of the essence. It is most important that they should fit in with the background and occasion. If the buffet is set in a well-appointed dining room, a white or pale damask, embroidered cotton, or lace cloth would be an appropriate table covering and the hostess' finest porcelain and silver should be utilized. If, how-

ever, the buffet is set in a recreation room or out-of-doors, appointments suitable to the setting should be employed.

Careful consideration should be given to the serving dishes and implements, for they will add to the beauty of the table. Some possibilities are copper or silver chafing dishes, colorful casseroles, hand-painted trays or wicker baskets for breads, patterned boards for cheeses, an out-size brandy snifter for salad or fresh fruit, a soup tureen for a ragout, or a porcelain épergne for cakes or cookies. Electric dishes and trays may be attractive and utilitarian additions.

The centerpiece is most important to the buffet and should be accompanied by appropriate candlesticks or candelabra. Where they will be placed will depend on the position of the table. If against the wall they will be put on the side next to the wall. If the table is in the middle of the room the centerpiece will be in the center.

In contrast to the décor of the dinner table, centerpieces and candelabra of considerable height are desirable for the large buffet table. Plenty of light is needed, so several candles in varying holders, of differing heights, placed beside, around, or in back of the centerpiece, if appropriate to the décor, would add to the total effect. Some possible centerpieces might include fresh flowers in a silver bowl, in tall glass vases, or on a porcelain compote; foilage or greens and gourds in a cornucopia; or a large bowl of fruit. On a small table or surface the principal dish may serve as the centerpiece.

The general décor may follow the mood or theme of the meal. Tasteful simplicity will promote an air of formality without detracting from conviviality. Or the entertaining area may be arranged to suggest a motif—early American coach house, the mauve decade, a French bistro, the south Pacific, a Greek taverna, or the Orient.

The suggestions for menus which follow are only a few of the infinite possibilities for a buffet dinner. But, whatever the choice of menu, let the food be decoratively arranged and artistically presented, and the time and effort devoted to the planning and preparation will be well rewarded by the pleasure of the guests.

GREEK TAVERNA BUFFET
(FOR 12)
MEZE (APPETIZERS)
STIFADO (BEEF STEW)
PILAFFI (PARSLEYED PILAF)
SALATA (SALAD)   GREEK BREAD
KARIDOPITA (WALNUT CAKE)
GREEK COFFEE

Since ancient times the Greek people have enjoyed informal dining, preferably accompanied by lyrical music and entertainment. They take great interest in their food and, as far as is known, were the first to write about it, including recipes. Today great attention is given to its preparation in the home. And in restaurants it is customary to trek to the kichen to inspect the dishes, chat with the cooks, and sample, if desired, some of the dishes before ordering. Most typical of the eating places is the rustic *taverna* where in the evening Greeks go not only to enjoy the delectable spicy dishes but to join in the singing and dancing. In the summer the tables are placed outdoors. But whatever the locale, a *taverna* is always a gay place. For the occupants make each meal a most convivial event.

This buffet is most suitable for a garden or patio in summer, or for a recreation-room meal in winter. Table appointments to create a rustic setting might include tablecloths of cotton or linen homespun, or cotton damask woven in small checks; patterned or plain-colored earthenware or pottery dishes; stainless steel or kitchen flatware; and colored candles in brass holders. A large bowl of fruit, which is an important part of each Greek meal, would make an appropriate centerpiece and could be served at the end of the meal.

MEZE
(Appetizers)
Arrange on a large platter or tray the following: Greek black olives, wedges of feta cheese (both available at Greek delicatessens; as substitutes use canned black olives and farmer cheese), *Avga Gemista, Manitaria Toursi,* and *Taramo-*

salata. Serve during predinner conversation or place on the table as a part of the buffet meal.

AVGA GEMISTA
(Stuffed Eggs)
12 hard-cooked eggs, shelled
½ cup minced cooked beets
4 teaspoons minced capers
3 tablespoons snipped fresh parsley
2 tablespoons vinegar
¼ cup mayonnaise
   Salt and pepper to taste
   Whole capers

Cut the eggs into halves crosswise. Remove the yolks. Cut a thin slice from the bottom of each egg-white so it can stand upright. Add next 7 ingredients to the yolks. Beat smooth. Spoon into the egg-white shells, forming a small mound on each. Decorate each with a caper. Makes 12 servings.

MANITARIA TOURSI
(Pickled Mushrooms)
1 pound small fresh mushrooms
¼ cup salad oil
3 tablespoons fresh lemon juice
1 garlic clove, halved
½ teaspoon salt
⅛ teaspoon pepper
2 bay leaves
   Pinch of oregano

Remove the stems from the mushrooms. Wipe the caps dry with paper towel. Put in a jar. Combine the other ingredients in a saucepan. Heat; pour over the mushrooms. Cool. Cover and refrigerate for at least 2 days. Shake now and then. Pour off any liquid and serve with toothpicks. Makes 12 servings.

TARAMOSALATA
(Red Caviar Spread)
   Juice of 2 lemons
1 jar (8 ounces) red caviar
1 medium onion, minced
5 slices of white bread, crusts removed
1 cup olive oil

Combine lemon juice, caviar, and onion. Mix well, preferably in a blender. Dip the bread slices into hot water. Squeeze dry and break into pieces. Add to the caviar mixture and blend smooth. Add olive oil and blend until no trace of the oil is left. Spoon into a mound on a plate or in a bowl. Garnish with chopped parsley and olives. Makes 12 servings.

STIFADO
(Beef Stew)
4 pounds beef chuck or round steak
⅔ cup cooking oil
1 can (6 ounces) tomato paste
1½ cups red wine
8 peppercorns
2 bay leaves
1½ tablespoons ground allspice
2 garlic cloves, halved
5 whole cloves
   Salt and pepper to taste
3 pounds small white onions, peeled

Cut the meat into 1-inch squares and sauté in oil until brown. Add the other ingredients except onions. Bring to a quick boil and simmer, covered, for 1 hour. Add more wine if necessary. Add the onions and cook until tender, another 30 to 40 minutes. Discard the garlic and cloves. The final stew mixture should be thick. Taste for seasoning before serving. Makes 12 servings.
Note: This dish may be prepared beforehand and kept for 1 or 2 days in the refrigerator. Or it may be frozen. Thaw at room temperature and reheat.

PILAFFI
(Parsleyed Pilaf)
3 cups uncooked rice
1½ cups chopped fresh parsley
⅓ cup butter
1 teaspoon salt
¼ teaspoon pepper
6 cups chicken consommé

Put all the ingredients in a large shallow casserole or baking dish. Mix well and bake in preheated moderate oven (350° F.) for about 50 minutes, until the liquid has been absorbed and the grains are separate. The ingredients in the dish may be refrigerated until just before cooking. Makes 12 servings.

SALATA
(Salad)
2 large heads romaine, cleaned and broken into pieces
2 medium cucumbers, peeled and sliced
2 green peppers, chopped
1 cup sliced radishes

½ cup olive oil
3 tablespoons fresh lemon juice
Salt and pepper to taste
¾ cup crumbled feta cheese

Combine all the ingredients and toss together. The vegetables may be prepared in the morning and the dressing, previously combined, added just before serving. Since the vegetables vary in size, the amount of salad dressing may be a little more or less than stated. Makes 12 servings.

GREEK BREAD

Loaves of Greek bread, some with sesame seeds, are available at many food stores and delicatessens. If not, use any type of bread.

KARIDOPITA
(Walnut Cake)

½ cup butter
2½ cups sugar
2 eggs, slightly beaten
2 cups sifted all-purpose flour
1 teaspoon baking powder
1 teaspoon baking soda
½ teaspoon ground cinnamon
⅔ cup sour milk
1 cup chopped walnuts
Grated rind of 1 lemon
1 cup water

Cream the butter. Add 1 cup sugar and the eggs. Blend well. Sift flour, baking powder, baking soda, and cinnamon and add alternately with sour milk. Mix in the nuts and lemon rind. Blend well. Pour into a greased rectangular baking pan (13 x 9 x 2 inches). Bake in preheated moderate oven (350°F.) for about 45 minutes.

In the meantime make a thick syrup by boiling together 1½ cups sugar and the water for 15 minutes. Pour over the cake while still warm. Turn off the oven and put cake back in it for 5 minutes. (Better

when served warm.) Cut into diamonds and serve. This may be prepared 1 or 2 days beforehand. Wrap in wax paper. Whipped cream, instead of syrup, may be served over the cake. Makes about 16 pieces.

GREEK COFFEE

In Greece the tiny cups of foamy dark coffee are usually called Greek coffee. But throughout the Middle East the same brew is known as Turkish coffee and is prepared in a long-handled small brass or copper container (ibrik). It is quite different from the clearer brewed coffee popular in America and must be made with finely pulverized grounds, available in coffee shops or Greek food stores.

Measure 4½ cups freshly drawn cold water into a small saucepan. Stir in 3 tablespoons sugar (less, if desired) and ¾ cup finely pulverized coffee. Bring to a boil, allowing mixture to froth up. Remove from the stove and repeat the boiling and frothing up two more times. Pour off some of the foam into each demitasse cup. Fill with the remaining coffee. Makes 12 demitasse servings.

SHRIMP CURRY BUFFET
(FOR 12)

STUFFED MUSHROOMS
SHRIMP CURRY   INDIAN PILAU
ASSORTED CONDIMENTS
WATERCRESS TOMATO SALAD
INDIAN BREADS
FRESH FRUIT PLATTER
TEA OR COFFEE

Since foods that can be eaten easily, without the aid of a knife, are preferable for buffets, curries are often chosen. This is not, however, the only reason for their popularity. For a curry, properly prepared and presented, is delectable to taste and delightful to behold.

For parties curry may be prepared a day or two beforehand and left in the refrigerator until ready to reheat. The latter can be done in the kitchen or in a chafing dish on the table. Customarily, the curry is accompanied by a rice dish, pilau—itself a well-seasoned combination —a colorful array of condiments in little bowls, and unleavened bread (chapatties, parathas, puris, or popadams). Darjeeling tea, a light green one, is the preferred Eastern beverage with curry. But cold beverages such as fruit drinks or ale may be substituted for it. Fruits or sherbet combinations are recommended desserts.

Table appointments for a curry buffet

should be as attractive as possible. The table may be covered with silk runners or saris from the Orient and set with large serving dishes of varying patterns and fitting colors, surrounded by any number of matching or mixed-patterned little bowls holding the condiments, as well as fresh fruits if desired. A possible centerpiece would be flower blossoms floating in low bowls and perhaps surrounded by Indian ornaments. If a chafing dish is used for the curry, the décor might be worked out around it. For example if it is copper, use brass candlesticks, a lazy susan for condiments, pottery plates, and a cloth of Indian-head material. If it is silver, however, select porcelain dishes, silver flatware, a crystal bowl of flowers, and a damask cloth.

STUFFED MUSHROOMS

Stem and wipe dry with a damp paper towel 24 large fresh mushrooms. Heat a skillet. Cover the surface generously with butter. Add the mushrooms in one layer. When the edges commence to brown, turn over and brown other sides. Cooking should only take 4 to 5 minutes. Drain on paper towel. Fill with deviled ham or any sharp cheese spread. Just before serving, heat for a few minutes, until warm, in moderate oven (350°F.). Arrange on aluminum foil trays, cover securely with foil, and freeze, if desired. Place in moderate oven (350°F.) for about 10 minutes before serving. Place toothpicks on the plate beside them. Serve as hors-d'oeuvre.

SHRIMP CURRY

5 pounds fresh or frozen raw shrimps
1 teaspoon salt
1 medium onion, sliced
2 lemons, sliced
6 peppercorns
½ cup butter
2 to 3 tablespoons curry powder
1¼ cups chopped onions
1½ cups peeled diced apple
2 bouillon cubes
2 cups hot water
1 tablespoon cornstarch
¼ cup cold water
1 cup evaporated milk, undiluted

Place shrimps in a large pan with enough water to cover. Add salt, onion, lemons, and peppercorns. Bring to a boil. Cook until pink, for 1 to 2 minutes, not more than 5. Drain and set aside. When cool, remove shells and dark veins. (This is the most economical and flavorful way to prepare the shrimps. But 2½ pounds cleaned shrimps may be used as a substitute.) Melt the butter in an extra-large skillet. Add the curry (the amount depending on its strength and the desired flavor), onions, and apple. Sauté for 10 minutes, stirring constantly. Add bouillon cubes and hot water. Simmer, stirring occasionally, for 10 minutes. Combine the cornstarch with cold water and mix into the hot liquid. Stir until thickened. Add shrimps and milk. Mix well and simmer, covered, for 10 minutes. When cool, this may be refrigerated for 1 or 2 days, or frozen. If the latter, reheat over low heat. Taste for seasonings. Makes 12 servings.

INDIAN PILAU
    3 cups raw rice
    6½ cups chicken consommé or 6 chicken
        bouillon cubes and 6½ cups cold water
    3 tablespoons butter
    1 teaspoon ground allspice
    2 cinnamon sticks
        Salt and pepper to taste
    6 tablespoons chopped blanched
        almonds
    ¾ cup raisins

Wash the rice and drain. Place it with the consommé, butter, allspice, cinnamon, salt, and pepper in a flat baking dish. Mix well. Cover with aluminum foil. Cook in preheated moderate oven (350°F.) for about 50 minutes, until the liquid has been absorbed and the grains are separate. Stir in the almonds and raisins. Take out the cinnamon sticks. Mix well and serve. The ingredients, except the almonds and raisins, may be placed in the dish beforehand and refrigerated until ready to cook. Makes 12 servings.

ASSORTED CONDIMENTS
There is no limit to the number of condiments that may be included with curry, but generally there are at least five of them. Possibilities include: finely chopped peanuts, chutney (1 or more kinds), grated coconut, chopped hard-cooked egg, chopped crisp bacon, chopped pickles, raisins, chopped fresh green onions, crumbled potato chips, preserved and candied gingerroot, shredded Bombay Duck (not duck but a dried fish caught off the Indian coast), chopped fruit peel, chopped green or ripe olives, snipped watercress, mustard pickles, chopped green pepper, watermelon pickles, chopped chives, pickled walnuts, sliced bananas, diced cucumber, diced pineapple, chopped parsley, and chopped tomatoes.

WATERCRESS-TOMATO SALAD
    2 bunches (about 4 cups) watercress
    5 tomatoes
    3 quarts Boston lettuce,
        broken into pieces
    2 tablespoons tarragon vinegar
    ½ cup salad oil
    1 teaspoon salt
    ½ teaspoon pepper

Wash the watercress. Snip off the leaves, discarding any wilted ones. Dip tomatoes into hot water. Peel, and slice thinly. Wash lettuce and drain. Mix together in a large bowl. Refrigerate until ready to serve. Have vinegar, oil, salt, and pepper combined in a jar. Pour over the vegetables and toss just before serving. Makes 12 servings.

INDIAN BREADS
In India a form of unleavened bread is generally served with curry. The most common are the chapatties, made from flour, salt, and water, rolled into circles, and baked on a dry griddle. Similar to them are the parathas which are baked on a buttered griddle. Popadams, made of rice or lentil flour, are fried tissue-thin wafers, whereas puris are deep-fried bread similar to fritters. One or all of these are sometimes available in supermarkets or delicatessens. If not, serve slices of white bread or soda crackers.

FRESH FRUIT PLATTER
Place 12 slices of fresh pineapple and 12 fresh peach halves on a platter. Sprinkle with orange juice. Refrigerate until ready to serve. In the meantime put 12 scoops of raspberry sherbet on a cookie sheet. Place in the freezer. When ready to serve take out of the freezer and arrange over the fruit. Garnish with sprigs of mint. Makes 12 servings.

Cocktail Parties

If one were to seek an appropriate adjective for the cocktail party, it would probably be "controversial." It is a function adored by many, abhorred by others. Regardless of preference, however, the cocktail party is an established part of the American scene. It is also a most useful and versatile form of entertaining.

From the standpoint of the hostess the cocktail party is a flexible affair that can serve many social purposes. The guests may be as few as ten in number, or the party may be expanded to the limits of available space. As it is a stand-up party, she is able to accommodate more people than at other affairs, and is also able to use dining room and living room, as well as porch and/or patio if she has them and the weather permits.

Still another advantage is that the cocktail party may be limited in time. Generally using the hours of late afternoon and early evening, most guests will drop in for an hour or so before going on to dinner or another engagement.

Conviviality is the keynote of the party, but the hostess is permitted a considerable degree of latitude in selecting her guests. She can range into various coteries of her acquaintance with considerably greater freedom than she could, say, for a small dinner. While limited in number of guests only by the space available, it would be risky to go beyond thirty or thirty-five without the assistance of a waiter or bartender.

It is not necessary to run the gamut of all the mixtures to which the name "cocktail" has been applied. Martinis and Manhattans are standard cocktails, Scotch and Bourbon should be available, together with tonic, soda, and water. Sherry is desirable and ginger ale or soft drinks are essential.

Food for the party may be limited to snacks, dips, and hors-d'oeuvre to be handled with fingers or toothpicks. Most of these will be served cold, but one or two, possibly three, hot dishes may be

featured. It should be remembered that the purpose of the food is to accompany the beverage; the object is to stimulate the appetite, not to satisfy it. It is doubtful that the guests will appreciate sweets.

Preparation of the cold hors-d'oeuvre can, of course, be accomplished beforehand. The hot dishes may be in the kitchen ready for the stove prior to or during the party. Drinks will, in the main, be prepared at the bar, although it may be desirable to mix some cocktails before the party, so that stirring with ice is all that is necessary.

In general, it is the host who will tend to the bar; if there is no host, the hostess may ask a friend to stand in. The hostess may pass certain of the cold dishes, particularly in the early stages of the party; thereafter, however, guests may be expected to serve themselves. The hostess is expected to make an initial offering of the hot dishes; the first should not be made ready until a good proportion of the guests have arrived, and the other dishes should be spaced at intervals. After this, they may be placed on warmers.

The dining table is excellent for the more substantial hors-d'oeuvre: left in the center of the dining room or dining area, more guests will have access to it. A light-colored cloth will best set off the food and centerpiece. Lighter snacks may be conveniently spread in small bowls around the entire entertaining area. It is wise to have an adequate number of ashtrays available.

The entertaining area should be well lit, for a cocktail party is not a somber affair. Music is helpful, particularly in the first half hour as the guests are beginning to arrive. The music should be light, however, and serve as background —neither loud enough to intrude, nor serious enough to demand exclusive attention.

A few suggestions for hors-d'oeuvre, both hot and cold, are given below. There are, of course, any number of prepared snacks and cocktail foods readily available. In selecting and making at least some of the hors-d'oeuvre herself, however, the hostess provides the personal and creative touch that distinguishes her party from any other.

CANAPÉ SPREADS

Crackers or thin slices of bread cut into triangles, rounds, diamonds, squares, or rectangles, may be spread with any of the following:

■ Flaked lobster, horseradish, chopped chives, dairy sour cream.

■ Liver pâté, paprika, ground nutmeg, bits of black olives.

■ Mashed sardines, cream cheese, grated onion, fresh lemon juice.

■ Anchovy paste, capers, Parmesan cheese, curry powder.

■ Ground almonds, cream cheese, smoked cheese.

■ Minced chicken, chopped sweet pickles, ground turmeric, mayonnaise.

■ Tuna fish, dairy sour cream, sweet relish.

■ Minced shrimps, French dressing, chopped fresh dill.

■ Blue cheese, cream cheese, sherry, chopped mint.

■ Minced turkey, chopped pecans, coconut, mayonnaise.

■ Deviled ham, minced pickled onions, stuffed Spanish olives.

■ Grated Parmesan cheese, yogurt, chopped chives.

■ Minced mushrooms, cooked sausage, ketchup.

■ Mashed kippered herring, dash of hot pepper sauce, fresh lemon juice.

■ Minced cucumber, chopped hard-cooked egg, dairy sour cream.

CLAM DIP

2 packages (8 ounces each) cream cheese, softened
  Juice of 1 lemon
½ cup mayonnaise
2 teaspoons Worcestershire
1 tablespoon prepared mustard
8 green onions with tops, minced
2 cans (7½ ounces each) minced clams, drained
  Salt and pepper to taste

Combine all the ingredients. Mix in a blender or with a fork until smooth. Chill in the refrigerator until ready to use. Serve with potato chips or crackers. Makes 1 quart.

SAVORY SHRIMPS

3 pounds raw shrimps in shells
1 medium onion, sliced
1 lemon, sliced
8 peppercorns
2 cans (10½ ounces each) condensed cream-of-mushroom soup
1 cup drained crushed pineapple
2 tablespoons sherry
2 teaspoons Worcestershire

Put the shrimps in a large pan with enough water to cover. Add onion, lemon, and peppercorns. Bring to a boil. Cook until pink, for 1 or 2 minutes, not more than 5. Drain. When cool, remove shells and dark veins. In the meantime combine the other ingredients and warm through. Add shrimps and cook for another 5 minutes, stirring often. Do not boil. Serve on a plate with toothpicks. Or put in a chafing dish. Prepare ahead of time and refrigerate. Or freeze. Defrost at room temperature and reheat just before serving. Makes about 20 servings.

ASSORTED COLD MEATS

Place thin slices of cold meats—roast beef, ham, turkey—in rows or in circles on a large platter. Put a plate of small buttered rolls and a dish of prepared mustard beside it so guests may prepare their own snacks. Refrigerate until ready to serve.

TERIYAKI STICKS

3 pounds sirloin steak
¼ cup soy sauce
¼ cup sugar
¼ cup sherry
1 garlic clove, crushed
2 teaspoons minced fresh gingerroot

Cut the steak into strips ¼ inch thick, ½ inch wide, and 2 inches long. Combine the other ingredients and pour over the meat. Marinate for at least 1 hour, mixing about occasionally. String, accordion style, on small bamboo skewers. Broil for 2 to 3 minutes on each side. (Prepare beforehand and refrigerate. Do not broil until ready to serve.) Makes about 60 skewers.

Note: Soy sauce differs in strength according to brand, therefore it is difficult to state exactly how much is needed. Since it is a strong flavoring, add sparingly at first. Taste after mixing with the other ingredients.

DILL MEATBALLS

2 slices of white bread
½ cup milk
⅓ cup minced onions
1½ tablespoons dillseed
3 tablespoons chopped fresh parsley
1¼ pounds ground beef
1 teaspoon salt
¼ teaspoon pepper
Oil for frying

Soak the bread in the milk. Squeeze dry and place in a large bowl. Add the other ingredients except oil. Mix well until all ingredients are blended. Roll into small balls the size of marbles. Arrange on a piece of wax paper. Heat enough oil to cover the bottom of a skillet. Fry meatballs, several at a time, until brown. Keep turning in skillet to cook evenly. Drain on paper towels. Serve at once with toothpicks. Or cool and freeze. To reheat, place on cookie sheet in hot oven (400°F.) for 5 minutes. Makes 8 to 9 dozen.

A CHEESE PLATE

Arrange 3 or 4 assorted cheeses—Roquefort, Stilton, Camembert, Bel Paese, Port Salut, or Gouda—on a large tray or platter. Place rows of assorted crackers or thin small slices of breads in between the cheeses. Leave at room temperature for 1 hour before serving.

CREAM-CHEESE MINIATURES

2 packages (3 ounces each) cream cheese, softened
½ cup drained crushed pineapple
½ cup chopped blanched almonds
1 jar (2½ ounces) dried beef

Combine cheese, pineapple, and almonds. Refrigerate until chilled. In the meantime snip the dried beef into tiny shreds with scissors. With a small spoon form the cheese mixture into tiny balls. Roll each in the dried beef shreds. Refrigerate until ready to use. Or freeze if desired. Thaw at room temperature. Serve with toothpicks. Makes about 35.

CHILI CON QUESO

1 medium onion, minced
2 medium green peppers, diced
3 tablespoons butter
2 cups (one 1-pound can) tomatoes
1 teaspoon chili powder
½ pound sharp yellow cheese (2 cups grated)

Sauté onion and green peppers in butter until tender. Add tomatoes and chili powder. Break the tomatoes apart with a fork. Simmer for 10 minutes. Add the cheese; keep over low heat until cheese is melted. Keep warm in a chafing dish. Place a bowl of corn chips next to it for dipping. This may be made up ahead of time and reheated. Makes 6 servings.

MARINATED ARTICHOKE HEARTS

2 packages (9 ounces each) frozen artichoke hearts
1 envelope (⅝ ounce) Parmesan Salad Dressing Mix
2 tablespoons fresh lemon juice
½ cup salad oil

Cook the artichokes according to directions. Drain and chill. Combine the Dressing Mix, lemon juice, and oil. Pour over the artichokes and leave in the refrigerator for at least 2 hours. Serve with toothpicks. Makes 6 servings.

Barbecues

To some it is an art, to others suburban madness. But, art or mania, at the drop of a briquette, numberless American males are eager to pursue the mystique of outdoor cookery with enthusiasm and zeal. This is a boon to the hostess, for she can make of the barbecue an attractive form of entertaining and a tribute to the hospitality of the household. Since in most cases she'll be able to place the task of cooking on the host, she can plan other details so as to add to the undoubted pleasure of dining outdoors.

It is not necessary to entertain on a grand scale to enjoy the pleasures of outdoor cooking. Millions of Americans find that a backyard, patio, garden, or porch provides an excellent setting.

From the standpoint of the hostess, the barbecue offers intriguing possibilities for entertaining. Although essentially informal in nature, it can be an elegantly served dinner on the terrace or patio. Again, it may be a stand-up meal for a number of grown-ups and their children. Its timing is naturally flexible and invitations may place the event at any hour from early afternoon to late evening.

The number of guests is limited only by the area and facilities available, and a convivial company is generally assured by the very nature of the barbecue. The essential good weather also tends to promote good humor. Fancy equipment is not necessary, and an amazing variety of foods can be cooked on a small *hibachi,* or Japanese grill. Accompanying foods, such as rice, vegetables, salads, and breads, can be prepared indoors and brought out at the appropriate time. If electric outlets are available in or near the cooking area, electric bean pots, skillets, and coffeepots can be utilized. Prior planning and preparation are musts in any event, and considerable practice is generally useful in outdoor cookery where precise timing is difficult at best.

Division of labor is the key to preparation and service, perhaps more so for a barbecue than for any other form of home entertaining. Generally, the host is only too eager to "rule the roast" and take care of the cooking actually performed outdoors. Some, of course, prefer to do everything themselves, from preparing salads to serving dessert. A smoother operation will probably result if responsibilities are divided. The hostess will, as usual, be responsible for overall planning. She may, for example, undertake all the preparation of items indoors, which she generally can plan so that most of it is accomplished beforehand and only a brief absence from her guests will be necessary. With the hostess for once in a supporting role, the host may star at the outdoor cooking with the degree of verve and élan he desires.

It is of utmost importance that all equipment—tongs, long fork, charcoal, lighter fluid, gloves, carving and serving implements, and proper seasonings and sauces—be set out before guests arrive so that numerous treks to procure them are not necessary.

While it is possible on some occasions to have guests stand, seating is more apt to promote comfort and add to enjoyment. Garden umbrella tables, bridge tables, picnic tables, a long folding table, even boards on sawhorses may be used to advantage. Sometimes it is possible to do the actual cooking on the patio or lawn and use an adjacent screened porch for dining.

After dark, candles in holders with wind protection are desirable for the dining and serving tables. These may be augmented by inexpensive candleholders or torches on poles inserted in the ground nearby. Insect-repellent candles are also available, should mosquitoes present a problem.

Unless the grill is of such magnitude that the entire meal can be prepared on it and served from it, a serving table or area is necessary. It should be as close to the cooking implement as possible and attractively appointed.

Solid-colored earthenware, decorated pottery or glass casseroles, baskets and wooden trays or boards, are suitable for a picnic-type table. But if an elegant porch or terrace is the setting, silver with porcelain serving dishes would be appropriate. Serve-yourself meals call for extra-large plates or trays, solid glassware, sturdy earthenware, plastic, or pottery plates, perhaps even attractive paperware.

Centerpieces are not always appropriate for outdoor dining. If used, they should be simple: a few flowers, evergreens, or lacy foliage in pewter or copper holders, a ring of petals around candlestick bases, or small baskets of fruit.

Simple or elaborate, the barbecue is almost certain to be an enjoyable event. For if nature will but collaborate to produce good weather, the air of informality will promote good humor, good appetite, and good talk.

BARBECUE COOKERY

■ Brush grill with oil before using. Be sure that it has been well cleaned.

■ Meat should be at room temperature. Take out of refrigerator at least 1 hour before cooking.

■ Cheaper cuts of meat are greatly enhanced by sprinkling liberally with tenderizer or marinating before cooking.

■ For steaks, allow ½ to ¾ pound per person. If several guests are invited, it might be preferable to buy 1 or 2 large steaks instead of individual ones.

■ Roasts are excellent for a large group. Any type can be cooked on a revolving spit. Balance is important. Be sure. the meat is centered securely on the spit. Slow fires are best for cooking. Place a pan made of foil under the meat to catch the drippings. The roast may be marinated before being spitted, or basted with any of your favorite barbecue sauces while cooking.

A SMALL BARBECUE
(FOR 4)
BROILED MUSHROOM CAPS
BARBECUED SPARERIBS
BAKED SPUDS   COLESLAW
WATERMELON WEDGES
COOKIES   COFFEE

BROILED MUSHROOM CAPS
Remove stems from 16 extra-large mushrooms. Arrange, cap sides up, in buttered shallow dish. Sprinkle with chopped parsley, a little sherry, salt, freshly ground pepper, and bits of butter. Put under broiler for 4 or 5 minutes. Serve on toast points. Makes 4 servings.

BARBECUED SPARERIBS
  5 pounds lean pork spareribs
½ cup chopped onion
⅓ cup red wine
   Salt and pepper to taste
1½ cups ketchup
   Juice of 1½ lemons (or 3 tablespoons)
½ cup firmly packed dark brown sugar
¼ teaspoon hot pepper sauce
  1 teaspoon Worcestershire
  1 teaspoon mustard seeds

Put spareribs in shallow dish. Cover with onion, wine, and salt and pepper. Marinate for 1 hour, turning occasionally. Combine remaining ingredients. Cook, stirring often, for 5 minutes, or until thickened. String ribs, accordion style, on skewer of grill and secure tightly with clamps. Brush well with the marinade. Have coals ready in rear of firebox.

Attach skewer and turn on motor. Put a drip pan under ribs. Cook for 1½ hours, or until tender, basting with the sauce during the last hour. Makes 4 servings.

BAKED SPUDS

Rub 4 washed large potatoes with oil and salt. Wrap each in double-thick foil. Put directly on hot coals and cook, turning with tongs once or twice, for 1 to 1½ hours, or until tender. To test, open foil and squeeze potato gently.

COLESLAW

2½ cups shredded green cabbage
1 cup shredded red cabbage
¾ teaspoon celery seeds
3 tablespoons salad oil
½ cup mayonnaise
1 tablespoon fresh lemon juice
1 tablespoon milk
½ teaspoon sugar
Salt and pepper

Combine cabbage, celery seeds, salad oil, mayonnaise, lemon juice, milk, and sugar in bowl. Mix well and season with salt and pepper to taste. Refrigerate, covered, until ready to serve. Makes 4 servings.

Note: All red or all green cabbage can be used if preferred.

HOLIDAY BARBECUE
(FOR 8)
COLD BROCCOLI SOUP
STUFFED FLANK STEAKS
MIXED BEAN SALAD
PINEAPPLE STICKS
COFFEE

COLD BROCCOLI SOUP

1½ cups finely chopped onions
2 celery stalks, diced
2 packages (10 ounces each) frozen chopped broccoli
4 chicken bouillon cubes
Salt and pepper to taste
3 tablespoons all-purpose flour
1½ cups light cream

Simmer onions and celery in ¾ cup water until tender. Cook broccoli in a little water for 8 minutes. Drain and add to celery and onions. Add bouillon cubes and 4 cups water; season with salt and pepper. Cook for 5 minutes. Stir a few tablespoons of liquid with the flour to make a smooth paste; mix into the soup. Bring to boil, strain, and cool. Add cream and chill. Makes 8 servings.

STUFFED FLANK STEAKS

2 flank steaks (about 1½ pounds each)
Meat tenderizer
½ cup red wine
¼ cup salad oil
¼ cup soy sauce
1 teaspoon ground nutmeg

1½ cups minced green peppers
2 onions, minced
1 cup finely chopped celery
6 tablespoons butter or margarine
4 cups coarse bread crumbs
2 tablespoons sweet pickle relish
¼ cup slivered blanched almonds
1 teaspoon salt
½ teaspoon pepper

Cut off any fat from both sides of flank steaks. With sharp knife, slit a deep pocket in each by cutting along one side, lengthwise, into interior. Work slowly so that none of the outside flesh is cut. Sprinkle all surfaces generously with tenderizer and a little water. Rub well with fingertips and score lightly with fork.

Combine wine, oil, soy sauce, and nutmeg. Pour over the steaks and marinate for at least 1 hour, turning occasionally. Sauté green peppers, onions, and celery in butter. Add crumbs and toss until moistened and mixed well. Add remaining ingredients and mix again. Carefully spoon into the steak pockets. Sew shut with large needle and coarse thread. Have coals ready in front part of firebox. Lay steaks on grill and cook for 12 to 15 minutes on each side. Carve on a slant, being careful that the stuffing does not ooze out. Makes 8 servings.

MIXED BEAN SALAD

About 2 cups (one 15-ounce can) red kidney beans, drained
1½ cups cooked baby Lima beans
½ Bermuda onion, separated into rings
½ cup sliced radishes
1 cup cucumber slices
1 tablespoon tarragon vinegar
¼ cup salad oil
½ teaspoon salt
½ teaspoon powdered mustard
Lettuce

Combine all ingredients except lettuce. Mix well and chill. When ready to serve, spoon into bowl lined with lettuce leaves. Makes 8 servings.

PINEAPPLE STICKS

Cut thick slices from the top and bottom of a fresh pineapple. With sharp knife cut out meat leaving shell in one piece. Cut center into halves lengthwise. Remove core. Cut pineapple lengthwise into spears. Roll each spear in sugar. Put back, one by one, into shell. Pour rum or any desired fruit juice over spears. Replace top and chill. Makes about 8 servings, depending on size of pineapple.

SOUTHERN BARBECUE
(FOR 12)
BLACK-BEAN SOUP
TEXAS BARBECUED CHICKEN
CHUCK-WAGON POTATOES
LETTUCE SALAD
PECAN PASTRIES   COFFEE

BLACK-BEAN SOUP

10 slices of bacon
3 cans (10½ ounces each) condensed black-bean soup
3 soup cans water
1 teaspoon crushed dried rosemary
Worcestershire to taste
Salt and pepper
2 hard-cooked egg whites

Cook the bacon until crisp. Crumble. Mix soup, water, rosemary, Worcestershire, and salt and pepper to taste. Bring to a boil. Add the bacon. In the meantime chop the hard-cooked egg whites. Pour the soup into cups. Sprinkle each with a little egg white. Serve as a first course. Prepare beforehand and heat, adding bacon and egg whites just before serving. Makes 12 servings.

TEXAS BARBECUED CHICKEN

1½ cups butter
¾ cup sugar
2 garlic cloves, crushed
1 teaspoon paprika
½ cup tarragon vinegar
3 cups ketchup
2 tablespoons Worcestershire
1½ teaspoons prepared mustard
1½ teaspoons salt
½ teaspoon pepper
2 teaspoons chili powder
6 broiler-fryer chickens (2½ pounds each), cut into halves
Meat tenderizer
Salt and pepper to taste

Combine all ingredients except last 4. Simmer for 20 minutes until thick, stirring occasionally. Makes 3 cups sauce.

Rub chickens with meat tenderizer and salt and pepper. Place, skin sides up, on the grill after the coals are ready. Cook, basting with the sauce and turning often, for about 1 hour, until the meat is tender and no pink can be seen. Makes 12 servings.

CHUCK-WAGON POTATOES

6 tablespoons butter

5 cups diced cooked potatoes
1 cup chopped Bermuda onions
2 cups chopped green pepper
¼ cup chopped pimientos
1 teaspoon salt
¼ teaspoon pepper

Heat the butter in an extra-large skillet. Combine the other ingredients. Mix well. Fry in the butter, stirring occasionally with a fork, until all sides are brown. Serve at once. Combine the ingredients beforehand and have ready to fry. Makes 12 servings.

LETTUCE SALAD

Clean 2 to 3 heads Boston lettuce and break into pieces (enough to make about 4 quarts). Place in a large bowl. Cover with a salad dressing made with 3 tablespoons vinegar, ¾ cup salad oil, 1½ teaspoons salt, and ¾ teaspoon freshly ground pepper. Toss and serve. Prepare the lettuce beforehand and refrigerate. Combine other ingredients in a jar and add just before serving. Makes 12 servings.

PECAN PASTRIES

Pastry for twelve 4-inch tarts, unbaked
2 cups chopped pecans
2 cups sugar
2 cups light corn syrup
4 eggs, beaten
2 teaspoons vanilla extract

Line tart pans with pastry. Combine the other ingredients. Mix well and spoon into the tart pans. Bake in preheated slow oven (300°F.) for 55 to 60 minutes. Serve cold, garnished with whipped cream if desired. Makes 12.

Dinners

"Strange," mused the indefatigable diarist Samuel Pepys in 1665, "to see how a good dinner and feasting reconciles everybody." True, but not strange. For a dinner is designed to reconcile everyone—not in the negative sense of resolving conflicts, but in the positive sense of promoting harmony, contentment, and congeniality.

In fact, of all the forms of hospitality, dinner is perhaps the most rewarding both for hostess and guests. In deciding that the occasion calls for dinner, the hostess knows that she will create something special: her well-planned menu, tasteful settings, and attractive décor will all contribute to an atmosphere of civilized well-being. And the guests, being generally small in number, will feel themselves a select group, especially chosen to enjoy this particular repast.

While the reasons for giving a small dinner party may vary, it is generally an occasion where a degree of intimacy will exist. Old friends, of course, may be so entertained. But friends who do not know each other may also be introduced at dinner—not just to meet, but to become acquainted. The same applies to a guest or guests of honor. On some occasions a holiday or anniversary may best be celebrated with a small dinner gathering.

As a sit-down affair, the number of guests will be limited by the size of the dining table. Eight generally makes a good group, but, the number may be six, ten, or twelve, whatever the facilities permit. Since the number of guests is small, they should be selected as carefully as a menu so that harmony and congeniality will prevail. Invitations should be extended at least ten days beforehand, and may be made by telephone. Considering all the pressures of modern living, however, it is wise to follow up the phone call with a written reminder on a simple visiting card or a printed invitation card—time, place, type of dress (only if black tie), and the purpose (if the dinner represents a special occasion or is held to honor someone). If it is preferred to extend written invitations only, notes may be sent on attractive notepaper "informals" or on printed invitation cards. Since it is essential to know that all guests will be present, the written invitations should include "R.S.V.P." The term is French and means "Reply, please!" asking the prospective guest to accept or decline the invitation.

In choosing a menu, balance is the primary consideration. The dinner, as in the case of a play, should have a beginning, a middle, and an end, although these must be modified with variety and climax. Thus, it would be quite possible to present an excellent dinner by serving hors-d'oeuvre with predinner beverages, climaxed at the table by a well-chosen casserole, salad, and rolls, and a simple dessert such as pie or fruit and cheese, followed by coffee.

The hostess may, however, prefer a variation on this theme by serving her guests a first course (soup, a mound of crabmeat on lettuce, stuffed tomatoes, or paté) in the course of predinner conversation, the company then repairing to the dining table for an entrée such as a roast, stuffed fish, planked steak, or lamb shish kebab, with appropriate potatoes, pasta, or rice, vegetables, salad, and rolls; followed by a light dessert such as a chiffon pie, sherbet, or Bavarian cream.

Or she might wish to climax the meal with flaming crêpes prepared in a chafing dish at the buffet or table.

Regardless of the menu selected for dinner, it is well to include only dishes with which the hostess has had some experience. She is thus in a much better position to plan the order of service and to know the degree of previous preparation that can be accomplished, and her self-assurance is not troubled with worry over the results of experimentation. Known preferences and/or prejudices of the guests also merit consideration and, unless the guests clearly understand and have accepted beforehand that the meal is to be somewhat exotic, extremely spiced or esoteric dishes should be avoided.

It is essential that the dinner proceed smoothly. Consequently, the hostess will work out her planning in regard to preparation and service with unusual care, and will also make sure that the host understands his own part in the proceedings. If possible, predinner conversation should not take place in the dining room or area. While the host remains with the guests, the hostess may slip out to attend to last-minute details—filling water glasses, checking food, lighting candles.

One device that facilitates service of the dinner, in the absence of help, is to serve the first course before the guests come to the table. After the guests are seated, the entrée is brought in. If a roast or fowl, and the host likes to carve, it may be placed before him and he will serve either to plates passed to him or stacked before him. Other types of entrée may be served by the hostess, or passed by her.

Salad may be served in different ways. Some prefer to toss and serve it at the table. Others merely to pass it with the vegetables. Fruit or molded salads, as well as some vegetable salads, may be arranged on small plates in the kitchen and set at each place. Salad may also be served as a separate course.

Service of dessert is also flexible. If appropriate, it may be placed, together with the necessary plates, on a nearby buffet or serving table prior to the meal, together with dessert silver if the latter is not placed above the dinner plates. Or some desserts may be placed on plates in the kitchen beforehand and brought in at the appropriate time. It is possible to serve dessert, together with coffee, after the guests have left the table. In most cases, however, this would destroy the function of dessert as the conclusion of the dinner, and coffee as the afterpiece.

Seating arrangements should be carefully worked out beforehand. If there are guests of honor, of course, the woman sits at the right of the host and the man at the hostess' right. Others will be seated as the hostess may decide, proceeding on the principle of alternating male and female, and not seating husbands and wives next to each other.

The occasion provides an opportunity for the hostess to utilize the household's best to create an attractive décor. An immaculate cloth of white or pale damask (properly laid over a pad), organdy, handerchief linen, lace, embroidered cotton, or mats of similar materials, provides an excellent setting for her gleaming silver, china, and crystal. Normally, each place will be set with a service plate or dinner plate, unless the serving arrangements dictate otherwise. Bread and butter plates are sometimes used, but would be omitted at a formal dinner. On occasion, the hostess may place a small plate to the left of the dinner plate, without a knife, as a combination salad-bread-relish plate. Silver in mixed patterns, if desired, will be appropriate to the number of courses and type of dishes. Dessert silver may be placed at the top of the plate (less formal), or brought in with the dessert service.

Crystal will depend on the accompanying beverages. A water goblet should always be present, placed just above the tip of the dinner knife. Wineglasses, if any, are placed to the immediate right of the water goblet, in the form of an arc and in order of use—the first to be used nearest the guest.

Additional items include salt and peppers, ashtrays, and, if desired, nut or candy dishes.

Centerpieces should be carefully worked out to agree with the table décor. Flowers are always in taste, and for a dinner may be in a fairly elaborate arrangement, but always low, so as not to interfere with anyone's vision. Holders should agree with the other appointments—silver, crystal, or porcelain would normally be appropriate. Other than flowers, foliage, greenery, fruits, and vegetables, arranged in suitable containers, are possibilities. Candlesticks or candelabra should not be too high.

FESTIVE DINNER
(FOR 6)
SEAFOOD BISQUE
BAKED ROCK CORNISH HENS WITH RICE
GREEN LIMA BEANS
GREEN SALAD   CHEESE TRAY
PINEAPPLE BAVARIAN CREAM
COFFEE

SEAFOOD BISQUE

1 can (5½ ounces) lobster meat
3 tablespoons butter or margarine
¼ teaspoon each of paprika and salt
Dash each of ground nutmeg and pepper
1 can (10 ounces) frozen cream-of-shrimp soup
1 can (6½ ounces) crabmeat
1 large can (14½ ounces) evaporated milk, undiluted
2 cups milk
½ cup snipped parsley

Break lobster meat into pieces. Sauté in butter with seasonings. Put in saucepan with remaining ingredients except parsley. Heat to boiling. Pour into cups and serve. Garnish with parsley. Makes 6 servings.

BAKED ROCK CORNISH HENS WITH RICE

3 frozen Rock Cornish hens (1½ pounds each)
Fresh lemon juice
Salt and pepper to taste
1 package (6 ounces) long-grain and wild-rice mix
Butter (about ⅓ cup)
White wine

Thaw hens by leaving in refrigerator overnight. Split each into halves. Cut off and discard the extra skin around the necks. Sprinkle with lemon juice and salt and pepper, and rub seasoning into hens. Put, breast sides up, in well-buttered shallow baking dish. Roast in preheated very hot oven (450°F.) for 15 minutes. Cook rice mix as directed but for only 15 minutes. Remove hens from oven. Reduce heat to moderate (350°F.). Turn hens over. Spoon partially cooked rice mix into cavities. Put a cube of butter over each and sprinkle with white wine. Return to oven and bake for 30 to 40 minutes longer, or until hens are cooked. Makes 6 servings.

GREEN LIMA BEANS

2 packages (10 ounces each) frozen baby Lima beans
2 tablespoons chopped chives or green onion
Salt and pepper
Butter or margarine

Cook Lima beans according to directions on package label. Drain off liquid. Add chives, salt and pepper to taste, and butter. Makes 6 servings.

Note: Frozen Fordhook or butter beans can be substituted if preferred. Seasoned salt and pepper can be used for variety.

GREEN SALAD

Prepare a green salad with 2 or more kinds of greens (Boston or bibb lettuce, romaine, escarole, chicory, watercress). Leaf lettuce makes a nice addition, if available. Or add fresh herbs if you happen to have them in your garden or can buy them easily. Break greens into bite-size pieces and chill in plastic bags until ready to use. Toss the salad just before serving with a plain olive-oil and vinegar dressing and serve with the Cheese Tray as a separate course. For variety, substitute Special French Dressing for the oil and vinegar.

Special French Dressing

Mix ½ cup fresh lemon juice or vinegar, 1½ cups olive oil, few gashed garlic cloves, 2 teaspoons salt, ¼ teaspoon pepper, 1 teaspoon paprika, 1 tablespoon prepared horseradish, and ⅓ cup chili sauce. Put in 1-quart glass jar and shake until blended. Refrigerate until ready to use. Makes about 2 cups.

CHEESE TRAY

For the cheese tray, select a variety of good, well-aged cheeses such as French Brie, German Muenster, Danish Crema Danica, and American Brick. These are all soft mild cheeses which are good foils for the crispness of the salad and crackers or breads. All cheeses, hard and soft, are better served at room temperature. Remove cheeses from the refrigerator a few hours before serving so that the flavors will be at their best. Very soft cheeses such as the Brie should be cut into small wedges or slices as soon as removed from the refrigerator. Cover lightly with foil or wax paper until ready to serve. Other cheeses can be cut as desired and re-shaped on the cheese tray. For the tray, you can use an attractive breadboard or a special wood cheese tray. An attractive arrangement of the cheeses on a suitable tray can serve as a centerpiece for the table. To serve with the cheese, select a variety of lightly seasoned crisp crackers such as rye, whole-wheat, or plain crackers with unsalted tops. Highly seasoned crackers are not suitable as they detract from the flavor of good cheese. Since you are not serving bread anywhere else in the meal, you might also serve some crisp French bread or hard rolls.

PINEAPPLE BAVARIAN CREAM

1 envelope unflavored gelatin
2 tablespoons cold water
2½ cups (one 1-pound, 4-ounce can) crushed pineapple, drained
3 eggs, separated
½ cup sugar
¼ teaspoon salt
Heavy cream (about 1¼ cups)
Maraschino cherries

Soften gelatin in cold water. Combine pineapple, egg yolks, sugar, and salt in top part of double boiler. Cook, stirring, until thickened. Remove from heat and stir in the gelatin. Cool. Whip separately egg whites and 1 cup cream until stiff and fold into pineapple mixture. Carefully pour into 1½-quart mold. Chill until firm. Unmold on pretty serving plate and decorate with additional whipped heavy cream and cherries. Makes 6 servings.

ROMAN DINNER
(FOR 10)
MELON WITH PROSCIUTTO
ROAST PORK TRASTEVERE
ITALIAN SCALLOPED POTATOES
GREEN-BEAN SALAD   BREADSTICKS
ZUPPA INGLESE
CAFFE ESPRESSO

MELON WITH PROSCIUTTO

2 large honeydew melons
1 pound prosciutto or boiled ham
Pepper
10 lemon wedges

Cut melons into halves. Remove seeds and cut off rinds. Slice melon into thin wedges. Arrange 2 or 3 on each of 10 small plates. Place 1 or 2 paper-thin slices of prosciutto over the fruit. Sprinkle with a few grains of freshly ground pepper. Put a wedge of lemon on each plate. Makes 10 servings.

ROAST PORK TRASTEVERE

1 pork loin roast (5 to 6 pounds)
Garlic salt
1½ teaspoons crumbled dried rosemary
Salt and pepper to taste

Have roast trimmed of excess fat and the backbone loosened from the ribs. Put, fat side up, in a roasting pan. Sprinkle with garlic salt, rosemary, and salt and pepper. Roast, uncovered, in preheated moderate oven (350°F.) until meat thermometer reaches 185°F., or for 40 to 45 minutes per pound. Remove backbone. Put on hot platter and let rest for 15 minutes before serving. Makes 10 servings.

ITALIAN SCALLOPED POTATOES

2 tablespoons instant minced onion
4 cups (two 1-pound cans) tomatoes
¼ cup chopped parsley
Salt and pepper to taste
6 cups thinly sliced peeled potatoes
Bread crumbs
Grated Parmesan cheese

Mix first 5 ingredients. Mash with fork so the tomatoes break apart. Put a layer of potatoes in buttered large decorative casserole. Cover with a few spoonfuls of tomato mixture. Repeat layers until all ingredients are used and casserole is full. Sprinkle lightly with bread crumbs and Parmesan. Bake, covered, in preheated moderate oven (350°F.) for 45 minutes. Uncover and cook until potatoes are tender. Makes 12 servings.

GREEN-BEAN SALAD

Cook 3 packages (10 ounces each) frozen cut green beans as directed. Drain. Add ⅓ cup salad oil, 3 tablespoons wine vinegar, 1½ teaspoons snipped dill, and salt and pepper to taste. Mix well and chill. Makes 10 servings.

ZUPPA INGLESE

This well-known Italian dessert has been given a most deceptive name, for in translation is means "English soup." Nevertheless, the decorative cake is delectable.

2 tablespoons butter or margarine
2 cups milk
¾ cup sugar
3 tablespoons cornstarch
½ teaspoon salt
2 eggs, beaten
1 teaspoon vanilla extract
12- ounce spongecake
6 tablespoons light rum
¾ cup raspberry jam
2 cups heavy cream
⅓ cup chopped candied fruit

Heat butter and milk to scalding. Mix ½ cup sugar, the cornstarch, and salt. Stir in hot liquid. Blend well and put in saucepan. Cook, stirring, until mixture thickens. Stir a little of the mixture into eggs and put back in saucepan. Cook, stirring, until thick and smooth. Add vanilla and cool.

Cut cake lengthwise into 3 layers. Put bottom layer on large flat plate or in shallow bowl. Sprinkle with 2 tablespoons rum. Spread evenly over it half of raspberry jam and then half of cooled custard. Put second layer over custard. Cover with same amounts of rum, jam, and custard. Add remaining layer. Sprinkle with 2 tablespoons rum. Whip cream until stiff. Add ¼ cup sugar and spread over top and sides of cake. Decorate with chopped fruit. Chill. Makes 10 servings.

CAFFÈ ESPRESSO
Measure 1 tablespoon espresso coffee for each demitasse cup of water. Brew in any coffeemaker. Serve with a twist of lemon, and sugar if desired.

ENTRECÔTE—The literal translation of this French word is "between the ribs." It is cut from the meat between the ninth and eleventh ribs of beef. It is one of the most universal of all French meat cuts and is usually broiled or sautéed. The cuts most nearly comparable in the United States are Delmonico steaks and roasts, short loin, and club steaks.

ENTRÉE—The word comes directly from the French word meaning "entrance." In culinary terms it is used to describe one of the dishes of a meal, or the course during which the dish is served. In American usage, an entrée is the dish served as the main course. In English usage, it is a rather elaborate made dish served before the roast; and in French usage, which helps explain the original meaning, it is any preliminary prepared dish served at luncheon or dinner which is neither hors-d'oeuvre nor soup.

ÉPERGNE—A centerpiece composed of an ornamental stem with branches holding three, four, six, and even eight dishes or receptacles. Épergnes are used to hold hors-d'oeuvre, or else fruits and little cakes.

ESCALOPE—A French word describing a prepared dish containing slices of meat or fish of any kind flattened slightly and fried in fat or butter. Nowadays, the dish is generally veal. In English the word is spelled escallop, in Italian, *scaloppine*.

VEAL ESCALLOPS, PLAIN
Dredge 8, or 1½ pounds, very thin veal escallops lightly with all-purpose flour. Melt 3 tablespoons each of butter and oil in a large skillet. When bubbly and hot, brown escallops quickly on both sides. Reduce heat, and cook gently until meat is tender. (This will take a very few minutes.) Season to taste. Makes 4 servings.

VEAL ESCALLOPS WITH WHITE WINE AND TARRAGON
8 very thin escallops (1½ pounds)
 All-purpose flour
3 tablespoons butter
3 tablespoons cooking oil
 Salt to taste
1 tablespoon fresh tarragon or 1½ teaspoons dried tarragon
 White wine

Dust escallops with a little flour. Melt butter and oil in a large skillet. When bubbly and hot, add escallops and brown quickly on both sides. Season with salt. Add the tarragon and just enough wine to cover meat. Lower the heat a bit, and continue cooking, turning escallops once or twice to be sure they are evenly bathed. When wine has cooked down and meat is tender, remove escallops to a hot platter, and add ¼ cup more white wine to pan. Turn up the heat, and cook rapidly for a minute or two. Pour juices over the escallops. Makes 4 servings.

Veal Escallops with Vermouth and Tarragon
Substitute dry vermouth for white wine in recipe above.

Veal Escallops with Dill
Follow directions for Escallops with White Wine and Tarragon, but substitute dillweed for tarragon.

ESCAROLE—This salad green is a type of endive with broad waved leaves. Often the heart is blanched. Its flavor is somewhat bitter. Escarole and endive can be used interchangeably in salads and in cooking.

Availability—Although usually considered a winter rather than a summer salad green, it is raised for both seasons and is generally available throughout the year.

Purchasing Guide—Look for crisp, tender, fresh plants with no brown edges or wilted leaves. Leaves should be easily snapped, and a yellow-green color.

Storage—Cover or wrap to retain moisture, and refrigerate.
☐ Refrigerator shelf: 3 to 8 days

Nutritive Food Values—As a green leafy vegetable it provides a fair amount of iron, is rich in vitamin A, and has small amounts of other vitamins and minerals.
☐ 3½ ounces, raw = 20 calories

Basic Preparation—Escarole is a sandy vegetable and needs soaking for at least 30 minutes. Leaves should be separated and the tiny roots cut off and discarded. Escarole can be used in a tossed green salad, a chef's salad, or a vegetable salad. While primarily a salad green, it can also be cooked as a green vegetable.

PANNED ESCAROLE

2 quarts finely chopped escarole (2 medium heads)
2 tablespoons bacon fat or butter
Salt and pepper

Add escarole to melted fat in large, heavy saucepan. Cook over high heat, stirring constantly, for 3 to 5 minutes. Season with salt and pepper. Makes 4 servings.

ITALIAN ESCAROLE AND LENTIL SOUP

1 pound lentils
8 cups water
3 tablespoons olive oil
1 onion, chopped
1 garlic clove, minced
1 tablespoon minced parsley
Olive oil
1 pound escarole
Salt
¼ cup grated Parmesan cheese

Wash lentils. Add to water in a large pan. Cover and bring to a boil. Lower heat and simmer for 1 hour, until almost all liquid has been absorbed. Sauté onion, garlic, and parsley in a little olive oil. Trim escarole, removing tough leaves. Cut leaves into 1-inch pieces. Wash thoroughly in cold water to remove sand. Add slightly drained escarole leaves to onion mixture. Cover and simmer for 15 minutes, stirring occasionally, until escarole is tender. Add escarole and pan juices to lentils. Season to taste wtih salt. Serve hot with grated Parmesan cheese sprinkled over the top. Mixture should be moist and soupy. Makes 4 to 6 servings.

ESCOFFIER—Georges Auguste Escoffier (1846-1935) was a chef of great renown who practiced his art consecutively for sixty-two years. Escoffier was a French-

man, but he was employed in London at the Hotel Savoy and at the Hotel Carlton. Both hostelries became world famous for their food while he was their chef. He was also associated with Caesar Ritz, the man who founded the Ritz hotels in London, Paris, Montreal, and New York.

During his lifetime Escoffier reaped fully the honors his outstanding gifts deserved. One of the greatest was a banquet given in his honor by the President of France. He was known as "the king of chefs and the chef of kings." Among the dishes he is known for, the most famous is Peach Melba, a peeled fresh peach resting on a bed of vanilla ice cream and covered by a raspberry purée with a dash of currant. He named it in honor of Dame Nellie Melba, the great Australian prima donna.

ESPAGNOLE—This is a classic French sauce, similar to Brown Sauce. Espagnole is so basic that it is called a *sauce mère,* or "mother sauce," from which spring innumerable other sauces.

Espagnole freezes well. It will keep for four to six weeks.

ESPAGNOLE

⅓ cup minced onions
⅓ cup minced carrots
⅓ cup minced celery
¼ cup boiled ham or raw bacon, finely chopped
¼ cup butter or cooking oil
¼ cup all-purpose flour
6 cups beef bouillon, boiling
2 tablespoons tomato paste
2 bay leaves
½ teaspoon ground thyme
1 garlic clove
3 parsley sprigs
Salt and pepper

Cook onions, carrots, celery, and ham in hot butter over low heat for 10 minutes. Stir flour into mixture. Cook over moderate heat, stirring constantly, for 10 minutes, until the flour is nut brown. Add bouillon all at once. Stir until smooth. Add tomato paste, herbs, and salt and pepper to taste. Simmer, partly covered, over low heat for 2 hours or more. Skim when necessary. If sauce thickens too much, add a little more bouillon. Strain and degrease sauce. If not used at once, store covered in refrigerator, or freeze. Makes about 4 cups.

ESPALIER—This is an open support or trellis on which a tree, most generally a fruit tree, or shrub is trained and pruned to grow in a flattened form. The word is also used for the tree or plant so trained. It comes from the Italian *spalla,* meaning "shoulder." Once trained, the tree may be kept on the trellis or transplanted against a wall or the side of a building.

Espalier training, which requires a considerable amount of skilled hand labor, is used to prepare a tree to grow against a flat surface; to make the most use of limited space; and, in cool and cloudy areas, to give trees the greatest possible exposure to the sun and to regulate their fruit bearing.

Espaliered trees are more common in certain parts of Europe, France, and Italy for example, than in the United States; but they were a feature of our colonial gardens, as can be seen today in the restoration at Williamsburg, Virginia.

ESPRESSO—A strong coffee, brewed by a distinctive method, which comes to us from Italy. An espresso coffeemaker is needed to brew the specially roasted, strong, dark coffee blend which is used. In coffeehouses, either American or Italian, it may be a large fairly complicated machine which forces steam through the coffee grounds. For home consumption, an espresso coffeemaker is a three-part coffeepot making from one to ten or twelve cups. Water is put in the lowest part; the special roast of coffee in the center basket; and the pouring container put on top. The water is heated to boiling, the pot is removed from the heat and then reversed, top to bottom, so that the water drips through the grounds.

ESSENCE—In culinary usage, an essence is a concentrated substance possessing the predominant qualities of a food: its coloring, flavor, or nutritive value. Often it is an alcoholic solution of an essential oil obtained by distillation, infusion, etc., as essence of peppermint, essence of oranges. It may also be a concentrated solution of meats, fish, or vegetable stock used to enhance the flavor of other foods.

EVAPORATE—To evaporate means to expel moisture from a liquid or solid, thus concentrating the solid portions. Evaporation is usually accomplished by heat, and any boiling process used in cookery involves evaporation to some extent. In canned evaporated milk, half the water has been removed, thus concentrating the milk solids.

EXTRACT—When this word is used in reference to food, it describes a concentrated product derived from herbs, spices, meats, vegetables, or liquors by solution or evaporation or both. Extracts are used most frequently as flavorings. They can be liquid, vanilla extract, for example, or solid, as in the case of a meat extract such as a bouillon cube.

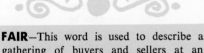

FAIR—This word is used to describe a gathering of buyers and sellers at an agreed time and place for the purposes of sale; an exhibition of products not held with sales chiefly in view, but rather as a competition, with prizes for excellence; and a festival and sale of articles usually held for a charitable purpose. The word comes from the Latin *feria,* meaning "holiday."

Fairs as "great markets," as occasions for the exchange of information and instruction, and as opportunities for merrymaking have a history reaching back to pre-Christian times. At the great European fairs the trade features have tended to predominate, whereas in American fairs agricultural education and the development of standards of quality have been stressed.

County-Fair Dinner
by Esther E. Wood

Five decades ago, the county fair was the climax of the summer in our rural Maine township. It attracted the old and the young, who came in all sorts of horse-drawn vehicles: top buggies, carriages, buckboards, and even jiggers and hayracks. On fair morning, folks were up early to do the chores, dispatch the necessary household tasks, and pack the picnic baskets. The first arrivals at the fair grounds were rewarded by finding room at the rail where they could hitch their horses for the day. Our family planned to fasten our Prince beside Grandfather's horse and to save places at the rail for the conveyances of our out-of-town relatives whose arrival was later than ours.

After we had hitched Prince, Grandmother, Mother, and I left for the hall to marvel at the displays of fruit, flowers, and vegetables, and to admire the quilts, rugs, and embroideries. Grandfather, Father, and my brothers headed for the cattle sheds. The small midway that featured a merry-go-round and a few fakirs was left for the afternoon when Father and our up-country uncles escorted us children and treated us to merry-go-round rides, spun sugar, and ice-cream cones.

At noontime we went back to our carriages to find our aunts and uncles waiting for us. The men hung feed bags over the heads of the horses, who by their impatient pawing signified that they knew it was dinnertime. The women first selected a grassy spot on which to spread a red tablecloth, and then supervised the moving of baskets, pans, and pots from the carriages to the picnic cloth. Mother always brought a pot of beans, kept warm by its wrapping of flannel, and a pan of buttermilk biscuits that had been baked at breakfast time. In another pan was Mother's dessert, a berry pie made either of crimson raspberries or purple blackberries.

Grandmother's contributions were always the same: a pan of scalloped potatoes, luscious and flavorful, and a baked chicken, stuffed with dressing seasoned by her own home-grown and home-cured sage. Grandmother also brought a four-egg custard pie, cooked in a deep yellow bowl and baked to a golden brown.

Our visiting aunts varied their picnic offerings. Sometimes they brought trout that Uncle Ernest had caught in his farm brook, or ham that Uncle Mark had cured in his own smokehouse. Because the aunts knew that Mother and Grandmother cooked pies for the fair dinner, they always baked cakes and cookies.

My brothers and I always looked forward to the sweets that our great-aunts had in their picnic baskets, and there was a good deal of disagreement as to which aunt was the better cook. My older brother loudly declared that Aunt Ri could out-bake Aunt Mary any day, but my younger brother and I maintained that our younger great-aunt was the better cook.

Aunt Ri, who had raised eight children and helped rear as many grandchildren, cooked on a large scale. Her Muster Cookies, which my brothers called "Half-Acre Cookies," were delicious and warranted to satisfy the hungriest boy. Not long ago one of her granddaughters gave me Aunt Ri's rule for Muster Cookies.

MUSTER COOKIES
¾ cup shortening
½ cup firmly packed brown sugar
2 eggs

1 teaspoon vinegar
1½ cups unsifted all-purpose flour
½ teaspoon each of ground cinnamon and ginger
1½ teaspoons baking soda
½ teaspoon salt
¾ teaspoon baking powder
¾ cup molasses
¾ teaspoon water

Cream shortening and sugar until light and fluffy. Beat in eggs, one at a time. Stir in vinegar. Sift dry ingredients. Add to first mixture alternately with molasses and water. Drop by teaspoons 2 inches apart on greased cookie sheets. Bake in preheated moderate oven (350°F.) for 8 to 10 minutes. Makes 8 to 10 dozen cookies.

Sometimes Aunt Ri brought a crumb cake which she cut into large squares and served with the comment, "Frosting does not travel well on a hot September morning. Crumbs are good travelers. Taste them and see if they are not as good as frosting." We often bake Aunt Ri's Crumb Cake and I never serve it without saying, "Crumbs are just as good as frosting."

CRUMB CAKE
½ cup butter
2 cups firmly packed brown sugar
2 cups unsifted all-purpose flour
1½ teaspoons ground nutmeg
1 egg
1 cup sour milk*
1 teaspoon baking soda

Cream butter and sugar until fluffy. Add flour and nutmeg and mix until well blended. Remove ½ cup of mixture and reserve. To remaining mixture add last 3 ingredients and mix well. Pour into well-

greased pan (9 x 9 x 2 inches). Sprinkle with reserved topping. Bake in preheated moderate oven (350°F.) for 30 to 35 minutes. Cool slightly before serving. Makes nine 3-inch squares.

*** Note:** If you can't get unpasteurized milk for souring, substitute buttermilk.

Aunt Mary was a great Grange-goer and it was her custom to collect recipes from her fellow Grange members. We always knew what her comment would be when she placed her plate of sweets on the red tablecloth. "These were made from a receipt that I got at Pomona Grange." And then she would go on to mention "Arbutus Grange" or "Rainbow Grange" or "Sand Hill Grange" or "Grange Number 280." We were always polite in our praise of Aunt Mary's offerings but I felt firmly that the Arbutus and Rainbow receipts were vastly superior to those from the plebian-named Granges.

Using Grange receipts, Aunt Mary made us tarts and cookies and puffs; she baked us cakes, white and chocolate, frosted and unfrosted, loaf and layer. I cannot recall that in all the years we shared our fair dinners she ever repeated a receipt. Perhaps that is why so few of her Grange receipts were saved. However, in Mother's Lemon Stream cook book, I do find two of Aunt Mary's receipts. Both are written on envelopes which are carefully pinned into the cook book and marked in Mother's rounded script, "Mary's Grange Receipt—real good."

The first receipt follows.

RAINBOW GRANGE RAISIN CAKE
2 eggs
1½ cups sugar
½ cup butter, melted
2½ cups unsifted all-purpose flour
1 teaspoon baking soda
1 teaspoon salt
¼ teaspoon ground nutmeg
½ cup sour milk*
1 cup raisins, chopped
1 large unpeeled orange, ground

Break eggs into mixing bowl and beat until frothy. Beat in sugar and melted butter. Sift dry ingredients and add alternately with sour milk to first mixture. Fold in raisins and orange. Pour into well-greased pan (9 x 9 x 2 inches) and bake in preheated moderate oven (350° F.) for 50 to 55 minutes. This cake is so rich that it needs no frosting. Makes nine 3-inch squares.
* **Note:** If you can't get unpasteurized milk for souring, substitute buttermilk.

The second recipe is for dropped cookies which we call "Arbutus Hermits." They are favorites with our family and guests. They are easy to make and they keep well. This is the rule:

ARBUTUS HERMITS
¾ cup soft butter
1½ cups firmly packed brown sugar
2 eggs
2 cups unsifted all-purpose flour
1 teaspoon each of ground cloves and cinnamon
¾ teaspoon salt
1 teaspoon baking soda
2 tablespoons hot water
1 cup chopped raisins
1 cup chopped nuts

Cream butter and brown sugar until light and fluffy. Beat in eggs, one at a time. Sift dry ingredients and combine half with first mixture. Add remaining flour mixture and hot water. Fold in raisins and nuts. Drop by teaspoons onto well-greased cookie sheets and bake in preheated moderate oven (350°F.) for 10 to 12 minutes. Makes about 8 dozen.

The county fair is still the climax of the summer season in my hometown. But today no one goes there in a horse-drawn vehicle; no one spreads a red tablecloth on which to place home-cooked beans, potatoes, chicken, and ham, with desserts of rich pies, cakes, and cookies. When I go to the fair these days, I eat today's holiday foods, hot dogs and hamburgers, purchased at a booth.

But if we picnic in the backyard we spread a red tablecloth and feast on home-cooked beans and biscuits, berry pie, Aunt Ri's Muster Cookies and Crumb Cake, and Aunt Mary's Raisin Cake and Arbutus Hermits. When we do this, someone is sure to exclaim, "Why, this seems almost like a fair-time dinner."

FARCE, FARCI—*Farce* is a French word meaning "forcemeat" ór "stuffing." *Farci* means "stuffed."

FARINA—This is a cereal, made from hard (but not durum) wheat, from which the bran and most of the germ have been removed. It is creamy-colored, rich in protein, and very easily digested.

Farina is used as a breakfast cereal, cooked in either water or milk. It is also made into sweet puddings. Since it is very bland, farina combines well with other foods. Farina is also a standard baby cereal, and the first solid food millions of European infants ever taste.

Caloric Values

☐ 3½ ounces, dry = 371 calories
☐ 3½ ounces, cooked = 42 calories

FARINA SPOON BREAD
3 cups milk
½ cup farina
1½ teaspoons salt
1 teaspoon baking powder
3 eggs, separated
1 tablespoon shortening

Scald milk in top part of double boiler. Slowly stir in farina and cook over boiling water until thickened. Add salt, baking powder, beaten egg yolks, and shortening. Fold in beaten egg whites. Pour into greased 2-quart baking dish and bake in preheated moderate oven (375° F.) for about 45 minutes. Makes 6 servings.

FARINA PUDDING
1½ cups milk
1 tablespoon butter
⅓ cup sugar
⅛ teaspoon salt
3 tablespoons farina
1 teaspoon grated lemon rind
3 eggs, separated
Cream

Put milk, butter, sugar, and salt in saucepan. Heat to scalding. Add farina and cook, stirring constantly, for 5 minutes. Remove from heat and add lemon rind. Cool. Beat egg whites until stiff. Then beat egg yolks until thick and lemon-colored. Stir farina mixture into egg yolks. Fold in egg whites. Pour into 1-quart casserole. Bake in preheated moderate oven (350°F.) for 35 to 40 minutes, or until firm. Serve warm with cream. Makes 4 servings.

FAT—In cookery, this is an edible oily or greasy substance occurring in animal cells, in milk, in olives, and in the seeds of certain plants. The most commonly used fats of animal derivation are butter, lard, bacon fat, suet, and poultry fat. Vegetable fats include the various oils such as olive, corn, safflower, cottonseed, soya, peanut, and sesame. Hydrogenated fats, the shortenings sold in cans for example, are generally composed of vegetable oils made solid by incorporating hydrogen into them. Some of them are combinations of animal and vegetable fats. Margarine may be wholly vegetable or a combination of vegetable and animal fats.

The principal uses of fats and oils in cooking are: 1) *To give richness and flavor,* as in the addition of fat to vegetables and to mayonnaise or French dressing. Butter, margarine, or bacon fat are preferred for vegetables, and olive oil is most prized for French dressing.

2) *To sauté, pan-fry, or deep-fry foods.* In choosing a fat for sautéing or frying the physical and chemical qualities of the fat are as important as the flavor. The best fats for frying are those which have a high smoking point and can be heated to high temperatures several times without burning or changing composition. Fats with very little flavor are best since they won't overpower the flavor of the food being fried. Good choices are the new-process (hydrogenated) lard, hydrogenated shortenings, and the oils. For sautéing, butter or margarine can be used when the flavor of these is desired. Margarine doesn't burn as quickly as butter and is more suitable for longer periods of sautéing or pan-frying. Any of the other fats or oils can also be used for pan-frying or sautéing. Bacon fat is especially popular for frying potatoes.

3) *For shortening (tenderizing),* as in cakes, pies, muffins, biscuits, etc. For shortening, any of the fats or oils can be used. Special recipes are necessary when using the oils since they add more liquid. Where flavor is important, as in some cakes and cookies, butter or margarine is usually preferred. However, hydrogenated shortenings can be used with good results. Lard makes especially flaky pastry, but oils or hydrogenated shortenings and often chicken fat are used. Suet is used generally for steamed puddings and occasionally pastry. It is also used for larding meat.

Storage—Butter, margarine, suet, bacon fat, chicken fat, and natural lard can be kept, tightly covered and refrigerated, for periods up to 2 weeks.

Hydrogenated lard and shortenings can be kept, tightly covered, on the kitchen shelf in a cool dry place away from foods with strong odors, for 2 to 3 months.

Oils can be kept, tightly covered, on the kitchen shelf in a cool dry place away from foods with strong odors for 1 to 2 months. Oils should not be exposed to light as it fades them. When exposed to air they will become rancid if moisture is present. Cans are better for storage than bottles.

Fat used for deep-fat frying can be re-used. To do so, cool fat in the frying kettle until it can be handled comfortably. Strain into the storage can through a strainer lined with a double thickness of cheesecloth. If strong-flavored foods have been cooked in the fat, a few slices of raw potato may be put into the strained partially cooled fat; reheat slowly. The potato will absorb some of the flavor. Cool fat and strain. Cover tightly and store in cool dry place.

Nutritive Food Values—Fats are the most concentrated form of energy in foods. One pound of pure fat yields about 4,000 calories. Fats give a general satisfaction to food because they slow down the rate at which it is digested. Fats and oils contain certain fatty acids that are essential to good nutrition.

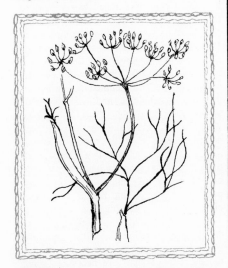

FENNEL—This is an aromatic plant belonging to the carrot family, and is native to the Mediterranean. There are three types of fennel, all of which have a feathery foliage of bright green. Common fennel, *Foeniculum vulgare,* is a tall perennial with finely divided feathery leaves and yellow flowers. It has a flavor reminiscent of anise. All parts of the plants can be utilized. The shoots are eaten raw or cooked; the leaves are used for salads and seasoning; and the seeds, which are oval, greenish- or yellowish-brown, are used as a culinary spice for cooking, candy, and liqueurs. Fennel oil is used in medicine, perfume, and soaps.

Sweet fennel, *Foeniculum vulgare dulce,* is a dwarf variety, also called finocchio or Florence fennel. It has a broad bulbous base which is used as a vegetable and has a flavor suggestive of celery.

The third type is *Foeniculum vulgare piperitum,* known as Italian or Sicilian fennel or carosella. Its tender young stalks are eaten raw.

Availability—Fennel is generally available during the summer months. Sweet fennel (finocchio) and Italian fennel (carosella) can be found in Italian food stores.

Fennel seed is available whole and ground.

Purchasing Guide—Choose bunches with fresh green leaves and crisp-looking stalks.

Storage—Refrigerate in moisture-proof wrapping.

☐ Refrigerator shelf: 3 to 5 days

Nutritive Food Values—All varieties of fennel are extremely rich in vitamin A with moderate amounts of calcium, phosphorus, and potassium.

☐ Common fennel leaves, raw, 3½ ounces = 28 calories

Basic Preparation—To cook sweet fennel, cut off the feathery tops and trim off tough outer stalks. Cut off hard base. Cut into slices, cutting with the grain. Cover with boiling salted water or braise with bouillon until tender. Dress with butter.

SWEET FENNEL FOR ANTIPASTO

Allow 1 medium size sweet fennel per serving. Trim off green stalks and tough outer stalks. Cut into wafer-thin slices. Arrange on shallow dish, barely cover with olive oil, and season. For added crispness, chill for at least 2 hours.

FENNEL PARMIGIANA

4 bulbs of sweet fennel
 Salt and pepper to taste
½ cup melted butter
¾ cup grated Parmesan cheese

Trim green tops and tough outer stalks from fennel. Trim base and slice the fennel from top to bottom into ¼-inch slices. Cook in boiling water until tender, about 5 minutes. Drain. Season with salt and pepper. Place half of fennel slices in shallow buttered baking dish. Pour half of melted butter over it and sprinkle with half of cheese. Top with remaining fennel, butter, and cheese. Bake in preheated hot oven (425°F.) for 10 minutes. Makes 4 to 6 servings.

FENNEL SEED TEA

1 tea bag
¼ teaspoon fennel seeds
1 quart boiling water
 Strained honey

Steep the tea and fennel seeds in the water for 5 minutes. Strain. Add 1 teaspoon honey to each cup. Makes 4 cups.

An equally good tea, and one tasting more of fennel, can be made by omitting the tea bag and steeping 1 teaspoon fennel seeds in 1 quart boiling water for 5 minutes. Either tea can be sweetened with sugar, either white or brown, instead of honey.

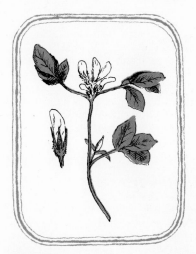

FENUGREEK (Trigonella foenumgraecum)—An annual plant of the pea family cultivated chiefly for its aromatic seeds. The name means "Greek hay." The plant is native to Asia and southern Europe. The seeds are formed in a slender, bean-like pod with a beaked point. They are threshed from the pods and dried by artificial heat. They are small, irregularly shaped, and yellow-brown in color. Their flavor is pleasantly bitter, somewhat like burnt sugar. The seeds are used for curry powders, chutney, and spice blends. They may be used also in soups, with meats, with such legumes as black-eye peas, in breads, spiced breads, and cookies. The fresh fenugreek plant is eaten as a vegetable in India.

FERMENTATION—A chemical change in food or other organic compounds caused by the action of enzymes produced by yeasts, bacteria, or microorganisms. The kinds most useful in foods and cooking are those which produce a gas or gases, most frequently carbon dioxide, within the food to give effervescence or leavening. The chemical changes, and they are widely varied, also may add flavor and change the appearance. Foods and beverages in which fermentation is most often usefully employed are breads; wines, spirits, and beers; cheeses, buttermilk, culture milks and yogurt; cider and vinegars.

Although even today the chemistry of fermentation is not fully understood, grapes were made into wine, wine was converted into vinegar, beers were brewed, dough was leavened, and cheese was made from milk before the start of recorded history, and it is impossible to place any date on the beginning of the art of fermentation.

FIASCO—An Italian wine bottle with a wide, round base and a thin neck. The neck can be long or short. The bottle is wrapped in straw, and has a straw base so that it can stand. The French word for this kind of bottle is *flasque,* the source of our word "flask."

The Italian plural for *fiasco* is *fiaschi. Fiaschi* are the traditional old-fashioned Italian wine or olive-oil bottles. They are especially characteristic of the red "Chianti" wines.

FIDDLEHEAD—An edible fern that grows on the shores of northern streams and lakes. It gets its name from the shape of the head of the frond. The soft budding stem of the fiddlehead fern is a delicacy of northern New England and Canada and it has a delicious flavor. The stems are picked when young, tender, and about eight inches tall. They are washed thoroughly, and served raw as a salad, dressed with vinegar and lemon juice. They are also steamed for 3 to 5 minutes only and served as a vegetable with salt and pepper, butter, hollandaise, or any other desired sauce.

Canned fiddleheads can be bought in specialty food stores.

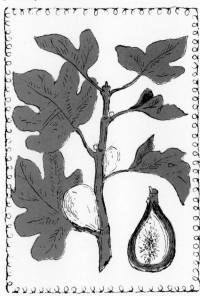

FIG—Figs are the fruit of the tree *Ficus carica.* Originally native to Asia, Africa, and southern Europe, the tree is now cultivated successfully in many parts of the world, particularly in mild, semiarid climates. The fruit consists of a soft pulp covered by a thin skin. There are between 600 and 800 varieties of figs, varying in shape from round to oblong and in color from almost-white to purple-black.

Figs are interesting botanical specimens. Some, the *Ficus carica, hortensis,* are self-pollenating and produce many of the best varieties for the table and for preserving. Others, the *Ficus carica, smyrniaca,* which produces the Smyrna

fig, must be cross-pollenated with still another variety, the Capri fig, which does not itself produce any edible fruit. This cross-pollenating is done by the fig-wasp which breeds within the Capri fig. Smyrna figs are the best variety for drying. The strangest variety of all the fig trees is the *Ficus carica, intermedia* which can mature one crop without cross-pollenization, but not a second.

The fig has been cultivated since earliest times. Apart from its value as a food tree, it was regarded as sacred by many people. The ancient Hebrews looked upon the fig tree as a symbol of peace and plenty. Mohammed's followers called it the "Tree of Heaven." The old Romans sacrificed the milky sap of the wild fig tree to Juno; and some central African tribes built huts for the spirits of their ancestors in the shade of the sacred fig trees. The fig is the first tree mentioned in the Bible (Genesis 3:7) "and they sewed fig leaves together, and made themselves aprons."

Availability—Figs are sold fresh, dried, and preserved in water or syrup. Candied figs, packaged whole or in halves, are available at Christmas time.

Fresh figs are available from June through October.

Dried figs are packed in two forms: *Layer* (or pulled) and *Locoum. Layer*-packed figs are pulled between the fingers and thumb to form a flattened disk shape. They may be packed in overlapping fashion in boxes and graded from "choice" to "extra fancy." Figs are also packed according to the size of spread which may range from 1¾ to 3 inches. Greek string figs are pulled figs which have been strung on reeds for shipment to this country. *Locoum*-packed figs are shaped into cubes. The word comes from a Turkish word meaning a "square-shape sweetmeat." Dried figs are sold in packages, on strings, and in cans.

Purchasing Guide—The following are the most common market varieties of figs:

Adriatic—A white fig with a bright green skin. Used primarily for drying.

Brown Turkey—A medium to large fig available fresh and also used for preserving. The fruit has a violet, brown, and greenish skin and is broad and pear-shape, with white to amber pulp.

Calimyrna—Derives its name from the combination of California and Smyrna. It is a large, squat-shape white fig, smooth and waxy with a thin yellowish-green skin. The fruit is used for drying and preserving and is also sold fresh.

Celeste—A small to medium fruit, pear-shape, with a violet to purplish-brown skin. The pulp is white to pink. It is used for preserving.

Kadota—A small variety with thick

yellow skin, practically seedless. It may be used for drying and preserving and is also sold fresh.

Magnolia or Brunswick—A large fruit with amber skin and a pinkish-amber pulp. It is most commonly cultivated in Texas and is used for preserving.

Mission—A dark purple, almost black fig, with small seeds. It is available fresh in addition to being used for drying.

When buying fresh figs, look for those that are fully ripe and fairly soft. They are at their best when tree ripened and rushed to the market on the same day they're picked. Size is not an indication of maturity or quality. Avoid bruised fruit as it will deteriorate quickly.

Storage—Fresh ripe figs are perishable and should be kept in the refrigerator. Plan to use them as soon after purchase as possible. Keep dried figs in a tightly covered container in a cool place. Canned figs, once they have been opened, should be transferred to a covered container and refrigerated.

☐ Fresh, refrigerator shelf: 2 or 3 days
☐ Canned, kitchen shelf: 1 year
☐ Canned, opened and covered, refrigerator shelf: 4 or 5 days
☐ Dried, kitchen shelf: 6 to 8 months

Nutritive Food Values—Fresh figs contain moderate amounts of potassium, riboflavin, phosphorus, calcium, and thiamin. Dried figs are a source of quick food energy, high in iron, with good amounts of calcium and phosphorus. They supply bulk for a natural laxative.

☐ Fresh, 3½ ounces, raw = 80 calories
☐ Dried, 3½ ounces = 274 calories
☐ Preserved, 3½ ounces, canned in water = 48 calories
☐ Preserved, 3½ ounces, canned in light syrup pack = 65 calories
☐ Preserved, 3½ ounces, canned in heavy syrup pack = 84 calories

Basic Preparation—For fresh figs, peel off the outer skin with a very sharp knife. Slice figs or leave whole. Serve with cream and sugar.

☐ **To Stew, Fresh Figs**—For one dozen fresh figs, bring to boil ¾ cup sugar and 1¼ cups water. Add peeled figs to boiling syrup and simmer gently for 5 to 10 minutes. Makes 4 servings.

Rinse in water and remove stems.

☐ **To Stew, Dried Figs**—Rinse in water and remove stems. Place fruit in a saucepan and cover with water. Add a cinnamon stick or a few whole cloves. Bring to a boil. Cook for 20 to 30 minutes, or until fruit is soft. Add 1 tablespoon sugar for each cup of figs during the last 15 minutes of cooking. Cool figs in liquid. Serve with cream if desired.

FIG BREAD

1 cup (8 ounces) dried figs

3½ cups sifted all-purpose flour
¾ cup sugar
1 teaspoon salt
4 teaspoons baking powder
3 tablespoons shortening
1 teaspoon grated orange rind
1 egg
1½ cups milk

Cover figs with boiling water. Let stand for 10 minutes. Drain and dry thoroughly. Remove stems and cut figs into thin slices. Sift flour with sugar, salt, and baking powder. Cut in shortening until mixture resembles coarse cornmeal. Mix orange rind with egg and milk. Add liquid to dry ingredients. Stir until just blended. Stir in figs. Grease a loaf pan (9 x 5 x 3 inches). Line pan with unglazed brown paper. Grease brown paper and pour mixture into pan. Bake in preheated moderate oven (375°F.) for 50 to 60 minutes, until bread is golden brown.

FIG PUDDING WITH PEANUT BUTTER
⅓ cup sugar
2 tablespoons all-purpose flour
1 cup water
1 cup peanut butter
1½ cups chopped dried figs
2 egg whites
⅛ teaspoon salt
Whipped cream

Blend sugar and flour in saucepan; add water and cook until thickened. Add peanut butter and figs; mix well and simmer for about 10 minutes, stirring often. Remove from heat; fold in stiffly beaten salted egg whites. Chill. Serve with whipped cream. Makes 8 servings.

FIG JAM
1 pound dried figs
2 tart apples
Rind and juice of 1 orange
Rind and juice of 1 lemon
4 cups water
3 cups sugar
Dash of salt

Wash figs; remove stems; chop into small pieces. Peel and core apples; chop fine. Or put figs and apples through food chopper, using coarse knife. Put figs and apples and grated rind of orange and lemon in large heavy kettle. Add water and boil for 10 minutes; reduce heat and cook for 10 minutes longer. Add sugar and salt; mix well and simmer for 20 to 25 minutes, stirring occasionally to prevent sticking. Add orange and lemon juices; mix well, remove from heat, and pour into hot sterilized glasses. Seal with paraffin. Makes about 7 8-ounce glasses.

═══════ 🐘 ═══════

FILBERT—This nut is the fruit of shrubs or small trees of the family *Corylus*. It is also known as a hazelnut or cobnut. Generally speaking the name "filbert" is applied to the oblong nuts of two varieties of hazel native to Europe, *Corylus avellana pontica* and *C. maxima;* "cobnut" to

another native European variety, *C. avellana grandis* which produces a large roundish nut; and "hazelnut" to the American varieties *C. americana* and *C. cornuta,* which bear small roundish nuts.

The nuts are borne in clusters and each nut is enclosed in a husk which opens as the nut ripens. They are harvested by being shaken off the bushes or gathered from the ground.

Filberts are drier than almonds or walnuts. When chopped or ground into a fine meal, they are used in baking, particularly in Central Europe.

Whole filberts can be salted, or sugared, or eaten as is. Chopped filberts can be used in candies, baked goods, and desserts. Sliced filberts can be added to salads and to main dishes.

Availability—Filberts are usually sold in the shell, in bulk or by the pound. Some shelled filberts are available packaged in film bags.

Purchasing Guide—Look for nuts with clean shells free from scars, cracks, or holes. They should be well filled so that the kernel does not rattle. Fresh-shelled kernels should be plump, meaty, crisp, and brittle. Avoid nutmeats that are shriveled or limp, indicating staleness.

☐ 2¼ pounds in-shell filberts = 1 pound shelled = 3½ cups

Storage—Keep tightly covered and away from light.

☐ Kitchen shelf: 1 month

☐ Refrigerator shelf: 3 to 4 months

☐ Refrigerator frozen-food compartment, prepared for freezing: 6 months

☐ Freezer, prepared for freezing: 1 year

Nutritive Food Values—Filberts provide protein, fat, iron, and thiamine.

☐ 3½ ounces = 634 calories

Basic Preparation—To shell filberts use a nutcracker. Remove the kernel intact. To slice or chop nuts, use a sharp knife and a cutting board.

☐ **To Roast in Oven**—Spread nutmeats in a shallow pan and place in a preheated hot oven (400°F.) for about 7 minutes or in a preheated very slow oven (275°F.) for 20 minutes. Stir nuts frequently to prevent scorching. For salted nuts, add 1 teaspoon salt per cup of nutmeats.

☐ **To Skillet-Roast**—Heat 2 teaspoons cooking oil in a skillet over low heat. Add nutmeats and 1 teaspoon salt per cup of nuts. Stir constantly until thoroughly heated. Drain well on paper towels.

☐ **To Grind**—Use a special nut grinder (or an electric blender); when butters and paste are desired, use a meat grinder.

FILBERT TORTE
12 egg yolks
1 cup sugar
2 cups (½ pound) shelled filberts

2 tablespoons dry bread crumbs
8 egg whites
Sweetened whipped cream

Beat egg yolks until thick and lemon-colored. Gradually beat in sugar. Beat until mixture is creamy. Grind nuts in a nut grinder or whirl in a blender. Stir nuts and bread crumbs into egg-yolk mixture. Beat egg whites until stiff but not dry and fold them into egg-yolk mixture. Pour mixture into 3 ungreased 8 inch layer-cake pans. Bake in preheated moderate oven (350°F.) for 15 to 20 minutes, or until cake tests done. Cool cake. Remove from pans and put layers together with sweetened whipped cream. Decorate top and sides with more sweetened whipped cream, and glacé fruit if desired. Makes 8 servings.

FILBERT CRESCENTS
1 cup soft butter
¼ cup sugar
2 cups sifted all-purpose flour
1 cup ground filberts
1 teaspoon vanilla extract

Cream butter and sugar until light. Add remaining ingredients and mix well. Chill until firm. Shape into small crescents. Put on ungreased cookie sheets. Bake in preheated moderate oven (350°F.) for about 10 minutes. Makes 8 to 10 dozen. Store airtight.

FILBERT SPICE COOKIES
1 cup soft butter
1 cup sugar
½ cup light molasses
3½ cups sifted all-purpose flour
1 tablespoon ground ginger
2 teaspoons each of ground cinnamon and cloves
½ teaspoon baking soda
¼ teaspoon salt
1 cup chopped filberts

Cream butter and sugar. Add remaining ingredients and mix well. Turn onto floured board and knead until smooth. Shape into rolls 2 inches in diameter. Wrap in wax paper and chill until firm. Slice thin; bake on greased cookie sheets in preheated moderate oven (350°F.) 8 to 10 minutes. Makes 6 dozen. Store airtight.

CINNAMON FILBERTS
2 cups (½ pound) shelled filberts
1 egg white
½ cup sugar
1 teaspoon ground cinnamon
¼ cup butter or margarine

Put nuts on shallow baking pan and toast in slow oven (325°F.) for 10 minutes. Beat egg white until foamy; add sugar and cinnamon gradually and beat until stiff. Add nuts and mix well. Melt butter in same baking pan. Spread nut mixture over butter. Bake in slow oven (325°F.) for 30 minutes, stirring every 10 minutes. Store in airtight container. (Other nuts can be substituted for the filberts.) Makes about 2½ cups.

FILÉ—This is a seasoning and thickening agent made from the dried and powdered young leaves of the sassafras tree. It is an essential element in Creole cooking, and one of the basic ingredients of gumbo.

Filé came to us through the Choctaw Indians who once lived in the New Orleans area in Louisiana, and who used filé constantly in their cooking. The sassafras leaves were gathered by the Indian women and spread out to dry in the sun. Then they were ground to a fine powder. This powder was brought to the French market in New Orleans, where it was adopted by the settlers.

Filé—the word may be derived from the French word *filé* meaning "made into threads"—was a useful thickening agent in an age that knew no gelatin, cornstarch, or other modern thickening agents. As the name implies, filé can go stringy in a dish. It must be added to a boiling liquid gradually, stirring constantly, *after* the dish has been removed from the heat. Under no circumstances must the dish be boiled again after the filé has been added.

HAM AND OYSTER GUMBO FILÉ

- 1 roasting chicken (3½ to 5 pounds), cut into pieces
- 2 tablespoons cooking oil
- ¼ cup butter
- 1 pound ham, cut into 1-inch cubes
- 3 tablespoons all-purpose flour
- 1 small onion, minced
- 2 medium tomatoes, chopped
- 1½ quarts boiling water
- 1 bay leaf
- 3 parsley sprigs
- 1 teaspoon ground thyme
  Salt and pepper
  Dash of hot pepper sauce
- 2 dozen oysters, shucked
- 1 tablespoon filé powder

Trim fat off chicken pieces. In deep large skillet heat together oil and half of the butter. Sauté ham in it until golden. Remove ham to Dutch oven or deep saucepan and reserve. Fry chicken pieces until browned but not cooked through. Remove chicken to Dutch oven. Stir flour into pan juices and cook until lightly browned. Add onion and cook until soft, stirring constantly. Add tomato and boiling water. Blend thoroughly. Pour sauce on ham and chicken in Dutch oven. Add bay leaf, parsley, thyme, salt and pepper to taste, and hot pepper sauce. Cook, covered, over moderate heat for about 30 minutes, or until chicken is tender. Stir occasionally. Add oysters and remaining butter. Cook over low heat, stirring occasionally, for 5 minutes longer. Remove from heat and stir in filé powder, blending thoroughly. Serve with cooked rice. Makes 6 to 8 servings.

FILLET, FILET—A fillet, the French word for the same thing is *filet,* is usually a flattish slice, strip, or piece of lean boneless meat or fish. When talking of beef or pork, a filet is also a specific cut, namely the tenderloin.

Fillets of meat or fish are often highly priced since they are choice cuts. However, there is no waste of any kind in them so that often it is advisable to buy fillets, especially fish.

FILLING—A sweet or nonsweet mixture used in a pastry shell or between layers of such foods as cake or bread to add content, flavor, or color. Sweet fillings are most generally found in pies, tarts, cream puffs, éclairs, cakes, and cookies; nonsweet fillings in sandwiches and nonsweet pastry shells. Omelets can have either type of filling.

SANDWICH FILLINGS, NONSWEET

■ Mix 1 can (2¼ ounces) deviled ham, ½ teaspoon celery salt, and ½ cup peanut butter. Makes ⅔ cup.

■ Mix crumbled crisp bacon with half as much chopped chutney.

■ Mix 1 cup minced cooked chicken, 2 tablespoons minced almonds, dash of monosodium glutamate, and ¼ cup mayonnaise. Makes 1 cup.

■ Mix 1 cup ground cooked ham, 1 tablespoon orange marmalade, ½ teaspoon powdered mustard, and ¼ cup mayonnaise. Makes 1 cup.

■ Mix 1 cup grated Cheddar cheese, 1 tablespoon soft butter, 2 tablespoons sherry, ½ teaspoon Worcestershire, and salt and pepper to taste. Makes about ½ cup.

■ Drain and flake 1 can (7½ ounces) salmon. Add 2 chopped hard-cooked eggs, ¼ cup minced celery, 2 tablespoons pickle relish, 1 teaspoon prepared mustard, mayonnaise to moisten, and salt and pepper to taste. Makes about 1 cup.

■ In top part of double boiler, melt 1 cup grated Cheddar cheese in 3 tablespoons milk. Stir in 4 chopped skinless frankfurters, 3 teaspoons prepared mustard, and 1 tablespoon mayonnaise. Makes about 1½ cups.

■ Mix ¾ cup ground bologna, 2 chopped hard-cooked eggs, 3 tablespoons chopped sweet pickle, ½ teaspoon instant minced onion, 3 tablespoons mayonnaise, and salt to taste. Makes about 1 cup.

SANDWICH FILLINGS, SWEET

■ Soak ¾ cup raisins in ¾ cup water for 30 minutes. Pour off liquid. Blend 4 ounces cream cheese, 3 tablespoons milk, and 1 tablespoon mayonnaise. Add raisins. Makes about 1½ cups.

■ Mix ½ cup finely chopped dates, ½ cup minced nuts, and ¼ cup mayonnaise. Add ½ teaspoon lemon juice. Makes about 1 cup.

■ Blend ½ cup maple syrup and ¾ cup soft butter or margarine.

■ Cream 3 tablespoons butter or margarine and 8 ounces cream cheese or cottage cheese. Add 2 tablespoons minced preserved ginger, 3 tablespoons ginger syrup, and 2 tablespoons minced nuts. Makes about 1½ cups.

■ Mix ¾ cup drained mincemeat and ½ cup finely chopped Brazil nuts.

■ Mix ½ cup each grated fresh or packaged coconut and minced cashews. Add 2 tablespoons orange marmalade.

■ Mix equal parts of honey and peanut butter.

■ Force ½ cup roasted peanuts and ½ cup moist dried figs through food chopper. Add 1 tablespoon lemon juice. Makes about 1 cup.

OMELET FILLINGS, NONSWEET

■ Creamed fish or shellfish; poultry; or dried beef

■ Cooked pork-sausage meat; ground or chopped cooked ham; or crumbled cooked bacon

■ Cooked chicken livers and minced onion; or minced stewed poultry giblets

■ Cooked peas; cooked corn; sautéed onion rings; sautéed eggplant cubes; or cooked sliced mushrooms

■ Spanish or Creole sauce

■ Chopped green pepper in tomato sauce; or diced avocado

■ Chopped fresh herbs such as parsley, chives, spinach, or sorrel

■ Grated cheese

OMELET FILLINGS, SWEET

■ Jams or jellies

■ Cream fillings

■ Stewed dried fruit; sweetened fresh fruits; or sliced bananas glazed in brown sugar and butter

■ Crushed macaroons

■ Chipped sweet chocolate

FILLINGS FOR NONSWEET PASTRY SHELLS

BASIC MEAT FILLING

2 cups firmly packed ground cooked or smoked meat or poultry
1 large onion, minced
½ cup fat
½ cup chopped green onions
2 eggs (about)
½ cup chopped parsley
Salt and pepper

Grind meat finely. Sauté onion in fat until golden. Add green onions. Stir in ground meat. Blend well. Beat in eggs until the mixture is moist and of the consistency of mashed potatoes. Stir in parsley and season to taste with salt and pepper. Cool thoroughly. Makes 2½ cups.

LIVERWURST FILLING

1½ pounds liverwurst
½ cup rendered chicken fat or butter or margarine
⅓ cup minced onion
¼ cup heavy cream
¼ cup brandy

Strip casing from liverwurst. Mash with remaining ingredients until very smooth. Makes 2 cups.

RUSSIAN EGG AND MUSHROOM FILLING

1 pound mushrooms
1 large onion, minced
3 tablespoons butter
1 cup fine dry white-bread crumbs
3 tablespoons dairy sour cream
Salt and pepper
2 tablespoons chopped parsley
1 tablespoon chopped dillweed
2 hard-cooked eggs, chopped

Chop mushrooms medium fine. Cook onion in butter until soft and golden. Add mushrooms, bread crumbs, sour cream, and salt and pepper to taste. Cook over low heat, stirring constantly, for about 10 minutes, or until mixture thickens. Cool, and add parsley, dillweed, and hard-cooked eggs. Makes about 4 cups.

SWEET FILLINGS

ALMOND CREAM FILLING

1½ cups milk
2 tablespoons all-purpose flour
⅓ cup sugar
Dash of salt
6 egg yolks, slightly beaten
½ teaspoon vanilla extract
½ teaspoon almond extract
¾ cup heavy cream, whipped

Scald milk in top part of double boiler over boiling water. Mix flour, sugar, and salt. Mix some of the hot milk into the mixture. Add to remaining milk. Cook over boiling water, stirring constantly, for 10 minutes, or until smooth and thickened. Beat hot sauce gradually into beaten egg yolks. Return to double boiler and cook for 5 minutes longer. Remove from heat. Cool. Stir in flavorings. Fold in whipped cream. Spread between cake layers or use to fill cream puffs or tart shells. Makes 2½ cups.

FRESH-COCONUT FILLING

2 lemons, grated rind and juice
1 medium-size fresh coconut, peeled and grated
Pinch of salt
2 cups sugar
1 cup boiling water
2 tablespoons cornstarch
½ cup cold water

Combine all ingredients except cornstarch and cold water in a saucepan. Bring to a boil. Mix cornstarch with cold water. Add cornstarch gradually to the coconut mixture. Cook over low heat stirring constantly, until very thick. Cool;

spread between cake layers or use to fill cupcakes or cream puffs. Makes about 3 cups.

ORANGE FILLING

½ cup sifted cake flour
1 cup sugar
¼ teaspoon salt
¼ cup water
1¼ cups fresh orange juice
¼ cup fresh lemon juice
2 tablespoons grated orange rind
Grated rind of 1 lemon
4 egg yolks

Mix flour, sugar, and salt in heavy saucepan. Add water and mix until there are no lumps. Add fruit juices and rinds. Cook over low heat until mixture thickens and becomes almost transparent. Beat egg yolks slightly; add hot mixture slowly, stirring constantly. Return mixture to saucepan and, stirring constantly, cook slowly for about 5 minutes, or until sauce thickens again. Cool. Makes enough filling for two or three 9-inch layers.

PINEAPPLE FILLING

¼ cup sugar
1 tablespoon all-purpose flour
Dash of salt
2 egg yolks, beaten
⅔ cup milk
1 tablespoon butter
1 cup (one 9-ounce can) crushed pineapple, drained

In top part of double boiler mix sugar, flour, and salt. Stir in egg yolks and milk. Cook and stir over boiling water until thick. Add butter and pineapple; cool. Spread between cake layers or use to fill tart shells. Makes about 2 cups.

RAISIN FILLING

Mix 1 cup each of dairy sour cream and sugar, ½ teaspoon salt, and 1 cup chopped seeded raisins in saucepan. Bring to boil and cook for about 10 minutes over medium heat, stirring constantly. Cool. Makes enough filling for 9-inch layer cake.

DATE-NUT FILLING

1 pound pitted dates
1½ cups sugar
½ teaspoon salt
2 teaspoons grated lemon rind
2 cups water
2 cups finely chopped nuts

Cut dates into small pieces. Put in saucepan with sugar, salt, lemon rind, and water. Bring to boil and cook for 10 minutes, or until thickened, stirring occasionally. Add nuts and stir in. Cool. Use for filled cookies. Makes about 3½ cups.

SOUTHERN CARAMEL FILLING

1 cup firmly packed light brown sugar
1 cup granulated sugar
½ cup butter
½ cup milk

Combine all ingredients. Cook over high heat, stirring constantly, for 2 minutes

by the clock (234°F. on a candy thermometer). Remove from heat and beat until cold. Spread between cake layers. Makes 1½ cups.

RICH LEMON FILLING

½ cup butter
Grated rind of 1 lemon
Juice of 3 lemons
1½ cups sugar
1 teaspoon salt
3 whole eggs
3 egg yolks

Melt butter; add rinds and juice. Stir in sugar and salt. Beat whole eggs and egg yolks and add to mixture. Cook over hot water, stirring constantly, until shiny and thick. Cool, cover tightly, and refrigerate. Spread between cake layers or use to fill tiny tarts. Makes about 3 cups.

CHOCOLATE BAVARIAN FILLING

1 envelope unflavored gelatin
⅔ cup sugar
¼ teaspoon salt
1¾ cups milk
1 package (4 ounces) sweet cooking chocolate
3 eggs, separated
1 teaspoon vanilla extract
⅔ cup flaked coconut

In top part of double boiler mix gelatin, ⅓ cup sugar, the salt and milk. Add chocolate. Put over hot water and cook, stirring, until chocolate is melted and gelatin dissolved. Beat with rotary beater until blended. Gradually stir into egg yolks. Put mixture back in double boiler and cook for 3 minutes longer, stirring. Cool for 10 minutes. Beat egg whites until foamy. Gradually add remaining sugar, beating until mixture stands in stiff peaks. Fold in chocolate mixture, blending well. Add vanilla and coconut. Spoon into 9-inch baked pie shell and chill until firm.

FINES HERBES—A French term meaning "fine herbs." In culinary language its precise meaning is a combination of two or more finely chopped fresh herbs, such as parsley, tarragon, chervil, basil, thyme, and chives. It is also used to describe chopped parsley, as in an *omelette aux fines herbes.*

Fines herbes are much used in French cookery, especially in omelets and in sauces. A properly composed combination of *fines herbes* adds great distinction to fish, chicken, meat, eggs, and salads.

FINES HERBES COMBINATIONS

■ **For Beef or Other Red Meats**—Thyme, chervil, and basil; or chives, basil, and parsley

■ **For Chicken, Meat, Eggs, or Salads**—Chervil, parsley, and chives

■ **For Fish, Chicken, or Veal**—Parsley, rosemary, and tarragon

FINNAN HADDIE—This is smoked haddock and was named for the village of Findon near Aberdeen in Scotland, which was famous for the curing of the fish. Haddock, a North Atlantic salt-water fish, is split open, the backbone is partly removed, and the head cut off. Then the fish is lightly salted and smoked. Originally, the smoking was done over peat fires which gave the fish a wonderful flavor.

Finnan haddie is a Scottish national product, and at one time all of it was imported from Scotland. Today the great bulk of the supply, which is excellent, comes from New England.

In England and Scotland, finnan haddie is considered an excellent breakfast dish. It is also good for lunch or supper. It may be cooked without soaking and is tasty broiled, with melted butter, or baked in milk.

Purchasing Guide—Finnan haddie is available whole or in fillets. It is sold by the pound and in small packages or cans.

☐ 1 pound finnan haddie = 2 cups cooked flaked fish

Storage—Wrap tightly and refrigerate.

☐ Refrigerator shelf: 3 to 4 weeks

Nutritive Values—Good source of protein.

☐ 3½ ounces, uncooked = 100 calories

Basic Preparation—Finnan haddie may be cooked without soaking.

☐ **To Broil**—Arrange fillets or a whole fish on a broiling rack over a little hot water. Dab with butter, and broil slowly until heated through and lightly browned.

FINNAN HADDIE BAKED IN MILK

2 pounds finnan haddie, whole or fillets
Boiling water
1 cup milk
2 tablespoons butter

Cover fish with boiling water and simmer for 5 minutes. Drain, and remove skin from whole fish. Place fish in baking dish. Pour milk over it and dot with butter. Bake in preheated moderate oven (350° F.) for 15 minutes, or until fish flakes apart. Makes 6 servings.

FINNAN HADDIE WITH SHRIMP SAUCE

2 tablespoons butter or margarine
2 tablespoons all-purpose flour
1½ cups milk
1 green pepper, chopped
6 stuffed olives, sliced
½ cup cooked sliced mushrooms
¾ cup cooked flaked finnan haddie
½ cup diced cooked shrimps
Salt and pepper to taste
Toasted crackers or bread

Melt butter in heavy saucepan; stir in flour; add milk slowly, stirring constantly. Cook over low heat, stirring constantly, until sauce is thickened. Add green pepper, olives, mushrooms, fish, and shrimps. Season with salt and pepper. Heat thoroughly. Serve on toasted crackers. Makes 4 servings.

100 Menus
to help you plan
more varied meals
for your family with
the recipes in this volume

Recipes for all starred dishes found in this volume.

BREAKFAST

Garnished Pears*
Spekannekoeken
(Pancakes with Bacon)*
with Molasses
Fennel Seed Tea*
___

Fresh Strawberries*
Miniature Puffy Omelets*
Austrian Crescents*
Crisp Smoked Sausage Links

Pineapple Sticks*
Braendende Kaerlighed
(Burning Love)*
Rugbrød (Rye Bread)* Toasted
Whipped Sweet Butter
___

Circles of Melon*
Crème Lorraine*
Oat Cakes*
Butter   Honey

Orange and Apricot Juice
Fried Chicken Livers
Eggs Hongroise*
Extra Toast
___

Stewed Damson Plums*
or Stewed Prunes
Ham à la Crème*
Croissants*

Dried Fruit Compote*
Poached Eggs
Marrow Toast*
Nut-Spiced English Muffins*
Elderberry Jelly*
___

Sliced Oranges with
Whole Cranberry Sauce
Finnan Haddie Baked in Milk*
Boiled Potatoes in Jackets
Crumpets*

LUNCH OR SUPPER

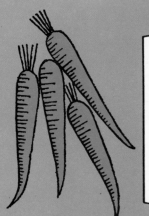

Sliced Fresh Pears
Fried Italian Sweet Sausage
Farina Dumplings, Roman Style*
Caffè Espresso*
___

Candied Apples
(with Cuminseed)*
Omelet Charentière*
Toasted English Muffins*
Damson-Plum Jam*

Cherry Chunky Applesauce
with Grated Nutmeg
Eggs au Beurre Noir*
Canadian Bacon
Cheese Bread Toast
Dewberry Jelly*
___

Sliced Peaches
and Mandarin Oranges
Creamy Scrambled Eggs
with Bacon*
Broiled Tomatoes*
Scottish Scones*
Ginger Marmalade

Vegetable Juice Cocktail
Alpine Eggs*
Toasted Buttered Corn Muffins
Asier (Pickled Cucumbers)*
Pears in Red Wine*
___

Dressed Crab*
Tomatoes Stuffed with
Dilled Cucumbers*
Assorted Crisp Breads
Arnaud's Ananas Flambés*

Italian Escarole
and Lentil Soup*
Hard Seeded Rolls
Zuppa Inglese*
___

Huevos Rancheros*
Mixed Bean Salad*
Shredded Lettuce
Pineapple Sticks*

Haringsla (Herring Salad)*
Rugbrød (Rye Bread)*
Whipped Cream Cheese
Grandpères (Grandfathers)*
___

Turkish Eggplant Salad*
Garlic Bread
Cheese Plate*
Stoofperen (Stewed Pears)*

Gule Aerter (Yellow Pea Soup)*
Croutons*
Pickled Cucumbers*
Sherbet Mold*
___

Seafood Bisque*
Toasted Cheddar Cheese
Sandwiches
Fresh Fruit Platter*
Arbutus Hermits*

Polevkas Jaternimi Knedlíky
(Soup with Liver Dumplings)*
Pumpernickel Bread
Sweet Butter
Cranberry Salad* with
Curry Mayonnaise*
___

Eggplant Clam Soufflé*
Watercress-Tomato Salad*
Assorted Crisp Breads
Macédoine of Fruit*

Gnocchi all'Italiana
(Dumplings Italian Style)*
Green Salad*
Fruit Cup
Chocolate Crispies*

―――――◆―――――

Cold Broccoli Soup*
Savory Croutons*
Crabmeat Molds*
Oranges à la Grecque*

Scotch Broth*
French Bread Croutons*
Agurkesalat (Cucumber Salad)*
Baked Custards*
with Grenadine

―――――◆―――――

Tuna Croquettes*
with Dill Sauce*
Beet Salad with
Roquefort Dressing*
Cold Strawberry Soufflé*

Fish and Chips*
Tarragon Vinegar
Cucumber Onion Salad*
Maids of Honour*

―――――◆―――――

Celery and Carrot Sticks
Frankfurter-Potato Dumplings*
with Skysovs (Spiced Drippings)*
Stewed Tomatoes and
Green Peppers
Prune Pound Cupcakes*

Arnauds' Breast of Chicken
en Papillote*
Pilaffi (Parsleyed Pilaf)*
Romaine-Avocado-Tomato Salad*
Hard Rolls
Strawberries with Kirsch

―――――◆―――――

Daube de Boeuf Provençale
(Beef Daube Provence Style)*
Green Noodles
Romaine Salad
French Dressing de Luxe*
Brennan's Bananas Foster*

Boned Roast Duckling
with Savory Rice*
Spiced Apricots and Prunes*
Curly Endive Stewed in Butter*
Chocolate Torte Burgundy*

―――――◆―――――

Hotel Ponchartrain Shrimp
Remoulade*
Telecí Maso s Vinnou Omackou
(Veal Roast with Wine Sauce)*
Sweet-Potato Croquettes*
Pommes Meringuées*

Roget Laks (Smoked Salmon)*
Steak and Kidney Pie*
Coleslaw*
Fresh Currant Ice*
Date-Nut Pinwheels*
English Tea*

―――――◆―――――

Soup on the Rocks*
Leverpostej (Liver Pâté)*
on Melba Toast Rounds
Individual Baked Eggplant
and Chicken*
Green-Bean Salad*
Linzer Torte*

Celery Hearts
Ripe and Green Olives
Ham and Oyster Gumbo Filé*
Rice
Heated Buttered French Bread
Individual Caramel-Date Pies*
Coffee with Chicory

―――――◆―――――

Flank Steak Roll-Ups*
Stamppot witte Kool
(White Cabbage with Potatoes)*
Sliced Tomatoes   Hot Rolls
Orange Chiffon
Refrigerator Cake*

Clear Oxtail Soup*
Roast Turkey English Style*
Spruiten Purée
(Purée of Brussels Sprouts)*
Cranberry Sauce
Trifle*

―――――◆―――――

Agurkesuppe (Cucumber Soup)*
Pork Chops with
Apricot Stuffing*
Gestoofde Prei
(Braised Leeks)*
Indian Pilau*
Devil's Food Cake
with Marshmallow Frosting*

Boiled Beef with Carrots
and Egg Dumplings*
Varm Peberrodssovs
(Hot Horseradish Sauce)*
Lettuce Salad*
Special French Dressing*
Orange Ambrosia*
Medaljekager
(Medal Cookies)*

―――――◆―――――

Roast Stuffed Pheasant*
Bread Sauce*
Gooseberry Jelly
Buttered Green Beans
Romaine Salad*
Mincemeat Roly-Poly*

Finnan Haddie
with Shrimp Sauce*
Dunbar's Stuffed Squash*
French Peas*
Hearts of Lettuce
Simple French Dressing*
Cherry Torte Glacé*

―――――◆―――――

Chicken with Figs*
Green Rice*
Brussels Lof
(Belgian Endive)*
Pickled Beet Slices
on Lettuce
Louisiana Pecan Cake*
à la Mode

Spring Vegetable Soup*
Grilled Sole
with Mustard Sauce*
Deviled Stuffed Potatoes*
Cherry Tomatoes and
Bibb Lettuce Salad*
Raisin-Pineapple-Custard Pie*

―――――◆―――――

Shrimp Curry*   Rice
East Indian Date Chutney*
Raw Cauliflower and
Spinach Salad
Sesame Cheese Sticks
Lemon Sherbet with
Preserved Kumquats
Filbert Spice Cookies*

Clam Juice Seasoned
with Horseradish
Ossenhaas à la Jardinière
(Fillet of Beef and Vegetables)*
French Bread
Whipped Sweet Butter
Apple Pie (Open English Type)*
with Cheddar Cheese Slice

―――――◆―――――

Lancashire Hot Pot*
Shredded Red Cabbage and
Carrot Salad with
Cooked Salad Dressing*
Hard Rolls
Damson-Plum Pie*

Gevulde Lamborst
(Roast Cushion Shoulder
of Lamb)*
Dandelion Greens
with Lentils*
Tomatoes, Cucumbers, Green
Peppers and Celery with
Oil and Vinegar
Coconut Custard Pie*

―――――◆―――――

Tomato Soup
Deep-Fried Croakers
with Tartare Sauce*
Braised Cucumbers*
Italian Scalloped Potatoes*
Orange Sherbet
Stuffed Sherried Dates*

Barbecued Spareribs*
Creole Black-Eyed Peas*
Hot Biscuits
Young Mustard Greens
and Lettuce Slaw
Karnemelk Pudding
(Buttermilk Pudding)*

―――――◆―――――

Lamb Stew with Okra
and Cuminseed*
Steamed Brown Rice
Vegetables Vinaigrette*
Flensjes (Thin Pancakes)*
with Honey and Whipped Cream

Menus

Butterklösse (Butter
Dumplings)* in Chicken Broth
Grillades*
Green Lima Beans*
Broccoli Amandine*
Applesauce with Brown Sugar
Bozi Milosti
(Celestial Crusts)*

Sliced Smoked Beef Tongue
Pot Cheese Dumplings*
Spinazie (Spinach)*
Buttered Rye Toast
Dried and Fresh-Fruit Soup*
Muster Cookies*

Commander's Palace
Stuffed Flounder*
Ratatouille Provençale*
Panned Escarole*
Wilted Cucumbers
Seven Layered Prune Torte*

Chicken Croquettes*
Vegetable Curry*
(Using Cauliflower)
Green Peas, Water Chestnuts
and Pimiento
Tomato Aspic Cubes and
Stuffed Eggs* on Chicory
Mayonnaise*
Melon Balls in Orange Juice

Eggplant-Yogurt Salad*
Chicken Curry*   Rice
Chutney, Chopped Green Onion,
Chopped Cashew Nuts,
Shredded Coconut
Makový Kolác (Poppy-Seed
Layer Torte)*

Beef Bouillon with
Farina Balls*
Assorted Cold Meats*
Nepalese Potato Salad*
Tomatoes Stuffed with
Cucumber on Watercress
Mayonnaise*
Pineapple Sherbet
Currant-Orange Cupcakes*

Roast Pork Trastevere*
Brunede Kartofler
(Sugar Browned Potatoes)*
Rødkaal (Red Cabbage)*
Waldorf Salad on Chicory
Cold Chocolate Soufflé*

Grilled Pork or Veal Chops
Frisk Stegt Løg (Fried Onions)*
Farina Spoon Bread*
Damson-Plum Conserve*
Green-Bean Salad*
Frothy Syllabub*

Benløse Fugle
(Boneless Birds)*
Candied Yams Amandine*
Asparagus with
Brennan's Hollandaise Sauce*
Orange, Grapefruit and
Onion Salad
Spanish Salad Dressing*
Raisin Spice Cake*

Rib Roast of Beef
Pan Gravy
Yorkshire Pudding*
Cabbage Curry*
Tomato-Cucumber Salad*
Strawberries à la Chantilly*

Pot Roast of Beef   Gravy
Spaetzle
(German Egg Dumplings)*
Sweet and Sour Red Cabbage
Chilled Carrots with Dill*
Simnel Cake*

Balkan Stuffed Eggplant*
Salata (Salad)*
Sliced Hard-Cooked Eggs
Sesame Seed Wafers
Karidopika (Walnut Cake)*
Greek Coffee*

Hamburgryg med Ribs Gelé
(Bacon with Currant Jelly)*
Stegte Kartofler
(Fried Potatoes)*
Deviled Mushrooms, Casino*
Green Cabbage Coleslaw
Aeblekage (Apple Cake)*

Baked Fish Sticks
Tartare Sauce*
Potatoes Anna*
Raw Dandelion Salad*
Garlic Bread
Sour Cherry or
Fresh Currant Pie*

Skewered Swordfish*
Italian Eggplant Parmigiana*
Dandelion Greens,
Italian Style*
Bread Sticks
Spumoni   Caffè Espresso*

Rullepølse (Meat Roll)*
Dill Pickles
Avga Gemista (Stuffed Eggs)*
Macaroni and
Vegetable Salad
Pumpernickel Toast
Sweet Butter
Almond Torte*

Dolmadakia me Avgolemono
(Greek Stuffed Grapevine
Leaves with Lemon Sauce)*
Wheat or Rice Pilaf
Lettuce Hearts and Anchovy
Salad with Feta or
Muenster Cheese Strips
Olive Dressing*
Squares of Rainbow Orange
Raisin Cake* with Warm Honey

Celery   Radishes   Gherkins
Creole Bouillabaisse*
French or Sourdough Bread
Whipped Butter
Chocolate Fruit Pie*

Baked Lamb Chops*
Delmonico Potatoes*
Green Peas and Onions
Bibb or Boston Lettuce
Chiffonade Dressing*
Charlotte Russe*

Gestoofde Kabeljauw of
Schelvis met Aardappelen
(Baked Fillets of Haddock
or Cod with Potatoes)*
Asparagus Salad
Hot Corn Muffins
Melon Slices* with
Raspberry Sherbet

Eggs in Aspic*
Stamppot van Boerenkool
met Worst (Kale with
Potatoes and Sausage)*
Stewed Tomatoes and Celery
Baked Apples
Speculaas (Spiced Cookies)*

Veprové s Krenem
(Piquant Pork with
Horseradish)*
Potato Dumplings*
Brussels Sprouts
Carrot and Green Pepper
Sticks
Dried Apple Cake*

Erwtensoep (Pea Soup)*
Jockey Club Eggs*
(with Veal Kidneys)
Toasted English Muffins
Cheese Tray*
Fresh Pears and Apples

Aal i Gelé (Jellied Eel)*
Beefsteak Na Kyselo
(Steak with Sour-Cream Gravy)*
Noodles with Buttered Rye
Bread Crumbs
Red Cabbage, Apple and
Raisin Salad
Devil's Food Squares*

Manitaria Toursi
(Pickled Mushrooms)*
Baked Rock Cornish Hens
with Rice*
French Green Beans
Mixed Green Salad
Orange Form Cake* with
Vanilla Ice Cream

◆

Duck Chow Mein*
Fried Noodles   Rice
Soy Sauce
Pineapple Slices
Chinese Almond Cookies*
Jasmine Tea*

Veal Escallops with
Vermouth and Tarragon*
Belgian Endive au Gratin*
Orange, Beet and Onion Salad
Vinaigrette Dressing*
Dumplings Baked in
Caramel Sauce*

◆

Varkensschijf
(Rolled Pork Rib)*
Svestkove Knedlíky
(Plum Dumplings)*
Buttered Diced Yellow
Turnips with Parsley
Celery, Green Pepper Slaw
Coffee Ice Cream
Date Sticks*

Ducklings in Claret*
Wild Rice
Cucumbers in Cheese Sauce*
Raisin and Carrot Salad
Simple French Dressing*
Apple Crème*

◆

Tomato Juice
Kaastruffels
(Cheese Truffles)*
Raisin-Rice-Stuffed
Veal Breast*
Creamed Carrots
Shredded Cabbage and
Green Pepper Salad
Appelschoteltje (Zwieback
with Apple in the Oven)*

Frikadeller
(Danish Meatballs)*
Stuffed Baked Potatoes*
Dilled Cucumbers*
Watercress
Rye Rolls
Rødgrød (Red Pudding)*
Filbert Crescents*

◆

Bubble and Squeak*
Assorted Pickles
Bread   Butter
Apricot-Rice Custard*

Consommé Madrilene*
Cheese Croutons*
Scalloped Chicken Supreme*
Corn on the Cob
Curry   Butter
Fresh Fruit Salad
Korean Sesame-Seed Cookies*

Baked Salmon with
Caper Butter*
Boiled New Potatoes
in Jackets
Curly Endive and Spinach
Salad   Russian Dressing*
Strawberries Romanoff*

Skinke med Madeira
(Ham with Madeira)*
Baked Acorn Squash
Green Lima Beans
Chinese Cabbage Slaw
Jam Tarts*   Special Coffee*

◆

Chilled Cucumber and
Tomato Soup*
The Sultan's Delight*
Rice
Almond Croquettes*
with Sliced Bananas
Chopped Dates and Honey

French Shrimp-Mushroom Flan*
Avocado, Tomato and Mixed
Green Salad with
Green Goddess Dressing
Sliced Peaches with
Vanilla Cupcakes*

Chicken Marengo*
Risi e Bisi
(Rice and Peas)*
Endive and Parsley Salad
Seeded Hard Rolls
Crème Brûlée*

Clams or Oysters
on the Half Shell
Brennan's Shrimp Clemenceau*
Green Bean Salad*
French Bread
Celery and Carrot Curls
Éclairs with Chocolate Glaze*

◆

Lamb Kofta Curry*
Stewed Rice and Lentils
Buttered Cauliflower
Sliced Pineapple and
Mangoes or Peaches
Coconut Cookies*
Iced Tea*

Melon with Prosciutto*
Poached Salmon Trout
with Tomato Hollandaise*
Broiled Mushroom Caps*
Greens, Onion
and Chicory Salad
Farina Pudding*

◆

Potato Chips
Taramosalata*
(Red Caviar Spread)*
Broiled Shoulder Lamb Chops
Eggplant Lasagna*
Fruit Platter

Chili Con Queso*
Corn Chips
Stuffed Flank Steak*
Mallung *
Pineapple, Apricot Salad
Lime Juice and Olive Oil
Mexican Flan*

◆

Stifado (Beef Stew)*
Potatoes in Foil*
Corn Relish
Crusty Rolls
Tutti-Frutti Mousse*

Browned Chicken Stew
with Cornmeal Dumplings*
Jellied Perfection Salad
on Lettuce
Chantilly Mayonnaise*
Fried Pies*

◆

Ragout of Eggs
and Mushroom*
Hot Garlic Bread
Tuna and Celery Salad
Orange Ice
Devil's Food Cake*

Onion Soup
Grilled Knackwurst
Spekkle Sla (Bacon Slaw)*
Applesauce   Crumb Cake*

◆

Fruited Spiced Beef*
Mashed Yams
Mixed Green Salad
Mustard   French Dressing
Filbert Torte*

Celery Hearts
Dill Pickle Chips
Kapr Peceny s Kyselou Omackou
(Carp with Sour-Cream Sauce)*
Buttered Noodles with
Poppy Seed
Stegte Tomater
(Fried Tomatoes)*
Fruit Twist Coffeecake*

◆

Hutspot met Klapstuk
(Hodgepodge with Boiled Meat)*
Cherry Tomato, Cabbage Salad
Horseradish   Mayonnaise
Stewed Pears   Fat Rascals*

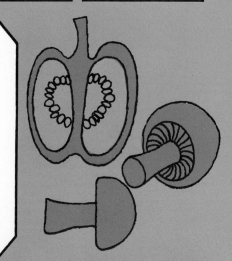

*Recipes for all starred dishes found in this volume.

GENERAL INFORMATION

The Ingredients and Measurements Used in Recipes

All recipes in this book have been tested in the Woman's Day Kitchens with standard American measuring cups (8 ounces = 16 tablespoons), measuring spoons (1 tablespoon = 3 teaspoons), and other standard kitchen equipment. All measurements are level. Liquids are measured in standard 8-ounce glass measuring cups, at eye level.

All sugar is granulated white sugar unless otherwise specified.

All flours, cake and all-purpose, are sifted before measuring unless otherwise specified. No self-rising flour is used.

All baking powder is double-acting baking powder.

All brown sugar is firmly packed when measured.

All confectioners' sugar is sifted before measuring.

All pepper is ground black pepper unless otherwise specified.

Fats and shortening are measured at room temperature, packed firmly into measuring cup and leveled with a straight knife. They are scraped out with a rubber spatula.

Salted butter or margarine, packed in ¼-pound sticks, is used unless otherwise specified. 1 stick = ½ cup = 8 tablespoons = ¼ pound.

1 tall can evaporated milk (14½ ounces) contains 1⅔ cups undiluted evaporated milk. Sweetened condensed milk is an entirely different product, and cannot be used interchangeably with evaporated milk.

⅓ to ½ teaspoon dried herbs can be substituted for each tablespoon fresh herbs. Crumble herbs before using to release flavor.

Before starting to cook or to bake, read the recipes carefully. Assemble all ingredients and equipment. Follow recipe exactly. Do not increase or decrease recipe unless you are a skilled enough cook to recognize what adjustments must be made as to ingredients, pan sizes, and/or cooking time.

Cooking Temperatures and Times

Cooking temperatures and times are approximate for meat. They depend not only on the weight and kind of meat, but also on its shape, temperature, and its bone and fat contents. A meat thermometer was used in testing.

Cooking times for meats are as recommended by the National Live Stock and Meat Board, 36 Wabash Avenue, Chicago, Illinois 60603.

Oven Temperatures

TEMPERATURES (Degree F.)	TERM
250 to 275	VERY SLOW
300 to 325	SLOW
350 to 375	MODERATE
400 to 425	HOT
450 to 475	VERY HOT
500 to 525	EXTREMELY HOT

Important—Preheat oven for 10 to 15 minutes before placing food in it. Many a cake has been spoiled by being placed in a barely heated oven. Baking times are based on the assumption that the oven is already at the stated temperature.

Check the oven temperature control frequently, especially if baking times vary from those given in recipes. (This can be done with a portable oven thermometer.) If a control is consistently off, call your public utility. They should be able to reset the oven temperature control.

Caloric Values

The caloric values, where mentioned, for each food are based on 100 grams, about 3½ ounces edible portion, as mentioned in Composition of Foods, Agriculture Handbook No. 8, Agricultural Service of the United States Department of Agriculture, Washington, D. C., revised December 1963.

COMPLETE RECIPE INDEX—Volume 4—666 Recipes

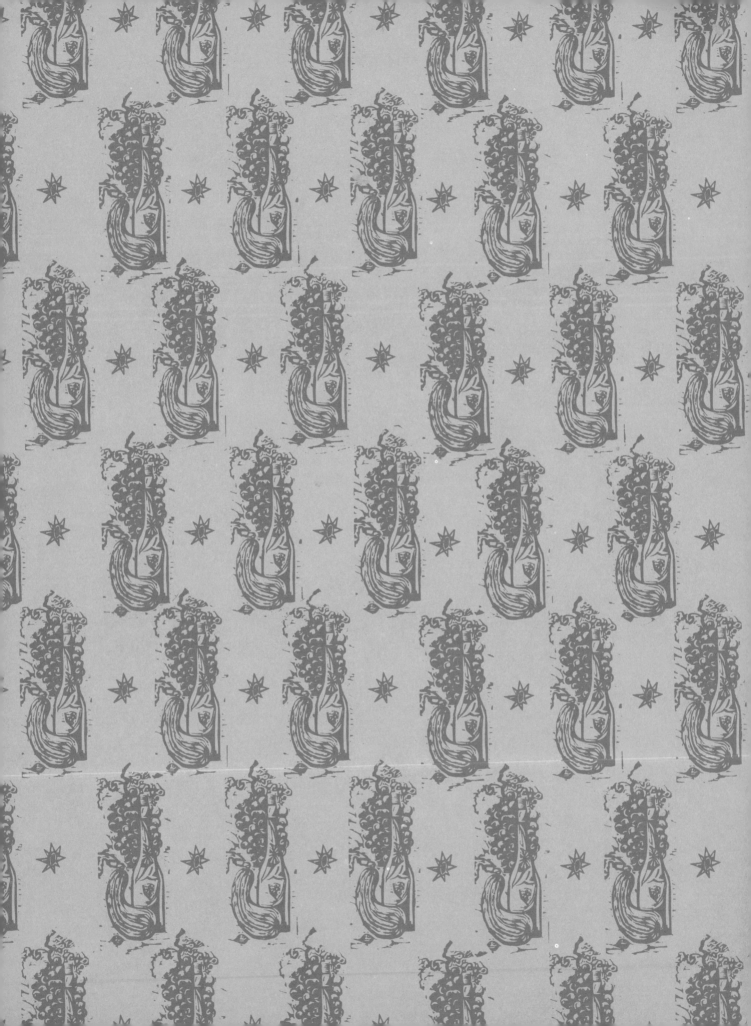